# *Plants of Haida Gwaii*

**X̲aadaa Gwaay gud gina k̲'aws** (Skidegate)
**X̲aadaa Gwaayee guu ginn k̲'aws** (Massett)

# Plants of Haida Gwaii

X̲aadaa Gwaay gud gina k̲'aws (Skidegate)
X̲aadaa Gwaayee guu ginn k̲'aws (Massett)

**THIRD EDITION**

**Nancy J. Turner, CM, OBC, PhD, FRSC**
Distinguished Professor Emerita
School of Environmental Studies
University of Victoria
Victoria, British Columbia

with

Florence Davidson, Willie and Emma Matthews, George Young,
Emma and Solomon Wilson, Maude and Agnes Moody, Watson and Sarah Pryce,
Kathleen Hans, Becky Pearson, and other Haida plant specialists.

Illustrations by Gitkinjuaas (also known as G̲iitsx̲aa; Ronald Wilson), Skidegate.

X̲aayda Xil Gan Sing.G̲a Suu/"Prayer for Haida Medicine"
by GwaaG̲anad (Dr. Diane Brown), Skidegate.

Epilogue by K̲ii'iljuus (Barbara Wilson), Skidegate.

Haida plant names of previous editions checked and revised by John Enrico;
many originally recorded by Robert D. Levine; writing system adapted from the
Skidegate Haida Immersion Program (SHIP).

**Front cover photo:** Florence Davidson carefully removes cedar bark from a young western red-cedar as the first step in preparing the thin inner bark used for weaving.

**Frontispiece photo:** Florence Davidson's granddaughter Helen Davis wearing a cedar-bark hat woven by her grandmother, 1972.

**Back cover photo:** Red huckleberries (sG̲iidllG̲uu - S, sG̲idlùu - M, sG̲idluu - A), in cedar-bark basket made by G̲iihlgiigaa Tsiit Git'anee, Todd DeVries.

**Opposite page:** Salmonberries, showing the range of colours.



1 2 3 4 5 — 25 24 23 22 21



**Published by:**
**Harbour Publishing Co. Ltd.**
**P.O. Box 219**
**Madeira Park, BC, V0N 2H0**
www.harbourpublishing.com

Cover design: Jim Brennan; Cover photos: Robert D. Turner
Back cover illustration: Gitkinjuaas (also known as G̲iitsx̲aa; Ronald Wilson)
Author photo: Christina Marshall, University of Victoria
Text design: Jim Brennan (previous editions); Robert D. Turner (third edition revisions)
All photographs are by Robert D. Turner & Nancy J. Turner or from their collection, except where otherwise noted.
All photos, maps and artwork are copyright © the artists and/or institutions noted in the credit lines.

Printed and bound in South Korea

Canada | Canada Council for the Arts / Conseil des arts du Canada | British Columbia Arts Council | British Columbia | Supported by the Province of British Columbia

Harbour Publishing acknowledges the support of the Canada Council for the Arts, the Government of Canada, and the Province of British Columbia through the BC Arts Council.

All author's proceeds from the publication of this book go to supporting Haida cultural and environmental education programs, at the discretion of the Haida leaders and knowledge holders of Skidegate and Massett.

**Library and Archives Canada Cataloguing in Publication**
Title: Plants of Haida Gwaii = X̲aadaa gwaay gud gina k̲'aws = X̲aadaa gwaayee guu ginn k̲'aws / Nancy J. Turner ; with Florence Davidson, [and 11 others], and other Haida plant specialists ; illustrations by Gitkinjuaas (also known as G̲iitsx̲aa; Ronald Wilson) ; Skidegate ; X̲aayda xil gan sing.ga suu/"Prayer for Haida medicine" by Gwaag̲anad (Dr. Diane Brown), Skidegate ; epilogue by K̲ii'iljuus (Barbara Wilson), Skidegate.
Other titles: X̲aadaa gwaay gud gina k̲'aws | X̲aadaa gwaayee guu ginn k̲'aws
Names: Turner, Nancy J., 1947- author. | Davidson, Florence Edenshaw, 1896-1993, author. | Enrico, John, 1947-
Description: Third edition. | "Haida plant names of previous editions checked and revised by John Enrico; many originally recorded by Robert D. Levine; writing system adapted from the Skidegate Haida Immersion Program (SHIP)." | Includes bibliographical references and index. | Text in English with prayer in Haida and English.
Identifiers: Canadiana 20200397176 | ISBN 9781550179149 (softcover)
Subjects: LCSH: Indigenous peoples—British Columbia—Haida Gwaii. | LCSH: Plants, Useful—British Columbia—Haida Gwaii. | LCSH: Ethnobotany—British Columbia—Haida Gwaii.
Classification: LCC E99.H2 T87 2021 | DDC 581.6/30899728071112—dc23

***Plants of Haida Gwaii* is dedicated to:**

***Barb, Linda, Terri-Lynn, Shirley, Nicole, Judson, Ernie, Robert, Reg, Penny, Helen, Joyce, Alice, Merle, Belle, Brenda, Lisa, Girl, Jaalen, Amanda, Gwaai, Niisii, Kung Staasl, Haana, Sean, Ari, Todd, Sev, Ganhlaans, Tiisaan and all the others: May plants always be central to your lives!***

Photographs in *Plants of Haida Gwaii* were taken by Robert D. Turner and Nancy J. Turner except where credits acknowledge other photographers or sources.

## ABOUT THE ARTIST

### Gitkinjuaas (also known as G̱iitsx̱aa; Ronald Wilson)

Gitkinjuaas, one of Haida Gwaii's most noteworthy carvers and artists, was born in Skidegate, British Columbia, in 1945, into the St'awaas Xaadaga Clan as the first nephew of G̱id Kinjuwas (Charles Wesley, Chief Cumshewa), and is now himself Chief Cumshewa. As a young boy Gitkinjuaas started his career as an artist by copying his Uncle Stan's pencil drawings. He also learned from watching carvers such as Tim Pearson, Ed Calder, Ike Hans, Arthur Moody, Jimmy Jones, Louis Collinson, Gordon Cross and Henry Young. Gitkinjuaas (G̱iitsx̱aa) attended the Vancouver School of Art in the late 1960s, where he studied watercolour, oil and acrylic painting, sculpture, photography, jewellery design and drawing. He also worked at Thunderbird Park in Victoria, BC, for one and a half years and learned totem carving from Henry Hunt Sr. At this time he carved a 9-foot (almost 3-metre) cedar pole for the Civic Centre in Prince Rupert, BC, as well as a replica of the Skedans burial box that currently sits over the entrance of the graveyard in Skidegate. He returned to Haida Gwaii in 1973 and has continued to live there over most of the time since then. Gitkinjuaas works with all mediums: wood, argillite, ivory, silver, gold and painting original designs. He is well known for his 52-foot (almost 16-metre) red-cedar totem pole, which stands near Skidegate at the site of the K̲ay Llnagaay Haida Heritage Centre. In 2007, G̱iitsx̱aa fulfilled his final obligations to his deceased maternal uncle G̱id Kinjuwas (Charles Wesley), erecting the headstone and holding a settlement potlatch. In 2008, with another potlatch, he validated his birthright to take the name Gitkinjuaas as head of the Cumshewa ruling family.

**List of Gitkinjuaas's Illustrations in *Plants of Haida Gwaii*:**


1. The Salmon People in Their Canoe 74
2. **X̱uya** [Raven] 75
3. **G̱ud** [Eagle] 77
4. Raven Transforms Himself into a Hemlock Needle 97 & back cover
5. Skunk-Cabbage Man 147
6. Raven in His Canoe 150
7. Devil's-Club Man 154
8. Mouse Woman with Sword Fern 189
9. Two-Headed Kelp and the Undersea World 201
10. Tree Fungus Man and **X̱uya** [Raven] 209

## X̱aayda Xil Gan Sing.G̱a Suu
by GwaaG̱anad

Sah nang iidxaaydas ahhay.yad siing.aay
sG̱aawdagii dang ga hll kil laa ga
X̱aaydaa xil sG̱aawdagii Sḵil jaad G̱a hll kil laa ga
X̱aaydaa xil G̱an t'ang yahgudang.aay waagii kilxii gang ga.
X̱aaydaa xil waadluxan iid G̱an laa 'uwanga,
wagyinuu iid hluu ging ng.aaysdll.yaay.
Assii waadluxan sG̱aawdagii dang G̱a hll kil laa ga.
Hawa'.

## Prayer for Haida Medicine
by GwaaG̱anad (Dr. Diane Brown)

Creator I thank you for today,
I thank Lady Luck for Haida medicines
We must respect Haida medicine
All Haida medicine is very good for us
also heals our bodies
For all this Creator I thank you.

# Contents

**The Story of *Plants of Haida Gwaii*: An Ethnobotany** 1
A Note on the Use of Terms 16
Warning and Notation on Haida Medicines and Foods 17

**Haida Gwaii, the Land, the Plants and the Haida** 21
The Land 25
Map of Haida Gwaii 27
The Plants 29
The Haida 35

**The Role of Plants in Haida Culture** 39
Food Plants 40
Toxic Plants 53
Plant Resource Management 54
Plants in Technology 57
Medicinal Plants 61
Plants in Language and Classification 65
The Spiritual and Ceremonial Aspects of Plants 71
Narratives about Haida Plants 72
Relationships between Plants and Animals 77

**The Plants, Their Haida Names and Cultural Roles** 79
Evergreen Trees 80
Deciduous Trees 100
Berry Bushes and Other Shrubs 106
"Root" Vegetables 134
"Leafy Herb" Plants 142
"Haida Flowers" 169
"Grassy Plants" 177
Ferns and Their Relatives 183
"Mossy Growth": Lichens, Liverworts and Mosses 192
Seaweeds and Other Marine Plants 195
Freshwater Aquatic Plants 206
A Terrestrial Alga 207
"Tree Biscuits" and Other Fungi 208

**Reflections and Conclusions** 213

**Epilogue: Conservation of Culturally Important Plants of Haida Gwaii**
by Kii'iljuus (Barbara Wilson) 215

**References** 218

**Appendices** 222
Appendix 1. Haida Language Symbols 222
Appendix 2. Haida Food Plants 225
A) Root vegetables 225
B) "Green vegetables" 226
C) Fruits 227
D) Tree inner bark 228
E) Casual or emergency foods 229
F) Beverage plants 229
G) Flavourings and/or sweetenings and/or confections 229
H) Plants for smoking or chewing 229
I) Plants used in food gathering or preparation 230
Appendix 3. Plants Considered Poisonous or Irritating 232
Appendix 4. Haida Plant Materials 233
A) Woods for implements, containers and construction 233
B) Woods for specialized fuels 234
C) Fibres and fibrous materials 234
D) Dyes, stains, paints, preservatives 234
E) Miscellaneous useful materials 235
Appendix 5. Haida Medicinal Plants 236
Appendix 6. Plants Having a Role in Traditional Beliefs and/or Stories of the Haida 238
Appendix 7. Examples of Plants Associated with Animals 241
Appendix 8. Unidentified Haida Plants 242
Appendix 9. General Botanical Terms in Haida 243
Appendix 10. Introduced Vegetables and Fruits and Other Plant Products Having Haida Names 245

**Index, English and Scientific Plant Names** 249

**Index, Haida Plant Names** 257

# The Story of *Plants of Haida Gwaii*: An Ethnobotany

This third edition of *Plants of Haida Gwaii* represents the culmination of over half a century of ethnobotanical research, learning about vibrant cultures and the plants they embrace. For me, it has been one of the most enjoyable, rewarding and educational experiences as an ethnobotanist. Researching and writing the book, and participating in many subsequent adventures, highlighted by so many friendships over multiple generations, are gifts that I will cherish and for which I am forever grateful.

The publication of this new edition of *Plants of Haida Gwaii* in 2021 came about after a fire destroyed the remaining stock of books of the 2010 edition, published by Sono Nis Press. Sono Nis was unable to republish the book, and I am grateful that Harbour Publishing, with its long interest in books about British Columbia and the history of its coast and its peoples, was pleased to publish this new edition. My special thanks go to Anna Comfort O'Keeffe, Amy Haagsma, Rebecca Pruitt MacKenney and the other Harbour staff. I also want to thank Dr. Bill Turner, my brother-in-law, for working

**OPPOSITE PAGE: Pole at Cumshewa, 1971.**

**RIGHT: Beaver at the base of Eagle totem pole at Skidegate, 1971, among the last of the older generation of poles.**

**Opposite page:** Poles at SG̲ang Gwaay Llnagaay (Nans Dins), UNESCO World Heritage Site, and the moss- and huckleberry bush-covered cedar house post and giant beam of one of the major houses in the village.

to obtain the rights and digital files for the original book from Sono Nis Press and for valued computer assistance, and my husband, Bob (Robert D. Turner), for his unfailing inspiration and help with this edition, and so much more.

Production of this new edition gave me the opportunity to update the Haida writing system in the book, and to acknowledge the new Chiefs' names: Gitkinjuaas (Chief Cumshewa, also known as G̲iitsx̲aa; Ronald Wilson) and Gidansda (Chief Skedans; formerly Guujaaw, and past president of the Council of the Haida Nation). Gitkinjuaas, whose beautiful paintings are a highlight of this book, has kindly given his permission to include them in this new edition.

For her continuing support and advice, in reviewing the Haida names and so much more, I am indebted to my dear sister K̲ii'iljuus (Barbara Wilson) of Skidegate, whose epilogue completes the book. I also extend my sincere appreciation to GwaaG̲anad (Dr. Diane Brown) who shared the **X̲aayda X̲il Gan Sing.G̲a Suu**/"Prayer for Haida Medicine" at the beginning of this book. GwaaG̲anad, along with eight other Haida language speakers—Gaayinguuhlas (Roy Jones), Yang K̲'aalas (Grace Jones), Ildagwaay (Bea Harley), Taalgyaa'adad (Betty Richardson), Jiixa (Gladys Vandal), Sing.giduu (Laura Jormanainen), SG̲aanajaadsk'yaagax̲iigangs (Kathleen Hans) and Niis Waan (Harvey Williams) —received honorary Doctor of Laws degrees at Vancouver Island University in June 2019, in recognition of their decades of work and dedication in documenting, teaching and revitalizing **HlG̲aagilda X̲aayda Kil**, the Skidegate dialect of the Haida language. Their work, along with many others', including speakers of the Massett (**X̲aad Kil**) and Alaska dialects of Haida, and experts in Indigenous languages throughout British Columbia and beyond, is so inspiring, and critically important. Dr. Marianne Ignace and Dr. Ronald Ignace deserve particular recognition for their ongoing work in Indigenous language revitalization, including Haida; in 2019, they received a Governor General's Award for Innovation for this work. The plant names provided here are only one aspect of the richness and embedded knowledge of **X̲aayda Kil**/ **X̲aad Kil** and other Indigenous languages.

The botanical names, and even family names, of some of the plants featured in the book have also changed since the last edition was published, so I have done my best to update these. I have, for the most part, followed the current nomenclature set out in *E-Flora BC* (*Electronic Atlas of the Flora of British Columbia*), with special thanks to Dr. Brian Klinkenberg, *E-Flora* editor and project coordinator, and all his collaborators, for producing this outstanding, extremely helpful and accessible resource. I also want to thank Ernest Ting Yu Wu, former UBC bryology graduate student, for his help in searching out some of the name changes that I have incorporated here. And thanks to Sean Young, collections curator for the Haida Gwaii Museum Society, for the new photo of the living tobacco plant from K̲ay Llnagaay. Special recognition, too, to Ariane Xay Kuyaas Medley, great-granddaughter of Florence Davidson, for her wonderful weaving talents; a photo of one of her spruce-root baskets is included here.

When *Plants of Haida Gwaii* was first published in 2004, and when the second edition followed in 2010, concerns about global climate change were being voiced by many. It has been only in the past decade, however, that climate change and its consequences for humanity and all our non-human relatives have become widely recognized. In 2019 Kii'iljuus completed her Master of Arts degree in the Faculty of Education at Simon Fraser University, with her thesis, **DamXan gud.ad t'alang hllGang.gulXads Gina Tllgaay** (*Working together to make it a better world*). With her research, she brought the topic of climate change and what people in her own community could do to help respond to and reverse the effects of climate change, in terms of housing, transportation, food production and other actions, to the fore. With this work, she reminds all of us that the precious plants and environments of Haida Gwaii, like those elsewhere in the world, are highly vulnerable to climate change impacts. Droughts, diminishing wetlands, storms, rising sea levels, increased insect pests and diseases, and loss of pollinators for berries and other flowering plants are all ongoing threats, and some of the effects are already evident: dying cedar and Sitka spruce trees, patches of dead salal, and fewer, smaller berries have all been noted on Haida Gwaii in the past few years. Added to the problems of overgrazing by the introduced deer, and damage caused by other introduced and invasive species, both plant and animal, these impacts are serious and extremely worrying.

Nevertheless, Haida Gwaii remains a spectacular archipelago. For me, it is one of the most beautiful and treasured places in the world. In 2017, I travelled by helicopter and truck with archaeologists Morley Eldridge and Jacob Earnshaw to interior parts of Graham and Moresby Islands where, over generations, Haida have travelled to harvest cedar bark and other plant resources, sometimes along ancient trails. As well, I have spent time, often with Kii'iljuus, in other parts of these beautiful islands. On Bluewater Adventures sailboats, we have both travelled with Randy Burke and his wonderful captains, crews and guests to Gwaii Haanas National Park Reserve, National Marine Conservation Area Reserve, and Haida Heritage Site. We have savoured delicious Haida meals at Keenawaii Roberta Olson's home, enjoyed interpretive walks and tours at the Haida Heritage Centre at Kay Llnagaay, sailed around numerous small islands and inlets, hiked through many special boglands and old-growth forests, and visited, with deep respect, the Haida village sites, steeped with history, all the way south to SGang Gwaay UNESCO World Heritage Site and Cape St. James. Always, at key village sites, we are greeted by Haida Gwaii Watchmen, who are devoted to these sites and their surroundings, guarding them and teaching visitors about their features and history. I want to continue, as with the previous editions, to use any proceeds from this publication to support Haida cultural and environmental education programs, at the discretion of the Haida leaders and knowledge holders of both Skidegate and Massett.

The original preface for the first two editions of *Plants of Haida Gwaii* (published in 2004 and 2010, respectively) is provided below, with minor updates. It tells much of the earlier story of the book's writing and is a tribute to the many people who made it possible.

**OPPOSITE PAGE: SGang Gwaay has a mystical attraction, and so, too, does the Haida Heritage Centre at Kay Llnagaay, near Skidegate (below), with its new generation of houses and poles, celebrating the living culture of the Haida (taken in 2007 at the opening of the centre; the poles were raised in 2001).**

**RIGHT:** Rediscovery canoe near Swan Bay, Gwaii Haanas. Canoe journeys are an important part of passing on cultural traditions.

**BELOW:** An eagle watches over Echo Harbour in Gwaii Haanas.

Spruce-root basket made by Ariane Xay Kuyaas Medley, great-granddaughter of Florence Davidson. Florence was the daughter of renowned artists Charles and Isabella Edenshaw. Ariane's relative and mentor Robert Davidson is a world-famous artist. Her grandmother Primrose Adams, her aunt Isabel Rorick and many other family members are also talented artists and weavers. This small, intricate basket fits in the palm of your hand; the enlarged illustration above is several times life-sized. A basket such as this takes great patience and many, many hours to create.

I first travelled to Haida Gwaii (then called the Queen Charlotte Islands) in 1971 with my husband, Bob, a graduate student in regional planning, to learn about Haida plants. I knew no one there, but came with a few letters of introduction from Dr. Roy Taylor, my graduate advisor and co-author with James Calder of *Flora of the Queen Charlotte Islands*. This flora was itself a great inspiration at the outset.

Over a period of three years, from 1971 to 1973, Bob and I visited Haida Gwaii several times, and we were overwhelmed by the generous hospitality of the island people. As I learned from the Haida elders about their plants and their culture, my respect for them, their ancestors and their families grew, and my love for their homeland deepened. We were tempted to stay on—never to return to the urban life of the southern coast of British Columbia—but somehow, we did leave, and our lives caught us up and spun us off in other directions. We finished graduate studies, moved to Victoria, had a family of three daughters and thought of Haida Gwaii only from afar, keeping up our contacts with people by phone, letters, Christmas cards and the occasional visit when friends travelled south.

Every film on the Haida, every news item, we watched on television with deep interest, and articles like the *National Geographic* feature of July 1987 brought great pleasure. Then, in 1990, Florence Davidson and her family invited me to her

**Near the Oeanda River on the windswept northeast coast of Graham Island.**

**LEFT: The remaining old-growth forests of Haida Gwaii, prime examples of coastal temperate rainforest—beautiful and irreplaceable. I was standing beside this magnificent spruce in 1973.**

**RIGHT: Cumshewa Village site, 1971.**

95th-birthday celebration. Meeting old friends and new, and seeing Nani Florence and her family again, was wonderful and inspiring. I promised myself I would finish the work I had started in the early seventies, to compile a book on Haida ethnobotany. I wanted this book to be a fitting tribute to Florence Davidson and all the other knowledgeable Haida elders who taught me, and I wanted it to be helpful to all the Haida and others, especially young people, in teaching about the plants and the rich heritage of the Haida.

Over the next three years I worked to bring the manuscript to reality, and, in the spring of 1993, I embarked on the next phase of the book's planning. I went back to Haida Gwaii to consult with the members of the Council of the Haida Nation about the book, and to arrange for verifications of details and general format. Many valuable suggestions and important corrections or clarifications were made by those who reviewed the manuscript, and I have done my best to meet the concerns and recommendations of all. At this time, I visited Nani Florence Davidson and Nuni Kathleen Hans again, and met Henry Geddes. Florence Davidson passed away in December 1993. Henry Geddes passed away in 1994. In June 1995, May 1996 and May 1998 I went to Haida Gwaii again, to share as best as I could the knowledge I had learned from my Haida teachers with the Haida Gwaii Watchmen of Gwaii Haanas National Park Reserve and Haida Heritage Site. In 1995, with Barbara Wilson, then coordinator for the Haida Gwaii Watchmen Program, and Maggie Stronge, also with Parks Canada, we travelled with Rob Pettigrew to the heritage village sites of Gwaii Haanas. During this trip I met many other Haida, all dedicated to preserving Haida

**Left: Florence Davidson in her famous kitchen, featured in *National Geographic*, working with cedar bark, 1972.**

**Right: George Young of Skidegate, 1971.**

cultural heritage and strengthening their ties with their elders and those who lived in Haida Gwaii long ago. We published, in limited form, the introductory section to this book as a handbook for the Haida Gwaii Watchmen Program.

In 1996 and 1998, my learning process continued, as I met and talked with friends old and new: K̲ii'iljuus (Barbara Wilson), Niis Wes (Chief Skedans; Ernie Wilson), Gitkinjuaas (Ron Wilson), Harold and Debbie Wilson, Mabel Williams, Golie Hans, Ada Yovanovich, Gwaag̲anad (Diane Brown), Captain Gold and Mrs. Captain Gold, Gidansda, Jaalen Edenshaw and many others. They have shared their perspectives, their hopes and their concerns about plant knowledge, conservation of plants and animals, loss and relearning of the Haida language, of basket weaving and carving arts, of the need for visitor education, lack of jobs, industrial forestry ... the list is endless. We have searched for plants distantly remembered, and rediscovered some of them. We harvested cedar bark and experimented with traditional pit-cooking techniques. And we will continue to research, test and celebrate plants into the future.

So many people have contributed to this book. The Haida elders who taught me about plants in the early 1970s include Edmund Calder, Elizabeth Collinson, Florence Davidson, Amanda Edgar, Henry Geddes, Kathleen Hans, Gertrude Kelly, Chief Willie Matthews and Emma Matthews, Agnes Moody, Maude Moody, Becky Pearson, Watson and Sarah Pryce, Emma and Chief Solomon Wilson, Chief George Young and Ada Yovanovich. Salish elders Violet Williams and Elsie Claxton are also valued contributors. Many of these people have passed away now, but their knowledge, generously shared with me and many others, will continue to enlighten people far into the future.

**Left: Ada Yovanovich, daughter of George Young, Skidegate, 1998.**

**Right: My friend Kii'iljuus (Barbara Wilson), en route to SGang Gwaay, 1993. She has been an advisor and active participant in the creation of this book.**

Kii'iljuus ("Born Big"; Barbara Wilson), if any one person can be singled out, has been the one whose steadfast interest, support and logistical advice has made this book a reality. I will never forget her friendship and help. In January 2003, she paid me the supreme honour of adopting me into her family, and giving me the name Kii'iljuus NaanGa, ("Grandmother of Kii'iljuus") because I, as her grandmother would have done had she been able, helped to introduce her to the rich and endlessly fascinating world of plants. Thank you, Barb, from the bottom of my heart. I take my responsibilities to you and your family very seriously and look forward to many more years of joyful botanical discovery with you.

Michael Nicoll Yahgulanaas, in 1993 Chief Councillor of Massett, and Gidansda (formerly Guujaaw), active practitioner of traditional medicine and Haida culture specialist, both kindly reviewed the first draft of the manuscript and helped to improve it in many ways. I am grateful to Gidansda for his patient counsel and advice in developing the succeeding drafts of this manuscript, and in raising my awareness of and sensitivity to issues of critical importance from the Haida perspective. Gidansda is former president of the Council of the Haida Nation (elected 2000).

Captain Gold (formerly Wanagan) and Dja da un koo ding us (Bernice; Mrs. Captain Gold) are also acknowledged with deep gratitude. Captain Gold, whom I first met at SGang Gwaay (Nans Dins), carefully read early drafts of this manuscript and helped me to make decisions on appropriate information to include. Captain Gold has continued to advise and help me in interpreting Haida cultural and plant knowledge. Bernice passed away in 2001, and her counsel is deeply missed.

I also acknowledge GwaaGanad (Dr. Diane Brown), respected traditional medicine practitioner and community health care worker in Skidegate and administrator of the Skidegate Haida Immersion Program (SHIP), for her advice, especially in discussions about how traditional medicines should be presented in a book such as this. The elegant and creative paintings of Gitkinjuaas (also known as G̱iitsx̱aa; Ron Wilson) bring the Haida plant stories to life.

Others whose advice and suggestions I deeply appreciate are Richard Baker, originally of Massett and later with Hey-way'-noqu' (Healing Circle for Addictions Society) in Vancouver; Golie Hans; Chief Cumshewa (Charlie Wesley) and Caroline Wesley; Miles Richardson (Kilslaay Kaajii Sding), formerly chair of the Council of the Haida Nation; and Woody Morrison.

I would like to thank the members of the Council of the Haida Nation and the Skidegate and Massett Band Councils for reviewing the manuscript and authorizing its publication. I especially acknowledge Cathy Pearson and Gidansda for their personal help in facilitating the review process.

Linguist Dr. John Enrico thoroughly reviewed the linguistic content of the first draft, and provided detailed corrections, comments and up-to-date transcriptions of most of the Haida terms, consistent with his own linguistic data, and in the orthography he has used in his publications on Haida language and narrative (e.g., Enrico 1995; Enrico and Stuart 1996). Unless otherwise noted, all Alaska Haida plant names, denoted (A), are provided by him, from his work in Alaska. This book would not have been possible without his careful work. In the end, however, it was decided to revise some of the linguistic characters used by Dr. Enrico, to make them more relevant to the Haida in learning to read the language. Thus, Dr. Enrico's "r" is now written as "G̱." The orthography I use here is closely aligned with that used by the current Skidegate and Massett language program (see Appendix 1).

Ḵii'iljuus (Barbara Wilson) has provided me with much additional assistance in correct spellings of Skidegate Haida plant terms, from her reference to the ongoing work of the Skidegate elders under the leadership of GwaaG̱anad (Dr. Diane Brown) with the Skidegate Haida Immersion Program (see SHIP *X̱aaydaa Kil Glossary*, 2016). In some cases, there is more than one version of a plant name, likely representing dialectic variations. The other island people who helped me over the years include Neil and Betty Carey, Charlie Hartie, Sergius DeBucy, Fran Fowler and Bill Ellis, Del Fowler, Rob Pettigrew, Audrey (Gladstone) Aiken, Virginia and Dave Hunter, Emily and Dave Goertzen, Knud and Merle Anderson, Emily White, Nora Koga, Agnes Jones, Robert Davidson, Reggie Davidson, Aggie and Sam Davis, Primrose and Victor Adams and their family, Claude and Vivian Davidson, and later, Sarah Davidson, Tom Adams, Penny Kerrigan, Alice Mountjoy and all their families. Florence Davidson's youngest daughter and her husband, Clara and Brian Hugo, who lived for many years in Vancouver, have also been very kind and helpful.

To my doctoral research advisor, Dr. Roy L. Taylor, then director of the University of British Columbia Botanical Garden, later director of the Rancha Santa Ana Botanical Garden in California, I am deeply indebted. He was ever helpful, supportive and encouraging as I was undertaking my fieldwork on Haida Gwaii in the early 1970s. My other doctoral committee members at the University of British

Wild rose (*Rosa nutkana*; **<u>k</u>'ung hl<u>k</u>'aayii - S; <u>k</u>'unhla hl<u>k</u>'aay - M**)

Columbia, Wilson Duff, Dr. Wilf Schofield and Dr. Gilbert Hughes, are also gratefully acknowledged. Other scholars who helped in this project in various ways are Dr. Michael Balick and Zoë Marchal, the New York Botanical Garden, Bronx; Dr. Marianne Boelscher Ignace, Secwepemc Cultural Education Society/Simon Fraser University, Kamloops, BC (who shared her unpublished notes of interviews with Emma and Willie Matthews and Adam and Ruth Bell, 1980–81, as well as photos and important feedback from Massett elders she worked with from 2001 to 2003, through the **<u>X</u>aad Kil** [Haida language] curriculum group and a Haida ethnobotany course in Old Massett, through Simon Fraser University, 2002; these elders included Adelia Adams, Norma Adams, Dorothy Bell, Ethel Jones, Mary Swanson, Gertie White and Nina Williams); Dr. Margaret Blackman, Department of Anthropology, State University College, Brockport, New York; Randy Bouchard and Dr. Dorothy Kennedy, British Columbia Indian Language Project, Victoria; Dr. I.M. Brodo, National Museum of Natural Sciences, Ottawa; Dr. Geoffrey Bursill-Hall, Department of Linguistics, Simon Fraser University; Dr. Adolf Ceska and Dr. Richard Hebda, botanists with the Royal BC Museum, Victoria; photographer Audrey Bernand; David Ellis, Vancouver; Daryl Fedje, Parks Canada and University of Victoria; Dr. Quentin Mackie, Department of Anthropology, University of Victoria; Dr. Joseph Kess, Department of Linguistics, University of Victoria; Dr. Brenda Callan, mycologist, Canadian Forest Service, Victoria; Dr. Brian Compton, Northwest Indian College, Bellingham, and Dr. Sandra Lindstrom, Department of Botany, University of British Columbia; Lavyna Alexander, University of Victoria; Dr. Robin June Hood, Sierra Club of Canada, British Columbia Chapter; John Broadhead, Gowgaia Institute; Robin Babiuk, Whistler; and Thom Henley, Skeena Valley. I am also grateful to Tracey Tanaka and Simon Franklin, Environmental Studies Program (now School of Environmental Studies), University of Victoria, who put in many painstaking hours typing and revising various versions of the manuscript, and to Peter Corley-Smith of Victoria, who was an invaluable proofreader and editor.

Dr. Robert D. Levine, who in the early 1970s was researching his doctoral dissertation on Haida grammar, was a collaborator in the recording of Haida plant names. Working mainly with Becky Pearson of Skidegate and Florence Davidson in Massett, he painstakingly checked the transcriptions of plant names gathered previously by me and others. We also made tape recordings of Becky Pearson and Florence Davidson pronouncing the names they were familiar with. Copies of these tapes, and others made with the Haida elders of interviews about plants, are housed with the Skidegate and Massett communities and at the Haida Gwaii Museum at Skidegate.

Field notes made by Dr. C.F. Newcombe around the turn of the 19th century are incorporated with permission of the American Museum of Natural History, Department of Anthropology (Belinda Kaye, Registrar for Loans and Archives;

**Mountains dominate much of the interior of Moresby Island and large parts of Graham Island, as shown at right in this view from Mount Matlock.**

C.F. Newcombe Accession 1897–1947). Permission to reproduce quotations from *During My Time: Florence Edenshaw Davidson, a Haida Woman* by Margaret B. Blackman (1982) has been given by Dr. Blackman and the University of Washington Press.

Our eldest daughter, Sarah Turner, and her friend Juniper Glass were excellent companions on my trip to Haida Gwaii in 1993. Sarah also prepared the botanical drawing of Haida tobacco. My mother, Jane Chapman, helped support this project in many ways. Finally, I want to acknowledge my husband, Bob (Robert D. Turner), who has been a steadfast companion, advisor, photographer, tape recorder, editor, photo scanner and indispensable support system throughout this project. His beautiful photos are featured throughout this book.

Completion of the first edition of this book in 2004 was made possible by University of Victoria Faculty Research Grants in 1993–94, 1995–96, and 2002–03 and by a Social Sciences and Humanities Research Council General Research Grant in 2001–02. Dr. Norman Sloan and Parks Canada Agency for Gwaii Haanas National Park Reserve and Haida Heritage Site generously provided funding for some of the illustrations and supported the book's production in many ways. I am grateful to Diane Morriss and Sono Nis Press for publishing the first two editions of this book, to Jim Brennan for his design work and to Dawn Loewen, for her copy editing skills. Thank you, now, to my friends at Harbour Publishing for bringing out this new edition.

Haawa, thank you again, to all those acknowledged in these pages. I will always treasure the friendships and the teachings from so many, both in Massett and Skidegate, and elsewhere on Haida Gwaii. I hope that this new edition will help to support all their efforts to keep this important knowledge of Haida plants alive for future generations.

Creek at Hlk'yah GawGa (Windy Bay), Gwaii Haanas.

Thimbleberry (**guugadiis xil**), right, and fireweed (**tl'laal**), left, both in full bloom at Skidegate.

## A Note on the Use of Terms

Throughout this book, I have tried to follow the recommendations and wishes of the elders and the Council of the Haida Nation, in the content of the book and in the use of terminology. Sometimes, this means using a word less familiar to others but more acceptable to the Haida, to whom this book is dedicated. The Haida plant names are from several different sources, with some variation. I have tried to follow the preferences of the Haida speakers, and have provided variants when there was uncertainty. Due to the complexity of spelling and to recent changes in spellings, there may be some errors, but I have done my best to minimize these. I deeply appreciate the elders' efforts in making the spellings as accurate as possible. The following are comments on specific wording used:

1 **Haida Gwaii**. The oldest Haida name of the island archipelago (formerly the Queen Charlotte Islands) is **diidaa kwaa gwaayaay** (literally 'out of concealment' or 'the visible world,' as opposed to the spirit world—John Enrico). The commonly used and politically preferred form among the Haida community is Haida Gwaii (**x̲aaydaa gwaay**), which is used throughout and is now the official name for the islands.

2 **Story** and **narrative** are used throughout to replace the term "myth," which is seen to have derogatory implications as a "fabrication." Similarly, "ancient times" or "long ago times" is used instead of "mythological times," and "supernatural being" replaces "mythical being."

3 **X̲uya** (Skidegate dialect) and **Yaahl** (Massett dialect) are featured over the English translation, "Raven."

4 **Nang'iitlagadaas** (Massett dialect) (literally 'respected, prosperous one'—Henry Geddes) is used, where possible, in preference to "chief," which is a term regarded by some Haida as colonial and not fully reflecting the attributes of the original Haida term. For simplicity, however, the word "chief" is retained within quotations from other sources, such as the narratives recorded by John Swanton.

5 **Massett**. This spelling, rather than "Masset" (which is generally seen on maps), reflects the preference of many Haida.

See also pages 21–24 for Haida sources and their abbreviations and pages 65–71 for explanations of conventions used for plant names, translations and abbreviations.

## Warning and Notation on Haida Medicines and Foods

Any plant medicines I mention in this book are not recommended for use, except under the advice of a physician or trained Haida herbal specialist. Traditional medicines have been used by the Haida under strictly controlled conditions and administered by skilled practitioners having the knowledge and experience of many generations behind them. The context in which such medicines are taken can be a critical factor; diet, lifestyle and physical and mental condition all affect the ways in which people respond to applications of medicine. Some medicines are highly toxic. They can cause illness, or even death, if used improperly.

**Devil's-club (ts'iihlinjaaw - S; ts'iihlanjaaw - M), a highly important medicinal and spiritual plant for Haida and other First Nations.**

Because of concerns of Haida elders and cultural and medicinal specialists for the safety of people who may misuse traditional medicines through lack of knowledge or experience, and for the privacy of traditional medical knowledge, this book does not provide specific information on plant medicines. Any information relating to medicinal or spiritual use of plants is of a general nature. This is to discourage individuals from attempting to experiment with the medicines and possibly harming themselves, and to prevent commercial interests outside the Haida community from capitalizing on their medicines. For the Haida community, a version of this text was prepared for the Council of the Haida Nation that contains more specific information relating to the Haida medicines. As Kii'iljuus states, "The plants are for healing, not for profit."

There is also a need to maintain the integrity of wild plant populations. Haida and other First Nations peoples all along the Northwest Coast have been deeply saddened to observe the destruction of western yew (*Taxus brevifolia*). Commercial harvesters have sought large quantities of bark from this slow-growing and relatively uncommon tree, now given a high commodity value as a source of the anticancer drug Taxol. Justifiably, Haida are extremely worried about commercial exploitation of other medicinal plants and forest products, and the implications of such exploitation on the ecosystems of Haida Gwaii.

Those wishing to try the Haida plant foods described here should be sure of proper identification of the plants, and that prescribed preparation and cooking techniques are used as appropriate. Please respect the plants and the people of Haida Gwaii, and do not harm plant populations, habitats or ecosystems through overharvesting or inappropriate collection methods.

*The special relationship between the Haida and plants is in fact considered private knowledge, and therefore the details in most cases are not presented in a book such as this. Each person has their own particular relationship with the environment and all the things in it expressed in one's own individual way. It is enough to know and to understand that this relationship exists and that it is sacred and private for each individual.*

Massett elders Adelia Adams, Mary Swanson and Dorothy Bell near Juskatla, 2003.
—PHOTO BY MARIANNE B. IGNACE

Massett from the air along the shore of Masset Inlet, May 22, 2006.

Poles at Cumshewa, 1971.

# Haida Gwaii, the Land, the Plants and the Haida

**Right:** The view from Maude Island, Skidegate Inlet, looking north towards Skidegate.

**Opposite page:** North Beach, Graham Island, looking towards House Point/ Naayi k̲un (Rose Spit).

Haida Gwaii has been home to the Haida since time immemorial. The mountains, the waters, the plants and the animals of Haida Gwaii are all part of a magnificent system, supporting and nourishing the Haida and, in turn, respected and embraced by them as an integral part of their culture and identity. Haida Gwaii was named "Queen Charlotte's Islands" in 1787 by Captain Dixon, an English explorer, after his ship (Akrigg and Akrigg 1969). Although the gazetteered name for this archipelago was Queen Charlotte Islands, the Haida were never consulted about this designation, and the name preferred by the Haida and many others is Haida Gwaii. That is the name I have used throughout this book, and it was officially recognized and renamed this way in 2009.

The Haida language reflects the close relationship of the people to the landscape and the other life forms of Haida Gwaii. Over 150 different plant names have been documented, and, as well, there are dozens of specialized terms pertaining to different characteristics, features, classes and parts of plants. A comparable vocabulary exists for animals and landscape features, seasonal and weather features, and other environmental aspects of life.

One of the first people "from away" [**yaatsx̲aaydaaG̲a** (S)] to undertake an in-depth study of Haida language and culture was John R. Swanton. He published several important books and papers on the Haida (e.g., Swanton 1903, 1905a, 1905b, 1908a, 1908b, 1911, 1912, 1913). Many of his notations on plants are incorporated

**Above left:** Emma Matthews and Willie Matthews (Chief Weah), Massett, 1971.

**Above right:** Golie Hans, Haida language teacher and daughter of Kathleen Hans of Skidegate, 1995.

**Right:** Captain Gold with Dja da un koo ding us (Mrs. Captain Gold; Bernice) and their granddaughter, 1995. Captain Gold and Dja da un koo ding us were married at SGang Gwaay.

here. In 1878, George M. Dawson explored the east and north coasts of the islands for the Geological Survey of Canada, and undertook the first major botanical observations on the islands, in conjunction with his descriptions of geology, topography and geographic features (see Dawson 1880; Cole and Lockner 1989). Another early ethnographer of the Haida was physician, naturalist and museum collector Dr. Charles F. Newcombe, who visited the islands many times between 1895 and 1923. He recorded many details of Haida plant use in his journals and notes, which are unpublished but available for review at the BC Archives of the Royal BC Museum (Newcombe 1898–1913), and at the American Museum of Natural History, Department of Anthropology (Newcombe 1897–47). Many others have written about Haida language and culture. The following sources were surveyed for information on plant names and/or uses: Blackman (1982, 1990); Boas (1889, 1991); Bursill-Hall (1962); Calder and Taylor (1968); Dawson (1880); Duff (1954, 1970); Duff and Kew (1958); Harrison (1895, 1925); Jenness (1934); Kess (1968); Levine (1977); Norton (1981); and Sapir (1923). Calder and Taylor provide a detailed history of the botanical explorations and research of Haida Gwaii in their *Flora of the Queen Charlotte Islands*, as well as meticulous descriptions of the vascular plants of the islands and their distributions and taxonomic affiliations.

Most of the information on Haida plants and plant names included here was contributed by the Haida elders consulted. These include (in alphabetical order):

**LEFT: Sol and Emma Wilson, Skidegate, 1971.**

**RIGHT: Mabel Williams peeling cedar bark, Skidegate, 1996.**

Eliza Abrams (EA), Massett (interviewed briefly in 1971)
Edmund Calder (EdC), Skidegate (interviewed in 1971)
Elizabeth Collinson (EC), Skidegate (interviewed in 1971)
Captain Gold (CG), Skidegate (discussed plants and Haida culture and history with me in 1995, 1996, 1998, 2000)
Florence Davidson (FD), Massett (interviewed in 1971, 1972, 1973; visited in 1993)
Amanda Edgars (AE), Massett (interviewed in 1971)
Henry Geddes (HG), Massett (visited in 1993)
Kathleen Hans (KH), Skidegate (interviewed in 1972; visited briefly in 1993)
Golie (Kathleen) Hans, daughter of Kathleen Hans, Skidegate (discussed plants with me in 1995, 1996, 1998)
Agnes Edenshaw Yeltatzie Jones (spruce root collection field work with Florence Davidson in 1972)
Gertrude Kelly (GK), Vancouver (interviewed in 1970, 1971)
Chief Willie Matthews (WM), Massett (interviewed in 1971, 1972)
Emma Matthews (EM), Massett (interviewed in 1971, 1972)
Agnes Moody (AM), Skidegate (interviewed in 1971)
Maude Moody (MM), Skidegate (interviewed in 1971)
Becky Pearson (BP), Skidegate (interviewed in 1972)
Sarah Pryce (SP), Skidegate (interviewed in 1971)
Watson Pryce (WP), Skidegate (interviewed in 1971)
Mabel Williams (MW), Skidegate (discussed plants with me in 1995, 1996, 1998)
Emma Wilson (EW), Skidegate (interviewed in 1971)
Solomon Wilson (SW), Skidegate (interviewed in 1971)
George Young (GY), Skidegate (interviewed in 1971, 1972)
Ada Yovanovich (AY), Skidegate (interviewed in 1971; discussed plants and this book with me in 1995, 1998)

In addition, information provided by Adam and Ruth Bell and Emma Matthews as told to Marianne Boelscher (now Marianne Ignace) (ca. 1978–1982), and notations of plant use as reported by Blackman (1982) in her work with Florence

Davidson, are included. Massett elders Adelia Adams, Dorothy Bell, Mary Swanson, Gertie White and Colleen Williams, working with Marianne Ignace, provided further feedback in 2001–2003; they are also featured in photographs in the book. The initials of the elders are given beside the Haida plant terms they provided or confirmed. Many aspects of plant knowledge are, or were, widely and generally known within the Haida speech community. In this book, when no reference citation is included with a piece of information, the reader can assume that it was known and contributed by three or more of the elders interviewed; details known to only one or two of the elders are acknowledged by their names. Throughout the book are notations of terms and associated information provided by Dr. John Enrico, from his review of the manuscript in the summer of 1993. These are simply cited as (JE) or, in the text, John Enrico. All are from his personal communication to me in 1993 and/or 1994.

## The Land

Haida Gwaii is an island archipelago in the northeast Pacific Ocean. The two major islands are Graham, at the north, and Moresby, to the south. These are separated by a narrow stretch of water, Skidegate Inlet and Skidegate Channel. There are several other large Islands—Langara, off the northwest tip of Graham Island; Louise, Lyell and Burnaby Islands off the east coast of Moresby; and Kunghit, at the southern extremity of the Moresby Island group—and many small ones are ranged around Graham and Moresby Islands. In all, there are approximately 150 islands in this archipelago, lying between 52 and 54 degrees north latitude and 131 and 133 degrees west longitude. The length of the archipelago is about 250 km (156 mi), the maximum width just over 80 km (52 mi), and the total combined area nearly 1,000,000 ha, or 10,000 $km^2$, or 3,860 sq mi. The islands are situated on the western rim of the continental shelf of western North America and are separated from the mainland of Canada and southern Alaska by a relatively shallow body of water, Hecate Strait, which ranges in depth from 15 to just over 90 m (50 to 300 ft) and in width from 50 km (30 mi) at the north end to 130 km (80 mi) at the south end. Geologists, geomorphologists and archaeologists have started a systematic survey of the ocean floor along the east coast of Haida Gwaii. There is increasing evidence to support the existence of ancient habitation sites, now under the ocean, from a time when the shoreline was considerably lower down than today. Haida lands were even more extensive once than they are now. The beds of ancient rivers, converging near ancient shores, are revealed by careful suboceanic surveys, and in 1999, for the first time, an artifact, a flaked stone tool, was recovered from an ancient shoreline site on the ocean floor. It was found in a sample of ocean floor of Hecate Strait at 53 m (174 ft) below present sea level, near Werner Bay on the central east coast of Moresby Island, in a place where a village or camp may once have been situated (Captain Gold, personal communication 2000; Quentin Mackie and Daryl Fedji, archaeologists, personal communication 2001). Many stories of Haida history have yet to be told.

The physiography, geological history and climate of Haida Gwaii are summarized by Calder and Taylor (1968). The reader is also referred to a more recent publication, *The Outer Shores* (Scudder and Gessler 1989), for detailed information on the environment and history of Haida Gwaii. Briefly, the islands can be divided into three major physiographic units: the Queen Charlotte Ranges, the Skidegate Plateau and the Queen Charlotte Lowlands. The mountains of the Queen Charlotte Ranges form the backbone of the islands and are very rugged, with some peaks reaching 1,230 m (4,000 ft) in height, and many between 770 and 1,075 m (2,500 and 3,500 ft) high. These ranges drop abruptly into the ocean on the western side, creating a steep, rocky coastline virtually devoid of beaches. Sloping northeastward from the Ranges is the Skidegate Plateau, a peneplain of table-topped hills and flat ridges, partially divided up by waterways. Most of the extensive forest

**Opposite page: Beach and headland on southern Gwaii Haanas with bull kelp (hlk̲yaama - S; hlk̲aa.m - M) washed up with the high tide, July 2010.**

communities are located on these plateau lands, and, in fact, much of the old-growth forest of this area has already been logged, in some cases with two or three cutovers.

At the edge of the Skidegate Plateau, farther to the northeast, are the extensive low-lying, boggy Queen Charlotte Lowlands, an undulating country of coniferous forest and raised bogs cut through by networks of sluggish streams and ponds. A few prominent hills, remnants of ancient volcanic activity, arise from this otherwise flat landscape. The best known of these is Tow Hill, along the northeast coast of Graham Island. More occur under the ocean and project out of the water as rounded, steep-sided islands. Along the eastern and northeastern coastlines are many beaches, ranging from the smooth, sandy expanses of **Naayii k̲un** (Naikoon; Rose Spit) and **Tll'aal** (Tlell), to gravel or cobble beaches and coves, to wave-cut rocky benches, as along the shore north of Skidegate Inlet.

All of the geological and physiographic features of the islands have been shaped by the diverse processes of volcanic activity, folding, uplift, erosion, sedimentation and glaciation. The earliest rocks, older than 200 million years, are altered basic volcanic rocks thousands of metres thick. By the end of the Triassic Period, there was an accumulation of thousands of metres of limestone and limy mud containing many invertebrate fossils. These materials were folded, uplifted, eroded and covered by layers of sedimentary rocks. Violent and varied volcanic activity lasted throughout most of the Jurassic Period, with great sheets of lavas alternating with thick accumulations of products of explosive eruptions, aggregating to more than 3,000 m (9,800 ft) thick. These form the primary rock masses of the islands. Further igneous intrusions and basalt flows, deposits of eroded materials from fluctuating sea levels, foldings, faultings and upliftings, culminating in the onset of Pleistocene glaciation—all have given the islands their unique characteristics, as described by geologists such as A. Sutherland Brown (1960).

**Opposite page: Haida Gwaii (formerly the Queen Charlotte Islands): major geographical features and Haida village sites.** –COURTESY OF JOHN BROADHEAD AND GOWGAIA INSTITUTE

The climate of Haida Gwaii is generally mild, with cool summers and mild winters. Especially in the fall and early winter, cloudy skies and strong winds prevail, with heavy seasonal precipitation, particularly on the west-facing slopes, where annual precipitation may exceed 700 cm (280 in). On the east coast, in the rain shadow of the mountain ranges, annual precipitation is lower, generally between 100 and 125 cm (40–50 in). In the mountains, much of the winter precipitation falls as snow, which may accumulate to depths of two or more metres (six or more feet), and, at upper altitudes, lasts well into the summer. The heavy rains of Haida Gwaii are recognized in at least one ethnobotanical tradition: the brightly coloured blooms of red columbine (*Aquilegia formosa*) and blue harebell (*Campanula rotundifolia*) are known respectively as **dall(-xil)-sgid** (M) ("red rain flowers") and **dall(-xíl)-guhlahl** (M) ("blue rain flowers"). Haida children were warned not to pick them or it would rain, making it impossible to dry the edible seaweed (*Pyropia abbottiae*).

"Haida Gwaii DEM" © 2003 the Gowgaia Institute, and amended with Haida place names with permission.

Mountains are the backbone of Haida Gwaii, and part of the geographically diverse landscape that is so important to the Haida. This view is from one of the important bogs on Moresby Island, between Skidegate and Mosquito Lakes.

Most of the old forests of Haida Gwaii have already been logged, and many areas of second growth have also been logged. Logging has disrupted the salmon streams and caused serious environmental damage.

## The Plants

The diverse landscapes of Haida Gwaii are reflected in the biodiversity of the islands, in terms of both their plants and their animals, and in the multitudes of biotic communities. The islands' relative isolation has allowed the development of several notably unique and endemic species, subspecies and varieties of plants and animals. However, most of the culturally significant species have ranges extending over a wide area. There are, in fact, several notable gaps in the flora of Haida Gwaii, including tree species that do not occur on the islands, but, in some cases, whose wood was imported by the Haida: black cottonwood (*Populus balsamifera* ssp. *trichocarpa*), paper birch (*Betula papyrifera*), Rocky Mountain maple (*Acer glabrum*), cascara (*Frangula purshiana*), bitter cherry (*Prunus emarginata*), true firs (*Abies amabilis*, *Abies grandis* and *Abies lasiocarpa*) and Douglas-fir (*Pseudotsuga menziesii*). Some of these have been recently introduced. Cottonwood and weeping willow (*Salix alba*) are growing at Skidegate Landing and elsewhere on the islands, and the Ministry of Forests has had Douglas-fir planted in some locations on an experimental basis.

The phytogeography of the islands is discussed in detail by Calder and Taylor (1968), and distribution maps for a total of 593 vascular plant species occurring on Haida Gwaii are included in that volume. More recently, the biotic and cultural features of Haida Gwaii are described in detail in *The Outer Shores*, a book edited by Scudder and Gessler and published by the Queen Charlotte Islands Museum Press (1989). Since that time, there have been many other publications about Haida culture and Haida Gwaii environments (see Fedje and Mathewes 2005; Steedman and Collison 2011; Kroeger et al. 2012; Turner 2014; and Williams-Davidson 2017).

**Most of Haida Gwaii consists of forest ecosystems dominated by Sitka spruce, western hemlock and western red-cedar.**

**For thousands of years Tow Hill, on the north coast of Graham Island, has been a culturally significant landmark.**

The various Haida Gwaii plant communities were identified and delineated by Calder and Taylor (1968). The lowland communities of particular relevance to the Haida are summarized in Table 1. Montane plant communities of upland meadows, talus slopes, cliffs and runnels and other rock outcrops are described, and representative plants noted, by Calder and Taylor (1968). The great majority of these species have not been reported to have specific significance to the Haida, but the places are nonetheless culturally important.

**Skidegate Inlet, sheltered from storms, divides Graham and Moresby Islands.**

**Clockwise from top left:**
Sac seaweed (*Halosaccion glandiforme*).

*Glehnia littoralis*, a type of "beach carrot" (celery family), a typical plant of Haida Gwaii coastal sand dunes.

"Red rain flowers" (red columbine); children were told that picking these flowers caused rain.

Stand of western red-cedar on the shore of Mosquito Lake, Moresby Island.

Devil's-club, a culturally important shrub becoming rare because of deer browsing.

**Clockwise from top:**

Mosquito Lake, on Moresby Island, is one of Haida Gwaii's many ponds and lakes.

Yellow pond-lily (xil gaydllgins - S; xil gii dlagang - M) is a common aquatic plant found around pond and lake edges. Its thick rhizomes are an important Haida medicine. The boggy areas on Haida Gwaii are key habitats for many important Haida plant resources, such as yellow pond-lily, Haida tea, sphagnum moss, and bog cranberries.

High-elevation bog on Moresby Island, above Crescent Inlet.

Boggy slope on Moresby Island at de la Beche.

The white, fluffy heads of cotton-grasses are conspicuous in many of the bogs.

**Table 1.** Summary of Lower-Elevation Plant Communities of Haida Gwaii (based on Calder and Taylor 1968), with Representative Plants of Known Cultural Importance.

| GENERAL CLASS | COMMUNITY TYPE | Some Representative Plants Known to and Used by Haida* |
|---|---|---|
| MARITIME | Subtidal | eelgrass, bull kelp, giant kelp, common rockweed, seagrass, edible seaweed |
| MARITIME | Shingle beach | springbank clover, American dune grass, glasswort, hemlock-parsley, beach lovage, mission bells, sea pea, seaside plantain, salal, stonecrop, seaside strawberry, giant vetch |
| MARITIME | Sand beach | American dune grass, beach lupine, sea pea, large-headed sedge, silverweed, seaside strawberry, beach tansy, beach wormwood, yarrow |
| MARITIME | Rock and cliff | common bedstraw, western buttercup, red columbine, blue harebell, hemlock-parsley, kinnikinnick, Nootka lupine, mission bells, yellow monkeyflower, seaside plantain, Nootka rose, salal, saskatoon berry, stonecrop, seaside strawberry, yarrow |
| MARITIME | Salt marsh | arrow-grass, springbank clover, eelgrass |
| BOG AND SWAMP | Swamp | mountain alder, Pacific crab apple, Labrador-tea, yellow pond-lily, skunk-cabbage, round-leaved sundew, Scouler's willow |
| BOG AND SWAMP | Mire | Pacific crab apple, Labrador-tea |
| BOG AND SWAMP | Bog | bog blueberry, mountain blueberry, bunchberry, cloudberry, cottongrass, Pacific crab apple, bog cranberry, crowberry, western hemlock, common juniper, swamp laurel, lingonberry, Labrador-tea, lodgepole pine, yellow pond-lily, western red-cedar, round-leaved sundew, yellow-cedar, sphagnum mosses |
| FRESHWATER AQUATIC | Lake and pond | field mint, yellow pond-lily |
| FOREST | Sand-dune forest | red alder, calypso, springbank clover, stink currant, red elderberry, western hemlock, red huckleberry, licorice fern, wild lily-of-the-valley, lodgepole pine, salal, salmonberry, single delight, sourgrass, Sitka spruce, sword fern, yarrow |

* Listed alphabetically by primary common name; for scientific and Haida names, refer to the index.

CONTINUED ...

**TABLE 1** (CONTINUED)

| GENERAL CLASS | COMMUNITY TYPE | Some Representative Plants Known to and Used by Haida* |
|---|---|---|
| FOREST | Meadow forest (alluvial flats and terraces) | red alder, false azalea, oval-leaved blueberry, red columbine, stink currant, devil's-club, red-osier dogwood, false hellebore, western hemlock, western red-cedar, Nootka wild rose, salal, Sitka spruce, thimbleberry, spiny wood fern |
| FOREST | Closed forest | red alder, false azalea, Alaska blueberry, oval-leaved blueberry, bunchberry, stink currant, western hemlock, red huckleberry, wild lily-of-the-valley, western red-cedar, salmonberry, single delight, skunk-cabbage, Sitka spruce, twistedstalk, spiny wood fern, western yew |
| FOREST | Forest clearings and edges | Alaska blueberry, oval-leaved blueberry, cow-parsnip, Pacific crab apple, highbush cranberry, red elderberry, fireweed, black hawthorn, red huckleberry, broad-leaved plantain, Nootka rose, salal, salmonberry, stinging nettle, thimbleberry, black twinberry, yarrow |
| FOREST | Upland forest | red alder, Sitka alder, red columbine, cow-parsnip, red elderberry, false hellebore, mountain hemlock, western hemlock, lodgepole pine, western red-cedar, salmonberry, Sitka spruce, yellow-cedar, yarrow, western yew |

* Listed alphabetically by primary common name; for scientific and Haida names, refer to the index.

## The Haida

**Ancient Sitka spruce at Windy Bay.**

**Opposite page, left and right: Spruce-hemlock forest at de la Beche Inlet, Gwaii Haanas.**

**Anne Nightingale stands beside the magnificent "Glory tree," an old-growth Sitka spruce, Windy Bay, estimated to be between 800 and 900 years old. It can take 10 or more people, arms stretched, to encircle the tree at its base. Many ancient Sitka spruce were logged for wartime aircraft construction.**

> People are like trees, and groups of people are like the forests. While the Forests are composed of many different kinds of trees, these trees intertwine their roots so strongly that it is impossible for the strongest winds which blow on our islands to uproot the Forest, for each tree strengthens its neighbour, and their roots are inextricably intertwined.
>
> In the same way the people of our Islands, composed of members of nations and races from all over the world, are beginning to intertwine their roots so strongly that no troubles will affect them.
>
> Just as one tree standing alone would soon be destroyed by the first strong wind which came along, so it is impossible for any person, any family, or any community to stand alone against the troubles of this world.
>
> —*Chief Skidegate (Lewis Collinson), March 1966*
> (Text provided by the Council of the Haida Nation)

The Haida have, from time immemorial, passed the details of their culture and history orally from one generation to the next. At the time of the arrival of the first Europeans, the Haida Nation occupied more than 20 permanent villages distributed along the coastline of Haida Gwaii and the Alexander Archipelago in southeastern Alaska. These villages, with estimated populations in the mid-1800s ranging from about 120 at **Naayii <u>k</u>un** (Naikoon) to about 750 at Skidegate (**s<u>G</u>iidagids** - S; from rock chiton—**s<u>G</u>iida**) (Blackman 1990:257), consisted of one or two rows of houses extending in a line along the shore, nestled against the treeline and facing the beach. The houses were of one or more matrilineal lineages, and that of the most important individual, or "town chief," better termed **Nang'iitlagadaas** (M) (literally "respected, wealthy one"—Henry Geddes, personal communication to Gidansda) and his family tended to be located either in the centre or at one end of the village. The characteristics and layout of the villages are described by Blackman (1990).

Swanton (1905a) delineated six major groupings of Haida Peoples (from north to south). Each group would have had its own particular dialect, although most dialects were similar enough that people could communicate with each other:

Kaigani, from Dadens on Langara Island (major villages: Sukkwan, Howkwan, Koianglas, Klinkwan and Kasaan);

North coast of Graham Island, from Rose Point (major villages: Yaku, Kiusta, Kung, Yan, Kayung, Massett [now Haida] and Hiellen);

**Skidegate Village, 1884. At that time over 30 poles were standing.** –ROYAL BRITISH COLUMBIA MUSEUM 16220 M136; PHOTO BY RICHARD MAYNARD

**Skidegate Village in a postcard view from the early 1900s. Note how the number of poles has decreased and the style of building construction has changed.** –RYAN PHOTO

Skidegate Inlet (major village: Skidegate);
West coast of Moresby Island (major villages: Chaatl and Kaisun, and later Haina—**xaay naa**);
East coast of Moresby Island (major villages: Cumshewa, Skedans and Tanu [Kloo]); and
Southern, or Kunghit people (major village: Nansdins [Ninstints] on SGang Gwaay [Skangwaii, Anthony Island]).

Another, anomalous group, the "Pitch-Town-People," from the west coast of Haida Gwaii, was identified by Swanton. Unlike the people of the other Haida villages, who had many crests (mostly significant animals) associated with their lineages and clans, these people were said to have lacked a crest system (Swanton 1905a).

Haida apparently migrated to Alaska relatively recently, around the year 1750 (Swanton 1911). The major Haida village sites are shown in the map on page 27.

An overview of the traditional culture and history of the Haida is provided by Blackman (1990), who has worked with Haida of both Haida Gwaii and Alaska since the early 1970s. The reader is referred to that publication for general information and references on the Haida, including sections on Haida territory, settlement patterns, house structures, subsistence, division of labour, trade and warfare, transportation, art, technology, cosmology, social organization, ceremonies, life cycles, history and population. Blackman also authored the biography of Florence Davidson, *During My Time* (1982), which contains many references to plants.

The Haida language, first described in detail by John R. Swanton (1911), has been more thoroughly characterized by Levine (1977) and Enrico (1980). Haida

**Massett: one of the earliest photographs of this village, taken in 1879. Over 30 poles or houseposts are evident in this photo.**
–Royal BC Museum 10980; photo by O.C. Hastings

**"Town Chief Weha's Home. Massett B.C." from a coloured post card, published in Germany in the early 1900s. (The current spelling is "Weah.")**

has no demonstrable relationship with any other language, and is thus considered a language isolate (see Thompson and Kinkade 1990). A description of the phonology, and the symbols used to represent the sounds of the Haida language, based on John Enrico's work and modified to the writing systems developed and used most recently by Skidegate (see Skidegate Elders and SHIP 2016) and Massett speakers, is provided in Appendix 1.

The demographic history of the Haida and the impact of Europeans and their activities is recounted by Duff (1964) and, more recently, Boyd (1990). As a result of the severe decline in population, from an original number of 7,000 to 10,000 on Haida Gwaii to under 600 people by 1915, the surviving Haida of British Columbia congregated at two main centres. Those from Moresby Island and vicinity assembled at Skidegate, and are now recognized as the speakership of the Skidegate dialect of Haida (S). Those from the northern villages around Graham Island and vicinity congregated at Massett (also known as Masset, Old Massett or Haida), and now comprise the speakership of the Massett dialect (M). The Alaskan Haida, mostly at Hydaburg, speak a dialect closely related to the Massett dialect, known as Kaigani (A). Descendency from original villages, and families, is still recognized; people are proud of their heritage and ancestral connections, clans and lineages, no matter where they reside today.

# The Role of Plants in Haida Culture

In all, over 150 specific types of plants are identified in this study. Many other plants, though not readily distinguished by name, were recognized by those consulted as being distinct kinds. Many plants were particularly important culturally, whether for food, material or medicine; some also played a role in ceremony or religious thought. However, even the plants that might be considered unimportant by virtue of not being "used" in some particular way were regarded as special and as living entities with their own power, their own spirit and their own ability to help those deemed to be good and respectful. In fact, everything in the Haida universe—plants, animals, water, rocks, mountains, stars and the sun and moon—all of these were, and are, seen as sacred and important.

In the following sections, the roles of plants under different categories will be considered, but the reader must keep in mind that it is each plant's whole entity and its essence that are important. Often it is truly impossible to separate

**OPPOSITE PAGE: The bald eagle is a common and magnificent bird of Haida Gwaii. The Eagle clan is one of the two Haida clans, the other being Raven.**

**RIGHT: Sunset on Skidegate Inlet.**

a plant's roles into material or spiritual spheres, or into applications of providing nutrition or healing powers, for example; these roles blend together, with no sharp division.

In this chapter, common English and commonly applied Haida names will be used in referring to the plants. For details of lesser-known Haida names and scientific names of the species mentioned, the reader should consult the specific plant write-ups, whose pages are referenced in the index.

## Food Plants

The traditional diet of the Haida is nutritious and well balanced. It is no wonder that the first Europeans who encountered the Haida characterized them as physically strong and generally healthy. Like all Indigenous Peoples of the Northwest Coast Culture Area (as described and defined by Suttles 1990), they relied and continue to rely heavily for their nutrition on animal foods from the ocean and rivers—fish, shellfish and marine mammals. They also hunted birds and used the eggs and young of some types. Land mammals were of lesser importance as food; the deer that now range so freely over Haida Gwaii were not there originally. They were introduced within the 19th and 20th centuries, although they were known to the Haida from the adjacent mainland areas. The deer and other introduced species, such as raccoon, muskrat, beaver and rats, have had a severe impact on the natural ecosystems of Haida Gwaii and on the availability of traditional resources, including certain berries and other plant foods. Recent research shows the far-reaching effects of the many exotic species introduced intentionally or accidentally to Haida Gwaii (Vila et al. 2001; Stockton et al. 2001; Engelstoft and Bland 2002).

Plant foods in the traditional Haida diet, although having a lower profile than the animal foods, were also crucial and, like other wild foods, are still significant today. Plant foods encompass a wide range of categories, from roots and other underground parts to green leaves and shoots, berries and other kinds of fruits, the inner bark of trees, and the fronds of some marine algae. Mosses, lichens and, surprisingly, mushrooms and other fungi were not generally utilized as food. This is a common situation on the Northwest Coast and across the northern part of the continent, where even edible types of mushrooms were regarded with some apprehension and were not generally eaten (Kuhnlein and Turner 1991; Turner 1995). Appendix 2 lists plant foods used by the Haida within the various categories mentioned. Also included are specific categories for casual or emergency foods, beverage plants, flavourings, plants for smoking or chewing and plants used in food gathering or preparation. The Haida names, as well as scientific and English names, are provided in the plant-use appendices.

Plants contribute a range of nutrients in the traditional diet. The "root vegetables," which generally comprise major storage organs of the plants, provide

**LEFT: Beaver were introduced to Haida Gwaii; there is evidence of their work in many places.**

**RIGHT: A Columbia black-tailed deer fawn, an introduced species, finds a hiding place on the beach.**

carbohydrates. The carbohydrate content is usually maximized at the end of the leaf-growing season, before new shoots appear. This is the usual time—fall through to spring—when the roots were harvested. Usually, root foods provide only relatively small amounts of vitamins. Green vegetables—including leaves, stems and shoots—are generally available (i.e., tender and palatable) in their young stages, in spring. As a group, they have a high moisture content; vitamins, including carotene (vitamin A), vitamin C and folic acid; and minerals such as iron, calcium, magnesium and various trace elements. Vitamin C is an example of a nutrient essential to human health for which plant foods were major contributors. It is notable that fireweed [**tl'laal** (S), **tl'ii'aal** (M), **tl'íi.aal** (A)], a species rich in vitamin C, was eagerly sought in the springtime as a raw green vegetable and spring tonic. Wild berries and other fleshy fruits are also generally good sources of vitamins C and A and folic acid, as well as of various minerals. The marine algae are exceptionally good sources of vitamins and minerals. Their carbohydrates may not be fully digestible, but might be broken down into more digestible compounds by the processing techniques applied to them. Beverage teas, as well as some of the medicinal infusions or decoctions ingested, would undoubtedly also have contributed to the vitamins and minerals in the diet (Keely 1980; Medical Services Branch 1985; Kuhnlein and Turner 1991; Turner 1995). Although there is little direct evidence

**Left:** Fireweed shoots at their edible stage; the inner portion is sweet and succulent in the spring.

**Centre:** Pacific silverweed roots prepared for a pit-cooking feast.
—PHOTO BY MARIANNE B. IGNACE

**Right:** Wild berries are as important as ever; here, frozen and slightly thawed berries are being prepared for mashing to make a dessert. The implement is Florence Davidson's yew-wood berry-masher.

of the quantities of plant foods consumed by Haida families traditionally, it can be assumed that plant products of one or more kinds were eaten with most meals throughout the year. Many baskets of berries would have been harvested—perhaps 50 or 100 litres (13 to 26 gallons) annually per family, with probably lesser quantities of root vegetables, greens, seaweeds and tree cambium.

Aside from their nutritional contributions, plant foods also enhanced and provided diversity in the diet. The important role of plant foods in Haida ceremonies and narratives, and in traditional and religious beliefs, is testimony of their high level of cultural importance.

In all, the Haida ate approximately 15 species of "root vegetables" (roots and other underground parts, including corms, rhizomes, bulbs and tubers) traditionally (Appendix 2-A). Some of these were used frequently and in quantity, while the use of others was more opportunistic or specialized. In the former category are the bulbs of "Indian rice," or northern riceroot [**'inhling** (S), **stla k̲'iist'aa** (M, A)], roots of Pacific silverweed [**ts'i'aal, ts'iiaal** (S), **ts'a.al, ts'a'al** (M), **k̲'wíi ts'a.aláay** (A)], and rhizomes of springbank clover [**naa'a** (S)], spiny wood fern [**sk'yaaw** (S, M), **sk'yáaw** (A)] and bracken fern [**saagun** (S), **ts'aagwaal hlk̲'a.aay** (M)]. Examples of the latter include the corms of the calypso, or false ladyslipper [**sk̲il tawaatl'l̲xaay** (S), **sk̲il taw, sk̲il tuu** (M), **sk̲íidaw** (A)], roots of the "wild carrot," or hemlock-parsley [**gyaagyaa k̲'al sguna** (S) and other terms], and, apparently, the rhizomes of sword fern [**ts'aagul** (S), **ts'aagwaal** (M), **ts'áagwaal** (A)] and stinging nettle [**G̲udangxaal** (S), **G̲udang.aal, G̲udang'al** (M), **G̲udáng.aal** (A)]. Aside from the wild root vegetables, potatoes [**sgawsiid** (S), **sguusiid** (M), **sgúusiid** (A)] were introduced to Haida Gwaii very early in the historic period. The Haida immediately adopted them and became renowned cultivators of these tubers, producing large quantities for their own use as well as for sale and trade to their neighbouring Nations, and to the Hudson's Bay Company. Other domesticated

**Top left:** Wild blueberries, an important Haida forest food.

**Top right:** Red huckleberries, a tart and delicious fruit of Haida Gwaii.

**Bottom left:** Salal berries, a delicious staple Haida fruit.

**Bottom right:** Highbush cranberries, a prized fruit that commonly features in Haida narratives.

root vegetables cultivated by the Haida in historic times include turnips, beets and carrots (see Appendix 10).

Green vegetables in the traditional Haida diet include such foods as shoots of fireweed [**tl'laal** (S), **tl'ii'aal** (M), **tl'íi.aal** (A)], giant horsetail [**k̲'ada sg̲awg̲a** (S), **dal x̲aw** (M) and other terms], cow-parsnip [**hlk'iid** (S, M), **hlk'íid** (A)], thimbleberry [sprouts: **k̲aysgwaan** (S), **dangaldagaa**, **dangaldgaa** (M), "**stl'agudiisalay**" (A)] and salmonberry [sprouts: **ts'ixaal** (S), **ts'asaal** (M), **ts'a.áal**, **tsa'áal** (A)], stems and leaves of western dock [**tl'aangk̲'uus** (S), **tl'aak̲'uus**, **tl'aak̲'uuj** (M), **t'láak̲'uj**, **tl'áak̲'us** (A)], and some of the marine algae, including giant kelp [**ngaal** (S, M), **ngáal** (A)] (usually eaten with herring eggs deposited on the fronds)

**LEFT: Soapberries, which do not grow on Haida Gwaii, are a valuable gift and trade item for the Haida.**

**RIGHT: Pacific crab apples, a highly regarded Haida food, were often stored for winter in boxes with water and oil.**

and edible seaweed [**sGyuu** (S), **sGiw** (M), **sGíw** (A)] of two or more different species. A total of 20 species are included in this category (Appendix 2-B). Within the historical period, some people also started using stinging nettle greens [**Gudangxaal** (S), **Gudang.aal**, **Gudang'al** (M), **Gudáng.aal** (A)] as a pot-herb. Domesticated rhubarb, which in Haida is named after western dock [**tl'aangk'uus** (S), **tl'aak'uus**, **tl'aak'uuj** (M), **t'láak'uj**, **tl'áak'us** (A)], was widely adopted (stalks only; the leaves are poisonous) as a dessert and jam vegetable. Spinach and beet greens were also cultivated, as well as cabbage, lettuce, chard and other leafy vegetables (Appendix 10).

A wide variety of wild berries and other fruits—30 species in all—were also utilized (Appendix 2-C). These can be harvested mostly beginning in the summertime through early fall, but many were, and are, processed for winter storage and used year-round. Important traditional fruits include bunchberries [**ts'ik'ab** (S), **ts'iik'ab**, **ts'iik'abaa**, **ts'iik'ab xil** (M), **ts'íik'ab** (A)], seaside strawberries [**hilGudaGaang** (S), **hillda.aang** (M), **hildaGáang** (A)], salal berries [**sk'idGaan** (S), **sk'idaan**, **sk'id'aan** (M), **sk'itáan** (A)], Pacific crab apples [**k'ay** (S, M), **k'áy** (A)], stink currants [**Gal-Gun** (S), **Gal.un** (M), **Gál.un** (A)], cloudberries [**k'aaxu ts'alaangGa** (S), **k'a.àw ts'alaangaa** (M), **k'aawts'aláangaa** (A)], thimbleberries [**gugadiis** (S), **stl'a gudiis** (M), **stl'a gudíis** (A)], salmonberries [**sk'awGaan** (S), **sk'aw.aan** (M), **sk'aw.áan** (A)], and various species of blueberries, huckleberries and cranberries in the genus *Vaccinium* [e.g., **hldaan** (S, M), **hldáan** (A); **sGiidllGuu** (S), **sGidlùu** (M), **sGidluu** (A); **dah** (S, M, A); **sk'agi tsaay** (S), **skaga tsaay**, **sk'ag tsaay** (M), **sk'ag tsáay** (A)]. Most of the juicier, sweeter types of berries were preserved by cooking, mashing and drying in cakes on skunk-cabbage leaves [**hlgun** (S, M), **hlgún** (A)] laid out on racks in the sun or set over a fire. The more acidic fruits, most of which were ready to harvest later in the year, including Pacific crab apples [**k'ay** (S, M), **k'áy** (A)], highbush cranberries [**hlaayi** (S), **hlaa.i**, **hlaayaa** (M), **hláay** (A)], bog cranberries [**dah** (S, M, A)] and lingonberries [**skaga tsaay**, **sk'ag tsaay** (M), **sk'ag tsáay** (A)], were generally stored in water in bentwood cedar boxes, topped with a layer of oil. Stored in this fashion, they kept well, becoming softer and sweeter as the winter progressed. These berries were often used as much appreciated gifts.

**Florence Davidson Recalls Picking Berries**

When we came back to Massett from the cannery, I used to pick berries with my mother. We went up to New Massett for salal [**sk'idaan**]. There weren't any white people there then, just all kinds of berries. My mother also used to go to Watun River for red huckleberries [**sG̲idlùu**] and I went with her. She'd bring the berries home and cook them with salmon eggs for thickening. She boiled them till they were dry. She put the berries in a bentwood box with a cloth covering over them, then thimbleberry leaves [**stl'a gudiis xil**] and skunk-cabbage leaves [**hlgun**] on top before she put the lid on. She cooked her berries in the shed behind the house where my dad carved, and she stored them there, too. She cooked salal berries the same way. My mother put up huckleberries, salal, and cranberries [**hlaayaa**] in boxes, five or six of them, for the winter. She used to jam blueberries [**hldaan**] in big jars, and she preserved maltberries [cloudberries] [**k̲'a.àw ts'alaangaa**] and crab apples [**k'ay**] in water. My dad had a little dugout ... and my mother, Emma Matthews' mother, and Alfred Adams' mother used to paddle out to Tow Hill to pick crab apples in October ... They'd spend days and days there and get real lots of crab apples. Sometimes they'd pick the stem off and preserve the apples in a barrel. Other times they'd cook the apples, just simmer them, and put them in a barrel. Wintertime they'd take the juice out. It tastes like apple cider. Then they'd whip up grease and mix the apples with grease and sugar ... They put the mixture in a bent box, put a clean flour sack on top, and put roasted thimbleberry leaves and roasted skunk-cabbage leaves on top of that cloth. They packed clean sand on top of the leaves so air doesn't get in. (Blackman 1982:82)

Certain berries found on the mainland, including soapberries [**'as** (S), **xagutl'iid** (M), **xagutl'íid** (A)], wild raspberries and blackcaps, do not occur on Haida Gwaii. Soapberries were obtained through trade and were an important feast and ceremonial food. In fact, several foods, including highbush cranberries [**hlaayi** (S), **hlaa.i**, **hlaayaa** (M), **hláay** (A)], Pacific crab apples [**k'ay** (S, M), **k'áy** (A)], and soapberries, are named time and again in Haida narratives, in the context of other "high class" foods served to chiefs and special guests. For example, in one story, "A Story of the Town of **A'nagun**," told by Walter, a member of the Rear-Town-People of Yan, one of the "Chiefs" (**Nang'iitlagadaas**) of the town made a feast: "They brought different sorts of food down out of the Stikine. They brought down [highbush] cranberries, soapberries, crab apples and dried fruits (or berries)" (in Swanton 1908b:537). Another example is in the story of Big-tail (told by Job Moody to Swanton 1905b:300): "Then Big-tail also went to Skidegate. After he had performed for a time ... all began giving him the food they had saved up. Cranberries [**hlaayi** (S), **hlaa.i**, **hlaayaa** (M), **hláay** (A)], wild crab apples [**k'ay** (S, M), **k'áy** (A)], **siG̲an** ["**sig.án**"—wild lily-of-the-valley berries], roots put up in cakes, berries put up in cakes, and grease [**t'aaw** (S)], they gave him ..." In another story, "A-Slender-One-Who-Was-Given-Away," the heroine was taken in a magical canoe: "The canoe was filled with good food, with cranberries, berries in cakes, soapberries, and the fat of all kinds of animals, grizzly-bear fat, mountain-goat fat, deer fat, ground-hog fat, beaver fat—the fat parts of all mainland animals ..." (told by John Sky to Swanton 1905b:164).

Within the historical period, apples, pears, cherries, plums and a variety of domesticated berries, including strawberries, raspberries, loganberries, gooseberries and currants, have been cultivated and utilized. Many are named after their wild counterparts (Appendix 10).

The inner bark (cambium) of two species of coniferous trees, Sitka spruce [**k̲ayd**, **k̲aayd** (S), **k̲iid** (M), **k̲íid** (A); edible inner bark: **sG̲aalaak'uu ts'ii** (S)] and western hemlock [**k̲'aang** (S, M), **k̲'aáng** (A); edible inner bark: **x̲i** (S), **x̲iga**, **x̲ig**, **x̲i** (M), **x̲i** (A)], was harvested and eaten for a short period of time in the spring. It was generally cooked, and some was dried for later use. Inner bark food is scarcely used at all at the present time.

Some of the major foods, as well as a few not normally eaten, were particularly sought during times of food scarcity or famine (see Appendix 2-E). For example, the fern "roots," including spiny wood fern [**sk'yaaw** (S, M), **sk'yáaw** (A)], sword fern [**ts'aagul** (S), **ts'aagwaal** (M), **ts'áagwaal** (A)] and bracken fern [**saagun** (S), **ts'aagwaal hlk̲'a.aay** (M)], were eaten in times of food shortage, as well as the rhizomes of beach lupine [**taG̲ansk'ya** (S), **ta.ansk'yaaw**, **ta.ansk'yaa** (M)] and skunk-cabbage [**hlgun** (S, M), **hlgún** (A)], and of some of the other root species that could be obtained during the winter or early spring when fresh food was unavailable. Especially at this time, storms or bad weather might prevent hunting or fishing activities, and plant foods, especially those whose location and availability were predictable, took on a critical role (Turner and Davis 1993).

Three species were used specifically for beverage teas (see Appendix 2-F). Traditionally, however, many types of Haida herbal medicines prepared as infusions (made by steeping plant products in boiling water) or decoctions (in which plant materials were boiled in water) were drunk in the form of teas, replacing all other fluids one might ingest over the period of the treatment. Many of these, used primarily for their medicinal effects, would also have provided required fluids as well as additional essential vitamins and minerals. Their healing effects would be enhanced by these contributions.

A few plants were used for flavouring or sweetening other foods (see Appendix 2-G). One particularly notable plant in this regard was licorice fern [**glaaying'waal** (S, M), **gláamaal** (A)], whose rhizomes leave a very sweet taste in the mouth when chewed. Many of the elders remarked that water drunk after licorice fern was

**Skunk-cabbage: The enormous leaves are used for wrapping food but are not themselves eaten.**

chewed tasted very, very sweet. This plant was also used to flavour and sweeten Labrador-tea [**x̲àaydaa tiiG̲a**, **k̲'using.a xilG̲a** (S), **xil k̲agann** (M), **xíl k̲agan** (A)].

A few plant products were chewed or smoked (see Appendix 2-H). Foremost among these was the native Haida tobacco [**x̲àaydaa gulG̲a** (S), **x̲àadas gulaa** (M), **x̲aadas guláa** (A)], whose history and use are discussed in detail under the description of this plant. It still remains somewhat of a mystery since it apparently became extinct sometime in the early part of the twentieth century, and no one living today remembers having experienced its use. Formerly, it played a highly significant role in Haida culture and featured in a number of stories. For example, Raven's sister [**siwaas** (S), **suwaas** (M)] was said to have planted this tobacco first at White Inlet, named for the calcined shells she threw out on the rocks.

A variety of other plants, though not consumed directly, were used in various ways in the collection and preparation of plant foods (see Appendix 2-I). These include such materials as skunk-cabbage leaves [**hlgun** (S, M), **hlgún** (A)] and thimbleberry leaves [**gugadiis xil** (S), **stl'a gudiis xil**, **stl'a gudiis hlk̲'a.aay** (M), **stl'a gudíis hlk̲'a.íi**, **stl'a gudíis xil** (A)], which were used to line cooking pits, wrap food and dry berries, and the stiff stems of yarrow [**xil sgunx̲ulaa** (S), **ts'ats'a k̲'u kamm** (M) and other terms] and the branches of waxberry [**k'u'iid** (S)], which were used as roasting skewers. A few other plants were used for collecting herring eggs. Some, like the giant kelp [**ngaal** (S, M), **ngáal** (A)] and eelgrass [**t'aanuu** (S, M), **t'anúu** (A)] might have been eaten together with these eggs, whereas the twigs and needles of western hemlock [**k̲'aang** (S, M), **k̲'aáng** (A)], whose boughs were used in this way, were removed before the eggs were eaten but certainly added a pleasant flavour to the herring eggs.

The harvesting of plant foods was an integral part of the seasonal round. Generally, people started out in early spring travelling from their winter villages in search of early greens and "winter" seaweed [**singga sG̲iiwaay** (S), **sangg sxiiwee** (M),

**sángg sG̲íiwaay** (A)]. Later in spring, the cambium and edible inner bark [**x̲i** (S), **x̲iga**, **x̲ig**, **x̲i** (M), **x̲i** (A)] of western hemlock [**k̲'aang** (S, M), **k̲'aáng** (A)] and Sitka spruce [**k̲ayd**, **k̲aayd** (S), **k̲iid** (M), **k̲íid** (A); edible inner bark: **sG̲aalaak'uu ts'ii** (S)] were "ripe," "summer seaweed" [**sG̲yuu** (S), **sG̲iw** (M), **sG̲íw** (A)] was ready to harvest, and herring were spawning on the kelp and other plants. From late spring, the first berries—for example, salmonberries [s**k̲'awG̲aan** (S), **sk̲'aw.aan** (M), **sk̲'aw.áan** (A)], wild strawberries [**hilG̲udaG̲aang** (S), **hillda.aang** (M), **hildaG̲áang** (A)] and red elderberries [**jitl'l** (S), **jatl'a**, **jatl'** (M), **jatl'** (A)]—started to ripen. The ripening of berries continued through the summer, from the huckleberries and blueberries [**sG̲idllG̲u** (S), **sG̲idlùu** (M), **sG̲idluu** (A); **hldaan** (S, M), **hldáan** (A)], to thimbleberries [**gugadiis** (S), **stl'a gudiis** (M), **stl'a gudíis** (A), salal berries [**sk'idG̲aan** (S), **sk'idaan**, **sk'id'aan** (M), **sk'itáan** (A)] and stink currants [**G̲alG̲un** (S), **G̲al.un** (M), **G̲ál.un** (A)], to highbush cranberries [**lhaayi** (S), **hlaa.i**, **hlaayaa** (M), **hláay** (A)], Pacific crab apples [**k'ay** (S, M), **k'áy** (A)], lingonberries [**sk'agi tsaay** (S), **skaga tsaay**, **sk'ag tsaay** (M), **sk'ag tsáay** (A)] and bog cranberries [**dah** (S, M, A)], which could be gathered late into the fall. In the spring and again in the fall, the root vegetables were generally harvested. Large quantities of "Indian rice," or northern riceroot [**'inhling** (S), **stla k̲'iist'aa** (M, A)], wild clover rhizomes [**naa'a** (S)] and Pacific silverweed roots [**ts'i'aal**, **ts'iiaal** (S), **ts'a.al**, **ts'a'al** (M), **k̲'wíi ts'a.aláay** (A)] were harvested and cleaned, and some were processed for winter storage to be used later in the year.

The harvesting and processing of plant foods was generally the responsibility of women. Harvesting could be difficult and tedious work, but was also a time for social interaction. Visiting and travelling together to berry-picking places or root-digging grounds would have made this an enjoyable time. Many of the elders remember the harvesting time with great pleasure. Women and families still go out to pick berries every year and to gather seaweed from the rocks, and even children participate willingly in these tasks.

Florence Davidson's story, as recorded by Blackman (1982:55–57), describes the "seasonal round," as she experienced it within her own lifetime:

> During her childhood years, Florence accompanied her parents at the end of February to Kung, the site of an old village in Naden Harbour; there they camped for a month or more to dry halibut. Returning only briefly to Massett, at the beginning of April ("gardening time") they left for Yatz, a former seal hunters' camp where the Haida now cultivated potato gardens. Here the men fished for halibut ... while the women planted their gardens. From Yatz, the Edenshaws returned again to Massett. Early May brought the women and children briefly back to Yatz where they picked and dried seaweed. During much of May, though, the Edenshaws resided in Massett, and Florence accompanied her mother on frequent treks to North Beach to gather and process the spruce roots for Isabella's weaving. In June the Edenshaw family

often left Massett ... for the mainland. Isabella sold her baskets and hats ... at Port Essington ...

Some summers the Edenshaws went instead to Alaska and Isabella worked at the cannery in New Kasaan ... When the family returned in late summer to the islands, Isabella and Florence picked huckleberries, crab apples, and salal berries. Late in the fall they gathered cranberries, and Isabella harvested her potatoes. The Edenshaws purchased or traded for their fall salmon ...

Blackman (1982:34) describes some aspects of the division of labour between men and women which are relevant to this study:

> Although some economic activities, such as collecting shellfish and cooking, were performed by both males and females, in general the Haida division of labor was marked. Men might beachcomb during the winter following onshore storms to collect clams and cockles that had washed ashore, but clam digging and the implement of procurement, the **gligú** (digging stick), were considered part of a woman's domain. The sexual division of labor was summed up for me by one elderly Massett man who offered the following comment on the essential property of a newly married couple: "Every man's got to have his fishing line and devilfish stick and every woman her digging stick."
>
> The gathering of plant resources was women's and girls' work; young boys did not normally accompany their mothers on such expeditions. What little gathering men did complemented that of the women. Both sexes, for example, collected spruce roots, but women dug the small delicate roots for hat and basket weaving, and men the large roots from which they made fish traps and snares. Similarly, both men and women collected cedar bark, but women sought the inner bark for weaving mats, and men the large sheets of outer bark for roofing.

A statement by GwaaG̱anad (Diane Brown) made before the Honourable Mr. Justice Harry McKay in British Columbia's Supreme Court (November 6, 1985), "Speaking in the Haida Way," expresses eloquently and with a depth of experience and feeling the close relationship the Haida have with their food resources. GwaaG̱anad talks of the spiritual nature of food such as **k'aaw** (herring roe on kelp [**ngaal** (S, M), **ngáal** (A)]):

> Finally the day comes when [the herring] spawns. The water gets all milky around it. I ... share this experience with all the friends, the lady friends, that we pick together this wonderful feeling on the day that it happens, the excitement, the relief that the herring did indeed come this year. And you don't quite feel complete until you are right out on the ocean with your hands in the

water harvesting the kelp, the roe on kelp, and then your body feels right. That cycle is complete ... And it's not quite perfect until you eat your first batch of herring roe on kelp ... your body almost rejoices in that first feed. It feels right ...

**Herring roe on giant kelp.**

The processing of foods was also extremely important—in some ways just as important as harvesting them. There are many variations on the techniques for preservation, depending on the types of food to be stored, the quantities and the ultimate purpose for which the food would be used. The most common method for preserving was drying, or dehydration. It was used for seaweeds and inner bark, as well as many of the berries and some of the roots. In most cases, the berries and roots would be cooked before being dried. Cooking removed some of the moisture; the remaining moisture was removed by the heat of the sun or a fire. Smoke, from fire-dried foods, also served as a flavouring and preservative.

As mentioned previously, some of the more acidic fruits were preserved by placing them in water, to be stored in wooden boxes or other vessels; generally they were mixed with, or topped with, animal grease or oil. The acidity of the fruit maintained the preservation, and people would use them over the winter as needed.

A very important method of processing food, which served at once to cook and flavour the food, was pit-cooking, or steaming in an "earth oven." With this method, a hole is first dug in the ground, or in the sand at the top of the beach, about two-thirds of a metre (2 feet) deep and as large as required to contain the food to be cooked—usually a metre (3 feet) or more across. A hot fire is lit in the bottom of the pit, and many dense, rounded rocks are placed in the fire and allowed to heat up until glowing red hot. At this point, unburned materials are removed from the pit, and the red-hot rocks spread around on the bottom. They are covered with dirt or sand, then with a layer of vegetation such as salal [**sk'iid**, **sk'iidG̲aanxil** (S), **sk'iihla**, **sk'iihl**, **sk'iihla hlk̲'a.aay** (M)] or other bushes, seaweed or skunk-cabbage leaves [**hlgun** (S, M), **hlgún** (A)], followed by a layer of the food to be cooked—usually root vegetables, tree cambium or seafood, especially shellfish. The food is topped with more vegetation. Water is poured in through a channel left as the pit was being constructed, enough to produce billows of steam, and the pit is carefully covered by a mat, or more recently, by a piece of canvas. The covering is topped with a thick layer of sand or dirt until the last vestiges of escaping steam are blocked. Then, the food can be left to cook overnight. In the morning, the pit is carefully opened, and the food, now cooked and flavoured by the surrounding plants, is removed. It can be eaten immediately, or, traditionally, could be dehydrated and stored for use during the winter. Pit-cooking is a traditional cooking method used throughout northwestern North America and in other parts of the world as well. It is an ingenious and highly sociable method of cooking and simultaneously flavouring large quantities of food—enough to serve a whole extended family or village, with a minimum of equipment and energy expended. The results are delicious and nutritious.

Dehydrated foods could be restored almost to their fresh state by soaking them in water overnight. This was done with berry cakes, dried roots and other dried foods. Alternatively, the dried foods could simply be added to soups or stews and allowed to rehydrate during the cooking process.

Seaweeds [**sG̲yuu** (S), **sG̲iw** (M), **sG̲íw** (A)], herring roe on kelp [**k'aaw** (S, M)] and berry cakes can be eaten in their dry state as snacks, or are often cooked with other foods such as fish, salmon eggs or other vegetables in soups or stews. Plant foods were, and are, served under many circumstances, at feasts and other formal gatherings, and family meals. Usually they are served together with meat or fish, and often with a dressing of oil from eulachon (oulachen, ooligan) traded from the Nisga'a of the Nass Valley, the Tsimshian of the Skeena, or other coastal First Nations, or with some other type of animal grease or oil. Eating these foods is a pleasurable experience, and many people, especially elders, remember the traditional foods with great fondness. Today, it is mainly the seaweeds and various kinds of berries that are used extensively by contemporary Haida. Few people still go out to dig the root vegetables or to get the traditional greens, or to scrape off laboriously the inner bark of the Sitka spruce or western hemlock. These are foods of the past which served the people well in their time. Perhaps those which are no longer harvested at present will be used again in the future.

Many of the harvesting areas were owned, or the rights to use the resources from them were controlled, by certain high-class people or particular families of a village. The owners were generous in the allocation of their harvest, sharing their food and the rights to harvest it with others, but they had the decision-making authority as to when the food should be harvested and where the food should be allocated. Patches or stands of fireweed [**tl'laal** (S), **tl'ii'aal** (M), **tl'íi.aal** (A)], springbank clover [**naa'a** (S)], Pacific silverweed [**ts'i'aal**, **ts'iiaal** (S), **ts'a.al**, **ts'a'al** (M), **k̲'wíi ts'a.aláay** (A)], crab apple [**k'ay** (S, M), **k'áy** (A)], highbush cranberry [**lhaayi** (S), **hlaa.i**, **hlaayaa** (M), **hláay** (A)], salmonberry [**sk̲'awG̲aan** (S), **sk̲'aw.aan** (M), **sk̲'aw.áan** (A)], salal [**sk'idG̲aan** (S), **sk'idaan**, **sk'id'aan** (M), **sk'itáan** (A)] and some of the huckleberries [**hldaan** (S, M), **hldáan** (A); **sG̲I̲idllG̲uu** (S), **sG̲idlùu** (M), **sG̲idluu** (A)] were all specifically owned by individuals and the rights to use them passed down from generation to generation through the mother's lineage.

John Swanton (1905a:71) alludes to this practice in the following passage about the seasonal round of Haida:

> When spring came, the people abandoned their towns and scattered to camp, where the men fished for halibut, salmon, and on the west coast for black cod, and hunted black bear, marten, seals, sea-lions, etc.; while their wives picked berries, dug roots, and cultivated tobacco, their only agricultural labour. Each Haida family had its own creek, creeks, or portion of a creek, where its smokehouses stood. Some of the smaller creeks are said to

> have had non-owners; and, on the other hand, some families are said to have had no land. In the latter case they were obliged to wait until another family was through before picking berries, and had to pay for the privilege. Any family might pick berries on the land belonging to another after the owners had finished picking, if it obtained the consent of the latter and paid a certain price.

Among the Haida, as among other northwestern groups, plant products were an important trade item. Boxes of highbush cranberries [**lhaayi** (S), **hlaa.i**, **hlaayaa** (M), **hláay** (A)] and crab apples [**k'ay** (S, M), **k'áy** (A)] were considered to be precious gifts and were often seen being transported by canoe between Haida Gwaii and the adjacent mainland, where they might be offered as gifts to Tsimshian friends and relatives or used as trading items (see Swanton 1908b). Seaweed [**sG̱yuu** (S), **sG̱iw** (M), **sG̱íw** (A)] was, and is, also traded over to the mainland. Preserved giant kelp [**ngaal** (S, M), **ngáal** (A)] with herring eggs [**k'aaw** (S, M), **k'áaw** (A)] has been another important trading item, as were halibut and Haida-crafted canoes (Adam Bell, personal communication to Marianne Boelscher 1980). Later, potatoes [**sgawsiid** (S), **sguusiid** (M), **sgúusiid** (A)] and other cultivated produce were traded by the Haida to their mainland neighbours. In exchange for Haida products, eulachons and eulachon grease [**t'aaw** (S)], soapberries [**'as** (S), **xagutl'iid** (M), **xagutl'íid** (A)] and other foods not plentiful on Haida Gwaii were imported. In the past, wild bog cranberries [**dah** (S, M, A)], lingonberries [**sk'agi tsaay** (S), **skaga tsaay**, **sk'ag tsaay** (M), **sk'ag tsáay** (A)] and some other wild berries were offered for sale at the co-op store on Haida Gwaii.

Many people still preserve wild plant foods for their own use. Thimbleberries [**gugadiis** (S), **stl'a gudiis** (M), **stl'a gudíis** (A)], salal [**sk'idG̱aan** (S), **sk'idaan**, **sk'id'aan** (M), **sk'itáan** (A)] and salmonberries [**sḴ'awG̱aan** (S), **sḴ'aw.aan** (M), **sḴ'aw.áan** (A)] are made into jams or simply jarred as preserves, and these items constitute valued gifts within the family or among friends.

Today Haida children continue to be taught the value of their traditional foods, and the knowledge and experience about this important facet of Haida traditional culture will not be lost, because people continue to live it. An ongoing project, partially completed, is a demonstration garden of Haida food and medicine plants around the Ḵay Llnagaay Heritage Centre at Second Beach, Skidegate.

## Toxic Plants

Very few plant species of Haida Gwaii are seriously toxic, but many can be harmful if improperly used. A number of these are listed in Appendix 3. One species well known for its toxic properties is false hellebore [**gwaayk'yaa** (S), **gwaayk'aa** (M), **gwáayk'aa** (A)], sometimes known as "skookum-root" ("skookum" is the Chinook Jargon word for "strong," or "powerful"). This plant, a lily relative, contains a number of poisonous alkaloids that act on the body's circulatory and nervous systems. It has been used commercially in the past to treat high blood pressure and some other ailments, but its effects are unpredictable, and thus its use as a pharmaceutical is not recommended. The Haida have been aware of the toxicity for probably hundreds if not thousands of years. Some use this plant in some ways as a medicine, but always there is the caution that it must only be used, if ever, under very specialized circumstances and under the direction of a knowledgeable person who understands the harmful properties of this plant as well as its virtues. It should never be taken in any capacity without the deepest knowledge of its qualities.

Other particular plants that might cause harm, or are known to the Haida as potentially harmful, include the following: stinging nettle [**Gudangxaal** (S), **Gudang.aal**, **Gudang'al** (M), **Gudáng.aal** (A)], widely known for its irritant properties; cow-parsnip [**hlk'iid** (S, M), **hlk'íid** (A)], which contains phototoxic compounds called furanocoumarins that can cause severe irritation, blistering and discoloration of the skin in the presence of ultraviolet light; skunk-cabbage [**hl-gun** (S, M), **hlgún** (A)], which contains sharp irritating crystals of calcium oxalate and whose leaves should never be eaten without very intensive processing; devil's-club [**ts'iihllnjaaw** (S), **ts'iihlanjaaw** (M), **ts'íihlanjaaw** (A)] and swamp gooseberry [**GudGa gi Gayd** (**-hlk'a'ii**) (S), **xaayuwaa** (M), **xáayuwaa** (A) and other terms], whose spines are known to be highly irritating to the skin; and western yew [**hlGiid** (S, M), **hlGíid** (A)], whose seeds, leaves and other parts are poisonous and whose fleshy tissues around the seed, though edible, are not recommended for eating. Finally, there are a number of other berries, such as black twinberry [**xuyaa GaanGa** (S), **yaahl Gaanaa** (M), **yáahl Gáanaay** (A); **k'aalts'idaa Gaan-Ga** (S)], twisted-stalk [**st'aw GaanGa** (S), **st'aw Gaanaa** (M), **st'áw Gáanaa**

**Gertie White of Massett, with gwaayk'aa (false hellebore), 2003.**
—PHOTO BY MARIANNE B. IGNACE

(A)] and waxberry [**k'u'iid GaanGa** (S)], that are either purported to be poisonous, or at least to have been eaten only by animals, not by humans. For more information on poisonous and potentially harmful plants of North America, the reader is referred to Turner and von Aderkas (2009).

**IMPORTANT NOTE:** Anyone wishing to try the Haida plant foods mentioned in this book should be extremely careful to first verify the identification of the plants, and to understand thoroughly the methods of preparation and ways they were eaten. It should also be noted that many of these food plants, though perhaps common and plentiful, are threatened by industrial activities, especially logging with its accompanying spraying of herbicides and pesticides, and therefore may not be as available as they were in the past. Their use should be undertaken only with the greatest of awareness and with concern for their conservation and preservation, and for the well-being of animals that also depend on them.

## Plant Resource Management

The Haida, with their ecological knowledge drawn from many generations of careful observation and experiential learning, certainly had more of an influence on plant resources than is generally acknowledged. The practice of aboriginal landscape burning, or burning of individual bushes or berry patches, is known to have occurred at least to a limited extent on Haida Gwaii (Hazel Stevens, personal communication to David Ellis, cited in Turner, 1999). Captain Gold (personal communication 1995) said that he had been told by Don Collinson that there was an area between Skidegate and Queen Charlotte City where people used to burn every few years. They stopped burning around 1920, and now it is all overgrown. Kathleen Hans believed that people used to burn areas long ago, but she never saw it herself. Burning was said to have enhanced the productivity of the berry bushes so treated. This stimulated growth probably occurred through the release of concentrated nutrients from the ash left after a fire and also as a result of the elimination or suppression of competing vegetation. Salal [**sk'idGaan** (S), **sk'idaan, sk'id'aan** (M), **sk'itáan** (A)] and probably red huckleberry [**sGiidllGuu** (S), **sGidlùu** (M), **sGidluu** (A)] were treated in this way as an intentional management strategy.

Logging was undertaken by the Haida especially around the villages, where fuel was needed, and where cedar logs and boards were the major construction material for houses. Captain Gold noted that cutting down trees around village sites had an additional benefit: the clearings enhanced the growth of berries, and the stumps provided an excellent substrate for berry bushes, including salal, huckleberries, blueberries and currants. Captain Gold pointed out an area near

**LEFT: An old stump with red huckleberry bushes growing from the top.**

**RIGHT: Edible bulbs of northern riceroot, with bulblets; each is capable of growing into a new plant. Ripe seed capsules are also shown.**

**Nans Dins** (Ninstints) village where trees had been felled by Haida many years ago. The stumps with their berry bushes are still visible, but the bushes are gradually becoming shaded out as the forest grows up around them.

Other management techniques may have included pruning berry-producing bushes through manual breaking of the branches, and, for root vegetables, selective harvesting. Green shoots were said to have grown better and larger when continuously harvested. Harvesting areas for these foods would be frequented year after year without apparent loss of productivity. In the case of root vegetables, productivity was probably enhanced, because only the largest roots and root parts were selected, leaving the smaller ones to grow in soil loosened and aerated through the digging and harvesting process. The release of seeds into the cultivated soil might also have enhanced the growth of these species. With the northern riceroot [**'inhling** (S), **stla k̲'iist'aa** (M, A)], the tiny bulblets surrounding the main bulb would have scattered to some extent during digging, allowing the continuing and ongoing propagation or dissemination of new propagules for new plants and future harvests. Fragments of the rhizomes of springbank clover [**naa'a** (S)], or of the roots

**Many areas of old-growth forest on Haida Gwaii have been cleared of undergrowth by browsing deer. These are crab apple trees at Cumshewa.**

of Pacific silverweed [**ts'i'aal**, **ts'iiaal** (S), **ts'a.al**, **ts'a'al** (M), **k̲'wíi ts'a.aláay** (A)] would have had the same effect, since new plants can grow from even small parts of these species' underground systems. Thus, the Haida lived on the land, using the food resources available to them year after year, without depleting them. They were able to keep their food systems intact from one generation to the next over hundreds, even thousands of years (Deur and Turner 2005; Turner and Peacock 2005).

Ownership of resource areas may have played an important role in the management of these resources (see Turner, Smith and Jones 2005). Many people today say that the berries and other resources are not as plentiful as they used to be. There are many explanations for this. One is that no one is looking after the resources (Turner and Peacock 2005). Another is that the deer introduced to the islands have browsed many of the native plants and have virtually removed the undergrowth from wide areas of old-growth forest. The deer, and introduced cattle as well, are specifically held responsible for dwindling supplies of seaside strawberries [**hilG̲udaG̲aang** (S), **hillda.aang** (M), **hildaG̲áang** (A)], highbush cranberries [**lhaayi** (S), **hlaa.i**, **hlaayaa** (M), **hláay** (A)] and cloudberries [**k̲'aax̲u ts'alaangG̲a** (S), **k̲'a.àw ts'alaangaa** (M), **k̲'aawts'aláangaa** (A)], which people say used to be much more abundant in the muskeg areas south of Massett. Curtailment of burning practices and the introduction of aggressive weeds are also blamed for depleting traditional plant resources (see Turner 1999; Deur and Turner 2005).

## Plants in Technology

Approximately 30 different species of plants have been used by the Haida as materials in their technology (Appendix 4). Virtually all the implements made and used by the Haida to procure their animal foods were made from plant materials. The fishing nets, lines, weirs, and hooks; the canoes, paddles and other implements used to hunt sea mammals and land mammals—all of these were made from plants. This fact adds a new dimension to the importance of plants in the Haida diet. The use of plant materials in fishing technology is described and illustrated in detail by Hilary Stewart (1977). A general reference to plants in the technology of British Columbia First Peoples is Turner (1998).

Like plant foods and plant medicines, plants used for technological purposes are highly respected by the Haida. Cedar, in particular, is revered for all that it offers. Prayers were and are said, and songs sung to the cedar trees whose bark was to be harvested or whose trunks were to be crafted into the large ocean-going canoes for which Haida canoe makers were famous. People were careful not to overharvest these materials. Under most circumstances, for example, cedar bark was removed from only a portion of the tree, so that it would be able to recover and would not be killed or weakened. Similarly, spruce-root gatherers took only a few spruce roots from each individual tree at any given time.

Haida woodworkers and artists have used more than a dozen different species of trees and shrubs for the specific qualities of their wood (Appendix 4-A). Some of these woods were used for making small items only. The wood from the larger trees was used in house construction or fashioned into large implements, totem and mortuary poles, and canoes. Some of the shrubs, such as red-osier dogwood [**sgiisgii** (S), **sG̲id xaadaal** (M)], were particularly valued for their long, straight, flexible branches, used for making frames and drying racks. Other species, such as Pacific crab apple [**k'anhl'l, k'aanhll** (S), **k'ayanhla, k'a'inhla** (M), **k'ayánhl** (A)] and western yew [**hlG̲iid** (S, M), **hlG̲íid** (A)], were valued for their tough, resilient wood, used for digging sticks, bows and other implements requiring a great deal of strength. Red alder [**k̲aal, k̲al** (S, M), **k̲ál** (A)], a light, easily carved wood, has been used specifically for making bowls and masks.

The most important wood of all is that of western red-cedar [**ts'uu** (S, M), **ts'úu** (A)], the "tree of life" (Stewart 1984). Cedar wood is used in large construction projects; the large houses, the house posts, the large beams and rafters, and the planks used to cover the sides and roofs of large houses all are made from this versatile tree. Red-cedar is also the major material for making large ocean-going canoes, although according to Charles F. Newcombe (1897), yellow-cedar wood [**sG̲aahlaan** (S), **sG̲ahlaan** (M), **sG̲ahláan** (A)] was also formerly important for making canoes. Another very significant application of western red-cedar is in the construction of storage boxes. Cedar planks, split from logs or even from standing trees,

**LEFT: K̲ii'iljuus (Barbara Wilson) holds a yew-wood digging stick carved by Gitkinjuaas (also known as G̲iitsx̲aa), her brother, 1993.**

**CENTRE: Bentwood cedar storage boxes from the old Prince Rupert Museum.**

**RIGHT: Western red-cedar tree.**

were curved or grooved in three parallel lines across the grain, steamed until soft, and bent into the four sides of the box. The corner where the ends meet is pegged or sewn with spruce root or other fibrous material, and the box is carefully fitted with a bottom and lid. A wide variety of sizes and styles was made. Many were beautifully painted with representative geometric features of animals or supernatural beings. As well as storing a wide variety of items and substances, these exquisitely crafted boxes were used for cooking; they are watertight, and if protected at the bottom by sticks or branches, and bound tightly around the outside with cedar-withe rope, can be used for steaming with hot rocks. Haida artists are still making these beautiful boxes, and they can be seen in gift shops and in museums on Haida Gwaii and throughout northwestern North America.

Aside from use in manufacturing and construction, some woods are particularly known for their qualities as fuels (Appendix 4-B). Red alder wood, for example, was and is a primary fuel for smoking fish, whereas western red-cedar is known to light easily and burn with a hot flame. Because of this and its easy-splitting quality, it is valued as a kindling. Originally, fires were made by friction, with the use of a hand drill and hearth of cedar or other easily kindled wood. The use of a fire drill to make fire was described by Charlie Edenshaw to Franz Boas (Swanton 1905b:139). Once kindled, a fire could be kept smouldering in a wad of red-cedar bark contained within the two halves of a clam shell; this device was called a "slow match." It could be buried in the ground at a camp spot or other location, and dug up many hours later to be used to ignite a fire.

Several plants were used for their fibrous materials (Appendix 4-C). Sheets of western red-cedar bark were used as the walls and roofing of temporary summer houses or even winter houses. To keep them from curling, they were drilled and

**Left: Yellow-cedar bark hat, woven by Florence Davidson.**

**Right: Woven Haida spruce-root hat from the Royal BC Museum collection.**

threaded at intervals with sharp, straight sticks of salmonberry, and then piled up and weighted to keep them flat until use. The inner bark of western red-cedar and yellow-cedar is perhaps the most important of all materials for making mats, clothing, baskets, hats and cordage. The techniques for harvesting and processing these barks are described in detail under the individual species. Sitka spruce roots [**hlllng.a** (S), **hlii.ng** (M), **hlíing** (A)] are another important traditional fibrous material. Painstakingly "cured" in the fire, peeled and then carefully split into a variety of widths, they were, and still are, used in the twining of many beautiful and intricate baskets and hats. Designs are woven right into the fabric using variations in twining techniques, and, as well, some of the baskets and hats are carefully painted with geometric designs. The arts of weaving and basketry with plant materials are still being practised, especially among Haida women. Thanks to the dedication of elder craftswomen like Florence

**Stinging nettle. Inset: A ball of stinging nettle fibre string from the Royal BC Museum collection.**

Davidson and her daughters Primrose Adams and Virginia Hunter, who have been careful to teach their art to younger members of their families and community, the making of these beautiful woven artworks will continue into the future.

In the past, the stem fibres of both stinging nettle [**g̱udangxaal** (S), **g̱udang.aal**, **g̱udang'al** (M), **g̱udáng.aal** (A)] and fireweed [**tl'laal** (S), **tl'ii'aal** (M), **tl'íi.aal** (A)] were spun to make cordage, used for fishing nets and for binding and tying. Another very important material in fishing technology was the long flexible stipe of bull kelp [**hlkyaama** (S), **hlkaa.m** (M), **hlkáam** (A)]. These stems were carefully cured, and then used as long lines for catching black cod, halibut and even salmon. For the deepwater fish, lines of many people would be tied together, and a series of hooks placed along them, so that, according to Niblack (1890), up to 50 or 70 black cod could be caught at one single casting of the long line.

A few plants yielded products that were used for colouring materials (Appendix 4-D). Primary among these is red alder [**kaal**, **kal** (S, M), **kál** (A)], whose bark yields a reddish brown stain for cedar bark or other materials. Indian paint fungus ["**tsigwán**" (possibly **tsigwáan**—JE) (A)], dried and powdered, was used as a red pigment and face paint when mixed with pitch.

Aside from these materials, which can be placed, more or less, into specific categories, a wide variety of plants were used in diverse, unclassified ways. For example, the horsetails [**k'ada sg̱awg̱a** (S), **dal xaw** (M) and other terms] were used as abrasives for polishing wooden items. Salal branches [**sk'iid**, **sk'iidg̱aan xil** (S), **sk'iihla**, **sk'iihl**, **sk'iihla hlk'a.aay** (M)], with their dark green, leathery leaves, are used in floral decorations. The roots of skunk-cabbage [**hlgun** (S, M), **hlgún** (A)] were employed as a substitute bait for halibut, and western hemlock boughs [**k'aang** (S, M), **k'aáng** (A)] were used as temporary shelters and hunting blinds. These miscellaneous useful materials are listed in Appendix 4-E.

The gathering of many plant materials took place at opportune times and places throughout the year, but for such materials as cedar bark and spruce roots, which had critical importance, special harvesting expeditions were undertaken at the optimum gathering times. Such trips were part of the seasonal round. For cedar bark and spruce roots, the time was early summer. For fireweed and stinging nettle fibre, late summer was the best time, when the plants were at their full state of maturity. In general, as was most common among the Northwest Coast peoples (Turner 1998), women were generally responsible for collecting plant fibres and fibrous materials such as cedar bark and spruce roots, whereas men were responsible for collecting and working with the wood products (Blackman 1990). One notable exception was bull kelp stipes, which were harvested by the men, diving to get the longest possible stems.

Like many of the plant foods, plant materials could be processed for further work later in the season. Cedar bark [**giixida** (S), **gi.id** (M), **giid** (A)], for example, when first harvested, was generally split away from its outer covering, possibly split again into two thinner layers, and at this stage could be hung up and dried, then bundled and stored away for winter, or for use in the evenings when other harvesting activities could not take place. The materials that were used for weaving could be restored to their natural pliability by soaking them in warm water for a short time. In many cases, the best materials were prepared to a relatively finished state. Cedar bark might be split into thin strips just the right width for use in basketry, or in making hats. Spruce roots [**hllnga** (S), **hlii.ng** (M), **hlíing** (A)] might be peeled and carefully split in pieces, then bundled, tied with strips of the root bark and dried.

The materials could then be stored away, but were readily available for the weaver to utilize immediately, simply by soaking them briefly. Bull kelp stipes [**hlk̲yaama** (S), **hlk̲aa.m** (M), **hlk̲áam** (A)] for use as fishing lines had to be carefully cured, a process that could take many weeks or months. They were generally impregnated gradually with oil so that they remained flexible and soft and would not be too brittle. Even so, before use, they were soaked in water for a while to give them optimum flexibility.

## Medicinal Plants

More than 60 different plant species and some lichens, fungi and algae, were and are used by Haida in some specific way in the maintenance of health or in the treatment of particular conditions or ailments. It is impossible to separate the concepts of healing from the concepts of spirituality and the power invested in natural things within the Haida culture. Medicinal plants, along with other natural objects, are treated with deep respect, and their potential for affecting peoples' lives and health is acknowledged from the outset by those seeking healing or practising traditional medicine.

A number of these healing plants were also used in more spiritual or "magical" contexts by people seeking special protection or power, or luck in whatever endeavours they were undertaking—maybe a young person at puberty, a hunter, a shaman seeking help to gain curing powers or someone, even a berry picker or fisher, wanting to have a good catch. It could also be someone in love who wanted to secure the affection of another person. Plant medicines were applied in these various ways, as well as in what might be considered the more traditional roles of curing specific ailments. Swanton (1905a:44–45) summarized the role of plants as medicines in Haida culture:

> Not only were medicines employed in cases of real sickness as we understand it, but their use was far more extended. Thus there was medicine for carving, medicine for dancing, medicine for acquiring property (such

> as **x̲at**, a rare plant, and devil's-club [**ts'iihllnjaaw** (S), **ts'iihlanjaaw** (M), **ts'íihlanjaaw** (A)]). The others are said to have been mixtures. These could be used by anybody who knew the prescriptions; but there were medicines which were the special property of certain families, and even if anyone else had known how to make them, it would not have been safe to do so. The result might have been war.

Solomon Wilson (personal communication 1971) told the legend of how medicine was acquired:

> At the time of creation, no one knew about medicines. Down south there was a young woman with a baby on her back who knew all about them, but you had to be exceptionally pure and clean to see her. One young man was pure and went to seek her. He chased and chased her and finally caught her, by turning backwards and grabbing behind his back. She told him about all the plant medicines, how they were used and what kinds and amounts and how to mix them. Then, at dawn, she had to be released before the raven [**X̲uya** (S)] crowed three times. She begged and pleaded, and finally he let her go. When she was released, she told him that there was one medicine she had not told him about: how to raise a person from the dead. The young man tried to catch her again and make her tell him about this last medicine, but he couldn't. That is why, to this day, no one knows how to wake a dead man.

Appendix 5 lists some important Haida medicine plants, including plants used in protection, purification or the acquisition of power.

Perhaps the plant that most epitomizes the critical role of many plants as physical and spiritual healers is **ts'iihllnjaaw** (S), **ts'iihlanjaaw** (M), **ts'íihlanjaaw** (A) (devil's-club). This beautiful and powerful shrub, with its large leaves and spiny stalks, has numerous medicinal applications for the Haida, as it does for most other First Nations whose territories fall within its range. In addition, however, and perhaps most importantly, it was used in both ancient and contemporary contexts for its role as a protective agent and a plant which is able to bestow power and strength to an individual who understands it and uses it with respect. There are many stories in which devil's-club is portrayed as a supernatural power giver. Some of these are recounted under devil's-club in the text. Additionally, many contemporary Haida know this plant and use it for their own purposes.

This book does not cover the specific applications or preparations for devil's-club or other Haida medicines. As noted in the Preface, it is because of concerns of Haida medicine specialists that their medicines may be overexploited or inappropriately used that they are not described here in detail. At the same time, it is important for outsiders to understand the immense importance and diversity of Haida medicinal and other cultural plants, so they are noted, with their names, and listed here with this in mind.

**Mabel Williams of Skidegate harvests spruce pitch for medicine, 1996.**

Some general discussion of Haida medicine is provided by McGregor (1981) and Deagle (1988). The former includes Tlingit and Tsimshian medicines in her article. Deagle provides the following information on cultural aspects of medicine (1988: 1579):

> Among the Haida people there is often a strong sense of family ownership of songs, dances, and medicines. Certain individuals are known to possess the recipe for medicines for certain types of ailments, and the exact ingredients of such medicines are well-guarded secrets. Traditionally, medicine would be collected by a member of the opposite clan or moiety. That is, if a member of the Raven clan was ill, a member of the Eagle clan would gather and prepare the medicine, and vice versa ...

Haida medicinal plants are used in a wide spectrum of health care needs: tonics and nutrient supplements; treatment of digestive tract ailments such as ulcers, diarrhea and constipation; medicines for colds, tuberculosis, influenza and other respiratory problems; poultices, salves or washes for wounds, infections, burns or sores; eye medicines; medicines for the aches and pains of arthritis and rheumatism; kidney or urinary tract medicines; medicines for some types of cancer; and gynecological and childbirth medicines for women.

One of the "women's medicines," spruce gum, is featured in a part of the "Raven Travelling" account told by John Sky of Those-Born-at-Skedans, and recorded by Swanton (1905b:120):

> On the next day, very very early in the morning, he [Raven] started off. After he had gone along for some time he came to some persons who burst into singing sweet songs and danced. They then asked him: "Tell us, what are you doing hereabout?" "I am gathering woman's medicine." "Well, what do you call woman's medicine? Is woman's medicine each other's medicine?" "Yes, it is

each other's medicine." Those women chewed gum as they sang. Then one of these gave him a piece. "This is woman's medicine." And one of them gave him directions: "Now, when you enter the house, pass round to the right. Chew the gum as you go in. And when your uncle's wife asks it of you by no means give it to her. Ask of her the thing her husband owns. When it is in your hand give the gum to her." And he went away from the singers. When he entered the gum stuck out red from his mouth. Then his uncle's wife said to him: "I say, Nañki 'lsLas-hlîña '-i, come, give me the gum." He paid no attention to her. He then sat down beside his mother, and to his mother he said: "Tell her to give me the thing my uncle owns. I will then give her the gum." Then his mother went to her. She told it her. And to her she gave something white and round. He then handed her the gum." While his uncle's wife chewed it and swallowed the juice he saw that her mind was changed ...

The effectiveness of Haida medicines, like those of other coastal First Peoples, has been attested to many times. Many medicinal plants contain antibiotic compounds or substances, and this would account, at least in part, for their efficacy. A study at the University of British Columbia (McCutcheon et al. 1992) demonstrated that a large proportion of British Columbia medicinal plants tested against a variety of harmful bacteria had antibacterial properties. Although there are few empirical studies to prove efficacy of traditional medicines in general, work done with Indigenous Peoples and traditional medicines in various other parts of the world substantiates the conclusion that they are generally effective when used within their cultural contexts (Bannerman et al. 1983). It must be stressed, however, that much more research is required in identifying the pharmacological constituents of these various medicines, and in relating the context of their application to their relative relative availability and efficacy.

Part of the Aboriginal philosophy of health and success was that a person seeking special powers or privileges should be ritually clean. This meant not only external cleansing, but also cleansing of the digestive tract through the use of various medicinal plants as purgatives, laxatives and emetics. Thus, a person who was seeking special powers would bathe, sometimes in many different locations, scrubbing himself thoroughly until the skin was completely clean. The person might also use a steam bath. At the same time, accompanied by fasting, a person might consume certain medicines to achieve internal catharsis as well. Only then would he or she be in the proper state to be able to ask for and receive supernatural help. This practice goes right back to the ancient days when many of the heroes described in the stories recorded by John Swanton and others undertake such ritual cleansing, fasting, bathing and purification before they seek help from supernatural beings or try to acquire power or good fortune.

## Plants in Language and Classification

The way people classify and name the objects in their environment has a great deal to do with their culture and general perspectives on the world. Not all people will relate to the same plants in the same way. Anthropologist Brent Berlin and his colleagues Peter Raven and Dennis Breedlove started, in the 1960s, to accumulate data on shared perceptions of the plant world in diverse cultures, as reflected in classification systems developed to categorize living things. They were among the first to explore what has become a well-studied field, known as folk biological classification or ethnoscience. They found certain patterns in folk biological classification systems, and published several major works on these patterns (see Berlin 1971, 1992; Berlin et al. 1968, 1973, 1974).

As Berlin and his colleagues describe it, there are a number of ranks or category levels that are related one to another inclusively, starting with the most inclusive rank—"kingdom" or "unique beginner." For plants, this is the category that corresponds with the broadest interpretation of the English word "plant." Within this category, there are, as recognized by most people, a relatively small number of broad classes suggested by Berlin to constitute the life form rank. These are categories that denote general obvious features of plants such as size, degree of woodiness and general habit. Included as life forms in Berlin's system are classes such as "tree," "bush," "grass," "vine" and so forth. Within the life form classes, in almost all cases, are a large number—Berlin suggests several hundred—of the most basic type of category, identified by Berlin as the "generic" rank. Generic categories are named usually by single, simple terms. Examples would be, within the life form category "tree": oak, pine, fir and alder. Examples within the category "bush" might be rose, raspberry, spiraea and waxberry. These generic taxa are, according to Berlin, the first terms to be encoded in the development of a language, and the first terms that a child might learn as she or he acquires the skills of speech. Taxa at other ranks are less common.

Sometimes, within the life form rank, there are categories of lesser inclusiveness that are named by Berlin "intermediates." Intermediates are not found in every case within life forms and are often covert, or unnamed. Some generics can be further categorized into the specific rank. For example, in English, there is "wild rose" and "garden rose." Sometimes within the specific categories, one might find further categories at the varietal rank. In the case of "rose," "garden rose" might be further subdivided into the large "hybrid roses" and the small "tea roses," or into "rambling roses" and "bush roses." These ranks are basic concepts which Berlin feels are virtually universal in various human languages. However, other researchers have found variations and anomalies in this system.

It is not the purpose here to investigate in detail the various arguments presented by Berlin and others about the validity of universal classification systems. As part of my doctoral research in the early 1970s, I focused on the classification of Haida plants and plant names (see Turner 1974), in a comparative study of Haida, Bella Coola (Nuxalk) and Fraser River Lillooet (Stl'átl'imx) botanical classification. Here I will briefly outline some of the major features of the Haida system.

In Haida there is no all-inclusive general term, or name, corresponding to "plant" (i.e., including all algae, bryophytes and vascular plants, with or without fungi and lichens). However, "plantness" is certainly recognized, and no Haida person would have difficulty identifying the boundaries of the "plant" category. Some of the major, more general categories of plants are implied through the designation of particular terms, used only in relation to members of a particular group, or taxon, e.g., "bush" or "evergreen tree," rather than the category being named per se. Gitkinjuaas (also known as G̲iitsx̲aa, personal communication 2001) explained the reason for the lack of a general term for "plant": it is because, for the Haida, all plants are living beings, individuals, just as individual humans are beings. Therefore, each individual type of plant has its own name, just as an individual Haida; there is no need to use a broader name.

There is somewhat of a named category for "tree," or perhaps more properly "evergreen tree," designated by the general application of the term for Sitka spruce: **k̲aayd** (S), **k̲iid** (M), **k̲íid** (A). The meaning of this term can be expanded under some circumstances to refer to a group of coniferous trees of various species, not just spruce, growing together. It might also incorporate red alder, which commonly grows in mixed forest situations, and at times, even Pacific crab apple and willows, the only other deciduous trees on Haida Gwaii.

However, another way of designating evergreen trees is through the application of the terms **hlk̲'amaál** (M) and **tlaas** (M) or their equivalents to the "boughs" of these species, and these species only. There is another term—**hlk̲'a'ii** (S), **hlk̲'a.aay** (M), **hlk̲'a.íi** (A)—that is applied specifically to branches of deciduous trees and of various types of shrubs. Some of the species to which this term is freely applied together with their Haida names include red alder, highbush cranberry, stink currant, wild rose, salal and lingonberry. Through the application of this term comes the inference of a major category of plants with leafy branches.

Yet another category is indicated by adding to certain Haida plant names, as a suffix or prefix, the term **xil** (S, M), which means at once "leaf" and "medicine." This semantic designation is particularly interesting since it pertains at once to anatomy and utilitarian application, thus linking the two together irrevocably. It is interesting that Berlin does not generally recognize use of plants as being a primary feature for making taxonomic distinctions, but others, such as Hunn (1982), are convinced that the utilitarian factor is important in folk biological classification. Plants in the **xil** (S, M), **xíl** (A) category, by virtue of containing this term in their names, include a variety of species, mostly herbaceous, leafy forms such as yellow pond-lily, trailing raspberry, twinflower and yarrow. Theoretically, all different kinds of leaves, and everything used for medicine by the Haida could be called **xil**. However, when **xil** is applied to plant names, it does delimit a particular group of plants, almost all of which fit the description of leafy and herbaceous.

Another major plant category for the Haida is that of "berries." The term for berry or fruit, **G̱aan** (S, M—some M speakers say **G̱aa.n**), **G̱áan** (A), is actually an element in many of the basic names for types of berries, such as the names for salmonberry [**sḵ'awG̱aan** (S), **sḵ'aw.aan** (M), **sḵ'aw.áan** (A)]; saskatoon berry [**G̱aan x̱aw'laa** or **G̱aan x̱aw.ulaa** (M), **G̱áan x̱áw'laa** (A) literally 'sweet berry']; and twisted-stalk [**st'aw G̱aanG̱a** (S), **st'aw G̱aanaa** or **st'uu G̱aanaa** (M), **st'áw G̱áanaa** (A) literally 'witch/saw-whet-owl-berries']. Some other berries, however, do not contain this name. For example, Alaska and oval-leaved blueberries are simply referred to as **hldaan** (S, M), **hldáan** (A).

A lesser and unnamed general category can be identified, incorporating "edible root vegetables." This category is implied by the common conversational association of plants such as silverweed, wild clover, northern riceroot, lupine, bracken and spiny wood fern. There is, however, no term specifically referring to all root vegetables.

Another major category is that for "grasses and grass-like plants," all of which are called **ḵ'an** (S, M), **ḵ'án** (A). A wide variety of plants, mostly in the grass, sedge and rush families, are called by this general name. Sometimes the name is supplemented with a descriptive modifier such as 'tall grass,' 'wide-leaved grass,' 'fine-leaved grass' and 'round grass,' but the use of these descriptors seems to be fairly informal. Sometimes the term **ḵ'an** is extended to include a number of herbaceous flowering plants. For example, George Young used it in naming buttercups and yellow flowers in general. Another general category includes various showy flowers. Although there is no Haida name for such a category, there is an anglicized expression, "**x̱aayda hlaawersG̱a**" (S), incorporating the English term "flowers." This general designation is employed by a number of Haida at the present time and might be considered equivalent to the English folk designation "wildflowers." Some of the species included in this category are listed in Table 2 (page 169).

Various other categories are quite general. For example, there are very few particular named types in the category incorporating mosses and lichens, **k'inx̱aan**, **k'iinx̱aan** (S), **k'in.aan** (M), **k'ín.aan** (A). Although there are very few named types in this and other general categories, this is not to say that people did not recognize the wide diversity of these small, "bushy" or low-growing plants of the forest floor, rock faces and tree trunks and branches.

It is interesting that there seems to be no one simple all-encompassing term for "seaweeds," although the Haida, of course, recognize many individual types of seaweed and utilize a wide variety of them. There are general terms for "mushroom, or toadstool": **st'aw dajingG̱a** (S), or **st'aw dajaangaa** ('owl hat'), **k'ak'u dajaangaa** ('owl hat'), **kagann dajaangaa** ('mouse hat') (M) (JE). There are also general terms for "tree fungus," including *Ganoderma* spp., *Fomes* spp. and *Polyporus* spp. and their relatives. However, despite the large number of species of mushrooms to be found along the west coast of British Columbia and Alaska, it seems that people did not generally distinguish them nomenclaturally, and used them very little.

A few mid-level or intermediate categories for Haida plants have been identified and are listed with specific examples of inclusive types in Turner (1974: 43–44). Some of these categories include green vegetables, ferns (further divided into fine-leaved ferns and coarse-leaved ferns) and thorny or spiny plants, which had specific application for use against bad spirits and other evil influences. Others include freshwater aquatic plants; plants that are strong medicines; blueberry-like forest shrubs; kelps; hollow-stemmed plants; and a variety of other lesser categories and alliances drawn among various plant species, generally in an informal way.

Approximately 150 Skidegate and 165 Massett generic-level names for plants were identified in the previous taxonomic study (Turner 1974). In each case, the majority of these represent a one-to-one correspondence between a Haida category and a scientific species category. Most of the remaining names relate to two or more closely related botanical species. A few relate to two or more botanically unrelated species, and a slightly higher number correspond to two or more related, but easily distinguished, species. Examples of Haida names having a one-to-one correspondence with a botanical species are the names for red-cedar, yellow-cedar, cloudberry, highbush cranberry and licorice fern. Examples of names referring to two or more closely related species are those for the edible seaweeds, the two species of hemlocks, two related species of lung lichen and the willows, which are very difficult to distinguish in any case. Examples of terms referring to two or more distinctly different but related species are the more inclusive names for lung lichen and dogtooth lichen, the names for Alaska blueberry and oval-leaved blueberry, and one of the terms applied to Labrador-tea and swamp laurel. Names referring to two or more unrelated plants include such terms as **taG̱ansk'yaa** (S), **ta.ansk'yaaw** (M) for bracken fern (some say sword fern) and beach lupine, both of which have edible rhizomes, and **yaanaang xilgaa** (S) (literally 'fog leaves'), applied by some to such different plants as yarrow, common horsetail and crowberry. The term **hlḵyaamaa** (S), **hlḵaa.m** (M), **hlḵáam** (A) applied variously to the hollow-stemmed species: bull kelp, dune grass and cow-parsnip.

New, expanded categories have been developed since the introduction of a variety of domestic plants and plant products, that have been equated with wild counterparts familiar to the Haida. These include jointly applied names for wild northern riceroot and the introduced grain, rice; for wild giant vetch and wild beach pea, and domesticated beans and peas; for wild swamp gooseberry and domesticated gooseberries; for wild western dock and domesticated rhubarb; for wild strawberries and domesticated strawberries; for wild rose and garden rose; for wild Haida tobacco and commercial tobacco; for wild Pacific crab apple and domesticated apples, and so forth.

In some cases, the original wild plant is sometimes designated by the modifier "Haida" [**x̲àad(as)**] to distinguish it from the now more salient term for the introduced product. An example is Pacific crab apple, now sometimes called **x̲àad(as) k'ayaa** (M) (literally 'Haida apples'), whereas the domesticated apple is simply called **k'ay** (M). In Skidegate, domesticated apples are called by the English name (JE).

Some Haida names have obviously been borrowed from other languages or have themselves been lent to other languages. In some cases the direction of borrowing is obvious, as with the Massett Haida term **dinax̲** for kinnikinnick. Variants of this name are widely used in Athapaskan languages for kinnikinnick (e.g., Ulkatcho Carrier **dunih**—Leslie Saxon, personal communication 1992; Turner 2014), indicating that the term was at some time in the past borrowed by Haida, possibly along with knowledge of the use of the leaves for smoking. The Haida names for highbush cranberry [**hlaayi** (S)] and bog cranberry [**dah** (S, M, A)] and possibly other plant names are related to Smalgyax, or Coast Tsimshian terms, but the directions of borrowing are unclear.

The Haida and other Indigenous Peoples of northwestern North America do not classify plants in exactly the same ways as some of the peoples included in the studies of Berlin and his colleagues (see Hunn 1982; Turner 1987, 1989). Nevertheless, as with the cultures described by Berlin et al., the Haida system for naming and classifying plants reflects a core of named, basic categories or taxa corresponding to the rank of "folk generic" as defined by Berlin et al. (1973; Berlin 1992), as well as categories of both greater and lesser generality, akin to the "life form" and "intermediate" ranks, and to the "specific" rank respectively as described by Berlin et al. (1973). A detailed analysis of Haida plant classification is provided in Turner (1974).

Some of the "basic" plant names are readily analyzable into smaller meaningful units. These are specified wherever possible under the individual plant descriptions in this book. Other names are apparently unanalyzable. In other words, they or their components have no meaning other than as applied as a name for that particular plant. Examples of unique plant names are: **ngaal** (S, M), **ngáal** (A) for giant kelp; **hlgun** (S, M), **hlgún** (A) for skunk-cabbage; **gwaayk'yaa** (S), **gwaayk'aa** (M), **gwáayk'aa** (A) for false hellebore; **hlk'iid** (S, M), **hlk'íid** (A) for cow-parsnip; **ts'uu** (S, M), **ts'úu** (A) for western red-cedar; **dlaaying'waal** (S), **dlaaying'waal** (M), **dláamaal** (A) for licorice fern; and **k̲aal**, **k̲al** (S, M), **k̲ál** (A) for red alder. These terms are generally assumed to be relatively ancient, their original meaning and analysis having been obscured over time. Another explanation is that these terms may have been borrowed from other languages in which the meanings would be obvious. Within those plants listed, however, a survey of neighbouring languages shows virtually no relationships for these terms except for one possible, interesting coincidence: the Tsilhqot'in (Chilcotin) and other Athapaskan peoples' word for "spruce" appears to be identical to the Haida name for red-cedar, **ts'uu**. This may be purely coincidental, but it possibly represents an ancient borrowing accompanied by a shift in reference from one important tree to another.

A few plants in Haida are named after their particular applications, or vice versa. For example, the name for western yew means "bow." Other plants are named for their associations with animals. There are a number of these in Haida, from "crow's mountain goat wool" for certain kinds of lichen, to "black-bear berries" for twisted-stalk (S), "raven's canoe" for giant vetch and its relatives, "grizzly bear's medicine" for alumroot and "land otter's medicine" for an unidentified plant, possibly *Microseris boreale*. Other plants are named for other identified characteristics of habit or habitat: "water *Ulva*" for sea lettuce; "deep ocean leaves/medicine" for some of the red algae; "earth leaves/medicine" or "ground leaves/medicine" for twinflower and trailing raspberry; and "rock leaves/medicine" for the dogtooth lichens.

Some plants are named for their own innate characteristics: "floating leaves/medicine" for yellow pond-lily; "it-sticks-to-you" for bedstraw; "round-thing-you-dig-out-with-the-finger" for northern riceroot; and "narrow furry object" for Labrador-tea, whose leaves are fuzzy underneath. Some plants give rise to more complex terminology. For example, the name **hldaan** for blueberries may pertain to a bruise or dark complexion in a person, as in the Massett saying **hldaansgingaan 'la fang.ii geenggaagang** "His face is covered with bruises" (literally 'looks like blueberries') (John Enrico, personal communication 1993). The term for crab apple (**k'aay**) can also be applied to any kind of sour taste, including that of a lemon [called **k'aayluus** (S), 'sour'].

Some plants are named for objects they resemble. For example, cottongrass is sometimes equated with eagle down: **k̲'a'll hltang̲waay** (S) ('muskeg bird down'—JE from C.F. Newcombe). Lingonberry is referred to as "dog salmon eggs." The sac seaweed is called by the term that means "fish's air bladder." Round-leaved sundew is given a name, "the heart of plenty," which relates to its use as a good-luck charm to bring plentiful resources, and calypso is called "black cod grease," apparently by virtue of its rich-tasting bulbs.

Some plants are named after other plants. For example, broad-leaved plantain is called "village skunk-cabbage," and thistle is called, for some unknown reason, "tobacco mother." More examples and more specific characteristics of Haida plant names are provided in Turner (1974). Gitkinjuaas (also known as G̲iitsx̲aa; personal communication 2001) noted that there were undoubtedly many other names for Haida plants in the past, but some of these would have been lost at the time of the terrible disease epidemics that killed so many Haida. At this time, significant knowledge passed away with those people who died from smallpox and other European diseases.

## The Spiritual and Ceremonial Aspects of Plants

As already mentioned in this chapter, Haida accord plants and animals innate powers to aid and support humans in their endeavours or to obstruct and deter them. These powers are recognized and respected, and those wishing to avail themselves of the special help to be provided by the trees and other plants are careful to follow the proper and respectful protocol. Regarding animals, John Swanton (1905a:16) observed:

> According to the Haida spirit-theory, every animal was, or might be, the embodiment of a being who, at his own pleasure, could appear in the human form. They seem to be looked at from two entirely different points of view. As animals, they were called **Gi´na te´iga**, birds, salmon, herring, devil-fish, etc.; as supernatural beings in disguise, **sG̲a´na k̲eda´s**, Forest-People, Salmon-People, Herring-People, etc. As animals, they might be hunted, or given as food to men by another animal, who was a supernatural being; as supernatural beings themselves, they might entertain men in their towns, intermarry with them, help or harm them ...

Later, Swanton (1905a:29) noted:

> Besides bird and beast powers, the existence of supernatural beings in the trees (**K̲a´-it sga´nagwa-i**) was recognized. When Raven went about as a woman, people asked her who her father was; and she replied, "Every one knows me. I am the daughter of a stripped hemlock [or spruce]." I might mention in this connection that cedar bark is said to be "every woman's elder sister." It would appear that not only animals and trees, but bushes, sticks and stones were alive with spirits; for when one of the great heroes is about to break a taboo or commit some similar error, "everything in the forest cries out to stop him."

Haida have shown respect in many ways to other life forms, in both early and contemporary times. Plant medicines, foods and materials are first addressed with special songs and words of gratitude. When the people got cedar bark, there was a song they sang asking the cedar tree to give of its bark. Similarly, many special songs are meant for medicines such as **ts'iihllnjaaw** (S), **ts'iihlanjaaw** (M), **ts'íihlanjaaw** (A) (devil's-club). Another example is in the use of special rituals. Swanton

(1905b:410–11) recorded a ritual use of kelp in an account told to him by Abraham of "Those-born-at-**Q!adAsgo** [sic]" of a war between the people of Kloo (T'anuu) and Nansdins (Ninstints) on SGang Gwaay (Skangwaii). The conquering warriors anchored their canoes in a large kelp bed, and a shaman performed a ritual, then symbolically whipped the souls of his enemies. He saw something in the air and pulled it towards himself. Then, "all the kelp [heads in the water] broke."

A girl at puberty or a woman in mourning was rubbed with soft cedar bark, which was then wedged into the cleft of a crab apple tree to make her strong and enduring (Curtis 1916). Another ritual for a girl reaching puberty was to hang hemlock boughs above her bed. The falling needles symbolized the property that would fall on her when she married (Curtis 1916).

Spiritual relationships of Haida with plants, including medicinal applications, are private knowledge and therefore the details of this aspect of Haida ethnobotany are not presented here. Each individual has her or his own particular connection with nature. It is important for all of us to understand that this relationship exists and that it has a profound influence on the way traditionally trained Haida perceive their lands, but equally important to respect its sacredness and essentially private nature.

## Narratives about Haida Plants

Plants are referred to many times in Haida traditional stories and legends. Appendix 6 lists some of the plant species noted to have some type of role in Haida stories. Most of these are taken from narratives recorded by Swanton (1905b, 1908b). Some plants are mentioned many times in Haida stories, others maybe once or twice. In some cases plants are named in the context of their natural roles as sources of food, materials or medicine for the supernatural beings and heroes around whom the stories revolve. In the story of "The One Abandoned for Eating the Flipper of a Hair Seal" told by John Sky, for example, a root-digging stick of yellow-cedar was chosen as the best after "all sorts of sticks," including red-cedar, had been rejected (Swanton 1905b:181). Red-cedar limbs are twisted to make rope in various stories (e.g., Walter McGregor's story told to Swanton 1905b:254).

In other cases, the plants themselves take on more of an acting role, participating in magical events, and sometimes even precipitating such events. Such is the case with the Skunk-Cabbage Being with the big belly who provided gifts of sockeye salmon to the young man in the story called "The Artisans," recorded by Swanton (1908b:460–66). The skunk-cabbage, originally in its plant form and later in the episode in the form of a supernatural being, provides a fascinating perspective, rarely seen by people today, on the role of plants. Another example of such an acting being

A drawing by Claude Davidson of an original argillite plate carved by his grandfather, artist Charlie Edenshaw. It depicts the story of the origin of women, with Tree Fungus Man as Raven's steersman.

was Tree Fungus, the steersman for Raven on his quest to obtain female parts so that he could create the first women. This story is also told by John Sky to Swanton within the series of episodes of "Raven Travelling" (Swanton 1905b:126).

Other plants, such as the giant tobacco tree, or the giant devil's-club mentioned in Willie Matthews' family story, also certainly have supernatural characteristics. In fact, in ancient times, crab apple trees (and other types of trees as well) were said to have been human beings (Dawson 1880).

The accounts and stories are full of episodes where magical transformations occur, for example: between hair combings and bushes or dense stands of trees (Swanton 1905b:499, 503, 521); from a two-headed bull kelp to the top of the housepost of a supernatural "chief" of the ocean world, in a story told by Walter McGregor (Swanton 1905b:245); from a fern clump to the entrance to the home of supernatural Mouse Woman [**jiigwal 'awG̲a** (S)]; or from a single cranberry to an entire meal for a supernatural hero. There is also the story of "He-Who-Got-Supernatural-Power-from-His-Little-Finger," told by Charlie Edenshaw to Franz Boas, in which "an old rotten tree with long roots" belonging to Master Canoe-Builder was transformed into a large canoe full of crying geese as paddlers, simply with the words, "Go into the water, canoe of my father" (Swanton 1905b:250).

**X̲uya** (S), **Yaahl** (M), **Yáahl** (A) [Raven] was a master of tricks, sometimes using small bits of plant materials. He used spruce needles to trick Low Tide Woman into thinking she was being pricked by sea urchins so that she would

***The Salmon People in Their Canoe*; painting by Gitkinjuaas (also known as G̲iitsx̲aa).**

*Xuya* [Raven]; painting by Gitkinjuaas (also known as Giitsxaa).

make the tide go down. He took stems of dune grass, covered them with moss and stretched them across a chasm to trick **Gud** [Eagle] or Butterfly into thinking they were fallen logs, walking across them and then falling to their deaths. On another occasion, he used spruce cones with grass stuck on rotten logs to simulate canoe loads of enemies (Swanton 1905b:126). Another trick involving hemlock branches is described in the story told by John Sky, "How Raven Got Water from Eagle." The following is a summary from John Sky's original story (Swanton 1905b:116):

> When **X̲uya** (S) [Raven] was trying to obtain water from Eagle, before there were lakes and rivers on the earth, he collected a hatful of pitch from roots in the woods [probably spruce roots] and gave it to Eagle, saying it was drinking water. When Eagle asked why it smelled like pitch, he answered that the water hole was in clay. The story goes on to tell how **X̲uya** finally did get water. He broke off hemlock branch tips "that had clusters of twigs sticking all around them" and set them ablaze. When Eagle took out his water basket to put out the fire, Raven scared him by breaking a clump of hemlock branches. Eagle ran to get away from the falling branches, and **X̲uya** grabbed the water basket, assumed his bird form, and flew away with it. Eagle pursued, but some of the water spilled, and rivers were formed.

Then, of course, in one of his biggest ruses, **X̲uya** changed himself into a hemlock needle, to be swallowed by a "chief's" daughter, thus making her pregnant. There are plenty of examples of such magical, superordinary plants, in most cases manipulated by beings with supernatural powers.

The foods of ancient supernatural beings reflect the diet of their modern counterparts. For example, one supernatural woman, Goose Woman, who ate only **ts'i'aal**, **ts'iiaal** (S), **ts'a.al**, **ts'a'al** (M), **k̲'wíi ts'a.aláay** (A) (silverweed roots), **naa'a** (S) (wild clover "roots") and **t'aanuu** (S, M), **t'anúu** (A) (eelgrass) stalks, not other kinds of human food, would later manifest herself as a goose [**hlgidg̲uun** (S)], and bring food to her husband's people, who were starving:

> They became nearly starved in the town. One day the woman said to [her husband] from the place where she was sitting: "Now my father is bringing food down to me." Behind the town geese were coming down making a great deal of noise, and she went thither. They went with her. All kinds of good food lay there, such as [silverweed] and wild clover roots. For this her father-in-law called in the people ... (told by Walter McGregor; Swanton 1905b:264)

The woman later fled when someone in the town said, "She thinks a great deal of goose food."

**Wild springbank clover flowers and edible rhizomes (naa'a - S).**

***G̲ud*** **[Eagle]; painting by Gitkinjuaas (also known as G̲iitsx̲aa).**

## Relationships between Plants and Animals

Plants and animals are naturally associated among the Haida and other Indigenous Peoples by networks of linkages based on observation of preferred foods, particular habitats and other interrelationships. For example, the story of Goose Woman quoted previously embodies significant information from Haida Traditional Ecological Knowledge about food sought by geese. In another account, skunk-cabbage is recognized as a food of deer. Various plants, particularly the "black-bear berry" (twisted-stalk), skunk-cabbage and the very poisonous false hellebore, are associated with bears. A number of the berries are named for animals that are said to use them for food. These various associations represent important ecological knowledge that had major significance in the Haidas' quest for subsistence. Some plants and animals with specific observed associations are listed in Appendix 7.

# The Plants, Their Haida Names and Cultural Roles

In this section, the plants are grouped according to a general Haida classification, which is discussed in detail in an earlier publication (Turner 1974), and also in this book in the previous chapter, in the section Plants in Language and Classification. The major groups are listed in the Contents at the beginning. The indexes will help the reader find specific types of plants by their Haida names, English common names or scientific names. The scientific names, in general, follow Taylor and MacBryde (1977) for the vascular plants; Schofield (1993) for bryophytes; Vitt et al. (1988) for lichens; and Scagel (1967) for marine algae. Common and scientific family names are also provided for the vascular plants. For simplicity, varietal and subspecific names are not provided, except when they are particularly relevant to Haida plant knowledge.

Haida terms from original sources (e.g., C.F. Newcombe, John Swanton, Franz Boas) that have not been verified by the Haida elders I consulted (see pages 21–24) are given in double

**Opposite page: Salmonberry flower (see pages 115–16).**

**Right: Cloudberry, a fruit of the muskegs; said to be much less common since deer were introduced to the islands (see pages 128–29).**

quotation marks. In some cases, some of the original diacritical marks used by these researchers are omitted here for purposes of practicality. Terms without quotation marks were checked with Haida elders; most were transcribed originally by linguist Robert D. Levine, who completed his doctoral dissertation on the Haida language in the mid-1970s (Levine 1977).

More recently, they were checked and annotated by John Enrico, who completed his Ph.D. dissertation on Massett Haida phonology in 1980 (see also Enrico 1992, 1995). Dr. Enrico's review of the manuscript resulted in many important clarifications and corrections based on information from his Haida Dictionary (Alaska Native Language Center). In certain cases, he rechecked the information with Florence Davidson (M), Kathleen Hans and Hazel Stevens (S). Dr. Enrico has completed a thorough revision of Skidegate texts and myths originally published by Swanton (1905b) (Enrico 1995). Local English plant names or non-literal approximations of Haida terms are given in double quotation marks, whereas literal translations or analyses of Haida names are given in single quotation marks. When known, plant names from the Skidegate dialect are indicated by (S), Massett dialect (M) and Alaska, Kaigani dialect (A). The initial N is also used occasionally to denote a term of the southernmost **Nans Dins** (Ninstints) dialect, where specified by Newcombe (1897).

The symbols used to represent the sounds of Haida are shown in Appendix 1. Appendices 2 through 7 list the plants according to the categories discussed in the section entitled The Role of Plants in Haida Culture (food, materials, medicines, traditional beliefs, etc.), beginning on page 39. Appendix 8 lists plants that have Haida names but whose botanical identification is uncertain. Appendix 9 gives Haida names for general botanical terms, such as "bough" or "root." Appendix 10 lists garden vegetables and other plants introduced to the Haida and for which there are Haida names.

## Evergreen Trees

### Yellow-Cedar, or Yellow Cypress

*Xanthocyparis nootkatensis* (D. Don) D.P. Little; Cypress Family (Cupressaceae)
**sG̱aahlaan** (S), **sG̱ahlaan** (M), **sG̱ahláan** (A)

These Haida terms were generally known to the elders consulted, and were also recorded by Newcombe (1897), Curtis (1916) and Norton (1981). Yellow-cedar wood, which is soft, yellowish and pungent, was valued for carving such items as digging sticks, adze handles, paddles, dishes, masks, rattles and, in historic times, bed-posts (Newcombe 1897; Swanton 1905b; Maude Moody), although Norton (1981) noted that one is warned not to use the wood in association with food because of its strong odour. The wood was specifically used for coffins, according to Newcombe, and the Haida word for "coffin" may be derived from the name for yellow-cedar. Yellow-cedar wood is valued by contemporary Haida carvers, who use it for ornamental paddles, wood sculptures and other items (Victor Adams, Massett, personal communication 1971).

The inner bark, called **giixida** (S), **gi.id** (M), **giid** (A) (JE; Boas 1891), the same as red-cedar bark (Florence Davidson), is valued for its soft, fibrous qualities. It was, and still is, used for weaving hats, mats and blankets. It is harvested in a similar manner to red-cedar bark, but is considered finer and of higher quality. Long strips of the bark are pulled from standing trees. The brittle outer bark is broken off and discarded, and the inner bark folded into flat bundles, which are tied with strips of the bark itself. While the bark is still fresh, the brown outer layer is peeled off with a knife. The satiny whitish innermost bark is then dried, in sheets or after being cut into strips, for later processing. Once dried, the bark is simply soaked in warm water to make it pliable again (Florence Davidson). Yellow-cedar mats and blankets are said to be more valuable than those of red-cedar (see Swanton 1905b:153). Yellow-cedar was also valued for its wood, which was used for shipbuilding and for other construction purposes (Michael Nicoll, personal communication 1993).

Yellow-cedar was the family crest of the "Chief of Skidailamas" (Newcombe 1904). This tree is referred to in a number of Haida stories. In one, the spark-throwing quality of the wood as a fuel is noted (Swanton 1905b:127). In another, a hero's supernatural wives asked him to get digging sticks for them. He made these out of many different kinds of wood, but the wives rejected all except those of yellow-cedar (Swanton 1905b:181). Both stories were told originally by John Sky.

## Western Red-Cedar

*Thuja plicata* Donn ex D. Don; Cypress Family (Cupressaceae)
**ts'uu** (S, M), **ts'úu** (A)
Inner bark (of small to medium cedars): **giixida** (S), **gi.id** (M), **giid** (A) (FD; JE) (also yellow-cedar)
Inner bark (thick, of big cedar): **g̲aay** (S, M), **g̲áay** (A) (JE)
Outer bark of old cedars: **gahlda** (S, M) (JE)
Withes (long, thin branches): **sgisgil** (S), **sgisgal** (M), **sgisgál** (A) (JE)

Red-cedar is one of the most important of all plants in Haida culture. Newcombe (1897) refers to it as "the most useful tree in these islands." The easily worked, rot-resistant wood is valued as a material for construction and carving. It is the main material for making traditional canoes, house boards and posts, totem poles, mortuary poles and a variety of smaller items, including boxes, cradles, snares, fish

**Left: Yellow-cedar.**

**Right: Yellow-cedar bark, cleaned and hung up to dry on Florence Davidson's clothesline, Massett, 1971.**

weirs and fire tongs (see Dawson, in Cole and Lockner 1989:468–69, who provides a description of the construction of a new house for "Chief Klue" at T'anu, from red-cedar posts and planks). Norton (1981) noted that one is warned not to use the wood for cooking fires or in direct contact with food because it will adversely flavour the food. Newcombe (1902) provides the following description of the cutting and preparation of cedar trees for planking at Kasaan, Alaska:

> A tree of suitable size was chosen. It was then cut half through on the side towards which it was desired to fall. Two deep notches were first made and the intervening wood was removed by means of wedges driven by sledge hammers. On the opposite side, a second but smaller cut was made. Before felling the tree several large logs were thrown where it was intended to fall so as to make it easier to turn over. The tree was then pulled down taking care that the side with the most branches was uppermost. The heavy work was always done by the owner, who was assisted by his nephew (sister's son) who did such light work as holding the wedges, etc. If others were required, they were always paid for their assistance.
>
> Once properly on the skids the top of the tree was cut through and removed. Next a long rope of cedar bark was taken and stretched on each side for the whole length of the trunk, supported where necessary by small pegs, and above the centreline of the tree. Notches were now made down to the line so marked, dividing the upper part of the trunk into several sections which were split off with the wedge and sledge hammer. The rough surface first made was next very carefully dressed down with stone chisels and latterly with the adze, and the log was then turned and accurately measured, if a plank was desired, to get an even thickness at each end. The rope was again attached to mark out this thickness and the second surface was prepared as before by notching with the stone axe and splitting off with wedges. The

**Left: Western red-cedar.**

**Right: Kii'iljuus (Barbara Wilson) looking at a large culturally modified western red-cedar with a hole chopped into the heartwood at Spirit Lake near Skidegate, 1998.**

plank so made might be used for flooring, or for the sides of the house, or might be split into small planks by wedges first inserted at the ends and assisted by levers at the side.

The use of cedar wood for fish weirs is described in a narrative recorded by Swanton (1905b:82), as told by Edward:

> Now the Head-of-creek woman of Skidegate creek had spoken as follows: "I will remember you. After the Food-giving-town people are all gone they shall become numerous again," she said. Then they cut down a cedar. They split it up and carried it out of the woods. Then they began to make a fish trap. And when they had finished it they named it "Small-hole-in-the-ground fish trap." [The maker of this] gave the fish trap to his son. His wife belonged to the **Giti'ns** and he (the son) was the first of the Big-house people.

Young cedar branches, or withes, were twisted or plaited together or used singly as a strong rope to "sew" the house planks together, particularly at the front and back of a house, and to bind canoes together and fasten their thwarts (Newcombe 1897, 1898, 1913; Swanton 1905b; Chief Willie Matthews). They were also used for the frames of baskets.

Red-cedar bark had a multitude of uses. Large sheets of the whole bark were used for covering temporary shelters and for roofing permanent structures (Newcombe 1897). Chief Willie Matthews described how the bark was prepared for roofing in the traditional way:

> They go to cedar trees about two feet [60 cm] in diameter near Naden Harbour. They cut all around the base of the tree with a chisel. Then they cut down a young cedar tree and, using the branches as a ladder, they climb up about

**Opposite page (clockwise from top left): Pulling off a strip of cedar bark; harvested cedar bark; pulling apart the layers of cedar bark; cedar-bark mat, woven by Florence Davidson; Florence Davidson and Nancy Turner splitting cedar bark, 1972.**

> seven feet [over 2 m] above the first cut and cut around. Then they make a cut from top to bottom straight down and peel the bark off in a large sheet, about four feet [1.3 m] by seven feet. They bundle about three together and carry them down to the canoe. The bundles are real heavy. To make them flat, they thread salmonberry sticks through the inner bark in several places, pile the bark up, and weigh it down with stones. These sheets are used for roofing or for covering things in canoes.

Cedar-bark roofing was formerly traded to the Nass River people (Nisga'a) at a price of one blanket per two sheets of bark, according to John Sky (Swanton 1905b:127). Harrison (1925) reported that September is called "**kitas,**" "the moon they get cedar bark," but John Enrico points out that **k̲'i k̲'iidas**, the seventh lunar month (roughly October) means 'split in half.' It fell between the six summer and the six winter months.

The inner bark is used for weaving mats, hats, cloaks and baskets. At one time it was made into ropes, fishing line and fishnets (Swanton 1905b; Dawson 1880; Newcombe 1897) and ceremonial neck rings for dancers (Dawson, in Cole and Lockner 1989). Tremendous quantities of this valuable material must have been harvested over thousands of years, all up and down the Northwest Coast. Newcombe (1902) described inner bark collecting at Kasaan:

> In May and June, when the sap is running, several women and girls go out early in the morning to gather cedar bark. They select young cedar trees about 12 inches [30 cm] in diameter, with few lower branches. A knife is used to cut the bark at breast height and to separate it from the wood at the bottom. The bark is then pulled outwards, and as the strip comes off the tree, a song is sung to a lively tune ... "We want a long strip, go up high, go up high!" [Note: John Enrico provides the actual Haida words for this song: **k̲'ahsgad-hlaa**, **k̲'ahsgad-hlaa** (literally 'strike-ground'—imperative), **háayaas-hl k̲'íiwii**, **háayaas-hl k̲'íiwii!** (literally 'hard'—imperative 'fall') (A). He notes that **háayaas** is a Chinook Jargon word.]
>
> The strip is pulled up as far as it will go, sometimes 20 or 30 feet [7–10 m]. The dry outer bark [**sk'al.uj** (M; 'outer layer of bark on young cedar'; can occur with a possessive determiner **k̲i.id**, **k̲iid** 'spruce,' or **k̲'aang** 'hemlock' only] is removed from the inner bark and discarded. The inner bark is bundled up, and the women return at midday, each carrying about 30 bundles strapped to her back. This bark is divided into two layers [**k̲'uts'** (M) "bark, general," on the outside, and **tsiihluu** (M) "phloem"; or better word for part next to tree: **duu** (M), the innermost bark]. These are cut in strips and hung in the sun to dry. They are folded into long bundles for storage. Cedarbark mats are woven on a wooden frame; **k̲'uts'** is used for perpendicular strands, and **tsiihluu** for horizontal strands. [Note: terms and information shown in square brackets

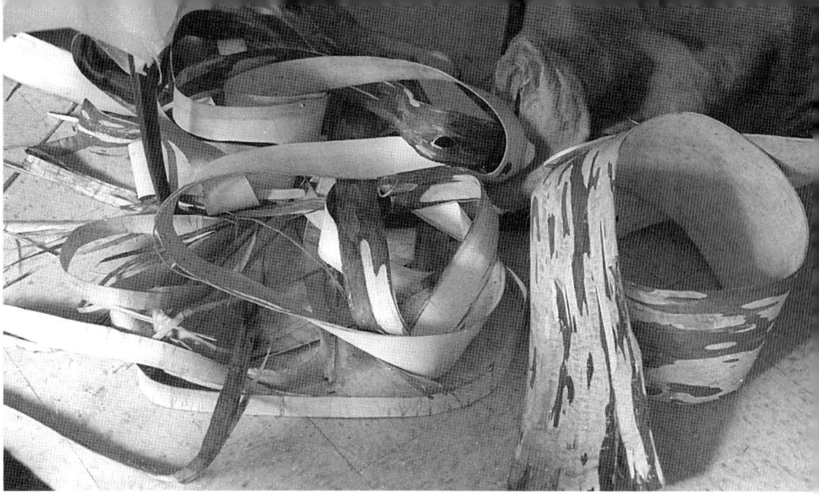

**LEFT: Florence Davidson harvests red-cedar bark, 1972.**

**RIGHT: Harvesting cedar bark; Nancy Turner pulling a long strip from a young tree.**

provided by John Enrico, personal communication 1993. Updated spelling and translation of the song are from his (coauthored) book *Northern Haida Songs* (Enrico and Stuart 1996)].

For decoration in weaving, bark strips are dyed black by soaking them in water with rusted iron (Eliza Abrams). Red alder bark is also used to colour cedar bark (Dawson 1880). Red-dyed cedar-bark head and neck rings were worn by the Haida on ceremonial occasions (Dawson, in Cole and Lockner 1989). Newcombe (1902) gave an account of the preparation of these "dance collars" and head-dresses:

> Long strips about five inches [12–13 cm] wide of the innermost bark of the red cedar are taken, dried over a fire, and then chopped across the grain over a paddle or a sharp-edged board, with a bone implement shaped like a meat chopper. To make the larger rope which has three strands, three long strips of the softened bark are taken and placed together, and one end of the bunch made fast to a stick, each strip is twisted separately while in a state of tension, and at short intervals. The three are all twisted together, and this is repeated until sufficient rope is made. Then the ends are brought together and tied in the form of a 'sailor's knot,' about a foot [30 cm] being left loose to form a fringe. The head-dress is made similarly, but the fringed ends are made to overlap, and are tied together by a separate piece. The red colour is made by chewing the bark of the red

**Left: Captain Gold has just removed a strip of cedar bark from a tree beside a much older culturally modified tree, or CMT, 1996.**

**Right: Florence Davidson bundles harvested cedar bark, 1972.**

alder, [**k̲aal**, **k̲al** (S, M), **k̲ál** (A)], and the colouring is sprayed from the mouth over these ornaments.

Shredded cedar bark, called **hltanhlk'yaa** (S), **hltanhlk'a** (M), **hltánhlk'a** (A) (JE) was used for towelling, bandages, infant bedding and diapers (Swanton 1905b; Newcombe 1897). It was also pulverized and ignited to cauterize swellings (Harrison, 1925), and was used for tinder (Newcombe 1897). Special cedar-bark cloaks were worn by girls at puberty (Blackman 1982). Swanton (1905a:29) noted, "Cedar bark is said to be 'every woman's elder sister.'"

A popular gambling game of the Haida, described by Tom Stevens to Swanton (1905b:52–57), involved bunches of sticks, usually of maple (imported to Haida Gwaii), yew or black twinberry wood, which were hidden under finely shredded cedar bark. These were divided into two or three piles, and the contestant had to guess which pile contained the **jil** (S), **jal** (M), **jál** (A) (literally 'bait'—JE), "a special undecorated stick."

Red-cedar was important in Haida narratives, and featured in many of the stories recorded by John Swanton (1905b). Young Cedar Woman was the name of a supernatural being; according to Edward, she was a cedar who stood behind a certain town. "She was unable to twist twine for a net because her skin was covered with hair" (Swanton 1905b:78). In stories told by John Sky, flickers were made by **X̲uya** [Raven] from cedar twigs with his blood on them; red-cedar wood was used to fashion the first orca, or killer whale; and certain rocks at the inner side of

Ramsey Island were said to be bundles of cedar-bark roofing left by **X̱uya** and other supernatural birds (Swanton 1905b:127, 149).

How **X̱uya** [Raven] Tries to Trick Eagle, and Fails

**X̱uya** [Raven] went fishing with his cousin, Eagle. He was only able to catch red cod, whose flesh was dry, whereas Eagle caught a black cod, which was full of grease. When they roasted their fish, **X̱uya** asked to taste Eagle's and, being jealous, said it tasted like cedar. He then excused himself, saying he was going to collect cedar bark. He told Eagle that a stump might approach him and that the flavour of his fish would improve if he rubbed it on the face of this stump. Eagle sensed a trick and, when a stump did come up to him, instead of rubbing his fish on it, he put red hot rocks on it. The "stump" retreated, and shortly afterward, **X̱uya** appeared with cedar bark and a noticeably blackened face. Eagle suggested that something must have burned his face, but **X̱uya** denied it, saying that bark had fallen on it. (told by "Chief of Kloo" to Swanton 1905b:129)

## Sitka Spruce

*Picea sitchensis* (Bong.) Carr.; Pine Family (Pinaceae)

**ḵaayd**, **ḵayd** (S), **ḵiid** (M), **ḵíid** (A) ('spruce tree/wood'; 'evergreen tree')

Branches: **hlḵ'am.aal k'i** (M) (literally 'sharp branches/boughs'; **k'i** 'be sharp') (see Appendix 9, under "Bough")

Roots (long, thin ones used in basketry): **hll.nga** (S—small roots, or roots, generic); **hlii.ng** (M), **hlíing** (A) (in M means 'long, narrow evergreen roots, spruce in particular')

Big spruce-root **bag: sk'aayx̱an** (S)

Edible inner bark: **sḵaalaak'uu ts'ii** (S) (**ts'ii** 'insides'—JE)

Suck juice out of spruce pulp: **hlk'uuk'aan** (S)

Spruce cones: **sk'a'anda sk'uwaal** or **skaa'anda sk'uuwaal** (S)

Pink spruce gum: **ḵ'aas, ḵ'aajii** (S), **ḵ'aas, ḵ'aaj** (M), **ḵ'áas** (A) ('gum, pitch, tar, wax, pitchwood,' general) (JE)

These terms were widely known to the Haida elders I consulted, and were also recorded by Newcombe (1898, 1901), Swanton (1905b), Curtis (1916) and Norton (1981). The terms **ḵaayd** (S) and **ḵiid** (M) are also applied in a general context to "evergreen trees," including hemlock, red-cedar and yellow-cedar. Some people may even include red alder within the generalized term, although most would deny that it encompasses Pacific crab apple. Nevertheless, this "expansion of reference" from "spruce" to "evergreen tree/tree" reflects its high profile and importance in Haida traditional culture. Indeed, it is the dominant forest tree over much of Haida Gwaii, and it is highly respected for its role in Haida life. A similar expansion of reference of a basic name for a tree or other type of plant of high salience to a general category name is a common occurrence in many languages of the world. Norton (1981) reported that among the Kaigani, **k̲'íid** is applied to "those plants which grow tall and straight," and that it is generic for "tree."

The sweet, juicy cambium and associated inner bark tissues of Sitka spruce, like those of hemlock, were scraped off the tree in mid-May and June, after a piece of bark had been removed, and were eaten raw (Curtis 1916; Emma Wilson, George Young, Florence Davidson, Emma Matthews). Emma Matthews (personal communication to Marianne Boelscher 1980) described the harvesting:

> When I was a little girl and Nonnie Selina was grown up, they used to go up there. They climb up the spruce tree, cut around it, peel the barks off. When there's enough on the ground, they take the [outer] bark off. You just swallow the juice, though. They used to put grease in it and a little bit of sugar and chew it a long time until all the juice comes off ... In summertime, that's when the inside of trees gets juicy and fat. [In winter] it's dry and nothing inside.

She noted that people ate the inner bark of hemlock as well. In fact, hemlock inner bark is generally much preferred over spruce because the many small lower branches of spruce make removing the bark very difficult, and the spruce inner bark has a reputation for tasting pitchy. Some people said that the practice of eating inner bark was learned from the Tsimshian people, who, as of the early 1970s, were still eating spruce and hemlock cambium. Formerly, it was sometimes dried into blocks or cakes for winter use. Dawson (1880) and Jenness (1934) stated that spruce boughs were used for collecting herring eggs, a practice more commonly employing hemlock boughs. Harrison (1925) reported that the white, hardened gum of spruce was chewed [for pleasure], and Norton (1981) noted a similar use for the Kaigani and that chewing the gum was thought to whiten the teeth. Several varieties of spruce pitch were gathered by children for chewing: **k̲'aas x̲andaaw** (S), **k̲'aas G̲ugahldiyaa** (M) was gathered by setting the tree alight (it was not highly valued because it was black); **k̲'aas stluutsiG̲adaang** (S), **k̲'aas k̲ults'àadaangaa** (M), **k̲'áas k̲últs'aadaang** (A) was dug out of woodpecker holes (it is pink when chewed and the best kind); and **k̲'aas x̲asaa** (M), simply scraped off trees (it was dirty and not highly valued) (John Enrico). Emma Matthews (personal communication to Marianne Boelscher 1981) recalled that pregnant women were not allowed to chew pink spruce gum because if they did, their afterbirth would stick to the womb and not come out.

Spruce wood and bark were used for fuel (Swanton 1905b; Norton 1981).

**Top left: Dorothy Bell (left) shows Colleen Williams how to harvest pitch from a spruce tree, 2003. –photo by marianne b. ignace**

**Top right: Sitka spruce.**

The wood was valued because of its heat, and because the smoke does not adversely flavour drying foods. The straight, young trees were used by the Kaigani to make splints for roasting salmon because the wood is neutral in flavour (Norton 1981). Newcombe (1897) noted that spruce wood was sometimes used for dishes, spoons and boxes, but not to any great extent. The strong knots and branches were sometimes employed in making halibut hooks (see under western hemlock, *Tsuga heterophylla*).

The roots are the most important part of the tree in terms of technology. They are used for weaving tightly twined baskets and hats, an art still practised by some Haida women.

**Haida spruce-root twined basket, from Royal BC Museum collection.**

**Opposite page, bottom left: Florence Davidson heating and peeling spruce roots, 1972.**

**Opposite page, bottom right: Florence Davidson digging spruce roots at North Beach with her granddaughters and Nancy Turner, 1972.**

**Florence Davidson Recalls Gathering and Using Spruce Roots**

Ever since I can remember, I used to go with my mother in May for spruce roots [**hlii.ng**]. Every fine day we'd go to North Beach early in the morning before sunrise. We'd pack water and food with us and mother would cook our breakfast in the woods. She used to have kindling ready and she left her pots and dishes there. We'd collect **hlii.ng** all day long ...

When it was noontime, we'd quit collecting **hlii.ng** and my mother would make lunch. Sometimes other ladies would come along and we'd have a nice time together—it was just like a picnic. Then we'd gather driftwood from the beach and make a big fire to "cook" the roots. My mother roasted them and I pulled the skin [bark] off. We'd collect piles and piles of them. My mother would know when to quit, when we'd had enough. The sun would be going down when we started for home. The bundles of roots were all tied together and we each packed a big bundle of roots ... When we got home my dad would cook for us ... Soon as my mother finished eating she'd start splitting the roots in half. She bundled them up and put all the same size ones together in a bent box. She packed them in real tight. She used to have so many boxes to keep the **hlii.ng** in. If you don't cover it, the roots turn brown, so she kept them in boxes.

My mother used to weave baskets and hats all winter long. When she was going to start her weaving she soaked the roots overnight, so they'd be easy to work. She'd get up early in the morning and cook and, after everyone was finished eating, she'd go to work splitting the roots again and weaving them into a hat or basket. She worked all day long, day after day, from the time she finished picking and putting up berries till the spring. It was just like having a business. When she finished a hat she put it in a dark place and then my dad would paint a design on it. Sometimes he painted placemats, hats, baskets with covers, seaweed baskets, baskets for carrying water. She even used to weave around bottles. She learned to decorate her baskets with grass [false embroidery] from a Tlingit lady in Ketchikan. What my mother wove all winter long she sold in June when we went to the mainland to work in the canneries. She sold her work at Cunningham's store in Port Essington. She used to get five dollars for a finely woven, painted hat. Mr. Cunningham paid her cash for her work and she bought our winter coats there. Mr. Newcombe used to come here from Victoria to buy things from my parents, too. (Blackman 1982:85–86)

Newcombe (1897) described the collection and preparation of **hllnga** (S), the long, thin basket roots:

> Large, deep pits are dug in the sandy soil near the shore, and the straightest spruce roots are pulled up and tied in bundles, called **<u>x</u>kîlkûtsiteñ** [**hlk'uts'id** (S), **hlk'uts'ad** (M) 'make into bundles' (plural); Newcombe's version is a sentence: **'la hlk'uts'iidan** 'she bundled them'—JE]. These are scorched to remove the bark, and then each root is pulled through wooden tongs until it is completely smooth and clean. The root is then split into a number of sections. The shiny, rounded outside strips, **hl<u>k</u>'ugaan** [see next paragraph], are used only as circular strands for hats and baskets. The choice piece, tsuni, rectangular in cross-section, is split from the center of the root and is dull in texture. It is used only for the long strands in weaving.

John Enrico elaborates on this description:

> The inner part of the root is **ts'uu.ii** (S, M); the outer part is called **duu** in M—these are basically the terms for warp and weft, respectively, transferred to the materials themselves. The verb meaning 'split roots' is **g'uga** (S, M, A) (Newcombe: **hl <u>k</u>'ugaang** 'I'm splitting them'). In M the first split of the root is down the line of the rootlets; a second split is then made parallel to this, giving a flat inner section—**ts'uu.ii** (S, M)—and two half-rounded lengths of **duu**.

Spruce-root baskets are of the finest quality. Twined with two, or sometimes three, active weft strands, they are so tightly woven as to be waterproof. The sandy-soiled spruce woods near Tow Hill yield good basketry roots for the Massett women.

Formerly, spruce-root "string," of finely split roots spun by hand into thread, was used to make halibut fishing line, to sew plants together, to tie adze heads to their handles and to bind and repair halibut hooks (Swanton 1905b; Swan 1885).

Spruce pitch is a valuable medicine, still used today. First Peoples throughout the Northwest Coast region used it to make a salve for treating skin infections, cuts and splinters. When James Swan (1885) was at Kiusta, he prepared a salve of spruce gum to heal a wound of Charlie Edenshaw's; he was rewarded with two large shark-design earrings.

The pitch was formerly rubbed on the face for protection against sunburn and cold (Dawson 1880; George Young). When a person died, the mourners mixed it with charcoal and applied it to their faces. It was also applied to the handles of tools, such as bark scrapers, to make them easier to grip (Newcombe 1897). Pinkish-coloured spruce gum (**<u>k</u>'aas**) was gathered, especially by the women, and chewed, first with cold water to harden it, and then as chewing gum, as Gertrude Kelly recalled.

This "red gum" is mentioned in several Haida stories, and was said to be a woman's medicine (Swanton 1905b).

In stories, **X̲uya** (S), **Yaahl** (M), **Yáahl** (A) [Raven] sometimes used spruce to fool others. Once he placed upright spruce cones, each with a grass stem sticking up beside it, on rotten logs, and floated them on the water, convincing his animal companions that they were distant enemies in their canoes, brandishing spears. Everyone was frightened away, and **X̲uya** ate all their hemlock bark and highbush cranberry cakes (Swanton 1905b:126). Another time, as told by John Sky, **X̲uya** deceived Old Man Tide into thinking that salal leaves with spruce needles stuck into them were sea urchins, so that he caused the tide to go down (Swanton 1905a:128). Similarly, he tricked Low Tide Woman into thinking that spruce needles were really sea urchin spines. She opened her legs, causing the tide to go down, thus allowing **X̲uya** to eat all the fish and shellfish stranded by the low tides (told by "Chief of Kloo" to Swanton 1908a:303).

Swanton (1905a) reported that one test of strength used by Haida men was to pull spruce branches off standing trees. Dawson (Cole and Lockner 1989:479) noted that "sprigs of fresh spruce were held by many of the dancers," when he attended a ceremonial dance at Skidegate on July 24, 1878. The Skidegate elders said that to prevent body odour, one could rub spruce cones or hemlock boughs under their arms.

**Agnes Edenshaw Yeltatzie Jones splitting spruce roots for basketry at North Beach, 1972.**

## Western Hemlock

*Tsuga heterophylla* (Raf.) Sarg.; Pine Family (Pinaceae)
**k̲'aang** (S, M), **k̲'aáng** (A)
Edible inner bark: **x̲i** (S) **x̲iga**, **x̲ig**, **x̲i** (M), **x̲i** (A); or **k̲'aang k̲aahlii** (S) ('hemlock inside') equivalent to **x̲i k̲aahlii** (M) ('inside of **x̲i**') (JE)
Hemlock bark gathering, pulling off the inner hemlock bark: **xiidang gwang** (S)
Hemlock needle: **t'aaw** (S)

The name for hemlock was widely known to the elders I consulted, and was also recorded by Newcombe (1897), Swanton (1905b), Curtis (1916) and Norton (1981). Newcombe (1897) identified the term **k̲'aang** as an "older hemlock," and also provided the terms **tlaaji** (S) ("adult tree") (literally 'limb butting into trunk'—JE), and **hlk̲'ang'waal** (S) ("young tree") (literally 'branch butting into limb'—JE). The cambium and inner bark tissues of young hemlock trees were formerly scraped off and eaten (Newcombe 1897; Swanton 1905b; Norton 1981; Florence Davidson, Emma Wilson). It was ready for harvesting in mid-May or June ("when the tree was 'fat'"—Norton 1981). Norton (p. 440) provides details of Kaigani use: "In late May or June large strips of bark were removed from the tree after being loosened with a wooden tool [**dllgu** (S), **dlagu** (M), **dlagw** (A) "digging stick" (JE), made of western yew

**RIGHT: Western hemlock.**

and in historic times made with a business end of copper (JE)]. The cambium was scraped from the inner bark, pounded, and pit steamed. It was then moulded into cakes and dried on wooden trays above the fire. After slow and thorough drying these cakes were stored in a wrapping of skunk-cabbage leaves and placed in baskets for later consumption. They were rehydrated before eating." Newcombe (1902) also noted that the cambium was eaten fresh or formed into "loaves" and baked into "bread." Hemlock food was still being used occasionally at the turn of the century, and before this time was widely used.

**Preparation of Hemlock Bark Food**

Young hemlock trees were felled, and then ... circular cuts were made above and below the places where the branches were given off, so that strips could be removed in convenient sections. Then by means of a small scraper (originally a sharp shell, e.g., the large mussel [**taax̱aaw** (S), *Mytilus californianus*]) made of iron and shaped like a fish knife, the tender sapwood was gathered, dried and made into square cakes measuring about 18 inches [45 cm] by 12 [30 cm] and an inch [2.5 cm] thick. Scraping and preparing were attended to by women and girls only. (Newcombe 1897)

Cambium cakes are said to be constipating unless eaten with eulachon grease (Norton 1981). Cakes of hemlock cambium mixed with highbush cranberries (*Viburnum edule*) were a favourite, high-quality food of the Haida, frequently mentioned in stories as the feast food of supernatural beings (Swanton 1905b).

Hemlock boughs, with the needles still intact, were used by the Haida to collect herring spawn, as they were by many other coastal groups. As the following excerpt demonstrates, this practice has ancient origins in stories.

Herring roe on hemlock branches. The lower branch has been cooked; the roe is peeled off to eat.

**The Story of How X̲uya [Raven] Helped the Haida Obtain Herring Eggs**

**X̲uya** went to the dance house of the Herring People, and when he looked at them dancing, they spawned upon his mustache. He ate the eggs but they tasted bad and **X̲uya** became disgusted and threw his mustache away. It became a seaweed, "**X̲uya**'s/ Raven's mustache," which the Haida sometimes used to collect herring spawn. Then X̲uya pushed a young hemlock bough into the house. When he drew it out, the fish eggs were thick on it and they tasted good when he ate them. This is why hemlock boughs are used in preference to "**X̲uya**'s mustache" for collecting herring spawn. (after Swanton 1905b:135; originally told by Walter McGregor)

Hemlock boughs were also used to make temporary shelters and blinds for shooting birds, according to John Sky (Swanton 1905b:121). Hemlock knots, particularly those formed by the ends of limbs in rotten stumps, were used to make halibut hooks [**taaG̲uu** (S)] and cod hooks [**k'uud** (S), "black cod hook"] (Newcombe 1897; Swanton 1905b), and the wood, occasionally, to make small items such as boxes and spoons. The ancient origin of the making of halibut hooks is related in the Skidegate story "Supernatural Being Who Went Naked," told by John Sky. This account contains numerous references to hemlock (Swanton 1905b:225). The fish hooks were oval or U-shaped and barbed with bone or iron. They were baited with pieces of octopus [**naaw** (S), "devilfish"]. According to Chief Willie Matthews, the ends of black cod hooks, also made of hemlock, were sprung apart with a small stick. The hooks were tied onto kelp fishing lines and lowered into the water from the canoe. The fish, attempting to get the bait, would spring the device, and its mouth would become clamped onto the barb. The stick floated to the surface, indicating to the fisherman that a fish had been caught. If more than one hook were tied to the line, the fisherman would wait until all the sticks had appeared on the surface before pulling up the line (Chief Willie Matthews). According to Niblack (1890), the Haida frequently put 100 hooks on a single line, and could catch 50 to 75 black cod at once.

Wood from bent hemlock trees, whose lower trunks are horizontal, was used for carving long feast dishes (Newcombe 1902). Hemlock sticks were used to make spears for octopus, and to construct fish weirs and grouse snares (Swanton 1905b). Hemlock wood was also used to make wedges, children's bows and ridge poles for portable lodges (Newcombe 1897). The roots were used to make snares (Swanton 1908b) and were sometimes spliced onto fishing lines to strengthen them. The twigs were used to fashion rings, used in the "hidden ring game" and the "ring and stick game" (Newcombe 1902).

Hemlock pitch, like that of spruce, is widely used as medicine, especially for wounds and skin infections. To prevent body odour, a person can rub under their arms with hemlock boughs.

Hemlock is frequently mentioned in Haida narratives. Hemlock-Bark-Scraping-Knife and Among-the-Hemlock-Boughs were the names of two supernatural beings. A common episode in stories is for **X̱uya** (S), **Yaahl** (M), **Yáahl** (A) [Raven] to turn himself into a hemlock needle, to be swallowed inadvertently by a supernatural chief's daughter. In this way, he impregnates her and is "reborn." See, for example, the story told to Professor Franz Boas by Charlie Edenshaw in Swanton (1905b:142).

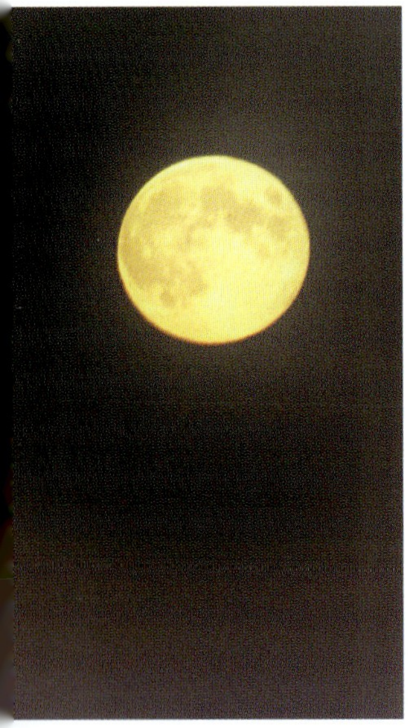

**X̱uya [Raven] Brings the Moon to the People**

After **X̱uya** [Raven] had traveled for a while he came to where a village lay. He then put himself in the form of a conifer needle [in other versions, a hemlock needle is specified] into a water hole behind the chief's house and floated about there awaiting the chief's daughter. The chief's child then went thither for water ... And when close to her he said: "Drink it." ... she became pregnant ... [Once born] the child ... cried so violently that no one could stop it. "Boo hoo, moon," it kept saying ... [Then] they gave it a round thing. There came light throughout the house ... Then he flew away with it ... He then bit off a part of the moon. After he had chewed it for a while he threw it up ... He then broke the moon into halves by throwing it down hard and threw [half of] it up hard into the air ... (as told by John Sky to Swanton 1905b:116–18)

In another part of the **Yaahl** (M)/ Raven Travelling tales told by Charlie Edenshaw to Professor Franz Boas, Raven, in the form of a hemlock needle, is swallowed by the chief's daughter and is reborn. As they travel from village to village, the baby (**Yaahl**) manages to eat everyone's eyes in the night, making all of them blind (Swanton 1905b:143).

A closely related species, mountain hemlock (*Tsuga mertensiana* [Bong.] Carr.), grows only in the subalpine and alpine regions of Haida Gwaii (Calder and Taylor 1968). Dawson (1880) reported that the cambium was eaten fresh or dried, but he may have been referring to western hemlock, even though he used the name "*Abies mertensiana*," an early name for mountain hemlock. According to Newcombe (1901), the names applied to mountain hemlock and its parts are the same as those for western hemlock.

Another relative of hemlock, Douglas-fir (*Pseudotsuga menziesii* [Mirb.] Franco), is called **x̲uuguuga** (S) (GY, BP; Newcombe 1901; Curtis 1916). Neither Douglas-fir nor the true firs (*Abies* spp.) are native to Haida Gwaii, but Douglas-fir, at least, was known to the Haida as driftwood, and possibly from their travels down the coast. There are a few Douglas-firs growing around Massett, where they were planted. The Skidegate Haida name may have been borrowed from some other language; there are apparently no names for Douglas-fir in the other dialects (JE).

***Raven Transforms Himself into a Hemlock Needle*; painting by Gitkinjuaas (also known as G̲iitsx̲aa).**

**Right: Lodgepole pine.**

## Lodgepole Pine

*Pinus contorta* D. Dougl. ex Loud.; Pine Family (Pinaceae)
**ts'ahl** (S), **ts'ahla, ts'ahl** (M) ('pine'), **ts'ahl** (A)

These names were widely known to the contemporary Haida speakers, and were also recorded by Newcombe (1901). The names for the cones and boughs apply generally to those of coniferous trees (see Appendix 9). Pine bark is used to make important Haida medicines, used both internally and externally. George Young said that one could see pine trees between **Tll'aal** (Tlell) and Port Clements with scars on their trunks where bark had been removed for medicine. In the case of accidents, Maude and Agnes Moody noted, lengths of pine bark, which naturally curls tightly around itself when removed from the tree, were bound around broken limbs to form a cast.

Florence Davidson said that the name for pine sounded like the word for "pillow" in Haida, but the significance of this similarity is unclear. The Tlingit name for lodgepole pine, "**chlatl**" (Krause 1956), may be related to the Haida.

## Western Yew, or Pacific Yew

*Taxus brevifolia* Nutt.; Yew Family (Taxaceae)
**hlg̲iid** (S, M), **hlg̲íid** (A) (also 'bow')

These names were well known to virtually all of the Haida elders consulted, and were also recorded by Newcombe (1901), Swanton (1905b) and Curtis (1916).

Yew wood is highly valued for its strength and resiliency. The Haida, like most other coastal peoples, used it for clubs, spears, boxes, awls, wedges, digging sticks and spades, halibut hooks, knives, small dishes, soopolallie (soapberry) spoons, masks, gambling sticks, paddles and bows (Newcombe 1897). The name for yew also means 'bow' in other aboriginal languages, including Halq'emeylem and

**Left: Western yew.**

**Right: Yew trunk, showing flaking reddish bark.**
–PHOTO BY MARIANNE B. IGNACE

Lil'wet'ul (Pemberton Lillooet), a testimony to this important traditional application of yew wood. Victor Adams of Massett often used yew wood in his carving, but noted, as of the early 1970s, that it was becoming difficult to obtain large pieces of the wood.

Yew wood was, and is, an important Haida medicine, as it is for other First Peoples of the Northwest Coast. Western yew has become world famous with the discovery in the 1960s of a potent anticancer drug, Taxol (paclitaxel), in its bark. This drug was patented by the pharmaceutical company Bristol-Myers Squibb. In order to obtain enough Taxol to proceed with clinical trials, and to meet demand as the drug was approved for treating various types of cancer from ovarian and breast cancers to kidney cancer, the company placed orders for vast quantities of yew bark. Within a short time, western yew trees all along the Pacific Coast were being exploited for their bark. Little or no recognition was given to the fact that yew has high cultural values, including medicinal values, for First Peoples. Before the commercial harvesting of its bark, yew was generally considered a "trash tree" in industrial forestry, and many yew trees were simply cut down and left or burned as slash. Wood carvers and medicine gatherers alike are now finding yew increasingly rare. Fortunately, researchers have developed techniques for synthesizing Taxol, for farming yew, for obtaining Taxol from the foliage as well as the bark, and for isolating it from other, more prolific yew species, so the harvesting pressure on wild western yew trees has evidently lessened in recent years.

Florence Davidson stated that the Massett people used to eat the "berries" of yew, but that if a woman ate too many, she would become sterile. Although the red flesh surrounding the seed of yew is edible, the seed itself is quite toxic, due to the presence of alkaloids. If the seed is swallowed whole, it is not harmful, but if it is chewed up, two or three seeds can be fatal (Turner and von Aderkas 2009).

Yew is a highly spiritual tree for First Peoples. According to Swanton (1905b), posts for a Haida shaman's grave house were always made of yew wood.

## Deciduous Trees

Several deciduous trees common in other parts of British Columbia do not occur naturally in Haida Gwaii. One of these is Rocky Mountain maple, or Douglas maple (*Acer glabrum* Torr.), which is found on the mainland and in Alaska. Nevertheless, Newcombe (1897) recorded a name for maple [**sin** (S), **san** (M)—JE], which applies to the tree, the wood and 'gambling stick' (JE), implying that maple wood was used to make gambling sticks [**sinda** (S), **sanda** (M) means 'play the stick (gambling) game'—JE]. None of the Haida elders I consulted had heard of this tree. Swanton (1905b:54) and Curtis (1916) also recorded the name "sin," but mistakenly referred to it as a type of "birch." (Birch does not grow in Haida Gwaii either.) Maple wood was apparently imported to Haida Gwaii from the mainland and from Kasaan, Alaska. It was, according to Newcombe (1901), used as a material for totem models, grease dishes, soopolallie (soapberry) spoons, sea otter clubs and dipnet handles. In the story of **Yaahl** (M)/ Raven Travelling, told by Charlie Edenshaw to Professor Boas and recorded by Swanton (1905b:143), **Yaahl** attempted to make canoes from several different types of wood in order to go and conquer the Southeast Wind, but all of them broke apart except the one of maple, with which he succeeded in making a good canoe, and with it he "vanquished the wind and made him his slave."

Another tree not found in Haida Gwaii, but apparently known at least to the Kaigani Haida at Kasaan, is a species of birch (*Betula* sp.), which was called "**attári**" [**adtagii**], a name apparently borrowed from Tlingit at **daayí** (Boas 1891; Newcombe 1897; Alaska Native Language Dictionaries 2003). The Kasaan people were said to import birch wood from the Nass River as a material for certain items such as seaweed chopping blocks.

Mountain-ash (*Sorbus sitchensis* Roemer) was cited by Newcombe (1897, 1901), who stated that the berries were eaten raw by the Haida. However, the names he gave for the berries, **k'ay** and **jatl'** (both M—JE), are the same as those for Pacific crab apples and red elderberries respectively, and one name he applied to the tree, "**k'ánhla,**" [**k'anhl'l** (S—JE)] is for Pacific crab apple tree. The other term recorded by Newcombe (1897) for the tree, "**hukia**," [**x̱a k'ayaa** (M), **x̱a k'ayaa** (A), mountain-ash fruit, literally 'dog crab apples'—JE] is uniquely applied to mountain-ash berries. It is still known in Massett (JE).

Scouler's willow.

## Scouler's Willow

*Salix scouleriana* Barratt and other willow species (*Salix* spp.); Willow Family (Salicaceae)

**chaanaang**, **tsaanaang** (S) (also applies to cottonwood) (Newcombe 1901; GY, WP, BP, EM), **sgiisga**, **sgiisg** (M) (JE; note that in M, **tsaanaang** is used for cottonwood, but apparently not willow)

"Small willow": "**tsá-ahl**" (Newcombe 1901)

Emma Matthews, George Young, Watson Pryce and Becky Pearson all knew of a kind of tree called **chaanaang**, and the last three said that it grew nearby, although they did not actually identify Scouler's willow as the tree in question. Newcombe (1901), however, identified **tsaanaang** as willow, and Scouler's willow is the most common species in Haida Gwaii (Calder and Taylor 1968). Emma Matthews said that **tsaanaang** is a tree "like alder" having big leaves and growing along the edges of rivers, but not occurring around Massett (see Cottonwood).

Newcombe noted that **tsaanaang** was used for both willow and cottonwood, but according to John Enrico, only in the Skidegate dialect. Boas (1891) identified the term **tsaanaang** ("**tchanang**") as Garry oak (*Quercus garryana*), a tree restricted to southern coastal British Columbia, mainly around Victoria, the southeast coast of Vancouver Island and the Gulf Islands. This tree would have been known only to those Haida travelling to the Victoria region.

Newcombe (1897) said that willow wood was used "in local houses," and George Young said that it was used for making spoons and other small items. The leaves were used in sweat houses (Newcombe 1897), apparently for purification or medicinal treatment. "Pussy willows" are used for decoration (Maude and Agnes Moody, Emma Matthews). Maude and Agnes Moody called them **kagan hlk̲'a'ii** (S) 'mouse-branches,' and Emma Matthews called them **duus-xil** [or **daaws-xil**], 'pussy-leaves.' **Duus** (~**daaws**) is Chinook jargon for cat (from English "puss").

Harrison (1925) stated that the original tobacco of the Haida came from the inner bark of a willow, and that it was ground in a stone mortar. This seems doubtful, however, in light of other information concerning Haida tobacco (see Turner and Taylor 1972; see also under Haida tobacco in this book).

## Black Cottonwood

*Populus balsamifera* L. ssp. *trichocarpa* (T. & G.) Brayshaw; Willow Family (Salicaceae)

**chaanaang**, **tsaanaang** (S, M—also pertains to willow in S), **tsáanaang** (A) (Newcombe 1901; Curtis 1916; JE)

This tree, also known as "balm of Gilead," is not native to Haida Gwaii, but is common at Hydaburg and elsewhere in southern Alaska. The sweet-scented buds were used to make a salve for skin ailments by Alaskan Haida as well as by the Nuu-Chah-Nulth and other Northwest Coast people. Cottonwoods have been planted at Skidegate Landing and possibly elsewhere on Haida Gwaii.

## Red Alder

*Alnus rubra* Bong.; Birch Family (Betulaceae)

Tree: **k̲aal**, **k̲al** (S, M), **k̲ál** (A)

Leaves: **k̲aal-xil**, **k̲al-xil** (S, M), **k̲ál-xíl** (A)

Branches: **k̲aal-hlk̲'a'ii**, **k̲al hlk̲'a'ii** (S), **k̲al hlk̲'a.aay** (M), **k̲ál hlk̲'a.íi** (A) (JE)

Red alder is the most common deciduous tree in Haida Gwaii. Its name was known to all of the elders I talked with, and was also recorded by Newcombe (1897), Swanton (1908b), Curtis (1916) and Norton (1981). The bark, which turns bright orange or reddish brown when exposed to the air, was an important source of brown or red dye. This was made by boiling the bark in water, and was used to colour cedar bark and to darken fishing lines to make them less visible in the water (George Young, Maude and Agnes Moody). Maude Moody noted that a half cup of the bark can be put into the wash water as a substitute for bleach (apparently as a disinfectant, since it would not be expected to whiten clothes). Newcombe (1897) said that a brighter dye was obtained by chewing the bark, then spitting the coloured saliva into a container, boiling it by means of hot stones, dipping cedar bark or other material into it and then drying it.

**Red alder.**

Alder wood is a favourite fuel for smoking fish. It was used for food containers because it did not impart any unpleasant flavour to the food (Norton 1981). It was also an important carving material for balers, masks, dishes and spoons (Newcombe 1897). The charcoal was said to have been used for tattooing (Willie Matthews; Curtis 1916).

Alder bark is a renowned medicine for Northwest Coast First Peoples; Haida and other medicine specialists value it greatly and use it medicinally in a variety of capacities. It has strong antibacterial activity and is used both internally, as a solution, and externally as a wash or poultice. It is well known up and down the coast as a medicine for tuberculosis. One medicine used in both Skidegate and Massett was said by Ed Calder and Willie Matthews to have been learned from the Kaigani Haida of Alaska.

"Alder" was the name of a man of Those-Born-in-the-Nansdins (Ninstints)-Country, and "**k̲als**," also pertaining to alder, was the name of a pole owner at Tanu (Newcombe 1902). In one story recorded in Swanton (1905b:238), a supernatural alder was used by a supernatural being to trap his son-in-law (He-Who- Got-Supernatural-Power-from-His-Little-Finger), but the young man outsmarted him and managed to destroy the alder. Kathleen Hans said that, long ago, alder used to be a woman, and therefore "you had to hug it before you cut it down, or it would fall on you."

## Sitka Alder, or Green Alder

*Alnus crispa* (Ait.) Pursh ssp. *sinuata* (Regel.) Hult.; Birch Family (Betulaceae)

**k̲'aahl'a** (S), **ka'as, ka.as, ka'aj** (M), **kaas** (A) (Newcombe 1897, 1901, 1902; Swanton 1908a; JE)

This is a small, bushy relative of red alder, not generally recognized to differ from it by contemporary Haida. However, Newcombe (1897, 1901, 1902) and Swanton (1908a) both characterized it as being similar to red alder, but not the same. They provided a number of versions of names for Sitka alder, confirmed by John Enrico as those given above. Newcombe and Swanton noted that the wood was used to make small articles such as spoons, small dishes, masks and rattles. Newcombe (1897) elaborated: "Wood white, used for making spoons, rattles, models of totem poles, etc. Is first soaked in fresh water for some time. (noticed in use at Skidegate, May 1901). Generally distributed. Very fragrant when young." Newcombe also noted that red alder wood is coarser than that of Sitka alder.

## Pacific Crab Apple, or Wild Crab Apple

*Malus fusca* (Raf.) C.K. Schneid.; Rose Family (Rosaceae)

Fruit: **k'ay, k'aay** (S, M), **k'áy** (A) [see **k'ayluus** (S), **k'aywahl** (M), **k'áywahl** (A) 'be sour' (JE)] (also applied to domesticated apples in M, A); **xàad**(as) **k'ayaa** (M) ('Haida apples'—applied to wild crab apples to distinguish from domesticated apples in M, A)

Tree: **k'anhl'l, k'anhll, k'anhyll, k'anhla** (S), **k'ayanhla, k'a'inhla** (M), **k'ayánhl** (A) ('crab apple tree/wood'—JE); **k'áy-xíl** (Dawson 1880), **k'ay-hlk̲'a.aay** (M) (Newcombe 1901; FD, EM)

Crab apples get really ripe: **chaalg̲asdl** (S)

This is a bushy deciduous tree often growing around lake edges and in swampy areas. The leaves are similar to those of cultivated apples, but usually have a coarse, pointed lobe along one or both leaf edges. The crab apples are ovoid and small (about 1 cm long), and borne in long-stemmed clusters. They are tart, but juicy and crisp, and they become sweeter after a frost or with storage. They were formerly a highly important fruit for the Haida, as for other Northwest Coast peoples (Turner 1995). This tree was notably plentiful at Sandspit, Point Skidegate and near Rose Spit, according to Newcombe (1897). Dawson (Cole and Lockner 1989:507) noted in his journal on August 20, 1878: "Many thickets of Crab apple fringing the shores on the Massett 'lakes' much fruit on them but not yet ripe. Told that next month ripen. Then collected, boiled, allowed to remain covered with water till mid-winter when gone over, stalks etc. removed & the whole mixed with eulachon grease [in sufficient quantity] forming a delicious pabulum."

**Left: Pacific crab apples.**

**Right: Pacific crab apple blossoms.**

Wild crab apples were known to all of the present-day elders, and the names for the fruit and/or tree were also reported, with slight variations, by Dawson (1880), Boas (1891), Newcombe (1901), Swanton (1908a), Curtis (1916) and Norton (1981). Formerly, the fruits were picked in the fall, often quite late in the season, then boiled, placed in cedar boxes, covered with water and allowed to remain until winter. At this time they were drained, destemmed, sorted, mixed with eulachon grease and eaten, often being served at large feasts (Dawson 1880; Elizabeth Collinson). Sometimes they were mixed with salal berries. In recent times, sugar was also mixed in. Recently, they have been preserved in jars, but nowadays, they are mostly frozen or made into jelly. Sometimes they are stewed in water, and the drained fruit is eaten while the juice is stored in jars for later use (Maude and Agnes Moody). Crab apple bark and leaves, like those of plum, peach and cherry, contain cyanide-producing compounds, and must be used with extreme caution (Turner and von Aderkas 2009).

Crab apple wood, which is strong and resilient, was used by the Haida, as by other Northwest Coast peoples, for making implements such as adze and axe handles and probably digging sticks (Newcombe 1901; Turner 1998). The bark was used variously for medicine.

A girl at puberty or a woman in mourning was rubbed with soft cedar bark, which was then wedged into the cleft of a crab apple tree to make her strong and enduring (Curtis 1916). In ancient times, crab apple trees (and other types of trees as well) were said to have been human beings (Dawson 1880). Crab apples, along with highbush cranberries and soapberries, were known in the stories and narratives as food of supernatural beings and high-class people (Swanton 1908b). For example, in the story of **Yaahl** (M) [Raven] and Butterfly, crab apples mixed with grease was one of a series of dishes served to **Yaahl**. However, Butterfly tricked him by telling the chief's wife that **Yaahl** did not know how to eat them; then Butterfly ate them instead (Swanton 1908b:297)

## Berry Bushes and Other Shrubs

**Common juniper.**

### Common Juniper

*Juniperus communis* L.; Cypress Family (Cupressaceae)
Plant: **kaayda kaxawaay** (S) (literally 'small trees sticking off here and there'—JE), **hlk'am.aal** (M) (also 'bough/evergreen branch') (FD), or **k'al.aa hlk'am.alee** (M), or **hlk'am.aal ginn gyaa. alaas** (M) (literally 'muskeg evergreen branch,' 'thing resembling evergreen branch') (FD; all terms checked and/or provided by JE), or **ɢaayang'waal hlk'a.aay** (M) (see Berries) (WM, EM)
Berries: **ɢaayang'waal** (M) (WM, EM, FD—recognized term, but not plant; JE)

This prickly shrub was usually called simply **hlk'am.aal** (M). Newcombe (1897) recorded the name "**kálhadsalá**" [possibly **k'al.aa-dsaalaa**] (M, A), which apparently translates as "swamp [muskeg] curls" (Newcombe's writing is difficult to decipher). The Skidegate elders I talked with did not recall a name for juniper, although George Young recognized it. Common juniper was used in a variety of ways for medicine, and was considered a highly spiritual plant, with important taboos and restrictions related to its use.

### Black Twinberry, or "Raven's Berry"

*Lonicera involucrata* (Rich.) Banks ex Spreng.; Honeysuckle Family (Caprifoliaceae)
Berries: **xuya ɢaanɢa** (S), **yaahl ɢaanaa** (M), **yáahl ɢáanaay** (A) ('raven's-berry'); or **k'aalts'idaa ɢaanɢa** (S) ('crow's-berry') (GY, WP)
Bush: **xuya gaanga hlk'a'ii** (S) ('raven's-berry-branches/plant')

The shiny, black, paired berries of this deciduous shrub were not considered edible for humans: "Only crows eat them." The name 'raven's-berry' was most commonly used and was also recorded by Newcombe (1897, 1901) and Swanton (1905b), but George Young and Watson Pryce both felt that 'crow's-berry' was also acceptable. They also mentioned another bush called 'crow's-berries' that had black berries hanging in bunches like cherries. Possibly this was black hawthorn (*Crataegus douglasii*) (see following species).

**Left: Black twinberry.**

**Right: Goatsbeard.**

**How Sounding-Gambling-Sticks Won Back His Possessions**

Sounding-Gambling-Sticks, a Chief's son at **Nans Dins** (Ninstints), gambled away his village and all his relatives. He travelled to the supernatural house of the ocean-dwellers by pulling on a two-headed kelp and was aided by his "powerful grandfather" there. He was told to "break off a bunch of gambling-stick wood for me which you will find at the corner outside." The Chief's son brought in pieces of "**sin**" (maple—*Acer glabrum*), then pieces of yew (*Taxus brevifolia*), and pieces of many other sorts of sticks, but all were rejected by the old man. Then he brought in pieces of **x̱uya g̱aang̱a hlḵ'a'ii** ("raven's-berry-bush"), which were accepted. They were made into a set of gambling sticks. The young man returned and, using these supernatural sticks—and bribing suspicious spectators with sweet tobacco seeds the old man had given him, Sounding-Gambling-Sticks was able to win back all he had previously lost. (adapted from Swanton 1905b:52–57, originally told by Tom Stevens)

Black twinberry was used medicinally in various ways. Kathleen Hans noted that the berries could be rubbed into the scalp to stop the hair turning grey.

Another bushy plant, goatsbeard (*Aruncus dioicus* [Walt.] Fern.; syn. *Aruncus sylvester* Kostel), having creamy white flower sprays but no berries, was nevertheless called **xuya ga̱anga̱** (S) ('raven's-berry') by George Young, and **taan ga̱anaa** (M) ('black-bear berries') by Chief Willie Matthews. Chief Matthews' name is more often applied to common twisted-stalk (*Streptopus amplexifolius*). Newcombe (1897) recorded the name "**gadakitxau**" (S) for it, but gave no further details. This name is apparently **ga̱da kidxaaw** (literally 'sticking off here and there white'—JE), and probably pertains to its whitish flowers, but was unknown to John Enrico's consultants.

## Black Hawthorn
*Crataegus douglasii* Lindl.; Rose Family (Rosaceae)
"**kanhla**" [see **k'anhl'l, k'anhll** (S) 'crab apple tree'—JE], "**wakla**" or "**wahla**" (Newcombe 1897, 1901)

The shiny black berries of this thorny deciduous shrub were apparently formerly eaten, although they are somewhat dry and seedy. Aside from the above terms reported by Newcombe, the plant was called **k'alts'ida ga̱anga̱** (S) ('crow's-berry') by George Young (see also previous species, black twinberry). Florence Davidson once called it **xaayuwaa hlk'a.aay** (M), but explained that this name was normally used for swamp gooseberry (*Ribes lacustre*), another spiny plant. Emma Matthews called the stout thorns **stlii.n** (M) (literally 'spine, thorn, quill of a porcupine'—JE).

LEFT: Black hawthorn.

RIGHT: Red-osier dogwood.

## Red-Osier Dogwood

*Cornus stolonifera* Michx.; Dogwood Family (Cornaceae)

**sgiis.gii** (possibly **sgiisgi** or **s<u>k</u>iisgii)** (S) (Newcombe 1897, 1901; JE), **s<u>G</u>id <u>x</u>aadaal** (M) (JE)

Newcombe's name was not known to the Haida elders I talked with, although all of them recognized this shrub, and John Enrico recorded the S and M names. The whitish berries were not eaten. However, the branches, which are thin and reddish, were used to make various frames, such as skin-drying frames for bear and other hides, and sweat-house frames (Newcombe 1897, 1901).

## Red Elderberry

*Sambucus racemosa* L.; Honeysuckle Family (Caprifoliaceae)

Berries: **jitl'l, jiitl'** (S), **jatl'a, jatl'** (M), **jatl'** (A) (Norton 1981; JE);or **laats'i** (S) (borrowed from Tsimshian) (GY)

Bush/wood: **jitl'l hl<u>k</u>'a'ii, jiitl' hl<u>k</u>'a'ii** or **staay** (S) (Newcombe 1897; JE), **jatl' hl<u>k</u>'a.íi** (A) (Norton 1981; JE); or **stiid**, **stiid-xil**, **stiid-hl<u>k</u>'a.aay** (M), **stíid** (A) (JE)

**RIGHT: Red elderberry.**

This is a large, deciduous shrub with compound leaves, creamy clusters of small flowers and small, bright red berries that are edible when cooked, but somewhat strong-flavoured. The Haida names, except the one given by George Young and said to be borrowed from Tsimshian, were known to all the elders, and were also recorded by Keen (1898), Newcombe (1909), Curtis (1916) and Norton (1981).

The ripe berries were eaten, but most people did not consider them to be choice. They were boiled for a long, long time until soft and mushy, then mixed with (eulachon) grease and eaten, at least within the historic period, with sugar and jam. The clusters of berries were picked in early summer, with the stems intact.

The stems were left on during cooking, and both stems and seeds were discarded, often being blown out of the mouth by the person eating the berries.

The pith inside the stems was used to fasten flint arrow points onto shafts, and as blunt tips for arrows. According to Newcombe (1897): "After removing sufficient pith from pieces of the stem, they are used as blunt tips for arrows, intended to stun birds etc. Skidegate and Massett."

Elderberry is widely used medicinally by Northwest Coast peoples. However, elderberry leaves, stems, bark and roots can be poisonous, since they yield a cyanide compound (Turner and von Aderkas 2009). Emma Matthews applied the name **skusaang.u** (M) (see "Roots" Appendix 9) to elderberry roots, noting that this term was used for "special" medicinal roots, and not just ordinary roots. "Elderberry Roots" was the name of a gambling stick (Swanton 1905b).

## Highbush Cranberry

*Viburnum edule* (Michx.) Raf.; Honeysuckle Family (Caprifoliaceae)
Berries: **hlaayii**, **hlaayi, hlaay** (or by Swanton **hlaayaa**—JE) (S), **hlaa.i**, **hlaayaa** (M), **hláay** (A)
Bush: **hlaayaa hlk̲'a'ii**, **hlaay hlk̲'a'ii** (S), **hlaayaa hlk̲'a.aay** (M)

**Highbush cranberry.**

This deciduous shrub used to be more common in Haida Gwaii, and the berries were eaten in large quantities. However, people say that the bushes have become very scarce following the introduction of deer to the islands. The berries, which are red and quite tart, were greatly prized and considered to be a "high class" food. Prime picking areas were owned and maintained by individuals and families, with permission required if anyone else wanted to harvest from these areas. For example, there were two highbush cranberry patches in the Miller Creek area near Skidegate [**Tl'llna** at the mouth, and **Taa.nga K̲yang.gas**], both of which were owned by Hazel Stevens' and Emma Wilson's father's grandmother, **Xaals sgunee** (John Enrico, personal communication).

Generally, the berries were picked in August and September, even if they were still green and hard, and put into boxes of warm water and eulachon grease [**t'aaw** (S)]. Then, around the end of December, they were drained and mixed with more grease, a little sugar and other berries, such as salal, then passed around at feasts (Emma Wilson). Newcombe (1897) described a different method of preparing the berries, employed by the Kaigani Haida. They were picked into an open-work cedar-bark basket, which was then plunged, berries and all, into boiling water and kept there a short time. The berries were then mixed with grease and stored in high cedarwood boxes for winter. Such boxes of highbush cranberries were important trade and gift items.

Highbush cranberries were the food most frequently mentioned in Haida stories (Swanton 1905b, 1908b), especially in the context of "good food" (e.g., 1905b:123, 164; 1908b:537, 539, 558; Turner 2014). They were often associated with salmon and were thought to be the food of supernatural beings, who often ate them mixed with hemlock inner bark cakes (see p. 125). In several of the episodes recorded by Swanton (1905b: e.g., 161, 213), the heroes are given a small piece of salmon and a single cranberry by a supernatural helper. No matter how much they eat of these miniscule portions, however, they can never finish them.

**How Yaahl [Raven] Brought Highbush Cranberries to Haida Gwaii**

**Yaahl** (M) [Raven] was visiting the Beaver People. Two days consecutively, he was served salmon, highbush cranberries and the inside parts of the mountain goat. On the second morning, **Yaahl** was taken behind a screen where there was a fishtrap in a creek filled with salmon, and several points on a lake which were red with cranberries. After the beavers had gone for the day, **Yaahl** ate the usual meal. Then he stole the salmon-filled lake and the house, rolling it up and hiding it under his arm, and climbed a tree with it. When the beavers returned, they tried to catch him by chewing down the tree, but **Yaahl** simply flew to another. Finally they gave up, and **Yaahl** flew inland and unrolled the lake there and kept the fishtrap and house to teach the people of Haida Gwaii and the mainland how to live. Since then, there have been many highbush cranberries in Haida Gwaii. (Adapted from original, told by Charlie Edenshaw to Professor Boas in Swanton 1905b:145–46)

Highbush cranberry was also used medicinally, according to Emma Matthews, Willie Matthews and Newcombe (1897).

## Stink Currant, or Greyberry

*Ribes bracteosum* Doug.; Gooseberry Family (Grossulariaceae)
Berries: **G̲alG̲un**, **G̲alG̲wan** (S), **G̲al.un** (M), **G̲ál.un** (A) (Norton 1981; JE)
Bush: **G̲alG̲un xil**, **G̲alG̲wan xil** (S) (GY), **G̲al.un hlk̲'a.aay** (M) (Newcombe 1901; FD)

This is a pungent-smelling shrub of swampy areas, with large, pointed, maple-like leaves and globular berries borne in a long cluster along a central stalk. The berries are

**Left: Stink currant.**

**Right: Trailing currant.**

light blue or greyish due to a waxy coating on the surface; if this is rubbed off, they are dark blue. They are edible and somewhat resinous in flavour.

"Greyberry" was known to all of the present-day elders, and the names were also recorded by Newcombe (1901) and Norton (1981). The same terms can also be applied to cultivated currants (Florence Davidson). Greyberries were eaten fresh, and probably were dried in the old days, as they were on other parts of the coast (Turner 1995). Norton (1981) noted that among the Kaigani they were, and still are, very popular. Formerly they were stored in watertight cedarwood boxes, and later in tins or drums lined with skunk-cabbage leaves and covered with grease. They were, and are, eaten with grease and sugar or mixed with salmon roe. Today they are frozen or "jarred" for winter use.

This shrub is also valued as a medicine by the Haida and other Northwest Coast peoples; almost all of the Haida elders were familiar with this medicine, and some people still use it.

This berry is featured in a story told by Walter, a member of the Rear-Town-People of Yan (in Swanton 1908b:448), "War Between the Land-Otter and Black-Bear People":

> The Black-Bears owned the lands where berries grow. They were very fond of their wild currants, because those were the only things they ate. The Land-Otter-People ate them ... all of them ... That was why the Bears were angry with them. So they made war ...

## Trailing Currant, or "Black Currant"

*Ribes laxiflorum* Pursh; Gooseberry Family (Grossulariaceae)

Berries: **k'aaydaGaanGa** (S) (possibly-'fruit') (JE); or **k'iit'agwaand** (S) (GY), **k'iit'agwaand, k'iidgwaan, k'iit'agwaan** (M) (Boas 1891; Keen 1898; Newcombe 1901; FD; JE) or possibly **kaw-xil** (M) (WM, EM), **k'íit'gwaang** (A) (Norton 1981; JE)

Bush: **yaanaang xilGa** (S) ('fog/cloud-leaves/medicine') (GY only); "**kaigigunlka**i" (S) (Newcombe 1897); **k'iit'agwaandaa hlk'a.aay** (M) (Newcombe 1901; FD; JE)

This wild currant often grows on rotten logs and stumps and has stems that grow long and root from the tips. The berries were eaten (Newcombe 1897; Norton 1981), and still are whenever they are available (Maude Moody), although one can seldom pick enough at a time for storage. Sometimes they were mixed with other berries to be stored for winter (Norton 1981). George Young considered them to be another kind of "greyberry" (see *Ribes bracteosum*).

Florence Davidson said that the leaves of this bush, called **k'iit'agwaandaa-xil** (M), were placed between layers of drying edible seaweed (red laver) to give it a good taste and fragrance: "They make the seaweed smell real good."

Trailing currant is a Haida medicine plant according to Reverend J. H. Keen (1900).

## Swamp Gooseberry, or Swamp Currant

*Ribes lacustre* (Pers.) Poir.; Gooseberry Family (Grossulariaceae)

Spines: **xaayuwaa** (M) (FD; JE—"resembling Tlingit"), **xáayuwaa** (A) (both translated as only 'swamp gooseberry fruit' by JE)

Bush: **Gudga gi Gayd (-hlk'a'ii)** (S) [probably literally 'run-backwards in fear (-plant/branch)' (also applied to shrimp—JE); see **gi** < **giGa**, **Gudgi** 'backwards'—JE] (Newcombe 1897—also for A; GY; BP; MM; AM); or **xaayuwaa** (M), **xáayuwaa** (A) (Newcombe 1901); or **xaayuwaa hlk'a.aay** (M) (FD)

Swamp gooseberry.

Florence Davidson warned that this prickly bush is "real poison," and can cause severe skin irritation if the spines are touched. She said that if they came in contact with one's hand, to soak it immediately in very hot water, otherwise it would swell up. She did not know of the berries, which are small, black, shiny and clustered, actually being edible, but noted that the cultivated gooseberry is called by the same name. Newcombe (1901) reported that the berries were eaten by the Haida. Kathleen Hans recalled eating them as a girl.

Swamp gooseberry is attributed similar protective powers to those of devil's-club, and the prickly stems can be used in the same way to give protection against evil for individuals or members of a household.

## Thimbleberry

*Rubus parviflorus* Nutt.; Rose Family (Rosaceae)

Berries: **guugadiis** (S), **stl'agudiis** (M) ('turn inside-out'), **stl'agudíis** (A) (Norton 1981; JE)

Bush: **xwadaluu, hlg̲aabaluu** (S) (JE), **guugadiis xil** (S); **madalaa.u, madlaaw** (**-xil/-hlk̲'a.aay**) (M) (EM, FD; Newcombe 1901; JE), **stl'agudiis xil, stl'agudiis hlk̲'a.aay** (M); **stl'agudíis hlk̲'a.íi, stl'a gudíis xil** ("the leaves") (A) (Norton 1981; JE)

Sprouts, shoots (edible): **k̲aaysgwaan** (S) (also 'body odour,' because eating the shoots makes you sweat) (JE), **dangaldagaa, dangaldgaa** (M) (nominalization of adjective 'sweaty'; see previous note) (JE); or"**stl'agudiisalay**" (A) (Norton 1981)

This shrub has large, soft, maple-like leaves and bright-red berries that are sweet and juicy, and fall off readily when ripe. The names were known to all of the present-day elders, and were also recorded by Newcombe (1897, 1901) and John Enrico. The young shoots in springtime were, and still are, peeled and eaten by the Kaigani, especially children, and formerly were also stored in grease for later consumption (Norton 1981). John Enrico notes that not everyone ate these shoots, because they are said to make one sweat (see Skidegate and Massett terms for them). The shoots were commonly eaten by other Northwest Coast groups (see Turner 1995). The berries were, and still are, enjoyed. Formerly they were dried in cakes or stored in grease [**t'aaw** (S)]; now they are sometimes made into jam. Thimbleberry leaves were used, like those of salmonberry, to line baskets, wipe fish or cover food in steaming pits (Norton 1981). Thimbleberry and salal leaves were placed between layers of dried spring salmon and sockeye to preserve the fish better (Emma Matthews, personal communication to Marianne Boelscher 1981).

**Left to right: Thimbleberry, young shoots; thimbleberry flowers; thimbleberries.**

## Salmonberry

*Rubus spectabilis* Pursh; Rose Family (Rosaceae)

Berries: **sk̲'awG̲aan, sk̲'aawG̲an** (S) (JE), **sk̲'aw.aan** (M), **sk̲'áw.aan** (A)

Berries, very dark ("black") colour form: **x̲ang k̲'aadaawaa** (M) ('red salmonberry' called 'sooty salmonberry' in S) (see **x̲ang** 'face'/'eye' in M) (FD; JE)

Berries, common ruby red colour form: **sk̲'áw.aansG̲id** (M) ('red-salmonberry') (FD)

Bush: **sk̲'aw, sk̲'aaw, sk̲'awii** (S), **sk̲'aw, sk̲'aw hlk̲'a.aay, sk̲'aw.aan hlk̲'a.aay** (M), **sk̲'áw, sk̲'áw hlk̲'a.íi, sk̲'áw.aan hlk̲'a.íi** (A)

Thick salmonberry bushes: **sk̲'aalang sk̲'aawG̲an gii aajaa** (S)

Flower, blossoms: **sG̲idG̲ang.xal, sG̲idG̲angxaal** (S), **sG̲idang G̲ang.aalaa, sG̲idang G̲ang.alaa** (M), **sG̲idáng G̲áangalaay** (A) (all JE)

Sprouts, shoots (edible): **ts'ixaal, ts'iixal** (S), **ts'asaal** (M), **ts'a.áal, tsa'áal** (A) (JE—see also note under Pacific silverweed, *Potentilla egedii*)

**Salmonberry sprouts (see also pages 43 and 78).**

Salmonberry, a prickly, raspberry-like deciduous shrub with three-parted leaves and early-blooming pink flowers, is one of the more important fruits of the Haida. Both the berries and the young shoots were eaten, and the berries are still gathered in large quantities. The young shoots were harvested in the spring, peeled and eaten raw (Newcombe 1897; Curtis 1916; Norton 1981; Emma Matthews; George Young). Formerly the Kaigani also stored them in grease (Norton 1981). (See also the notation under wild rose, following, about eating "briar" shoots.)

The berries, which come in several colour forms ranging from golden to red to almost black, start to ripen in early June. They are generally eaten fresh, but were sometimes dried or stored in grease. They are thought to be constipating if eaten in quantity unless eaten with grease. Today they are "jarred," or made into jam. In this century, women jarred them by the case for winter use (Norton 1981).

Emma Matthews (personal communication to Marianne Boelscher 1979) said that when her husband Willie

Matthews was a little boy at the village at Yakan Point, they used to go out with a slave in the summertime to pick salmonberries. The slave had four-gallon tins in a basket; that is how the berries were carried. They ate so much [as much as they wanted], and then they gave the rest to those who could not get them.

Salmonberry leaves were used, like those of thimbleberry, to line baskets, wipe fish or cover food in steaming pits (Norton 1981). Long, straight sticks of salmonberry were peeled and driven through cedar-bark roofing sheets to flatten them and prevent them from curling too much (Newcombe 1901; Curtis 1916). Newcombe (1897) elaborates: "Mature branches [of salmonberry] often used to straighten large sheets of cedar bark with which now [1890s] temporary, formerly permanent houses are shingled. A hole is first bored by a curved bone knife made from the rib of a large seal or sea lion, and then the sticks are interwoven through the fibrous bark and cut off even with the edges of the strips ..." The sticks were also used as throwing spears in the "kelp game" (see under bull kelp, *Nereocystis luetkeana*), and in other games as well (Swanton 1905a).

Salmonberries were pulverized and mixed with eulachon grease and other types of fish oil, and this mixture was rubbed on the hair to make it grow long and glossy (Harrison 1925). The thorns were mixed with other ingredients for poultices. The mixture is called **kiisd kit'agung** (M) (literally 'poking for pus'—JE) (Newcombe 1897, from Reverend J.H. Keen).

Salmonberry was frequently mentioned in Haida stories. For example, supernatural animal skins were stretched on salmonberry bushes. The branches were used to replace missing limbs in bringing skeletons back to life. The branches were used to make a bed frame by the hero **sG̱aana G̱unaan ḵaas** (Swanton 1905b). In one story on the origin of people, Raven turned grass and salmonberry bushes into human beings; that is why people are so short-lived. They die just like the leaves fall (told by Walter of the Rear-Town-People of Yan and another man of the Cod-People, in Swanton 1908b:319).

Swainson's thrush is called **wiid** (S, M) in Haida; it is known as the "salmonberry bird." It was believed that the singing of this thrush caused the salmonberries to ripen. In spring, people sang a song to this bird: "To Salmonberry bird, who makes the berries ripe—bring many large and well-coloured ones" (Newcombe 1902). The name of a house at the village of **Qaisun** was **wiid na'as** after the salmonberry bird (Newcombe 1902).

Garden raspberry is called **sḵ'aw.aan giid'ii** (**hlḵ'a.aay**) (M) ['salmonberry-offspring(-bush)']. George Young recalled another salmonberry relative from his residential school days in Chilliwack. He used to call trailing wild blackberries (*Rubus ursinus* Cham. & Schlecht) **tllgaa sḵ'aawG̱aanG̱a** ('earth/ground-salmonberries'). These are edible and delicious, but do not grow as far north as Haida Gwaii (see also Appendix 10).

Wild rose.

## Wild Rose, or Nootka Rose

*Rosa nutkana* Presl; Rose Family (Rosaceae)

Fruit, or hips: **k̲'ung** (S), **k̲'unhla**, **k̲'unhl** (M), **k̲'únhl** (A) (also pertains to the young green ovaries below the flower buds—EM)

Flowers: **sg̲idg̲ang.xaal** (S) ('red-blossoms') (WP, BP; JE—"salmonberry blossoms only"), **k̲'unhla xilaay** (M) (FD)

Bush: **k̲'úng hlk̲'a'ii** (S), **k̲'unhla hlk̲'a.aay** (M)

The names for this common, prickly deciduous shrub, and its reddish "hips," were known to most of the present-day elders, and were also recorded by Newcombe (1897, 1901) and Curtis (1916). Newcombe (1897) and Curtis (1916) stated that the hips were eaten by the Haida raw or steamed. Most people I consulted had not heard of this, but Gidansda (Guujaaw) used to eat them as a boy, and said that children still do eat them. He recalls using the slivery seeds for itching powder (personal communication 1993). Norton (1981) states that the Kaigani people did not use them in the past, but recently have sometimes dried and powdered them and added them to tea. Kaigani women formerly peeled and ate the young shoots of "briar" [referring either to wild rose or salmonberry], as a tonic and beauty aid, along with the shoots of fireweed (*Epilobium angustifolium*).

**Above:** Dishes of soapberry whip, ready to serve.

**Right:** Soapberry, showing underside of branch. Soapberries do not grow on Haida Gwaii today, although they apparently did in the distant past.

## Soapberry, or Soopolallie

*Shepherdia canadensis* L.; Oleaster Family (Elaeagnaceae)
Berries, whole or whipped: **'as** (S) (borrowed from Tsimshian); or **xagutl'iid** (M), **xagwtl'íid** (A) (borrowed from Tlingit)
Bush: **xagutl'iid hlk̲'a.aay** (M)

Soapberries do not grow in Haida Gwaii (Calder and Taylor 1968), but were, and still are, obtained from neighbouring peoples. The Skidegate name, **'as**, is related to the Tsimshian name for soapberries, whereas the Massett and Alaskan Haida names are related to the Tlingit. Florence Davidson said that the name **xagutl'iid** pertains to sipping the berry whip. As well as being known to the people of the present day, the names were recorded by Boas (1891), Newcombe (1897) and Curtis (1916). Many Haida now obtain their soapberries from the Hazelton and Prince Rupert areas. The Kaigani people are said to obtain them from the Haines and Hoonah areas to the north (Norton 1981).

The berries are usually obtained as a jarred product, immersed in water, and often with sugar already added. They are then mashed up, mixed with water and whipped with the hands, a bunch of huckleberry branches or a bundle of cedar bark or, recently, with an electric beater, into a frothy dessert, sometimes called "Indian ice cream." They should never be allowed to come in contact with grease or they will not whip.

The whip is more than just a food. It is often served at feasts and gatherings.

Waxberry, showing soft, white, inedible berries.

Formerly at least, the whip was served in special yew-wood dishes and eaten with specially carved long, paddle-like spoons of willow, maple or cottonwood imported from the mainland (Newcombe 1897). Today, it is still considered a special party food, enjoyed by young and old alike. Becky Pearson recalled that people used to "fight" with the whip, throwing it around and turning bowls of it over each other's heads. The term recorded by Sapir (1923), **'ajaa** (S) (literally 'have soapberries on'—JE; "smeared with soapberries"), testifies to this practice.

Despite the lack of botanical records for soapberries in Haida Gwaii, there is a story reference to soapberries occurring at "Peninsula Point" (Spit Point, at the southeast entrance to Skidegate Inlet). Certain soapberries made by supernatural beings mentioned in this Skidegate story were said to "look like Peninsula Point soapberries, yet they were different" (Swanton 1905b:301). In another story, Master Carpenter's canoe was filled with good food, including highbush cranberries, berry cakes and soapberries (Swanton 1905b:32).

## Waxberry, or Snowberry

*Symphoricarpos albus* (L.) Blake; Honeysuckle Family (Caprifoliaceae)
Berries: **k'u'iid G̲aanG̲a** (S) (Newcombe 1901; JE)
Bush: **k'u'iid** (S) (Newcombe 1901; GY; JE)

This shrub has small pinkish flowers and soft, white inedible berries. George Young stated that the sticks were sometimes used as skewers for drying clams. Newcombe (1897) provided more details: "Twigs are peeled, and the clean white slimy sticks are used as skewers for spreading salmon, trout etc. when drying them in smoke houses for winter use. Circumstance was noted at 'Skidegate Creek,' 17th May, 1901."

Salal berries.

## Salal

*Gaultheria shallon* Pursh; Heather Family (Ericaceae)

Berries: **sk'idGaan** (S), **sk'idaan**, **sk'id'aan** (M), **sk'it'áan** (A) (for berries or bush—Norton 1981); or **taan Gaanga** (S) ('black-bear berries') (BP only—"another name for them")

Plant/leaves: **sk'iid**, **sk'idGaan xil** (S), **sk'iihla**, **sk'iihl**, **sk'iihla hlk'a.aay** (M)

To pick a whole cluster of salal berries: **hlk'waakuusda** (S)

Salal is a well-known plant in Haida Gwaii. Its Haida names are known to all speakers of the language, and were recorded by Dawson (1880), Newcombe (1897), Curtis (1916), Norton (1981) and John Enrico. The berries are still used in considerable quantities. Florence Davidson recalled that formerly they were boiled in large pots, often in a special little shack behind the main house. The cooked berries were then poured into rectangular wooden moulds set on skunk-cabbage leaves and allowed to dry on racks over the fire into cakes. In winter these salal cakes were soaked in water, then eaten with grease [**t'aaw** (S)]. Nowadays, people eat them fresh or make them into jam, jelly or syrup. The berries were sometimes used to thicken salmon eggs.

Salal leaves were placed between layers of dried spring salmon and sockeye to preserve the fish better (Emma Matthews, personal communication to Marianne Boelscher 1981). Today the leaves are used in floral decorations. Salal leaves were also used medicinally according to Adam Bell (personal communication to Marianne Boelscher 1980).

Saskatoon berry.

## Saskatoon Berry, or Serviceberry

*Amelanchier alnifolia* Nutt.; Rose Family (Rosaceae)
Berries: **G̲aan x̲aw'laa, G̲aan x̲aaw'laa** (S), **G̲aan x̲aw'laa, G̲aan x̲aw.ulaa** (M), **G̲áan x̲áw'laa** (A) (literally 'sweet-berry')
Bush: **G̲aan x̲aw'laa hlk̲'a.aay** (M) (FD)

This oval-leaved, deciduous shrub is well known for its edible, sweet-tasting blue berries. The names were known to all the present-day elders consulted, and also recorded by Newcombe (1901). George Young commented, "All berries taste good, but there is only one they call **G̲aan x̲aw'laa** ('sweet-berry')." However, at Massett, Florence Davidson and Emma Matthews both said that bog blueberry (*Vaccinium uliginosum*) was also called 'sweet-berry.' Florence Davidson said, "They know they [the two types of berry] are different. They tell each other where they grow and then they know [which one is being referred to]." The berries were formerly dried in cakes (Newcombe 1901).

## Alaska Blueberry and Oval-Leaved Blueberry

*Vaccinium alaskaense* Howell and V*accinium ovalifolium* Smith; Heather Family (Ericaceae)
Berries: **hldaan** (S, M), **hldáan** (A)

Berries of Alaska blueberry: **hldaan gidga** (M), **hldáan gidga** (A) (JE)
Berries of oval-leaved blueberry: **hldaan G̲adaga** (S), **hldaan G̲adaga** (M), **hldaan G̲adga** (A) (JE)

**Oval-leaved blueberries.**

Bush: **hldanhla**, **hldanhl** (M) (bushes without berries) (FD); or **hldaan hlk̲'a'ii** (S), **hldaan hlk̲'a.aay** (M) ("when it had berries") (FD, EM, WM)

Both species of wild highbush blueberries, Alaska blueberry and oval-leaved blueberry, were recognized and differentiated, but most people call them by the same Haida name. There is an expression used for a person whose face is covered with bruises: **hldaansgingaan 'la fang. ii geenggaagang** (literally 'looks like blueberries') (Florence Davidson; John Enrico). The berries of both types were eaten fresh or dried in cakes. Oval-leaved blueberries, which have a greyish coating and usually earlier to ripen, are considered to be sweeter, whereas Alaska blueberries, which are darker and later ripening, are a little less tasty. The Kaigani Haida distinguished the two types as "**hldáan k̲itk**" for Alaska blueberry and "**hldáan g̲at**" ('light blueberry') for oval-leaved blueberry (Norton 1981). Hunters travelling in the mountains often talked about going through "thick, bushy blueberries"—**hldaan hlk̲'a.aay** (Florence Davidson).

Some people have noted that blueberry wood gets harder as it grows older, and that it was used for house pegs, like nails, to attach planks to the frames (Henry Geddes).

Bog blueberry (*Vaccinium uliginosum* L.) was also well known to Haida berry-pickers, although it seems to be little used today. It was given various names. Although Boas (1891) recorded the term "**sk̲'awg̲aan giidg̲ii**" ('salmonberry-baby') for it, this identification is unlikely; the term probably refers to another species, such as trailing raspberry (*Rubus pedatus*). George Young called it **tllgaa g̲aang̲a** (S) ('ground/earth-berries'), a name he used for several low-growing types of berries, including lingonberry and kinnikinnick. Florence Davidson and Emma Matthews called it **g̲aan x̲aw'laa**, **g̲aan x̲aw.ulaa** (M) ('sweet-berries'), a name they also applied to saskatoon berry (*Amelanchier alnifolia*), whose fruits are somewhat similar, although recognized by Nani Florence and Nani Emma as being distinct.

Red huckleberries.

## Red Huckleberry

*Vaccinium parvifolium* Smith; Heather Family (Ericaceae)
Berries: **sG̲idllG̲uu**, **sG̲iidllG̲uu** (S) [see **sG̲id** 'red'], **sG̲idlùu** (M), **sG̲idluu** (A)
Bush: **sG̲idllG̲uu hlk̲'a'ii**, **sG̲iidllG̲uu hlk̲'aay.yii** (S), **sG̲idlúu hlk̲'a.aay** (M)
Picking huckleberries by brushing them off the branch: **sk̲'udgwii** (S)

These colourful berries are known to almost everyone and are still picked and enjoyed by many. Their names were familiar to all of the present-day elders, and were also recorded by Newcombe (1897, 1901), Curtis (1916), Swanton (1911) and Norton (1981). Gertrude Kelly recalled that the berries sometimes weigh down the bushes until they touch the ground. The bushes can produce copious quantities of the juicy berries, making them easy to pick. Today the berries are eaten fresh, cooked in muffins and pies, or made into preserves. Kathleen Hans recalled that her grandmother used to make red huckleberry jam with pieces of lemon added for flavouring.

The Reverend J.H. Keen (Newcombe 1897) noted that the stems were used medicinally by Haida.

## Bog Cranberry

*Vaccinium oxycoccos* L.; syn. *Oxycoccos* spp.; Heather Family (Ericaceae)
Berries: **dah** (S, M, A)
Vine: **dah hlk'a.aay** (M) (FD), **dah xil** (A) (Norton 1981; JE)

This berry and the following one are generally considered to be closely related. Some say that the term **dah** can be used for both types, but it is more typically applied to bog cranberry. **Dah** was known to all of the present-day elders and was also reported by Boas (1891) and Newcombe (1897). Emma Matthews noted that when women wanted to pick cranberries, they would say "let's buy," and that the name for cranberries also means "buying." (John Enrico believes, however, that the name has nothing to do with buying.)

Bog cranberry is distinguished from lingonberry by its small vines that lie on the ground in the muskeg, with the red berries borne singly on thin stalks. Lingonberry has short, more upright stalks and grows in the muskeg or under trees, with clustered, red berries. Although bog cranberry is often referred to as the "summer form," and lingonberry the "winter form," both types are gathered around October, and are prepared and eaten in a similar fashion. They are usually cooked for a long time before being eaten (Elizabeth Collinson, Gertrude Kelly, Emma Matthews, Florence Davidson). They are sometimes made into jelly or jam, and were sometimes dried with other berries (Norton 1981).

Bog cranberry patches were apparently owned by some families and were passed from generation to generation by a system of matrilineal inheritance.

**Bog cranberries.**

## Lingonberry, Low Cranberry, Rock Cranberry or Moss Cranberry

*Vaccinium vitis-idaea* L.; Heather Family (Ericaceae)
Berries: **sk'aagii chaay**, **sk'agi tsaay** (S), **skaga tsaay**, **sk'ag tsaay** (M), **sk'ag tsáay** (A) [all literally 'dog-salmon eggs'); or **tllgaa g̲aang̲a** (S) ('ground/earth-berries') (GY)
Plant: **skaga tsaay hlk̲'a.aay** (M)

The name **sk'aagii chaay/skaga tsaay** ('dog-salmon eggs') for these berries was the most commonly used among the elders consulted, all of whom associated them with the previous species, bog cranberry. The small, red, clustered berries do indeed resemble dog-salmon roe. They are also known as "winter cranberries."

In September 1990, when Florence Davidson was celebrating her 95th birthday, I showed her some of these berries I had gathered on my way from Skidegate to Massett. She looked at them carefully, asked where I found them and then said, with a twinkle in her eye and a smile I will never forget, "Let's go there tomorrow. We'll pick a big bowlful!"

These berries, and bog cranberries, used to be sold at the co-op store in Massett. Many people still go to pick them, and make preserves from them, although Norton (1981) reported that the Kaigani people were not using them very much anymore.

Lingonberries.

### Kinnikinnick, or Bearberry

*Arctostaphylos uva-ursi* (L.) Spreng.; Heather Family (Ericaceae)

Berries: **tllg̱aang̱a, tllgaa g̱aang̱a** (S) ('ground/earth-berries') (Newcombe 1901; Curtis 1916; GY, BP); or **dinax̱** (M) (Boas 1891; Newcombe 1901; FD, EM, WM)

Plant: "**sk̲'utsgai**" (S) (Newcombe 1901); or **tllg̱aang̱a hlk̲'a'ii** (S) ('ground-berry-branches/plant') (GY); or **dinax̱ hlk̲'a.aay** (M) (Newcombe 1901; FD)

This trailing, evergreen shrub with bright red berries was known as a smoking substance to Indigenous Peoples all over North America. Dawson (1880) reported that the Haida mixed the leaves with tobacco "to eke out the precious narcotic," and George Young also recalled that people used to smoke the leaves. The Massett name, **dinax̱**, is of Athapaskan origin, having cognate forms in Tanaina, Tsilhqot'in, Nicola Valley Athapaskan and Chipewyan (see Kari 1987; Marles 1984; Turner 2014; Turner et al. 1990).

The berries, though somewhat dry and with hard seeds in the centre, were eaten by Haida, as by other peoples (Turner 1995). They were first soaked in water and were cooked in grease, lard or butter to reduce the dryness (Newcombe 1901; Swanton 1905b, Curtis 1916, George Young, Watson Pryce). Florence Davidson said they were not common around Massett, but recalled that the Kaigani Haida of Alaska ate the berries with grease and sugar, and that they were said to be dry and "tasteless." Becky Pearson, on the other hand, enjoyed them very much. George Young recalled that this plant is abundant on Tree Island. Kinnikinnick leaves are widely used in both North American and European medicine to treat kidney diseases and infections of the urinary tract. They are known as "uva ursi" in the herbal medicine trade.

Kinnikinnick.

Twinflower (*Linnaea borealis* L.), a small, trailing, evergreen plant of the honeysuckle family (Caprifoliaceae) with delicate pairs of pink flowers, was also called **tllgaa xilg̱a** (S) ('ground/earth-leaves/medicine') by George Young, as was trailing raspberry (*Rubus pedatus*) of the rose family (Rosaceae). This last plant was called **tl'ants'uud g̱aanaa (-xil)** (M) ['Steller's jay berry (-leaves/medicine)'] by Chief Willie and Emma Matthews, who also used this term for twinflower on occasion.

## Crowberry

*Empetrum nigrum* L.; Crowberry Family (Ericaceae)

**x̱uya g̱aan** (S) ('raven's-berry'—see also black twinberry, *Lonicera involucrata*), or **yaanaang xilg̱a** (S) ('fog/cloud-leaves/medicine') (GY); or **x̱a skaa.awaa (hlḵ'a.aay)** (M) (Boas 1891; Newcombe 1897; FD; JE); **ha skáawaa** (A) (spelling uncertain) (literally 'sticking off ground in little bunches here and there'—JE); or **ts'ahl tlaas** (M) ('pine-boughs') (EM only); or **hlk'yaan hlḵ'am.alee** (M) ('forest-boughs/branches') (EM only)

This small muskeg shrub, whose branches resemble miniature fir trees, was recognized by all of the elders, but, as can be seen above, was given a variety of names. The name given by George Young is similar to that of yarrow (*Achillea millefolium*) and horsetails (*Equisetum*), but he was well aware that they were all different plants. The small, black berries were eaten, but Newcombe (1897, 1901) noted that if too many are consumed, they can cause "ruptures." The plant was known as a Haida medicine.

**Crowberries.**

**Seaside strawberries, a favourite berry common to the sand dunes of Haida Gwaii, especially at Rose Spit.**

## Seaside Strawberry

*Fragaria chiloensis* (L.) Duchesne; Rose Family (Rosaceae)
Berries: **hilG̲udaG̲aang, hilG̲udaG̲ang** (S), **hillda.aang** (M), **hildaG̲áang** (A) (Norton 1981; JE)
Plants: **hillda.aang xil** (M) (FD), **hillda.aang hlk̲'a.aay** (M) (WM, EM)

All the present-day elders remembered picking wild strawberries. The above names were also recorded by Boas (1891), Newcombe (1897) and Curtis (1916). Both George Young and Emma Matthews stated that strawberries were formerly much more plentiful than now; one used to be able to fill large buckets of them within a few hours. The deer and cattle introduced to Haida Gwaii, they said, have drastically reduced the crop, apparently by browsing the young shoots and flower buds as well as eating the berries themselves. The Kaigani people gathered wild strawberries on the Coastal Islands and also imported them from Massett and from Haines on the Alaskan mainland. They did not preserve them but ate them fresh (Norton 1981). However, Newcombe (1897) noted that the berries were eaten both fresh and "boiled down" by the Skidegate and Massett people. He reported that the plants were "generally distributed but especially plentiful on Sandspit Point, Skidegate, and just above the beach between Massett and Rose Spit. Also at **Tll'aal** [Tlell] River."

Many people grow domesticated strawberries in their gardens, and these are called by the same name as the wild ones (see Appendix 10). The wild ones are often quite pale, even whitish, but are nonetheless considered to be even more flavourful than the garden varieties.

Strawberry leaves have been used medicinally by Haida in various ways.

**Cloudberry.**

## Cloudberry, "Mars Apples," "Malt Berries" or "Fox Berries"

*Rubus chamaemorus* L.; Rose Family (Rosaceae)
Berries: **k̲'aax̲u ts'alaangG̲a, k̲'aax̲u ts'alaang.G̲a** (S) (see **k̲'aax̲u** 'fallen tree'), **k̲'a.àw ts'alaangaa** (M), **k̲'aawts'aláangaa** (A) (Norton 1981; JE)
Plant: **k̲'a.àw ts'alaangaa xil** (M)

This is a low but upright, herbaceous, berry-bearing plant of muskeg areas. It has paired scallop-edged leaves, single white flowers and raspberry-like fruits with large, orange to reddish drupelets. Florence Davidson explained the origin of the Massett name of the berries from 'cracking noise': "When it's not ripe, you can hear one chewing it. That's why they call it that."

Cloudberries have been a popular fruit of the Haida, especially the Massett people. The Massett name was recorded by Keen (1898), as well as being known to several of the modern-day elders. Becky Pearson, Florence Davidson and Emma Matthews all believed them to be formerly much more common than recently. They say the deer and cattle, both introduced to Haida Gwaii, have eliminated most of the berries.

People picked the berries in July, while many of them are still hard and unripe, then stored them in water or grease in large boxes or barrels. Some people said the unripe berries were parboiled before storage. They were also imported to Haida Gwaii from the Skeena River. Canned "malt berries" were sold at the co-op store in Massett for as much as $1.25 per pound (450 grams). They were very well liked. Florence Davidson said it made her mouth water just to see them again. Watson Pryce said they made excellent jam. Norton (1981) noted that when the Kaigani in Alaska stored the berries in containers with grease, the containers were sealed with a "sand top," a bag containing fine sand placed on top of the grease to ensure that the berries remained submerged and did not become mouldy.

## Trailing Raspberry

*Rubus pedatus* L.; Rose Family (Rosaceae)

Berries: **tllgaa G̲aanG̲a** (S) ('earth/ground-berries'), or **tl'aay tl'aay G̲aanG̲a**, **kl'aay kl'aay G̲aanG̲a** (S) ('Steller's jay berry') (Newcombe 1901), **tl'ants'uud G̲aanaa** (M) ('"bluejay" [Steller's jay] berries'); **tl'ants'uud G̲aanaa** (A) (Norton 1981)

Vines: **tl'ants'uud G̲aanaa hlk̲'a.aay**, **tl'ants'uud G̲aanaa xil** (M)

**Trailing raspberry.**

These names were known to several of the present-day elders, and were recorded by Newcombe (1897) and Norton (1981). Haida used to eat the berries (Newcombe 1897), but they are difficult to pick because they are so small and low-growing. They were cooked a long time and sometimes eaten with other berries such as bog cranberries (Elizabeth Collinson). Norton (1981) noted that the Kaigani sometimes dried them with other berries. Chief Willie Matthews also called twinflower, a small, pink-flowered trailing vine (*Linnaea borealis*), "bluejay-berry leaves," apparently after trailing raspberry.

## Bunchberry, Dwarf Dogwood or "Frogberries"

*Cornus canadensis* L. and *Cornus unalaschkensis* Ledeb.; Dogwood Family (Cornaceae)

**ts'ik'ab**, **ts'iik'ap** (S), **ts'iik'ab** or **ts'iik'abaa**, **ts'iik'ab xil** (M), **ts'íik'ab** (A) (borrowed from English "Jacob," from "Jacob's berry," or "Jacobberry") (Norton 1981; JE; M.B. Ignace)

These names were known to all of the elders, and were also recorded by Newcombe (1897, 1901). The apparent origin of the Haida name from English "Jacobberry" is intriguing, and may suggest a recent origin of the use of the berries as well. Bunchberries are low, patch-forming plants with whitish, dogwood-like flowers, and dense clusters of bright red, edible berries. The berries are good-tasting, but have a hard "stone" in the centre. Nevertheless, they were commonly eaten, raw or cooked, by the Haida as by other coastal First Peoples, and were usually served with sugar and

Bunchberry.

eulachon grease. They were sometimes preserved in grease for winter, according to Chief Willie and Emma Matthews. Norton (1981) stated that the seeds themselves were also eaten by the Kaigani Haida of Alaska.

## Wild Lily-of-the-Valley, or Two-Leaved Solomon's Seal

*Maianthemum dilatatum* (Wood) Nels. & Macbr.; Lily Family (Liliaceae)

Berries: **siG̲an, siiG̲an** (S) (Newcombe 1901; Swanton 1905a; JE), **sa.an, sa'an** (M), **sa'áan** (A) (Norton, 1981; JE)

Plant: **sk'aax̲aay** (S) (Newcombe 1901); **siiG̲an hlk̲'a'ii** (S), **sa.an xil, sa.an hlk̲'a.aay, sk'aang.iid** (M) (Newcombe 1901), **sk'aang.iid** ("**sk'angiit**") (A) ("the leaves") (Norton 1981)

Ripe berries: **sa.an tsaalaa** (M) ('soft/sweet **sa.an**') (FD; JE) (the adjective **tsaalaa**, "soft and sweet," can also be applied to **k'ay**, crab apples—JE)

This is a low, bright green plant with paired, heart-shaped leaves, growing in moist clearings and under trees, often in extensive patches. Its flowers are small and white, clustered at the top of the stem, and its small berries are mottled brown and green when unripe, turning soft and red when fully ripe. The above names were known to most of the Haida elders consulted, and, as noted, some were also recorded by Newcombe (1901), Swanton (1905a) and Norton (1981).

The berries were commonly eaten, apparently formerly in large quantities. George Young said that they were usually picked while still green, then stored in water until

**Wild lily-of-the-valley.**

ripe. Children ate them raw from the plants, but they were not considered to be very good this way. Chief Willie Matthews recalled that they were dried partially in the sun, cleaned, boiled in a basket for just a few minutes, then mixed with other berries, such as salal. Norton (1981) said that the Kaigani formerly scalded them for a few minutes, then ate them with grease, or grease and sugar.

George Young and Becky Pearson recalled that the leaves of this little "weed," growing in mossy places in the forest, and about the size of one's finger (curled up), were picked and eaten. These are called **sk'aax̲aay**. The Kaigani Haida boiled and ate the new "folded" leaves as a vegetable (Norton 1981). Newcombe (1901) reported that the young leaves were eaten as a "spring purge." The leaves of this plant were also widely used by Northwest Coast peoples as a poultice for wounds, burns and skin infections.

One narrative, told by Job Moody to Swanton (1905b:300), mentions a feast for supernatural beings in which these berries were eaten, along with highbush cranberries, Pacific crab apples, berry cakes [probably of salal], lupine-root cakes, and grease [**t'aaw** (S)]. Haida tobacco was also given out at this important occasion.

## Common Twisted-Stalk

*Streptopus amplexifolius* (L.) DC.; Lily Family (Liliaceae)

Berries: **st'aw G̲aanG̲a**, **st'aaw G̲aanG̲a** (S), **st'aw G̲aanaa**, **st'uu G̲aanaa** (M), **st'áw G̲áanaa** (A) (all literally 'witch/saw-whet-owl berries'—JE) [note that the Skidegate elders also call saw-whet owl **st'aaw**]; or **st'awliij G̲aanG̲a** (S) (JE); or **taan G̲aanaa** (M) ('black-bear berries')

Plant: **taan G̲aanaa xil** (M)

This herbaceous plant of moist shaded areas has simple elliptical leaves, small bell-shaped flowers and, later, elongated reddish orange translucent berries hanging individually under each leaf along the upper stem. The berries were not eaten by the Haida (although they are by some people in Alaska). Some Kaigani people now occasionally use the root (rhizome) in salads for its cucumber flavour (Norton 1981). The Lime Village Tanaina of Alaska call this plant "**k'ijeghi giga**" ('horned owl's berry'), and the Outer Inlet Tanaina call it "**ggagga gek'a**" ('brown bear's berry') (Kari 1987), interesting parallels to the Skidegate and Massett Haida names. The Tanaina also do not eat the berries.

Most of the Haida elders I talked to recognized this plant, but no one mentioned any medicinal or other uses for it. The implication was that one stayed away from it because it was associated with witchcraft, owls and bears.

A smaller relative, *Streptopus roseus* Michx., was reportedly also called 'bear-berry' (**taan G̲aanaa**) in Massett (Newcombe 1897, 1901). Newcombe also recorded the names "**st!olisganga**" (S) and "**t'anána**" (M) for star-flowered Solomon's-seal (*Maianthemum stellatum* (L.) Link.), or false Solomon's-seal (*Maianthemum racemosum* (L.) Link.), neither of which grows in Haida Gwaii, and said that the stem

**Left: Common twisted-stalk.** —PHOTO BY AUDREY BERNAND

**Right and below: Stonecrop, with edible, berry-like leaves.**

was used medicinally. It is therefore unclear to which plant he was actually referring. He noted, under this plant, "stem scraped and applied to cuts" (Newcombe 1897).

### Stonecrop

*Sedum divergens* S. Wats; Orpine Family (Crassulaceae)

**saad <u>G</u>aan<u>G</u>a**, **shaad <u>G</u>an<u>G</u>a** (S) (GY, WP; Newcombe 1901), **saad <u>G</u>aanaa** (M), "**sa'ián**" (A) (Newcombe 1901); or **t'iisgu skaahlln** (S) (literally 'little round thing [i.e., leaf] on the rock'—JE) (Newcombe 1901)

The reddish, fleshy, berry-like leaves and whole plants of this small rock plant were eaten in spring, "when young and tender" (Newcombe 1897) and were regarded more as a berry than a green vegetable. Newcombe (1897) collected its relative, roseroot (*Rhodiola rosea* L.; "*Sedum rhodiola*") on the Limestone Islands [**<u>k</u>'aa <u>G</u>aananang** (S)], near Skedans. Stonecrop was known to George Young, Watson Pryce and Emma Matthews as commonly growing on offshore islands. Kathleen Hans recalled that the leaves were chewed as a mouth freshener after one had taken fish grease laxative. This plant was also used medicinally.

## "Root" Vegetables

**LEFT AND RIGHT: Northern riceroot, a Haida root vegetable.**

### Northern Riceroot, Mission Bells or "Chocolate Lily"

*Fritillaria camschatcensis* (L.) Sweet; Lily Family (Liliaceae)
**'inhling** (note **hllnga** 'root'—JE) (S), **stla k̲'iist'aa** (M, A) ('round-thing-you-dig-out-with-your-finger': see **stla** 'finger'; **k̲'ii** 'round'—JE)
Bulbs, bulblets: **'inhling ts'ing** (**'inhling** 'teeth') (JE)

Northern riceroot is a lily with brownish purple, bell-shaped flowers clustered at the top of the stem, and several whorls of elongated leaves at intervals along its length. The edible bulbs are white and spherical, surrounded by many small rice-like bulblets, hence the name "riceroot." The names were recorded by Newcombe (1897, 1901), Keen (1898), Curtis (1916) and Norton (1981). (Curtis incorrectly identified the plant as tiger lily, *Lilium columbianum*, which does not occur in Haida Gwaii.) The Skidegate and Massett names were well known to all of the Haida elders speaking the respective dialects, although none had actually tasted the edible bulbs since childhood. Dawson (1880:114) mentioned a wild lily whose bulbs were eaten, undoubtedly northern riceroot, but said that it was not actively collected after 1880, except where they were used abundantly. The fact that the names are so well remembered testifies to the popularity of the food. Some say that when rice was introduced, it was called by the name **'inhling ts'ing** (S), or **'inhling** "teeth," which was originally used for the bulblets surrounding the bulb of northern riceroot.

For eating, the bulbs were collected in May, before flowering, or July, after flowering. The Massett and Kaigani Alaska names suggest they were simply dug out with one's finger. They were boiled in water and eaten as a thin paste, or steamed "like cauliflower," as Florence Davidson and Maude Moody recalled. Sometimes they were roasted in the embers of a fire and eaten with sugar or molasses, and eulachon grease (Newcombe 1897; Norton 1981). Norton (1981) noted that the Kaigani boiled them alone or with the chopped leaves of "Indian rhubarb" (*Rumex aquaticus* var. *fenestratus*). They were slightly bitter-tasting (see also 'Ksan, People of, 1980), but George Young and Solomon Wilson both commented that there are some places, such as near Tasu on the west coast of Haida Gwaii, that yield better-tasting bulbs than others. George Young said that the bulbs could remain alive even when washed by the sea, and that they taste very good afterwards. Newcombe (1897) collected the plant at Limestone Island near Skedans. Nowadays, the plant is said to be less common, and is considered to be quite rare (Marchant 1981; Turner and Kuhnlein 1983). It is found in the rocky headlands along the coastline between Skidegate and Queen Charlotte City.

Riceroot was also used medicinally by the Haida.

**How He-Who-Was-Born-from-His-Mother's-Side Used 'inhling to Vanquish the Salmon People**

He-Who-Was-Born-from-His-Mother's-Side was being chased by super-natural beings (coho salmon) in canoes with red bows. His powerful grandfather, Great Blue Heron, told him, "Now, brave man, have the town people pull **'inhling** out of the ground and spread it before them." He did this, and in a short time the salmon people rolled their eyes upward. Then some people came with vertical stripes on their canoes. Again his "grandfather" told him to have his people pull up **'inhling** and throw it about before them. Once again the supernatural people's eyes rolled upwards. They were dog salmon. He-Who-Was-Born-from-His-Mother's-Side made them cowards by putting **'inhling** teeth into their mouths ... (originally told by John Sky to Swanton 1905b:229*)

* In a footnote (19), Swanton identifies **'inhling** only as "a low plant with white seed vessels." He notes that "there are said to be sharp points around the bottom of its stalk referred to as **'inhling ts'ing**, or **'inhling**-teeth." Although the description is inaccurate in portraying the **'inhling** as white seed vessels, it is undoubtedly *Fritillaria* being referred to.

## Hemlock-Parsley, or "Wild Carrot"

*Conioselinum gmelinii* (Cham. & Schltdl.) Steud.; Celery Family (Apiaceae)

**gyaagyaa k̲'al sguunaa** (S) [tentatively, literally 'crest object with smelly skin'—JE] (Newcombe 1897, 1901 No. 22—"*Angelica*"), or "**na'uskausitaxil**" [possibly **naw-sgaawsidaay xil**] (S) ['?-potato-leaves/medicine/plant'; "indecipherable"—JE] (Newcombe 1901); or "**ts'itsix̲**" [**ts'ats'a** —"carrot"] (M) (Newcombe 1897—"*Coelopleurum gmelini* Ledeb."); or possibly **x̲àadas ts'ats'a** (M), **x̲aadas ts'ats'á** (A) (JE—"unidentified," but possibly this species) or **hlk'inx̲a sgaawsidaay** ['forest/"stick" potatoes'; also apparently applied to water-parsley, *Oenanthe sarmentosa*] (S) (Newcombe 1897, 1901; GY; JE); or **hlk'yaan sguusadee** (M) ('forest/"stick" potatoes') (Newcombe 1901; JE); or **hlk'iid sgaawsidaay** (S).

**Hemlock-parsley, or "wild carrot."**

Ethnobiologist Dr. Brian Compton (1993) finally unravelled the mystery of the Northwest Coast edible root called "wild carrot" by a careful search of the early literature and by interviewing North Wakashan (Heiltsuk and Haisla) speakers, using specimens of various native carrot-like plants. He found that hemlock-parsley ("*Conioselinum pacificum*") is the "wild carrot," and his conclusions are supported by the miscellaneous notations from Haida Gwaii by C.F. Newcombe and others. Newcombe (1897, 1901), for example, noted that the carrot-like roots were boiled, cut into squares and eaten with grease [**t'aaw** (S)]. Elsewhere, Newcombe stated that roots of the plant called "stick potatoes" (see discussion, following) were roasted and eaten, especially at Cumshewa. In another part of his notes, Newcombe (1901) reported that *Conioselinum* roots were used as a medicine but were not eaten. Emma Matthews (personal communication to Marianne Boelscher 1979) recalled that people used to get some kind of roots that looked like parsnips. They washed them clean, pounded them on cedar blocks and, when this was finished, they shaped them into cakes. They made little boxes for them. When they got quite a few, they dried them over a fire. Emma had never seen this done, but had heard people talking about it from the old days. Apparently, she was referring to *Conioselinum*. One of John Enrico's Alaskan Haida consultants, the late Christine Edenso, recalled that the plant called **x̲aadaas ts'ats'á** (A) had "big white flowers on top" and that the roots were eaten. John Enrico notes that this plant was probably the original referent for **ts'ats'á**, more recently applied to domesticated carrot.

There is also some apparent confusion between hemlock-parsley and the related water-parsley (*Oenanthe sarmentosa* Presl), a plant reportedly strongly purgative (see Turner et al. 1983), but nevertheless identified as "forest/stick potatoes" by George Young, and also by Newcombe (1897, 1901), with the implication that it was eaten. Likely, however, the real "stick-potatoes" is hemlock- parsley. *Oenanthe* was also called **hlk'iid giidg̲ii** (S) by George Young (see below). These plants are both related to the highly poisonous water-hemlock (*Cicuta* spp.) (which does not occur in Haida Gwaii), and *anyone not very familiar with the identification of plants in the carrot family should leave all of them strictly alone.*

The root of hemlock-parsley has not been eaten for many years and did not seem to be very familiar to the Haida elders I consulted. George Young simply called it **hlk'iid giidg̲ii** (S), meaning 'child/offspring of cow-parsnip' (*Heracleum maximum*). He also used this name for several other smaller umbelliferous plants such as *Glehnia littoralis* Schmidt and *Oenanthe sarmentosa*. Chief Willie Matthews, too, simply called hemlock-parsley "cow-parsnip baby." George Young and Agnes and Maude Moody noted that the long, fleshy roots of *Glehnia* were eaten like parsnips.

Since the name "stick potatoes," mentioned many times in Newcombe's notes (1897–1906), originates from the word for potato, **sgawsiid**, and since potato was introduced and the term possibly derived from the English "good seed" (Appendix 10), there is an implication that the use of hemlock-parsley as a root vegetable may be relatively recent, perhaps learned from mainland peoples during the fur-trade era.

## Beach Lupine

*Lupinus littoralis* Dougl. ex Lindl.; Bean, or Legume Family (Fabaceae)
Roots: **tag̲ansk'yaa** (S) (Newcombe 1901; Swanton 1913; EW), **ta.ansk'yaaw, ta.ansk'yaa** (M) (Swanton 1913; WM, EM, FD; JE)
Plant: **ta.ansk'yaaw xil**, **ta.ansk'yaaw hlk̲'a.aay** (M) (FD)
Flowers: **ta.ansk'yaaw x̲illee** (M) ('lupine blossom'—see also under "Flower" in Appendix 9) (FD)

The thick, fleshy roots of this perennial blue-flowered plant were eaten by the Haida in the old days but are no longer used, according to those elders who knew the plant by name. Beach lupine roots, about as thick as one's finger, can grow up to one metre (three feet) in length, and the plant forms large colonies on the coastal dunes at **Tll'aal** (Tlell) and Rose Spit (Swanton 1913; Calder and Taylor 1968). Swanton (1913), who provided the original identification of **tag̲ansk'yaa** (S)/ **ta.ansk'yaa** (M),

**LEFT: Beach lupine, whose roots were roasted and eaten.**

**CENTRE: Massett elders and members of the X̲aad Kil (Haida language) curriculum group at Cemetery Beach remembering how beach lupine, ta.ansk'yaaw (M), was used. From left to right: Dorothy Bell, Ethel Jones, Norma Adams and Mary Swanson are all elders in the Haida ethnobotany course taught by Marianne Ignace (SFU, August 2002). —PHOTO BY MARIANNE B. IGNACE**

**RIGHT: Nootka lupine.**

noted that the roots were dug in September and were sometimes roasted slowly in the embers of a fire in which fish was being toasted. The whitish inner pith, with roasting, becomes "as sweet as sugar" (Swanton 1913). Emma Matthews and Florence Davidson noted that the roots were also steamed in pits dug in the sand and lined with skunk-cabbage leaves. The cooked roots were then peeled and eaten with sugar and grease. They were also prepared for winter storage by pounding them, moulding them into cakes and drying them. The dried cakes were also eaten with sugar and grease.

Emma Matthews (personal communication to Marianne Boelscher 1985) was told about these roots ("**sk'yaaw**"—normally applied to fern roots), which were dug from sand dunes, by her elders: "They used to get lots of it and dry them, make a big hole and put rocks of fist size into it. When they get red hot you put them in the hole and put skunk-cabbage on top of it, and those roots on top of it." She never tasted the roots herself, but they were said to taste very good. She thought they used to dry them for winter, then soak them before use.

In one Haida narrative, lupine root cakes were eaten, along with berries of wild lily-of-the-valley, at a feast by supernatural beings (Swanton 1905b). In another, **Yaahl** [Raven] steamed, peeled and ate these roots (Swanton 1908b).

Lupines are known to be potentially toxic to humans and livestock (see Turner and von Aderkas 2009), but no mention was made of this problem for the Haida. Evidently the roots of this species, when well cooked, do not pose any threat. The Kwakwa̲ka̲'wakw (Southern Kwakiutl) people who ate lupine roots, however, noted that they make one dizzy and "drunk" (Turner and Bell 1973), and Krause (1956), who noted their use by the Tlingit, said that they had narcotic properties.

Newcombe (1897, 1901) noted the use of another species, Nootka lupine (*Lupinus nootkatensis* Donn ex Sims) by the Haida. He and Boas (1891) gave the name **ganduu** (S) for the roots of this species. John Enrico recorded the Alaskan Haida form, **gúnduu** (A). Newcombe said that these roots were dug before the plants flowered in spring and were roasted and eaten. He collected it on Maple Island in Skidegate Inlet and also noticed it at Sandspit Point, Skidegate, Skincuttle [**sk'in G̲aatl'**] and Massett near the village (Newcombe 1897). These names are apparently unknown today, and none of the present-day elders recall having eaten the roots. Willie Matthews and George Young, on seeing the pea-like seedpods of this lupine, called it "Raven's canoe" (see under beach pea and giant vetch—"Raven's canoe plants"). Nootka lupine roots were also formerly eaten by the Nuxalk (Bella Coola) and Kwakwa̲ka̲'wakw (Turner 1973, 1995).

## Springbank Clover, or Wild Perennial Clover

*Trifolium wormskioldii* Lehm.; Bean, or Legume Family (Fabaceae)
Rhizomes: **naa'a** (S) (Newcombe 1897,1901; Curtis 1916; GY, WP, BP; JE)
Plant: **naa'a hlk̲'a'ii** (S) (Newcombe 1901); or possibly **xil laabs** (M) (WM, EM; not known to FD—JE)

This perennial root vegetable, with "clover" leaves and long, whitish rhizomes, was known to most of the elders consulted, although several did not actually recognize the plant itself. It was described as having "roots" "like spaghetti, but even finer," and is known to grow in patches on the upper part of the beach. Watson Pryce noted that the narrows on Hotspring Island was a good place to gather them. The rhizomes

**Left: Edible rhizomes of springbank clover.**

**Right: Springbank clover.**

**Pacific silverweed.**

were formerly dug with a cedarwood or yew-wood shovel or pointed digging stick (Newcombe 1897). They were boiled or steamed, and eaten with sugar and grease [**t'aaw** (S)]. Occasionally they were eaten raw (Newcombe 1897). They are said to taste something like a sweet potato. Geese are also known to like these "roots."

Springbank clover still grows at Skedans, around Tlell and at Mayer Lake. The rhizomes were eaten by virtually all Northwest Coast peoples and are generally associated by the Haida and other groups with another, similar root vegetable, Pacific silverweed (*Potentilla egedii*) (Turner and Kuhnlein 1983; Kuhnlein and Turner 1991).

## Pacific Silverweed, "Cinquefoil" or "Wild Sweet Potatoes"

*Potentilla egedii* Wormsk.; Rose Family (Rosaceae)

Roots: **ts'ii'aal, ts'iiaal** (S), **ts'a.al, ts'a'al** (M), **k̲'wíi ts'a.aláay** (A) (**k̲'wíi** 'soil'—JE) (**ts'a'áal** in A now means 'salmonberry shoots,' the original word for the latter having been lost—JE)

Plants: **ts'ii'aal xil, ts'iiaal xil** (S), **ts'a.al xil** (M), or **x̲íid ts'a.aláay** (A) (a "mud sprout"—Norton 1981; literally 'white-fronted goose **ts'a'áal'**—JE)

This is a yellow-flowered herbaceous perennial of salt marshes, river estuaries and shorelines, often growing together with the previous species, springbank clover. Its leaves are silvery on the underside and are pinnately compound, the leaflets borne in a feather-like arrangement along a central stalk. The Haida names were known to the present-day elders, and were also recorded by Newcombe (1897, 1901), Swanton (1905b, 1908a) and Curtis (1916). The first names, although they apply specifically to the roots, can be used to refer to the whole plant as well. The Alaskan Haida

**Edible roots of Pacific silverweed.**

name for the roots represents an interesting case of potential homonymy, explained John Enrico: "Due to sound change in the northern [Haida] dialects, the words for salmonberry shoots and cinquefoil roots have become the same. M [Massett] then differentiated them by adding a medial s in the word for salmonberry shoots. A [Alaska] turned to a compound for one of them instead."

The roots, like those of springbank clover, were formerly an important food for the Haida and for other Northwest Coast peoples (Turner 1995). Florence Davidson said that the roots were dug in the springtime and were very good, although slightly bitter. A yew-wood shovel was used for digging them (Newcombe 1897). They were generally pit-cooked, and their taste is described as like sweet potatoes. Adam Bell (personal communication to Marianne Boelscher 1980) recalled that the roots were dug in May and June, and that they taste good. They were prepared for winter simply by washing the sand off and drying them, or by mashing them into cakes and drying them. Becky Pearson recalled seeing people digging these roots at Burnaby. The Skidegate elders noted that people eat the roots with **t'aaw** (grease) and sugar. Norton (1981) noted that the Kaigani people formerly cleaned the roots and boiled them with grease, and also dried them for winter use.

Formerly, good patches of silverweed were hereditary property of individual village members, and one had to pay the owner of a patch to dig roots there.

In Haida stories, steamed silverweed roots were the only human food eaten by Goose Woman (Swanton 1905a). People still note that geese like to eat these roots. (Geese are also known to like springbank clover rhizomes; see previous species.) In a Kwakwa̱ka̱'wakw (Southern Kwakiutl) story, the roots were eaten by Mallard Duck Women (Turner and Bell 1973).

## "Leafy Herb" Plants

### Cow-Parsnip, or "Indian Celery"

*Heracleum maximum* W. Bartram; Celery, or Umbel Family (Apiaceae)
**hlk'iid** (S, M), **hlk'íid** (A)

This is a large herbaceous perennial with broad, three-parted leaves, big, white, umbrella-like flower clusters and flat, winged fruits ("seeds"). It is known to almost everyone in Haida Gwaii, and its name, known to all the Haida elders I consulted, was also recorded by Newcombe (1897, 1901). The whole plant was called **hlk'iid**, or sometimes **hlk'iid hlk̲'a'ii** (S). The flowering stalks are called **hlk'iid x̲ilaahgaay** (S) (see Appendix 9, under "Flowers"), or **hlk'iid k̲aj** (M) ('**hlk'iid hair/head**'). When the plant comes into bloom and the flowerheads expand, people say "**hlk'iid k̲aajénjes dlaan**." Florence Davidson noted that the blooming of cow-parsnip is an indication that seagull eggs [**sk̲'iin k̲aaw** (S)] are no good for eating anymore. Rolled oats are sometimes called **hlk'iid k̲aja** (M) after their resemblance to the seeds of cow-parsnip (Appendix 10).

The stalks are called **chiijii k'waaluu** (S), **hlk'iid hlk̲aamee** (M) or **hlk'íid hlk̲áamaay** (A) (see **hlk̲aa.m** 'bull kelp'—M) (Becky Pearson, Florence Davidson).

The young stalks were peeled and eaten in the spring, before the flower buds started to expand. They were always peeled because the skin was said to be poisonous (Newcombe 1897: Maude and Agnes Moody, Kathleen Hans, Willie and Emma Matthews). When one eats the leaf stalks, he must never allow them to touch his lips, or he will get mouth sores; the bud stalks, after they are peeled, can touch the lips. Cow-parsnip and several other members of the celery family contain phototoxic furanocoumarins, concentrated in the skin of the plant. When these come in contact with the lips or skin, and then are exposed to full sunlight (with ultraviolet rays), they can cause severe irritation, including blistering and discoloration, which may last for days or weeks. This is why the elders warn that the stalks must always be peeled and certain parts must not touch the lips (Kuhnlein and Turner 1987).

George Young recalled that cow-parsnip shoots were eaten only in times of famine and were not highly regarded. He also stated that the stalks growing in the shade were good, but those in the sun were inedible. However, many other elders had more positive recollections of them, saying that they really enjoyed them. It seems, though, that few people eat them today in Skidegate, although some Massett people still harvest them, and Norton (1981) said that children still ate them among the Kaigani. She reported that the stalks were formerly stored in quantity for winter use, being peeled, and then packed away in grease. Some of the Kaigani women told her that the plants grew much taller when they were regularly harvested, and that they "need to be picked."

Cow-parsnip (left), whose peeled shoots (right) are eaten as a springtime vegetable.

The roots are used medicinally by Haida. Ed Calder said that Haida learned to use cow-parsnip roots for medicine from the Tsimshian people at Prince Rupert.

As noted, under hemlock-parsley, several smaller umbelliferous plants were named after cow-parsnip, simply being called **hlk'iid giidg̲i** (S) ('child/offspring of cow-parsnip').

## Western Dock, or "Wild Rhubarb"

*Rumex aquaticus* var. *fenestratus* L. (Greene) Dorn; Knotweed Family (Polygonaceae)
**tl'aang.k̲'uus** (S) (Newcombe 1897, 1901; GY, WP), **tl'aak̲'uus, tl'aak̲'uuj** (M) (also applied to garden rhubarb) (WM, EM, FD), **t'láak̲'uj, tl'áak̲'us** (A) (Norton 1981); or **x̲àadas tl'aak̲'ujaa** (M) ('Haida rhubarb') (in contrast to domesticated rhubarb) (FD); or **stladaal sgyaan** ("**slhda!lskien**") (M) (Newcombe 1897; Keen 1898; JE notes that this name is for the introduced curly dock, *Rumex crispus* L., which is not eaten)

This plant, including both leaves and stalks, was commonly eaten in the old days like rhubarb stalks or spinach, as recalled by George Young and Florence Davidson. It is still occasionally used. The Kaigani formerly boiled it with northern riceroot (*Fritillaria camschatcensis*) [**'inhling** (S), **stla k̲'iist'aa** (M, A)], and also used it in soup or stew. The stems were cooked separately (Norton 1981). The red leaf stalks were boiled to make **tl'aak̲'uus jaamgaa** (literally 'jammed rhubarb,' borrowed from English "jam") in more recent times (Florence Davidson).

**Left: Western dock, a leafy green vegetable.**

**Centre: Sea asparagus, or glasswort.**

**Right: Skunk-cabbage.**

Florence Davidson (Blackman 1982:85) recalled, "Near the end of May, ladies would go on boats across Yan [from Massett] to get wild rhubarb, just like they'd go for seaweed. When I was old enough to pull some, I'd go with my mother. I used to [desire] it so much. I worked fast to collect it and I used to try all my best to get real lots. We'd carry home bundles of wild rhubarb tied up in a tablecloth. My mother cut the rhubarb up and boiled it for dessert. We ate it with lots of sugar and grease." Dock roots are widely used for medicine by Northwest Coast peoples, including Haida, and several elders knew of their use.

A related plant, sourgrass (*Rumex acetosella* L.), is called **k̲ayluus** ('sour') (S).

## Sea Asparagus, or Glasswort

*Sarcocornia pacifica* (Standl.) A.J. Scott; Goosefoot Family (Chenopodiaceae)

The Kaigani Haida use this plant as a green vegetable today, but it was apparently not used in the "old days." The food use is commonly believed to have been learned from the Norwegian settlers in the area. "The plant is picked from late May through July, or until it flowers and is too woody for use. It is picked in quantity, a gallon or more at a time, canned, 'jarred,' frozen, or used fresh. It is first boiled or scalded in several waters to remove the salt. Hot, it is eaten with butter or bacon; cold, it is used in salads with onion and dressed with mayonnaise or oil and vinegar" (Norton 1981:441).

## Skunk-Cabbage

*Lysichiton americanus* Hult. & St. John; Arum Family (Araceae)

**hlgun**, **hlguun** (S, M), **hlgún** (A) (Norton 1981—"refers particularly to the leaf") ("whole plant or leaf"—JE)

This giant-leaved plant of swampy places is well known for its bright yellow flower sheaths and bright green, pungent-smelling leaves. All the elders I talked to were familiar with the Haida names. The greenish, club-like flower spike, or spadix, is called **hlgun/hlguun chiiji** (S) ('**hlgun** penis') or **hlgun/hlguun tsaay** (S, M), **hlgún tsáay** (A) ('**hlgun** fish eggs'—JE) (also recorded by Newcombe 1897). Becky Pearson said that the name **hlgun tsaay** can also pertain to knitting when it is close and even, like the texture of the stalk.

The leaves of skunk-cabbage are poisonous to eat for humans. They contain needle-like crystals of calcium oxalate, which can become embedded in the tissues of the tongue and throat and cause intense irritation. In severe cases, the resulting swelling can cause choking and lead to death (Turner and von Aderkas 2009). Harrison (1925) reported that two young girls pretending to have a tea party ate the leaves, and one of them died from them. Emma Wilson said that a child once ate a spadix of a skunk-cabbage flower and died (possibly this is the same case). However, Emma Wilson also mentioned a certain centre-stalk portion that is very rarely found but is excellent to eat and tastes like banana. When she was small, her father found one and gave it to her to eat. Perhaps this was one of the very young shoots, which are said by some to be edible and quite good when cooked. Deer are known to eat the young shoots and leaves without ill effect (John Enrico, personal communication), and formerly people cooked and ate the roots (rhizomes) in the early spring as a starvation food (Turner 1995). Also, several elders said that the roots are eaten by bears when they come out of their winter sleep in the spring. It is also said that the roots were eaten by Indian doctors (shamans); because they are so strong, and "burn," they provide good protection against evil.

As long as the leaves are not consumed, they are extremely useful in many aspects of food preparation, since they are so large. Their waxy surface protects the food from any of their pungent or poisonous properties. They were used for makeshift drinking cups and berry containers, and to carry salmon eggs, line baskets, wrap fish for steaming and line cooking pits and berry-drying racks (Newcombe 1901; Maude Moody). They were also placed in boxes of salmon eggs being stored for winter, apparently helping to preserve them, according to Solomon and Emma Wilson. Emma Matthews (personal communication to Marianne Boelscher 1985) noted that more recently, the leaves are used to line four-gallon tins before the salmon eggs are placed inside. Norton (1981:440) elaborates on the importance of this plant in food preparation:

> The leaf is strong, firm and very pliable. The central vein was softened by heat to make it malleable so foods could be wrapped in airtight packages, stored for long periods, or cooked in their own juices. The leaf was useful to keep foods separate when more than one family was cooking at the same fire or when the juices of the foods being cooked should not mix.

**Poached Halibut**

A number of people recall that skunk-cabbage leaves were used to wrap food for cooking. Norton (1981:440) relates, "A typical 'contact' recipe from the early part of this century that is well remembered is poached halibut, king salmon, or deer. The fish or meat was placed in skunk cabbage leaves along with 'spuds' (potatoes), covered with tomato sauce, sealed and placed on hot ashes to cook. All three dishes could be cooked at once because they were sealed in the leaves and could not flavor one another. Skunk cabbage leaves ... do not impart a flavor to food ..." Other remembered recipes include carrots, onions and other vegetables being cooked in this dish. The food was laid in the bottom of a pit, covered with sand and a fire lit overtop. The fire was allowed to burn a couple of hours, then salt water was poured on. The meal was left to cook about half an hour more, then the pit was opened, the leaves cut open and the food taken out to make a delicious meal.

Skunk-cabbage roots were occasionally used as bait on halibut hooks, which were made of yew wood. The white roots look like octopus trailing in the water. (When the halibut opens its mouth to take the bait, it creates such a vacuum that the hook is pulled right in.) This information is reported in Swanton (1908b:574) in the story of "The Famine of Ti'An," told by Walter of the Rear-Town-People of Yan: "Since they had nothing with which to catch fish, they baited their hooks with skunk-cabbage roots." They caught lots of halibut with this method.

Skunk-cabbage also had a number of medicinal uses for the Haida, as for other Northwest Coast peoples. Adam Bell (personal communication to Marianne Boelscher 1980) recalled one incident when an Alaska woman had her thigh "all smashed up" [broken]:

> They put a stick there and sliced skunk-cabbage and put one on each side of the leg. Then they land and pack up their sister. They change the skunk-cabbage every day. They put her in the hospital in Sitka. They take off the skunk-cabbage. In those days they had no X-rays. It was all healed up. Then they told her to stand up. She could walk around all right. It was the skunk-cabbage that did it. They warmed up the skunk-cabbage before they put it around.

Newcombe (1902) recorded a place apparently named after skunk-cabbage, a point on the south side of Chaatl Island, which was called **hlgundii kun** (possibly 'skunk-cabbage point'; translation not definite—JE). Skunk-cabbage is mentioned in some of the narratives recorded by Swanton (1905a, b). In one, there is a reference to a "swampy place where skunk cabbage grew," meaning Skidegate Channel. In another, there is a suggestion that skunk-cabbage roots are related to having supernatural power; the hero in this particular story, Deer, stated, "I can pull out any skunk cabbage root with my teeth" (Swanton 1908a:317). For this ability, **Yaahl** [Raven] allowed Deer to marry his [**Yaahl'**s] sister. In another story called "The Artisans" (#31), told by Walter of the Rear-Town-People of Yan (Swanton 1908b:460–66), the hero, who had been abandoned by his entire village except his grandmother, was returning home when he came to a big skunk-cabbage. He dug a trench around it in readiness for the time when he should be thirsty. The next day, he came to the skunk-cabbage again and in the trench he had dug there was a sockeye salmon. He dug the ditch a little larger. Then he took the salmon to

***Skunk-Cabbage Man*, "a large person with a big stomach"; painting by Gitkinjuaas (also known as Giitsxaa).**

Broad-leaved plantain.

his grandmother and they ate part of it. The next day there were two salmon. Again he enlarged the trench. The next time, there were three, then five, ten, twenty and finally "a great quantity." Each time he dug the trench a little larger. Then he noticed that someone had come and was eating all the salmon. It was a large person with a big stomach. The boy shot arrows at him. Later, he discovered this was a supernatural being, Skunk-Cabbage. It was he who had been helping the boy by giving him the salmon.

In another narrative, also told by Walter of the Rear-Town-People of Yan, of "Deer and Beaver," Deer, who lived in Tlingit country, was said to keep the skunk-cabbage he ate just like a garden (Swanton 1908b:446).

## Broad-Leaved Plantain

*Plantago major* L.; Plantain Family (Plantaginaceae)
**'laanaa hlgun<u>g</u>a** (S), **'laanaa hlgun** (M) (both literally 'village skunk-cabbage');
OR **'laanaa xil<u>g</u>a** (S) ('village-leaves/medicine') (KH)

This small, wide-leaved herbaceous plant, appropriately called 'village skunk-cabbage,' was known to Florence Davidson, George Young, Becky Pearson and several other elders. The name was also recorded by Keen (1898) and Newcombe (1897, 1901). The plant is known for its resemblance to skunk-cabbage as well as for its ability to grow along footpaths and trampled places near human settlements. As an emergency medicine, the leaves are widely used by people in Europe and North America as a poultice for sores, wounds, burns, infections and eczema. They are bruised or mashed and applied directly to the skin.

Giant vetch.

## Beach Pea and Giant Vetch: "Raven's Canoe" Plants

*Lathyrus japonicus* Willd. and *Vicia nigricans* ssp. *gigantea* Hook. & Arn. (Hook.) Lassetter & C.R. Gunn; Bean, or Legume Family (Fabaceae)

**X̲uya tluuG̲a** (S), **Yaahl tluwaa** (M), **Yáahl tluwáay** (A) (all 'Raven's-canoe')

Beach pea.

"Raven's canoe" applies specifically to the black, pea-like pods of these two beach plants, which resemble miniature canoes. One can say **Yaahl tluwaa hlk̲'a.aay** (M) when referring to the vines. Cultivated garden peas and green beans (Appendix 10) can also be called by this name, which was recorded by Newcombe (1897, 1901) and Swanton (1905a, 1911), as well as being known to the present-day elders. Additionally, the pods of Nootka lupine (*Lupinus nootkatensis*) are sometimes called by the same term. The name originates from an episode in a narrative (see following).

The "peas" of these wild plants were not generally considered to be edible, although Newcombe (1897, 1901) reported that the seeds of young giant vetch were eaten, and Norton (1981) said that several of her Kaigani consultants boiled and ate the peas after the pods were dried, although one woman said they were dangerous. Some Kwakwa̲ka̲'wakw (Southern Kwakiutl) were also said to eat them (Turner and Bell 1973). It is interesting to note that giant vetch is called "canoe-plant" in the Straits Salish and Makah languages of southern Vancouver Island and the Olympic Peninsula, respectively (Violet Williams and Elsie Claxton, Salish elders, personal communication 1989; Gunther 1945; Turner and Hebda

*Raven in His Canoe* (a giant-vetch pod); painting by Gitkinjuaas (also known as G̲iitsx̲aa).

2012). John Enrico mentioned a man who lived in the bush for many years and often ate the pods of "raven's canoe" plants.

> **X̲uya [Raven] Rescues a Supernatural Woman**
>
> **X̲uya** [Raven] saw a "woman" sticking out of the water at the mouth of Bentinck Arm. He made three attempts to reach her, with three different kinds of canoes, but every time he approached, she sank into the water. Then he opened a wild pea with a stick and used the pod as his canoe. This time when he drew near, she did not sink. He took her into his canoe and set her ashore at Haida Gwaii on the west arm of Cumshewa Inlet (called **xawu k̲uns**, a campsite at the mouth of Pallant Creek—JE). The woman was known as **jilaa k̲uns**, 'Creek Woman' (JE). (from a story told by John Sky and recorded originally by Swanton 1905b:115)

Single delight, or "snowflower."

## Single Delight, "Snowflower" or "Wild Snowdrops"

*Moneses uniflora* (L.) Gray; Heather Family (Ericaceae)

**xil guugaa** (S) (Newcombe 1901; Swanton 1905a, b; GY, EM), or **xilaawg** (M) (Newcombe 1897, who gave same name for A; Keen 1898; EM, FD)

This small, white flower growing on mossy rotten logs on the forest floor was recognized by all of the elders consulted and was widely known as a medicine. The meaning of the names is not known. The leaves are extremely peppery and bitter. Newcombe (1901), unsure of its identity, suggested that it might be *Cardamine*, a peppery plant of the mustard family; elsewhere in his notes, however (1897), the identification as *Moneses* is confirmed.

Swanton (1905b) recorded a story episode in which a whole mountain full of this plant was eaten by the hero to give him supernatural strength. Other similar episodes are recounted in Swanton (1908b:689, 742). For example, in the story of **xanaa** (p. 742), told by Isaac of Those-Born-at-**hl'yaalang** the hero wanted to be a chief, so he went up upon a mountain (of Massett Inlet) to eat medicine (*Moneses*). He ate grease with it. He then saw a great supernatural being, who taught him many songs. Elsewhere, Swanton (1908a:745) noted, "When people wanted to be chiefs, they ate bitter leaves."

## Round-Leaved Sundew

*Drosera rotundifolia* L.; Sundew Family (Droseraceae)

**ta'inaang k'uug** (M), **ta'ináang k'úug** (A) (JE) ('the heart of plenty'; see **ta'inang** 'be a season of plenitude [lots of fish and berries],' referring to the desired effect of this plant as a charm—John Enrico, personal communication 1993) (WM, EM, FD)

This tiny insectivorous muskeg plant, with reddish gland-tipped hairs covering its leaves, was important as a good-luck charm. Massett fishermen hung small bunches of it on their seine nets set across river estuaries, and this was believed to increase

Round-leaved sundew.

the catch. Willie Matthews warned that its use should be kept secret, however, or it would not work. It was also carried by hunters to ensure luck in catching game. Florence Davidson noted that red woodpeckers' feathers were used in the same way.

## False Hellebore, Green Hellebore or "Skookum-Root"

*Veratrum viride* Ait.; Melanthium Family (Melanthiaceae);
formerly in Lily Family (Liliaceae)
**gwaayk'yaa**, **gwaayk'ya** (S), **gwaayk'aa** (M), **gwáayk'aa** (A) (JE—refers to the root only); or **gwaayk'ya hlk̲'a'ii** (S) (Harrison 1925)

***Caution:* Highly toxic. Use of any part of plant, or solution from it, on eyes or broken skin, as snuff, or any internal application, is not recommended.**

This powerful plant was known to all of the Haida elders I talked with, and its name was also recorded by Boas (1891), Newcombe (1897, 1901) and Swanton (1905a, b). John Enrico notes that the name refers specifically to the root, or rootstock. The plant is a tall, bright green herbaceous perennial with large, elliptical, deeply pleated leaves and somewhat drooping clusters of greenish yellow flowers at the top of the stem. It grows in moist places and is common in some areas of Haida Gwaii. It is very toxic, due to the presence of several chemically related alkaloids, but it is widely used medicinally and ritually by First Peoples in northwestern North America (see Turner and Bell 1973; Turner 1973; Turner and von Aderkas 2009).

Because it is so poisonous, it must be used with extreme care and respect. The Haida have had many different uses for it, but these are considered to be private knowledge, and because of this, and the danger of misuse, uninformed people should keep away from this and other medicinal plants.

In the ancient times, false hellebore root, often called "blue hellebore," mixed with urine and allowed to ferment in a watertight basket, was used to conquer supernatural beings, such as under-ocean shamans. If this potent solution was sprinkled on or near them, they would lose their supernatural powers. This root was used for protection against evil supernatural forces by virtually all Northwest Coast and other First Peoples within the range of the plant.

False hellebore flowers.

Emma Wilson suggested that Haida people used to import false hellebore root from the Tsimshian of the Skeena River (even though the plant is common in Haida Gwaii).

**Left:** False hellebore, a culturally important but poisonous plant.

**Right:** Devil's-club.

## Devil's-Club

*Oplopanax horridus* (Sm.) Miq.; Ginseng Family (Araliaceae)
**ts'iihlinjaaw, ts'iihllnjaaw** (S), **ts'iihlanjaaw** (M), **ts'íihlanjaaw** (A)

***Caution:* Devil's-club spines can be extremely irritating if touched. The spines can act as slivers and are difficult to remove. They often fester under the skin. Some people are allergic to devil's-club and can have a severe reaction to it, even from just superficial contact.**

**Devil's-club's spiny stems.**

Devil's-club, with its spiny, straggly stems and large, maple-like, prickly leaves, was one of the most important medicinal and protective plants of the First Peoples of northwestern North America (see Turner 1982). Haida still use it for many purposes, and respect it highly for its spiritual and medicinal powers.

Devil's-club berries were rubbed in the hair and on the scalp of children to get rid of lice and dandruff and to make the hair nice. Willie Matthews recalled that his aunt, Mrs. Weah, had beautiful hair when she was young because her grandmother treated it in this way. Perhaps because of the special protective properties of its sharp spines, devil's-club is important for protection against evil and illness. Lengths of stem can be placed above a doorway or under one's mattress, or in the four corners of a room, to protect the members of a household and keep them safe.

Aside from its medicinal and protective properties, devil's-club sticks were used to make black-cod lures, according to Chief Willie Matthews. The wood was also used for fish lures by the Ditidaht people of the west coast of Vancouver Island (Turner et al. 1983). Gamblers often used devil's-club as a good-luck charm (Newcombe 1902).

In one story told by John Sky, devil's-club was eaten, along with two other plants, to gain supernatural powers (Swanton 1905b:212–13). Many accounts include the use of devil's-club for gaining wealth and power. For example, in the story of the Copper Salmon, told by Walter of the Rear-Town-People of Yan (Swanton 1908b: 689–700), a man who had lost all his possessions gambling placed devil's-club sticks all around him in a circle and ate the skin of each in turn, until they were all finished. Then he put the sticks under his head. Where he had defecated, there was a lot of single delight (*Moneses uniflora*), all of which he ate. He then became sick and lost consciousness, but when he awakened, after eating still more of this plant, he got a powerful song and found a copper salmon and was able to regain his wealth.

***Devil's-Club Man*; painting by Gitkinjuaas (also known as G̲iitsx̲aa).**

There are a number of names in Chief Willie Matthews' family that pertain to wood spirits or "fairies," **skil jaadee**. These names go back to a time when one of his ancestors, searching for power, fasted for a month on a hill beside Ain (**'aay.n**) River and encountered a giant devil's-club plant. He took part of the plant as medicine and fell asleep. When he awoke, he saw a special wood spirit, or "fairy," **skil jaadee**. She was "cute" and had a baby on her back. Willie Matthews' own name, **skilda k̲'ahljuu**, meant "waiting for a fairy maid." (This story was told to me by Willie Matthews, and to Marianne Boelscher by Emma Matthews. Other versions were known to Henry Geddes and Maude Moody.)

Devil's-club, **ts'iihlinjaaw**, is the name of a town on "Hellebore Island" (Newcombe 1897). "**Tsít'lat'lints**," a round rock islet near North Island, was named after an important leader named **ts'iihlinjaaw** ('devil's-club') (Swan 1885).

## Swamp Laurel, or "Poisonous Hudson's Bay Tea"

*Kalmia microphylla* (Hook.) Heller; Heather Family (Ericaceae)
**G̲agan xil** (M) (**G̲agan** 'breathe'; probably originally **G̲agan xilG̲a**—JE)

This shrub of boggy places is sometimes called by the same name as Labrador-tea, **xil k̲agann** (M) (Newcombe 1897) or **xíl k̲agan** (A; Norton 1981) (see note under following species), although most people agree that the two plants are distinctive. Willie and Emma Matthews noted that, although it is called by the same name, swamp laurel is distinguished from Labrador-tea by being called "**xil k̲agann**-used-for-medicine," whereas Labrador-tea is called "**xil k̲agann**-used-for-tea." Swamp laurel was used as medicine alone or mixed with other plants. It must be used with great caution, however, because it is known to be toxic (Turner and von Aderkas 2009). Norton (1981) noted that Alaska Haida distinguish it from Labrador-tea because the leaves of swamp laurel point up, not down, and they call swamp laurel "**sagáang k̲'áwhlaa**" (A) ("leaves grow up"). Tea from swamp laurel is said to "make you drunk." It is known as the "poisonous Hudson's Bay tea."

**Swamp laurel.**

**Labrador-tea, showing younger and older leaves.**

## Labrador-Tea, Haida Tea, Hudson's Bay Tea

*Rhododendron groenlandicum* (Oeder) K.A. Kron & W.S. Judd; Heather Family (Ericaceae)

**x̱àaydaa tiiɢ̱a** (S) (literally 'Haida-tea'; borrowed from English "tea"); or **x̱aaydaa x̱aaw** (S); or **ḵ'using.a xilɢ̱a** (S) ('tuberculosis-leaves/medicine'; see **ḵ'using.a** 'tuberculosis') (GY, BP); or **xil ḵagann** (M), **xíl ḵagan** (A) (also applied to swamp laurel, see previous species; according to JE, **ḵagann** is a degenerative form of an adjective based on the root word **ɢ̱agan** 'breathe,' a noun meaning 'breath') (Boas 1891; Newcombe 1897; Norton 1981—A; FD, EM, WM); or **ɢ̱awaa sk'ajaaw** (M) (literally 'sticking off cylindrical or curled and furry'—JE) (WM, EM, FD)

This muskeg shrub, whose furry-backed leaves are commonly used for tea, was known to all of the present-day elders. Boas (1891) suggested that the name **xil ḵagann** translated as "mouse neck," but this meaning was considered doubtful to Florence Davidson (see notation from JE under this name). Most people called the plant "Haida tea" or "Hudson's Bay tea," a name derived from the former practice of Hudson's Bay Company traders of selling the leaves for tea. It seems likely that prior to the coming of the Hudson's Bay traders, the plant was not used by the Haida as a beverage, but only as a medicine.

Some people prefer the leaves as tea when picked in spring before the plants flower; others say they can be picked in July or August, as long as they are still young and tender and growing upright, not hanging down. Becky Pearson recalled that the leaves were formerly dried in open baskets. Nowadays, the leaves are placed in paper bags and hung over a stove or heater to dry. A handful of the dried leaves is put into a pot of water and boiled until the solution is quite dark. Sometimes the pot is left simmering at the back of the stove for up to two days; one can just help himself, and add more water as the fluid disappears. Most people prefer to drink the tea with plenty of sugar. Labrador-tea was also used medicinally by the Haida, alone or mixed with other medicinal plants. Adam Bell (personal communication to Marianne Boelscher 1980) noted that when Hudson's Bay tea has blossoms, it is used as a medicine; without blossoms, it is used as a tea.

## False Azalea

*Menziesia ferruginea* Smith; Heather Family (Ericaceae)

**ḵ'as**, **ḵ'aas** (S, M, A), **ḵ'as hlḵ'a.aay** (M), **ḵ'as xil** (M) (Newcombe 1897, 1901; FD)

Of the contemporary elders consulted, only Florence Davidson recalled the name for this deciduous forest shrub recorded by C.F. Newcombe. Florence Davidson said that berry-pickers were warned never to use the branches of false azalea to fasten down a skunk-cabbage leaf covering for a full berry basket. Twigs of almost any other shrub

**False azalea. LEFT: Showing *Exobasidium* fungus on the leaves. RIGHT: The small pinkish flowers.**

could be used for this purpose, but if false azalea sticks were used, it would bring bad luck, and the one who used it would never get plentiful berries. The name **k̲'aas** (pertaining to "ear wax") possibly relates to a fungus [*Exobasidium vaccinii* (Fuckel) Woronin] that sometimes grows on the undersides of the leaves.

Newcombe (1897, 1901) reported that the branches and stems of false azalea were frequently placed under bodies in coffins to prevent the "death virus" from spreading, or "to prevent relatives and friends from dying soon after" (Newcombe 1897). He reported instances of the plant's use at **Nansdins** (Ninstints) and at Yan, near Massett. This use was confirmed by Henry Geddes, who noted that a wood "like huckleberry, but with no berries" was put into coffins with the corpse, but he did not know why this was done. Swanton (1905a) noted that young girls at puberty were passed through a ring of **k̲'as** four times, and then the ring was left in a dry place in the woods. This is also apparently the shrub referred to by Curtis (1916) as "buckbrush," the charcoal of which was said to be used in tattooing. Curtis (1916) described a ritual using "buckbrush" similar to the one reported by Swanton: when a girl reached puberty, her mother rubbed four shoots of the "buckbrush" plant on her, then thrust them upright in elevated ground in four different places. This ritual was to induce modesty and a retiring disposition in the girl. It also reportedly eliminated underarm body odour in young women.

Thus, this rather inconspicuous shrub, lacking edible berries or spectacular flowers, was apparently attributed significant powers and was highly respected.

Young stinging nettle plants.

## Stinging Nettle

*Urtica dioica* L.; Nettle Family (Urticaceae)
Plant: **g̱udang.xaal** (S) (possibly related to **g̱uu** 'burning'), **g̱udang.aal**, **g̱udang'aal** (M), **g̱udáng.aal** (A)
Roots: **kun'aan** (S), **kun.aan** (M) (Newcombe 1901; Curtis 1916)
Nettle fibre: "**a-a'ada**" (**ahx̱ada**) (Newcombe 1897) (this term literally means 'net')

Stinging nettle is a tall, leafy herbaceous plant of rich soils, often growing in patches around village sites. It was known to all of the present-day elders, and, as well, its names were recorded by Keen (1898), Newcombe (1901), Swanton (1905b) and Curtis (1916). Nettle roots, which are long and white, were apparently eaten "raw or roasted" in the old days (Newcombe 1901; Emma Wilson, Willie Matthews, Watson Pryce). Watson Pryce recalled that the young plants were also eaten, just as they appeared above the ground, but this use may have been learned from Europeans (Turner 1995).

The white stem fibre from dried, mature nettles was formerly spun for twine and netting (Newcombe 1897). John Enrico notes that in Swanton's texts, there is a claim by the **daayuu'ahl 'laanaas** lineage, now extinct, that they were the first people to weave nettle-fibre nets on Haida Gwaii; Kathleen Hans' father knew this story (JE). Notably, according to the Skidegate elders, one name for a net full of fish is **dang** (S), apparently after nettle.

Stinging nettle was widely known up and down the coast, and throughout British Columbia and even elsewhere in North America and Europe as a "counter-irritant" treatment for rheumatism and other pains of the joints and muscles. Generally, bundles of nettles were used to beat the afflicted area. Newcombe (1897) noted: "Leaves used as a counter-irritant and to relieve pain are whipped over the affected part, the person applying the remedy guarding the hand by wrapping it in a cloth (case noticed at Skidegate June 1901)." The Haida also used stinging nettle for several other types of medicines. It is well known in European herbal medicine as a remedy for asthma and bronchial disorders.

In one story recorded by Swanton (1905b), the hero came to an old canoe on which moss and nettles were growing.

## Yarrow

*Achillea millefolium* L.; Aster Family (Asteraceae)

**xil sgunxulaa** (S), **xil sgun.ulaa** (M) ('fragrant leaves/medicine') (also apparently used for beach-tansy, *Tanacetum huronense* and beach wormwood, *Ambrosia chamissonis*) (BP); or **kuuga k'u'inda** (S) (literally 'short rocks'—JE) (Newcombe 1901; Swanton—**guga k'u'aanda**); or "**xIlskIuwa**" (**xil sk'yaawaa** 'tail-leaves') (S, M) (Newcombe 1901); or **sk'yaw hlk'a.aay** (M) ('tail-branches/plant') (WM, EM); or **kamkamm**, or **k'u kamm**, or **ts'ats'a k'u kamm** (M) (see **ts'ats'a** 'carrot,' **kémdelaa** 'something fine'; a reduced form of the verb, perhaps **k'u kamnanang** 'chew up fine'; **kam** is a classifier meaning 'many-small pieces'—JE) ('carrot-something-soft'; Percy Brown notes that these names refer to the stem only—JE) (M, A) (FD; Newcombe 1898—"**dsits kokama**"; Keen 1898)

**Yarrow, an aromatic plant.**

**Beach-tansy ('sloppy yellow leaves on the beach').**

This greyish aromatic plant with finely divided leaves and flat-topped clusters of white flowers was known to all of the elders I consulted, but many different names were applied to it, both by them and by Newcombe (1898, 1901). In addition, George Young referred to it as **yaanaang xilg̱a** (S) ('fog/leaves/medicine'), a name he also gave to horsetail (*Equisetum*) and club-moss (*Lycopodium*), although he was careful to note that these are different plants, despite being called by the same name. Emma Matthews on one occasion called it **tsàa.u ts'áagwaal** (M) ('beach-fern').

Amanda Edgars recalled that the Naden Harbour people at Kung used to pull the leaves off the stiff stems and string butter clams on them for smoke-drying. The plants imparted an excellent flavour to the clams, which were stored on the stems, then eaten later from them. The aromatic oils of the plant may also have had some preservative properties.

Yarrow roots and leaves were used medicinally by the Haida, as by other First Peoples. Yarrow is also well known in European herbal medicine, where it is used to stop bleeding and to help wounds heal, as well as to treat toothaches.

Beach wormwood ('fragrant leaves/ medicine').

## Beach Wormwood, or Sand-Bur Ragweed and its Relatives

*Ambrosia chamissonis* (Less.) Greene; Aster Family (Asteraceae)
**sk̲'iina xil** (S) (see **sk̲'in** 'gull'—JE) (Newcombe 1897, 1901); or **xil sk'yaawaa** (M) (see **sk̲'iinaay**, **sk̲'iinee**; **sk'yaawaa** 'have a tail') (Newcombe 1897, 1901; Keen 1898); or **xil sgunx̲ulaa** (S), **xil sgun.ulaa** (M) ('fragrant leaves/ medicine') (probably mainly applied to beach-tansy, *Tanacetum huronense*) (GY)

Beach wormwood was used medicinally by Haida.

Yellow beach-tansy (*Tanacetum huronense* Nutt.), a related plant, was called by a similar name (**xil sgunx̲ulaa**—'fragrant leaves/medicine') by Newcombe (1901). Florence Davidson described the plant in a phrase, **tsàa.u salii xil k'anhlahl jahjuu** (M) (literally 'sloppy yellow leaves/medicine on the beach'; see **tsàa.u salii** 'beach,' **xil** 'leaves/medicine,' **k'anhlahl** 'yellow' and **jahjuu** 'sloppy'). She said simply, "They call it how it looks." Emma Matthews identified it by another descriptive phrase; **tsàa.us k̲'un saagulee** (M) ('beach-fern'), because of its finely divided leaves.

Pineappleweed (*Matricaria matricarioides* [Less.] Porter), another aromatic plant in the aster family, has been used recently by some Kaigani people to make a herbal tea (Norton 1981).

## Alumroot

*Heuchera chlorantha* Piper; Saxifrage Family (Saxifragaceae)
**xu'aji xilG̲a**, **xuuajii xilG̲a** (S), **xuu.uj xilee** (M) (literally 'grizzly-bear's leaves/ medicine') (Newcombe 1897, 1901; EM, BP)

The names and original identity of this herbaceous perennial plant of rocky cliffs were provided by Newcombe (1897, 1901), who noted that the leaves were used for medicine, mixed with another type of plant. Becky Pearson had heard of the name, but did not know to which plant it referred. Emma Matthews described "grizzly-bear leaves" as a plant somewhat like broad-leaved plantain (*Plantago major*), but with differently shaped leaves, and growing in the muskeg. This is not a usual habitat for alumroot, so she must be referring to another type of plant.

## Wild Cress

*Cardamine angulata* Hook.; Mustard Family (Brassicaceae)
**G̲aagan xil** (S), **G̲agan xilee** (M) (possibly 'breath leaves') (Newcombe 1897, 1901; Curtis 1916:139)

Newcombe (1897) described this as a plant growing "by springs and water-courses," and generally distributed, an assessment confirmed by Calder and Taylor (1968), who note that it is relatively rare on the Pacific Coast outside of Haida Gwaii. It was used medicinally by the Haida, both for treating ailments and for bringing good luck to sea hunters.

Western bitter cress.

## Western Bitter Cress

*Cardamine oligosperma* Nutt.; Mustard Family (Brassicaceae)
**danhl xil** (S), **danhlaa xilee** (M) (literally 'medicine for swelling'—JE) (Newcombe 1897)

Yet another, very small flower, western bitter cress was named **danhlaa** (M, A) by Newcombe (1901) and **danhlaa xilee** (M) by Keen (1898). This small annual was noted as a probable Haida medicine by Reverend Keen (as cited by Newcombe 1897).

Fireweed.

## Fireweed

*Epilobium angustifolium* L.; Evening-primrose Family (Onagraceae)
**tl'laal(-xil)** (S), **tl'ii'aal** (**-xil**) (M), **tl'íi.aal** (A) (Norton 1981)

This tall, leafy plant with pointed clusters of reddish-purple flowers is well known to the Haida. Its names were also recorded by Newcombe (1897, 1901) and Keen (1898). In spring Haida women and girls used to gather large quantities of fireweed shoots, along with new branches of "briar" (wild rose or, more likely, salmonberry). They peeled and chewed them to purify their blood and "make them handsome" (Harrison 1925). Haida men also ate the peeled stems, often with sugar and grease [**t'aaw** (S)]. They are considered to be a good tonic, and somewhat laxative; they help to "move stuff around one's insides." The usual method of eating the shoots is to split them lengthwise with the thumbnail, sprinkle sugar over them, then pull off the tender inside part with the bottom teeth (George Young, Maude and Agnes Moody, Gertrude Kelly; Newcombe 1897). Kathleen Hans recalled that "high class" people used to own patches of fireweed, and permission had to be asked from them before people could harvest shoots from these patches. Recently, among the Kaigani, fireweed shoots are considered to be children's food and are mainly eaten by them (Norton 1981). Chittenden (1884) said that fireweed roots were also eaten.

When the stems were eaten, the outer fibrous skins were saved. Later, they were soaked in water and spun to make twine and fishing nets (Chief Willie Matthews, George Young). Newcombe (1897) also noted the manufacture of cordage from fireweed stem fibres: "From the fibrous skin or bark after the outer layer had been got rid of by prolonged immersion in water, a string used to be spun, which was afterward made into nets" (Newcombe 1897). The dried, partly processed stems were called "**k'lialk̲ak̲uu**" [possibly **tl'ii.aal**- with suffix] (M), and the prepared fibre, **tl'ii.aal k̲'al** (M). A seine net of fireweed fibre was called **tl'ii.aal 'àade**e (M). Swanton (1905b:74) recorded a story told by Edward in which the Food-giving-town women made nets of fireweed "bark" (identified only as **ll'aal** by Swanton).

Fireweed "roots" (rhizomes) were used medicinally by the Haida. Newcombe (1897) reported that another, related species, willowherb (*Epilobium glandulosum* Lehm.; syn. *Epilobium watsonii* Barbey) was used as a medicine.

The reddish-purple flowers of fireweed are called **tl'ii.aal x̲illee/x̲ilayee** (M), and the seed fluff is called **tl'laal hltaanawa** (S) or **tl'ii.aal hltan.uwee** (M) (literally 'fireweed-down feathers'). According to Swanton (1905a:60), a game called "a Woman's Pubic Bones" employed fireweed ["a slim plant called **ll'aal**"] stalks as items wagered.

## Hedge Nettle

*Stachys chamissonis* var. *cooleyae* Benth. (A. Heller) G. Mulligan & D. Munro; Mint Family (Lamiaceae)

**x̲udaan**, **xudaan** (S, M) (Newcombe 1901, from Swanton; WP, GK, AE, FD, Dora Brooks)

There is some uncertainty about the identification of the plant(s) called **x̲udaan**. The name, "**húdang**" was also applied by Newcombe (1897, 1901) to self-heal (*Prunella vulgaris* L.), another, shorter plant of the mint family, but Watson Pryce rejected this identification. Florence Davidson's description of the plant called **x̲udaan** also fits hedge nettle better than self-heal: a tall, shade-loving plant with a single, thin celery-like talk, growing under salmonberry bushes. She said that in the old days, Haida children chewed the stems and sucked the juice. According to John Enrico, Harrison (manuscript dictionary) noted that **x̲udaan** has a flower "the shape of a halibut [**x̲aagu** (S)]." This description could apply to the lower part of the hedge nettle blossom, but more likely refers to the elliptical leaves.

**Left: Hedge nettle.**

**Right: Bedstraw.**

### Bedstraw, or Cleavers

*Galium aparine* L.; Madder Family (Rubiaceae)

**ts'ahl t'awsgiid**, **ts'ahl t'awsgid**, or **ts'ahl t'awt'iis** (S), **ts'ahl t'awsgiid**, **ts'ahl t'uusgiid** (M), **ts'ahl t'áwsgad** (A) (all literally 'its-seeds-stick-to-you'; see classifier **t'aw**, **t'uu**, describing "seeds"—JE); or **xil ts'ahlsgidaa** (S) (GY only)

This scrambling herbaceous plant is common along the upper shoreline of Haida Gwaii, in the driftwood zone. It has elongated leaves in whorls along the stem, and small, round "burrs." The burrs, and the entire plant, are very "sticky" due to the presence of small hooked hairs on the stems, leaves and fruits. The plant was recognized by all of the present-day elders, and the names were also recorded by Newcombe (1901). No uses were reported for it, however.

**Dried fruiting plant of *Nicotiana quadrivalvis*, the closest known relative to the original Haida tobacco, grown in 2003 by Jaalen Edenshaw, from seeds contributed by Donn Todt of Ashland, Oregon.**

## Haida Tobacco

*Nicotiana quadrivalvis* Pursh var. *multivalvis* (Lindl.) Mansf.; Nightshade Family (Solanaceae)

**gul**, **guul** (S, M), **gúl** (A) (applies to both Haida tobacco and commercial tobacco); or **x̱aayda gulG̱a** (S), **x̱àadas gulaa** (M), **x̱aadas guláa** (A) ('Haida-tobacco'); or **skil t'aaxul** (S)

Names for tobacco, both the original and commercial types, were reported by Dawson (1880), Newcombe (1897, 1898, 1901), Boas (1891), Swanton (1905b) and Curtis (1916). They were also known to most of the present-day elders, although none had had the opportunity to see the original Haida tobacco.

The identity and fate of "Haida tobacco" has been one of the most perplexing and intriguing problems in Northwest Coast ethnobotany. It is one of the few clear-cut examples of aboriginal plant domestication within the Northwest Coast culture area. It is also a rare example of the use of a narcotic plant by Northwest Coast peoples. Much has been written about the plant. It is prominent in Haida narratives, and although the last reported cultivation of it was nearly 120 years ago, most of the elders, as of the 1970s, still knew of it, and some had even heard stories of its origin.

The "mystery" of Haida tobacco is discussed by Turner and Taylor (1972) and Meilleur (1979). The earliest written report of its use was made in 1787 by Beresford, an anonymous chronicler of Dixon's voyage. He stated that the people of Yakutat Bay (Tlingit) were fond of chewing a plant "which appears to be a species of tobacco" and that they mixed it with lime and the inner bark of pine. Various other explorers provided accounts of a kind of tobacco that was cultivated by the Haida, which was not smoked, but rather chewed with burnt shells (Turner and Taylor 1972). Before use, the "tobacco" leaves were dried on a framework over a fire, finely bruised with a stone mortar and pressed into cakes. They were then mixed with a little lime from the burnt clam shells and chewed or held in the cheek. Stone mortars were used solely for grinding tobacco (Dawson 1880). Commercial chewing and smoking tobacco imported by the fur traders gradually gained dominance over the indigenous tobacco, until by the late 1800s its cultivation ceased altogether, and the indigenous tobacco apparently became extinct. According to Dawson (1880) and Swan (1885), one old woman grew it at Cumshewa up to the 1880s. It was also commonly grown at Skedans, according to Henry Brown, one of the Haida men consulted by C.F. Newcombe (1897).

According to Henry Brown, the seed pod was about the size of a bean, but quite round. It contained a number of small seeds. These were planted at the end of April, at the same time as potatoes. One pod was placed on each small hill of earth, as in planting potatoes. At the beginning of September, the plants were harvested and cured by drying, and at this time the grower would put rotten wood in the ground to enrich the soil for the next year. Henry Brown said that abalone shells [**G̱aalG̱ahlyan** (S)] were burned, then put into water to yield a fine, floury substance, the "lime" that

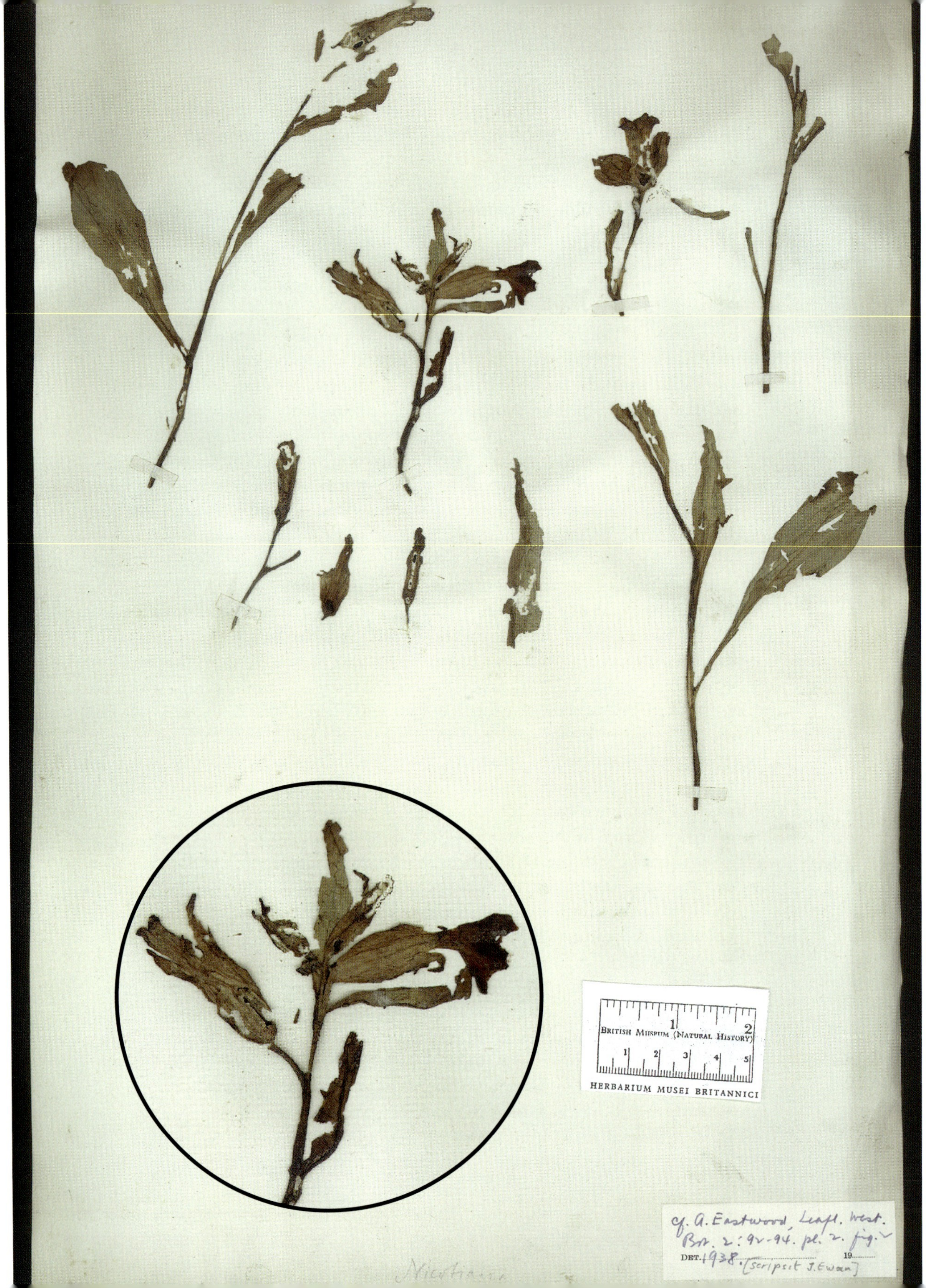
BRITISH MUSEUM (NATURAL HISTORY)
HERBARIUM MUSEI BRITANNICI
cf. A. Eastwood, Leafl. West. Bot. 2: 92-94. pl. 2. fig. 2
DET. 1938. [scripsit J. Ewan] 19

**OPPOSITE PAGE: Photograph of last remaining specimen of Haida tobacco, labelled "Nicotiana," in the collection of the British Museum, London [BM000815987] (with inset, closeup of flower); notation on the back reads "Queen Charlotte Islands on the Northwest Coast of America. Capt. Dixon. Used by the inhabitants as Tobacco." –PHOTOS BY ROBIN SMITH**

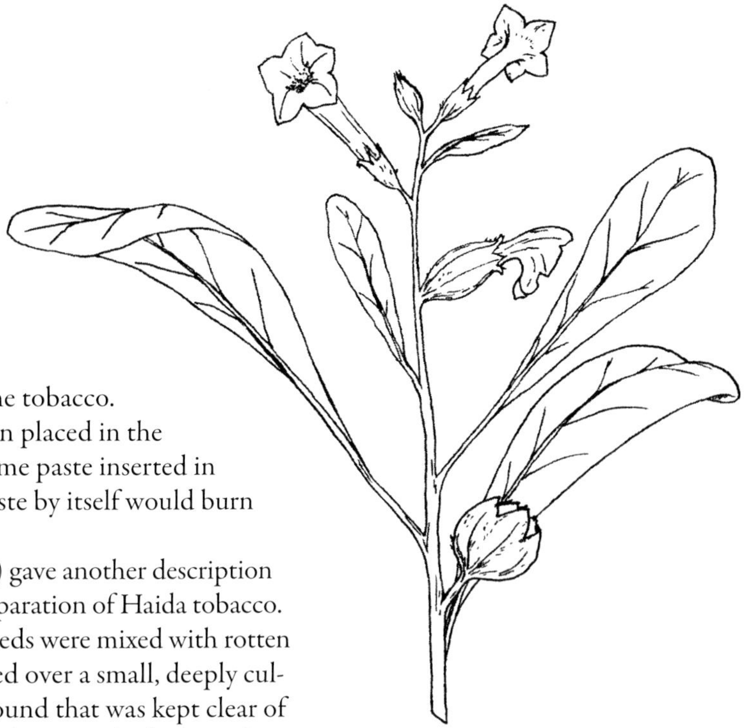

**RIGHT: Artist's reconstruction of Haida tobacco based on Captain Dixon's collection, as well as photos and collections (including one at the Royal Botanic Gardens herbarium at Kew, made by David Douglas near the mouth of the Columbia River in 1829) of *Nicotiana quadrivalvis*, its closest known relative. –DRAWING BY SARAH E. TURNER**

was chewed with the tobacco. It was stored separately from the tobacco. The latter was then placed in the mouth, and the lime paste inserted in the centre; the paste by itself would burn the mouth.

Curtis (1916) gave another description of the use and preparation of Haida tobacco. In planting, the seeds were mixed with rotten wood and scattered over a small, deeply cultivated plot of ground that was kept clear of weeds. The plants (apparently the leaves) were harvested when they were a foot high, and were tied in bundles. In 1850, five bundles of leaves were sold for a $5 blanket [**gyáad** (S)]. The shells were prepared by wrapping them in spruce bark and steaming them overnight. They were then crushed, roasted and mixed with mashed tobacco leaves and stems. They were chewed, never smoked. Some people even kept a wad of leaves in their mouths overnight.

Swanton (1905b) recorded several Haida narratives referring to Haida tobacco and indicating its power. In one told by John Sky, He-Who-Was-Born-from-His-Mother's-Side came to some people shooting leaves off a tall tree and eating the leaves that fell. The hero shot an arrow at the tree itself, causing it to fall, then collected the "eggs of the tree." These were later planted to form the source of this plant (p. 233). In another story, the hero laid tobacco and calcined shells beside beached killer whales. The whales took these materials and, with them, were able to get back to the ocean (p. 296).

Tobacco apparently belonged originally to the Eagle clan, because **X̲uya** (S) [Raven] obtained the seeds from his cousin **G̲ud** [Eagle], and distributed them. Tobacco "seeds" (probably seed pods) were often used in stories to bribe or reward people because they were so "sweet" (Tom Stevens, in Swanton 1905b:54) or to give power (p. 245). They were a common gift and trade item. White Inlet originally got its name because **X̲uya**'s sister, **Siwaas**, planted tobacco in front of the inlet, but she prepared calcined shells before it was ready to chew, so she threw them out, making the rocks white (Walter McGregor, in Swanton 1905b:137). A town at the mouth of a river flowing into Dixon Entrance at the base of Tow Hill was called Tobacco-Drying-Town, according to Isaac of Those-Born-at-**hl'yaalang** (Swanton 1908b:754).

**Jaalen Edenshaw with his daughter Haana, holding the tobacco (*N. quadrivalvis*) he grew from seed.**

### How Tobacco First Came to Haida Gwaii

Long ago the Indians [first people or ancient people, **tlldluu x̲àadaG̲aay**, or more contemporary equivalent **tllsdaa x̲àaydaG̲aay**—JE] had no tobacco and one plant only existed, growing somewhere far inland in the interior of the Stickeen country. This plant was caused to grow by the deity, and was like a tree, very large and tall. With a bow and arrows a man shot at its summit, where the seed was, and at last brought down one or two seeds, which he carried away, carefully preserved, and sowed the following spring. From the plants thus procured all the tobacco afterward cultivated sprung. (Dawson 1880:152)

**Note:** This is similar to the version from the story *He-Who-Was-Born-from-His-Mother's-Side,* told by John Sky (Swanton 1905b:233).

**Descendant of original tobacco plant grown by Jaalen Edenshaw on display at K̲ay Llnagaay.**
—PHOTO BY SEAN YOUNG

## "Haida Flowers"

*(See also the flowering plants in the previous categories, as well as yellow pond-lily under Freshwater Aquatic Plants; the plants in this section are known particularly for their flowers.)*

Many types of flowering plants were simply called **x̱aaydaa hlaawersG̱a**, **x̱aaydaa hlaawersgaay** (S) ("Haida flowers"; borrowed from English) if one could not recall any more specific name, especially if the plant had no particular use. Although the term **x̱aaydaa hlaawersgaay** is not traditional, it represents adaptation of language and taxonomy that is of definite interest to those who want to better understand how languages evolve. The category of Haida flowers is somewhat of a "catch-all" in this regard (see Turner 1974, for a description of this category). Examples of some plants classified as "Haida flowers" are provided in the following table.

**Table 2.** Examples of "Haida flowers" (**x̱aaydaa hlaawersG̱a**) identified by George Young (GY) and/or Maude Moody (MM) and/or Emma Wilson (EW) of Skidegate. Some are also known by more specific names to other people.

| **Common Name (*Scientific Name*)** | **Source** |
|---|---|
| Yarrow (*Achillea millefolium*) | MM |
| Beach wormwood (*Ambrosia chamissonis*) | GY |
| Kinnikinnick (*Arctostaphylos uva-ursi*) | MM |
| Goatsbeard (*Aruncus dioicus*) | MM |
| Sea rocket (*Cakile edentulata*) | MM |
| Blue harebell (*Campanula rotundifolia*) | MM |
| Lambsquarters (*Chenopodium album*) | GY |
| Coralroot (*Corallorhiza maculata*) | MM |
| Sundew (*Drosera rotundifolia*) | MM |
| Crowberry (*Empetrum nigrum*) | MM |
| Bedstraw (*Galium aparine*) | MM |
| Large-leaved avens (*Geum macrophyllum*) | GY |
| Swamp laurel (*Kalmia microphylla*) | MM |
| Twinflower (*Linnaea borealis*) | MM |
| Beach lupine (*Lupinus littoralis*) | MM |
| Silverweed (*Potentilla egedii*) | GY |
| Selfheal (*Prunella vulgaris*) | EW |

CONTINUED ...

"Haida flowers" (**x̲aaydaa hlaawersg̲a**).

**Left:** Large-leaved avens (*Geum macrophyllum*).

**Right:** Arctic starflower (*Trientalis arctica*).

**Table 2** (continued)

| Common Name (*Scientific Name*) | Source |
|---|---|
| Buttercup (*Ranunculus acris*) | MM |
| Nootka wild rose (*Rosa nutkana*) | MM |
| Blue-eyed grass (*Sisrynchium littorale*) | MM |
| Hedge-nettle (*Stachys chamissonis* var. *cooleyae*) | MM |
| Twisted-stalk (*Streptopus amplexifolius*) | MM |
| Waxberry (*Symphoricarpos albus*) | MM |
| Foamflower (*Tiarella trifoliata*) | MM |
| Youth-on-age (*Tolmeia menziesii*) | MM |
| False asphodel (*Triantha glutinosa*) | MM |
| Arctic starflower (*Trientalis arctica* ) | MM |
| White clover (*Trifolium repens*) | MM |

## Calypso, or False Ladyslipper

*Calypso bulbosa* (L.) Oakes; Orchid Family (Orchidaceae)
**sk̲il taawaatllx̲aay, sk̲il taawaatl'x̲aay** (S), **sk̲il taw, sk̲il tuu** (M), **sk̲íidaw** (A) ('black-cod grease') (GY, FD; Newcombe 1901)

The small, whitish corms of this beautiful purple-flowered forest orchid were eaten raw (Florence Davidson) or boiled and eaten like northern riceroot bulbs (*Fritillaria camschatcensis*) (Newcombe 1901). Black cod grease, after which the plant is named, is a prized food and is said to be "as white as butter," in Florence Davidson's words. The corms of this plant have the same colour and consistency

Calypso.

(George Young). Florence Davidson recalled that Massett girls used to eat the corms to give them a good figure. (According to Swanton (1905a), a girl at puberty should eat only black cod for four years. Other fish, if eaten by a pubescent girl, would become scarce.) Nowadays, with wildflowers being threatened by logging and development, calypso's use as food is probably not justified.

A tiny relative of calypso is a minute bog orchid, *Malaxis paludosa* (L.) Sw., which most of the elders did not recognize, but Emma Matthews remembered it from her times in the muskeg picking cranberries, and said it was called **G̲asàa** (M), **G̲asaa** (A). On another occasion, she applied this name to another bog plant, deer cabbage (*Fauria crista-galli* [Menzies] Makino). She said the name means "what deer eat," and said that the plant was used medicinally. Another plant known to Emma Matthews from her berry-picking times in the muskeg is Canada burnet (*Sanguisorba canadensis* L.). She knew of no use for it.

Newcombe (1901) tentatively attributed the name "**hlunhit**" (**hlunxid**) (not known to JE) to wild geranium (*Geranium richardsonii* Fisch. & Trautv.), but this term is similar to the name he used for Siberian miner's-lettuce (*Claytonia sibirica*) (see entry for that plant).

The English word "flowers" in its "Haida-ized" form, "**x̲aaydaa hlaawersG̲a**" (S) or **hlaawersgee** (M), is commonly used for any type of wild or garden flower. For example, Florence Davidson used the name **sk̲'in hlaawersgee** (M) ('seagull's flowers') for wild violets growing on the beach (*Viola adunca*) (see also next entry). Later, in an interview with JE, she said the name did not refer to beach violet, but could not recall to which plant it did refer.

There are other anglicized plant terms, or translation borrowings applied to flowers. Emma Matthews gave a Haida name meaning "don't-forget-me-leaves/medicine" (**gumdi jiik̲iis gedans xilaiyu**) to forget-me-not flowers (*Myosotis laxa* Lehm.), and also to butterwort (*Pinguicula vulgaris* L.), a small bog plant. She would use the name for "any little blue flowers they didn't have names for."

## Blue Harebell and Red Columbine: "Rain Flowers"

*Campanula rotundifolia* L.; Campanula Family (Campanulaceae)
*Aquilegia formosa* Fisch.; Buttercup Family (Ranunculaceae)

"Blue rain flowers": blue harebell.

Both of these flowers were called **dall** (plant—**dall-xil**) (M) ['rain(-leaves/medicine')] by Florence Davidson. She noted that if one wanted to distinguish between them, blue harebell, with its sky-blue, bell-like flowers could be called **dall-G̲uhlahl** (or **dall-xil-G̲uhlahl**) (M) ('blue-rain-leaves/medicine'), and red columbine, with its intricate scarlet and yellow flowers, could be called **dall-sG̲id** (or **dall-xil-sG̲id**) (M) ('red-rain-leaves/medicine'). Both of these were also simply called **x̲aaydaa hlaawersG̲a** (S) ('Haida flowers') by many people. Newcombe (1901) recorded the name "**kalaxilG̲a**" (**k̲'al.aa xilee**) (M) ('muskeg flowers') for blue harebell. Red columbine, which was seen by Newcombe (1897) at Skedans and Tasu, and noted as "plentiful on shores of west coast inlets," was called **daal sgilG̲a** (S) ('rain's belly button') by Watson Pryce and Becky Pearson, and **t'iis hlk̲'a.aay** (M) ('rock-branches/plant') by Emma Matthews.

Other flower names similar to those of blue harebell and red columbine were applied to shooting star (probably *Dodecatheon jeffreyi* Van Houtte, the more common of the two species in Haida Gwaii). Newcombe (1901) lists its names as **dall sgilG̲a**, **dall xilG̲a** (JE). Although he translates both as "navel flower," they seem to be versions of 'rain's belly-button/navel' and 'rain-leaves/medicine.' He collected it ("*Dodecatheon*") at Limestone Islands (April 28, 1901), as well as seeing it on the west coast and at Skincuttle a month later. Yet another "rain flower" reported by Newcombe (1897, 1901) is violet, including wild blue violet (*Viola adunca* Smith) and yellow violet (*Viola glabella* Nutt.), both recorded as "**dall sgi**," without a translation [**daal sgii** 'rain's belly-button']. Newcombe gave no use for either shooting star or the violets. Florence Davidson included shooting star as a kind of **dall xil**, but not violets. However, she told John Enrico that **dall** refers to "any kind of flowers growing on rocks."

Florence Davidson recalled that in the old days, children were warned not to pick, transplant or even touch any of the "rain flowers," especially during the spring seaweed harvest, or they would cause rainstorms and prevent the seaweed from drying.

**Siberian miner's lettuce.**
–PHOTO BY ROBIN BABIUK

## Siberian Miner's Lettuce

*Claytonia sibirica* (L.) Howell; Miner's Lettuce Family (Montiaceae; formerly in Portulacaceae)

**hlk'uux̲aay** (S) (Newcombe 1897; KH; JE); or **hlk'ung.iid**, **hlk'ungiid** (M) (Swan 1885; Newcombe 1897; FD; JE); or **tl'aangk̲'uus xil** (S) (Newcombe 1901); or "**lkanatxil**" (Newcombe 1901); or "**lhk!uñx.il**" (S), "**lhkunetxil**" (M); or **'ankos** "village plantain" (Newcombe 1897).

Swan (1885) and Newcombe (1897, 1901) stated that the succulent lower parts of the stem ("roots"—Newcombe 1897) were eaten with eulachon grease [**t'aaw** (S)], although most of the present-day elders had not heard of this use, nor did they offer any special names for this plant. Newcombe (1897) noted, "Root eaten after roasting on hot stone." This notation represents the only suggestion I have encountered of the roots of Siberian miner's lettuce having been used as food on the Northwest Coast. Newcombe identified it only as "*Claytonia*" (*Montia* is a synonym). There are only three species of *Claytonia* /*Montia* on Haida Gwaii (Calder and Taylor 1968). John Enrico noted that in the Provincial Archives of British Columbia Newcombe papers is a letter to Dr. Newcombe from J.K. Small of the New York Botanical Garden, dated July 1903, in which a plant specimen sent by Newcombe to Small was identified by the latter as "*Montia sibirica* [ssp.] *bulbifera*." This would seem to be the subspecies referred to by Newcombe in his notes. There are still a few questions. This subspecies was not reported by Calder and Taylor (1968). Furthermore, George Young and Watson Pryce both denied that the plant they knew as **hlk'uu<u>x</u>aay** (S) was Siberian miner's lettuce. They stated that **hlk'uu<u>x</u>aay** (S) was a small plant growing on the west coast of Haida Gwaii, in mountainous areas on scree slopes. They said that plants were boiled and eaten, that the leaves were small and that there were no noticeable flowers or berries. They, and Becky Pearson, said that **hlk'uu<u>x</u>aay** was highly valued as a food in the old days.

Kathleen Hans, however, identified **hlk'uu<u>x</u>aay** as Siberian miner's lettuce from a photograph of the flowers (JE). When this information is added to the letter received by Newcombe, confirming his specimen as "*Montia* [now *Claytonia*] *sibirica* [ssp.] *bulbifera*," one must conclude that this is a likely identification, unless it is an unreported species of tuberous *Claytonia*. Florence Davidson recalled the plant **hlk'ung.iid** only from eating the root; she did not remember the plant (JE).

The second Skidegate name given by Newcombe (1901) is the same as that of western dock or "wild rhubarb" (*Rumex aquaticus* var. *fenestratus*), discussed previously. Perhaps Newcombe was confusing the identity of these two plants. A similar name to the others was given on another occasion for wild geranium (*Geranium richardsonii*) by Newcombe.

## Buttercups and Other "Yellow Flowers"

*Ranunculus acris* L., *Ranunculus occidentalis* Nutt. and other *Ranunculus* species of the Buttercup Family (Ranunculaceae); and other types of yellow-flowered plants

**xil k'anhlahl** (**hl<u>k</u>'a.aay**) (M) ['yellow(-leaves)-plant/branches'; a descriptive phrase only—JE] (FD, EM)

This name, or variants of it, was applied generally to any kind of yellow flowers, but especially to buttercups, including both indigenous and introduced species (Florence Davidson, Emma Matthews). Florence Davidson said if one wanted to be more specific about the type of yellow flower, she could describe where it was growing. George Young also implied that there was one, general name for "all the yellow stuff growing on **<u>k</u>'an**," but could not recall the term (**<u>k</u>'an** usually pertains to grasses and grass-like plants, as well as hay, but seems to refer in this context to

**Western buttercup.**

flower stalks, or perhaps grassy meadows). Gertrude Kelly, too, recalled that there were "a lot of yellow flowers up home [Skidegate] we used to talk about."

Buttercups were known to be poisonous and irritating to the skin. As Florence Davidson said, "**xil k'anhlahls poisen gáageng**" ('buttercups are poisonous'; note borrowed English term "poison"). They, and various other plants of the buttercup family, are widely used as counter-irritants in Indigenous medicine (see Turner 1984). The Haida used the pulverized, moistened seeds of western buttercup (*Ranunculus occidentalis*) and probably other species, as a rubefacient, to intentionally blister the skin (Newcombe 1897, 1901). The name for these pulverized seeds, **doctor** ("**daktaa**") **xil<u>g</u>a** (S), **doctor xilee** (M) (Keen 1898; BP, WP; JE; Newcombe 1897 [H. Edenshaw, Reverend J.H. Keen], 1901), incorporating the English word "doctor," may indicate a recent origin for this medicine. Becky Pearson referred to **daktaa xil<u>g</u>a** as "an 'ugly,' nondescript weed used for medicine."

Newcombe also recorded names for western buttercup plants (*Ranunculus occidentalis*), but gave no analysis of the terms: "**sahildjigai**" (M) (Newcombe 1897), **saahldajiigaay** (N—from Tom Price; apparently unanalyzable—JE) (Newcombe 1897, 1901). He also mentioned a Skidegate name for a kind of name for a kind of buttercup, "**xilskutsklan**" (or **xil k'ud tl'an**—JE; literally 'plant that sucks') ("milk stalks") [note: "milk" is **tl'an'u**, a nominalization—JE], but gave no further details. John Enrico suggests that such a name would more likely apply to a latex-producing plant such as dandelion (*Taraxacum officinale*); see entry for that plant. Newcombe also noted that the small-flowered buttercup (*Ranunculus uncinatus* D. Don, "*Ranunculus tenellus*") was called by the same name as *R. occidentalis*.

Other plants of the buttercup family, including marsh-marigold (*Caltha biflora* DC.), coptis, or fairy lamp-posts (*Coptis asplenifolia* Salisb.) and monkshood (*Aconitum delphiniifolium* DC.), were noted by Newcombe (1901) as having been asked about but not named or used as far as he could determine. Boas (1891) applied the name **xil gii dlagang** (M) ('medicine above swim'; i.e., 'floating leaves/medicine') to marsh-marigold, but this name is generally applied to "water-lily," or yellow pond-lily (*Nuphar polysepala*), and probably represents a mistaken identification by Boas.

## Large-leaved Avens

*Geum macrophyllum* Willd.; Rose Family (Rosaceae) (see p. 170 for illustration)

This yellow-flowered herbaceous plant would probably belong in the class of "yellow flowers," as discussed previously, but it was given a distinct name, **gaaluuga k'uu** (S), by Newcombe (1897, 1901), who noted that the roots were used externally as a medicine.

## Heart-leaved Arnica

*Arnica cordifolia* Hook.; Aster Family (Asteraceae)
"**Hit haua:c**" (see **xil x̲awaas** 'liquid, **wet'** plus present tense **-s**—JE) (A) (Boas 1891)

This is another yellow-flowered plant, for which the only information available was provided by Boas (1891). He noted that the Tlingit called this plant "town on medicine," but the meaning of the Haida name is not known.

Hairy cinquefoil.

## Hairy Cinquefoil

*Potentilla villosa* Pall. ex Pursh; Rose Family (Rosaceae)
**t'iisgu skaahlln** (S) ('small round thing up on rock outcrop'—JE) (Newcombe 1897; Swanton—JE)

Newcombe (1897, 1901) mentioned no use for this silvery-leaved, yellow-flowered plant, but noted that it was common on rocky shorelines; his names evidently pertain to the rocky habitat of the plant.

Yellow monkeyflower.

## Yellow Monkeyflower

*Mimulus guttatus* DC.; Lopseed Family (Phrymaceae; formerly in Scrophulariaceae)
**sG̲aal ts'iit'iisG̲a**, **sG̲aal tsit'iisgu**, **sG̲aal chiit'iisguu** (S) ('bee's-coat/jacket') (Newcombe 1897, 1901; WP), or **sG̲aal hlaawersG̲a** (S) ('bee-flowers'; borrowed from English "flowers") (GY, MM, AM); or possibly **xil 'ang dan tiidaals** (M) ('climbing-leaves/medicine') (EM)

The meaning of the first term, originally reported by Newcombe (1901), was somewhat obscured by his notation of "yellow jacket" beside it, a term confounded by the inclusion of "jacket" in the name for the insect and in the Haida name for this flower. Actually, the name, **sG̲aal**, translates as "bee," or possibly "bumblebee," and the name for "coat/jacket" seems merely coincidental and unrelated to the "jacket" of "yellow jacket" wasp. Several Skidegate elders knew of the association between monkeyflower and bees, but only Watson Pryce knew of the original name, 'bee's-jacket.' The name given by Emma Matthews, 'climbing leaves/medicine,' was not known to Florence Davidson, and may have actually pertained to another plant, since monkeyflower is not a vine and does not really "climb." No uses were reported for monkeyflower.

**Bull thistle.**

## Bull Thistle

*Cirsium brevistylum* Cronq.; Aster Family (Asteraceae)
**gul 'awga** (S) ('tobacco's mother') (WP, GY)

George Young commented that "there is some kind of tobacco medicine in the name [for thistle]," but did not know how the name originated or of any use for the plant, apparently introduced to Haida Gwaii. Becky Pearson recognized the name, but said that it was just "a weed." The name may be general for any thistle.

## Dandelion

*Taraxacum officinale* Weber; Aster Family (Asteraceae)

This common introduced flower is known by its English name. George Young noted that the white latex from the stems could be used to remove warts. The stems are broken and the latex applied directly to a wart, and the process is repeated over many days until the wart disappears. Kathleen Hans confirmed this use (JE) (see note on "milk stalks" under buttercups). Other First Peoples also know of the use of dandelion latex to remove warts.

---

# "Grassy Plants"

Grasses and grass-like plants, as well as hay, are generally called **k'an** (S, M), **k'án** (A). Although many different types were recognized, the elders I consulted generally did not distinguish different grasses by name, but only, if necessary, by description. Species discussed and given this name include: several sedges (*Carex canescens* L., *Carex laeviculmis* Meinsh., *Carex lenticularis* Michx., *Carex mertensii* Prescott, *Carex obnupta* Bailey and *Carex pauciflora* Lightf.); other members of the sedge family (Cyperaceae) (*Eleocharis macrostachya* Britt. and the cotton-grasses *Eriophorum angustifolium* Honck. and *Eriophorum chamissonis* C.A. Meyer ex Ledeb.); members of the rush family (Juncaceae) (*Juncus articulatus* L., *Juncus bufonius** L., *Juncus effusus* L., *Juncus ensifolius* Wikstr., *Juncus falcatus* E. Meyer, *Luzula multiflora* [Retz.] Lejeune, *Luzula parviflora* [Ehrh.] Desv.); arrow-grass or salt-grass, in the arrow-grass family (Juncaginaceae) (*Triglochin maritima* L.); false asphodel (*Triantha glutinosa* [Michx.] Baker), in the lily family (Liliaceae); and the true grasses, both native and introduced, in the grass family (Poaceae) (e.g., *Agrostis aequivalvis* [Trin.] Trin., *Agrostis palustris* Huds., *Alopecurus geniculatus** L.,

*Ammophila arenaria** (L.) Link., *Dactylis glomerata** L., *Deschampsia caespitosa* (L.) Beauv., *Elymus hirsutus* Presl., *Glyceria occidentalis* (Piper) J.C. Nels., *Holcus lanatus** L., *Hordeum brachyantherum* Nevski., *Poa douglasii* Nees and *Puccinellia pauciflora* (Presl) C.L. Hitchc. (Introduced species are indicated by an asterisk * after their names.)

Some of these "grassy plants" were also named at a more restricted level by some people, sometimes with a unique term, or by applying a modifier to the general name, **k̲'an**. For example, the large-headed, sharp-fruited dune sedge, *Carex macrocephala* Willd., which is common at **Tll'aal** (Tlell) and along the north coast, was given a singularly appropriate name by Emma Matthews: **x̲ahlk'ats'a hlk̲'a.aay** ('porcupine plant/branches'), but this was not known to the other elders interviewed, who simply called it **k̲'an** and noted how sharp the heads were.

Emma Matthews also knew a "special" name for Mertens' sedge (*Carex mertensii*), a handsome sedge with dark reddish, drooping flowerheads. She called it **sG̲iid** ('red; wine-coloured'), a name also applied to large red chitons [**sG̲iida** (S)]. In addition, Emma Matthews used the name **k̲'al.aa k̲'anee** (M) ('muskeg grass') for grass-like plants growing in the muskeg, including *Eleocharis macrostachya*, common rush (*Juncus effusus*) and false asphodel (*Triantha glutinosa*), whereas most of the other elders simply used **k̲'an** for these.

Maude and Agnes Moody noted that the leaves of some sedges were used in basketry, and were sometimes dyed red with alder (*Alnus rubra*) or red ochre. Tall basket sedge (*Carex obnupta*) is the species most commonly used in other areas of the coast to make closely twined baskets (Turner 1998; Turner and Efrat 1982; Turner et al. 1983), and may also have been used by Haida basket weavers. Common rush (*Juncus effusus*) was another species Maude Moody said was used for baskets, but it is often considered too brittle to be woven easily (Turner 1998).

Some of the more important kinds of "grassy plants" are discussed in more detail in the following entries.

## "Cut-Grass," or Small-flowered Bulrush

*Scirpus microcarpus* K.B. Presl; Sedge Family (Cyperaceae)

This grass-like plant, having extremely sharp-edged leaves, is probably the plant referred to as "Raven's knife," **x̲uya sG̲awG̲a** (S), known to George Young and Watson Pryce, and cited by Newcombe (1901) and Swanton (1905b). "Raven's knife," identified only as "water grasses in a stream," was mentioned in a story (Swanton 1905b). "Cut-grass" features in the stories of other northwestern peoples, usually used as a knife to cut off the private parts of Coyote or other supernatural animal characters (see Turner et al. 1990).

## Cotton-Grasses

*Eriophorum angustifolium* Honck., and *Eriophorum chamissonis* C.A. Meyer ex Ledeb.; Sedge Family (Cyperaceae)

**Cotton-grass (*Eriophorum angustifolium*).**

These attractive grass-like plants with whitish, cottony fruiting heads are widely recognized as growing in the muskeg where people went to pick bog cranberries (Emma Matthews). The two species are not usually distinguished, and the general name for "grassy plants," **k̲'an**, is the only name used by some. However, a variety of names pertaining to the fluffy quality of cotton-grass are also known. Becky Pearson called it **hltang̲waay** (S) ['(bird)-down'] and Kathleen Hans preferred **k̲aajii hltang̲waay** (S) ('down head') (JE). Newcombe (1897, 1901) recorded the name **k̲'a'll hltang̲waay** (S) ('muskeg-down') for it, but this was rejected by Kathleen Hans. Newcombe also noted that some people refer to it as **hltan.u ki hlk'ujuu** (M), the name for a device of feathers hung on a pole to show wind direction and force as an indicator of safety for canoe travel. This name was not known to Florence Davidson (JE); however, Willie and Emma Matthews knew of this name, and also applied the name **hlk'yaanàa t'amdalaa** (M) ('forest soft/fine'; "something fluffy from the woods"—EM). This name was unknown to Florence Davidson as well (JE). Maude and Agnes Moody simply called it **hlt'amjaaw** (S) ('soft'), a name not used by Kathleen Hans (JE).

No particular use was recorded for the cotton-grasses. Emma Matthews said that deer eat the leaves.

**Left:** Arrow-grass.

**Right:** Seaside plantain.

## Arrow-Grass, or Salt-Grass

*Triglochin maritima* L.; Arrow-grass Family (Juncaginaceae)

Florence Davidson called this plant **hlgid.un t'aangal** (M) ('goose-tongue'), and said that the Kaigani people gather quantities of the young leaves in spring and eat them fresh or, more recently, can (jar) or freeze them for winter use. It is possible, however, that she was referring to seaside plantain (*Plantago maritima* L.), which is very similar to salt-grass, and is commonly known in Alaska as "goose-tongue" (see Heller 1976; Kari 1987). However, Norton (1981) also identifies "**hlgit'un t'aangal**" (A) as *Triglochin*, and notes that the fleshy, white leaf bases were boiled and eaten alone or used in soups and stews. Young arrow-grass leaf bases are eaten by the Sechelt and other Coast Salish peoples (Turner 1995), but the mature plants are considered toxic because they contain cyanide-producing compounds (Turner and von Aderkas 2009). Norton (1981) states that the water in which these greens were boiled was changed at least three times; this apparently dispelled the harmful substances.

George Young and Becky Pearson simply called this plant **k̲'an hlgamg̲anda** (S) ('round grass'; see **hlgamjuu** 'round'), and Emma and Willie Matthews called it by a similar name, **k̲'an sk'ang.andaa** (M) ('cylindrical grass'). This term was also used for the fruiting heads of American dune grass (*Leymus mollis*). These terms were unknown to other consultants. George Young recalled that salt-grass grew at Copper Bay.

American dune grass.

## American Dune Grass

*Leymus mollis* (Trin.) Pilg. ssp. *mollis*; Grass Family (Poaceae)
**hlkyaama** (S) (Swanton 1905b:148—"a tall, stiff grass growing near the shore of the sea") (see also the following paragraph)

This common, coarse, bluish green grass of beaches and sand dunes was known to all of the elders. It was called by a variety of names, including the general name for "grassy plants," **k'an** (S, M), **k'án** (A) (George Young, Emma Wilson, Florence Davidson). Chief Willie and Emma Matthews called it **k'an tl'ang.andaa** (M) ('flat grass'), and applied the name **k'an sk'ang.andaa** (M) ('cylindrical grass') to the fruiting stalks (see also previous species). Florence Davidson recognized **k'an tl'ang.andaa** as a "thick beach grass, not sharp" (JE). Maude Moody called it **tsixu k'an** (S) ('bead grass'), but this name was not used by other consultants (JE). Swanton (1905b) recorded the name "false grass" or "resembling grass," **k'an 'aalgaa**, for young dune grass plants in the spring, and Newcombe (1901) gave the name **k'an kaajii** ('grass head') for the fruiting heads. Newcombe (1901) and Swanton (1905b) also applied the term **hlkyaama** to dune grass, as well as to bull kelp (*Nereocystis luetkeana*). This name was also used for cow-parsnip (*Heracleum maximum*) stalks; presumably it relates to the hollow, cylindrical nature of all of these plant parts.

Maude Moody and Emma Matthews recalled that the green stems (culms) were formerly gathered, split in half, dyed and used in basketry, apparently for decorative overlay or imbrication. The leaves themselves were not used.

Dune grass features in several Haida stories, particularly in connection with **X̱uya** (S), **Yaahl** (M) [Raven]. There is some confusion about the plant, because it is called **hlḵyaama** in these stories, and this term is also used for bull kelp (Swanton 1905b:148), but in some cases, Swanton confirms the identity. In one incident recounted by John Sky and Walter McGregor to Swanton (1905b:135, 148), for example, **G̱ud** [Eagle] was eating all the berries **X̱uya** [Raven] wanted. To get even with him, **X̱uya** broke off a stalk of **hlḵyaama**, laid it across a gulf, and put moss on it to make it look like a fallen log. Eagle, fooled by this trick, started to walk across, but when he was halfway, the grass stem broke and he fell into the gulf. Raven ate the remaining berries. Newcombe (1902) also refers to a story in which **X̱uya** [Raven] made Eagle cross a log bridge, which broke. He maintained that this "log" is represented on a totem by a hat with many crowns on it. These "crowns" may actually represent the nodes (joints) on a dune grass stalk.

In another story (Swanton 1905b), a member of **X̱uya**'s [Raven's] father's household was making sarcastic references to the destruction of the people of **ḵinggi** [the killer whale spirit living under Mount de la Touche, and the mountain itself—JE]. One of the jibes he made was, "Supernatural beings came to look at a ten-jointed **hlḵyaama** growing in front of the village of the Master of Stories, **ḵinggi**, and were destroyed." (A ten-jointed dune grass would be a gigantic specimen, compared with normal plants.) It seems that great significance is attached to the joints of the dune grass, and there is some implication that the rings on the hats of the Watchmen figures, for example, at the tops of some totem poles, are symbolic of the dune grass nodes.

### X̱uya [Raven] Obtains Fern Roots

**X̱uya** [Raven] went to visit Fern Woman with a canoe full of oulachen. He invited her to help herself to the fish, and as she was filling her basket, he stepped on a stalk of **hlḵyaama** and said, "A-a-a. I feel my canoe cracking." He pushed it from the land, and when Fern Woman reached out to get more oulachen, he pulled out the hairs under her armpit. She called her sons, who knew how to throw objects by means of a stick. They shot at him and broke ten of his paddles, but the eleventh had a knothole in it, and the stones went right through it. Thus, **X̱uya** escaped with Fern Woman's armpit hair, really fern roots, which were eaten from that time on. (Told by John Sky to Swanton 1905b:117)

**Left:** Giant horsetail, vegetative plants.

**Right:** Giant horsetail, spore-bearing stalks.

## Ferns and Their Relatives

### Horsetails

*Equisetum* spp.; Horsetail Family (Equisetaceae)

Common horsetail (*Equisetum arvense* L.) and giant horsetail (*Equisetum telmateia* Ehrh.) are called variously **yaanaang xilGa** (S) ('fog/medicine') (GY, AY), **k'ada sGawGa** (S) ('beach knife') (Newcombe 1897, 1901), **dal xaw** (M) ('rain liquid') (FD); or **sk'in** ('sandpaper'—also applied to dried dogfish skin) (S, N) (Newcombe 1897, 1901)

The young shoots, and possibly the rhizomes, of horsetail used to be eaten, according to Newcombe (1897), who did not identify the species involved; undoubtedly it was *Equisetum telmateia*, a species whose shoots were commonly eaten elsewhere on the coast (Turner 1995).

Branchless horsetail or scouring rush (*Equisetum hiemale* L.) was also called **dal xaw** (M) ('rain liquid') by Florence Davidson, but was known by a different name, **saan xila** (M), to Willie Matthews. A similar name, **saan xilee**, was also given by Keen (1898) for "*Equisetum* spp.," and is possibly the same as a term given by Newcombe (1897) for marsh cinquefoil, *Potentilla palustris*. The name was unknown to Florence Davidson (JE).

The rough stems of the horsetails were used as abrasives, like sandpaper, especially for polishing gambling sticks and other wood work (Newcombe 1897).

Willie Matthews and George Young both said that the stems of the branchless horsetail were used for medicine.

Running club-moss.

## Running Club-Moss

*Lycopodium clavatum* L.; Club-moss Family (Lycopodiaceae)

**k'aad dlljigawaay** (S) ('deer's-belt') (BP—who did not know the plant; name unknown to KH—JE); or **k'aad dlajgaa.wee** (M), **k'áad dlajgáawaay** (A) ('deer's-belt') (Boas 1891; Newcombe 1901; FD, WM); or "**sli*u*xilhkidunan**" (N) [possibly **styuu xihl kidxunang**; possibly 'sea urchin'—**styuu** or 'remove leaves with the end of an elongated object (like a stick)' **xihl kidxunang**—JE] (Newcombe 1897); or **y'aanaang hlk'a'ii** (S) ('fog branches') (GY); or **k'al.aa k'in.anee** (M) ('muskeg moss') (WM; also applied to *Sphagnum* mosses by WM, FD and others)

Some of these terms may also apply to fir club-moss, *Huperzia selago* (L.) Bernh. ex S. & M. (syn. *Lycopodium selago* L.), a shorter, "bushier" club-moss. Notably, the Tlingit word for running club-moss is **kuwakaan síigi**, which also means 'deer's-belt' (see Tlingit **kuwakaan** 'deer'—JE) (Boas 1891). The Nuu-Chah-Nulth name for this plant, "**t'apw'anim'ak muwach**," also means 'deer's-belt'). The origin must be an ancient story theme, and the name must have spread through translation borrowing, probably from an area outside Haida Gwaii, since deer are not indigenous to the islands. The relationship between club-moss and 'fog,' suggested by George Young's name, is likewise not understood.

Running club-moss was also a Haida medicine, according to Maude Moody.

## True Ferns

Several names are applied to ferns, sometimes to particular types, sometimes to the general group. These include **ts'aagul**, **ts'aaxul** (S), **saagwaal**, **ts'aagwaal** (M), **ts'áagwaal** (A), **saagwaal xil**, **ts'aagwaal xil**, **saagwaal hlk̲'a.aay** and other variations of these terms. In the older literature it is often difficult to determine whether a specific type of fern, or the general group, is being referred to, since only "fern" is given as a translation. Furthermore, the elders consulted often varied in their use of fern terms. As can be seen, the terms **saagwaal** and **ts'aagwaal** seem close linguistically as well as semantically. To complicate matters, the edible rootstocks of several fern species were given different names from the plants themselves. As George Young stated, when talking about the name for sword fern and other types of ferns, "One word can mean so many names. It's all in the way the sentence or the subject is brought up. You can have one word for two completely different kinds of plants ... "

Dried ferns of various types were used for bedding and were placed between dried fish in cedar boxes to keep the fish from getting mouldy (Maude Moody). Newcombe (1903) reported that a certain pattern woven into Haida baskets was called **ts'aagul dagaang** ('fern design').

Swanton (various notes and plant collection—JE) and Newcombe (1901) cite **hlt'an'anda**, 'bracken fern.' Newcombe gave specific names for two other types of ferns, but provided no further details of their use. These include: maidenhair spleenwort (*Asplenium trichomanes* L.), whose Haida (Skidegate) name was recorded as **xil tl'xida** (literally 'leaf that shakes its hands') (Newcombe 1897; Swanton, various notes and plant collection—JE); and oak fern (*Gymnocarpium dryopteris* [L.] Newm.), called **hlt'an'anda** (S) (Newcombe 1897, 1901) (see also bracken fern, *Pteridium aquilinum*). Both are in the spleenwort family (Aspleniaceae). Newcombe (1901) also seems to list **snaaljang** or **snaaljaang** (M) for *Asplenium*.

Fern Woman, **Snanjang jaad** (S), is another prominent supernatural being, mentioned in a couple of stories recorded by Swanton (1905b) (see also under American dune grass, *Leymus mollis*). The identity of the fern is not known. Fern roots used for medicine are called **snanjang k̲'ul** (S), according to the Skidegate elders.

### Big-tail and the "Fern" Spirit Being

One story describes a famine in Skidegate. "A long time after that they again began to starve ... Then they gathered edible fern stumps right behind them. Those they ate. They hunted outward and inward." Finally, after the hero, Big-tail, performed shamanistic rituals all night, Supernatural-Being-Looking-Landward promised to feed his people if they would "stop making the little supernatural being living along the shore cry ..." He was referring to the fern spirit woman, who cried because the ferns were being eaten ... "But still they all went out to look for food again up and down the inlet ... That night, [Big-tail] again sang a song for himself. In the night the wind blew in from the sea. At daybreak he stopped singing. The day after that one went out very early ... Now they were saved. They stopped starving ..." (John Moody, quoted from Swanton 1905b:302)

**Note:** The ferns referred to in this story are called **sG̲aana jaad xad.dalaa** 'little killer-whale women' or 'little spirit women' and **sk'yaaw k'ad.dalaa** 'tiny **sk'yaaw** (rootstocks of spiny wood fern)'; these names have not been found elsewhere (JE) (see Williams-Davidson 2017).

## Maidenhair Fern

*Adiantum aleuticum* (Rupr.) Paris.; Maidenhair Fern Family (Pteridaceae)

This delicate, black-stemmed fern of moist, shady creeksides was called **ts'aagul** (S) by George Young and **ts'aagwaal** (M) by Willie Matthews. Neither knew of any particular use for it. The stems may have been used in basket decoration.

## Lady Fern

*Athyrium filix-femina* (L.) Roth.; Spleenwort Family (Aspleniaceae)

This common, finely dissected fern of swampy areas was called **ts'aagul** (S) by George Young, and **saagwaal** (M) by Florence Davidson and Chief Willie Matthews. Willie Matthews added that it could be called **jáadaa sáagwaal** ('woman's fern'), apparently a translation borrowing from the English name (this is an unlikely word combination in Haida—JE). Many people seemed to categorize this fern together with sword fern, or possibly confuse the two. For example, Emma and Solomon Wilson called it **snan-jaang** (S), a name more commonly applied to sword fern, and said that the rootstocks were eaten, although most elders consider lady fern inedible (see Turner et al. 1992). As mentioned previously, the classification of ferns in Haida and other northwestern languages is extremely complex.

## Spiny Wood Fern

*Dryopteris expansa* (K.B. Presl) Fraser-Jenkins & Jermy; syn. *Dryopteris austriaca* (Jacq.) Woynar ex Schinz & Thell., *Dryopteris assimilis* S. Walker, *Dryopteris dilatata* (Hoffm.) A. Gray and *Aspidium spinulosum* Swartz var. *dilatatum* Hook; Spleenwort Family (Aspleniaceae)

**RIGHT: Spiny wood fern.**

Spiny wood fern, whose rootstocks were eaten traditionally by many northwestern peoples (see Turner et al. 1992), were also used extensively by the Haida. The plant itself is called **ts'aagul** (S) (GY), or **saagwaal** (M) (FD; Swanton 1905b). Willie Matthews carefully distinguished between the terms **saagwaal** (M), for wood fern, and **ts'aagwaal** (M) for sword fern. Gertrude Kelly recalled that wood fern is more delicate and "curly" than sword fern. The edible rootstocks of wood fern are usually called **sk'yaaw** (S, M), **sk'yáaw** (A), according to most of the elders consulted, as well as Newcombe (1897, 1901), Curtis (1916) and Norton (1981—misidentified here as "*Thelypteris limbosperma*"). Newcombe (1897) called the plant "**sk̲!iaoxil.**" George Young, however, referred to the edible rootstocks as **snanjang**, a term usually applied to sword fern. In any case, there seems to be a definite linguistic distinction between the rootstocks and the tops of the fern. Watson Pryce, for example, commented that "**sk'yaaw** has ferns on it," with the implication that it is associated with fern fronds, but conceptually separate from them. For many fern fronds together, Florence Davidson would say **saagulee k̲waan.gang** (M) ("There are lots of wood ferns/lady ferns."—JE).

The edible rootstocks were described as resembling clusters of bananas, two hands clasped together or "little fingers." They were collected in the spring, before the new leaves emerged, and placed into large bags. They were then washed and cooked overnight in steaming pits lined with skunk-cabbage leaves and covered with layered skunk-cabbage or canvas. They could also be cooked for a long time over an open fire. More recently, people also prepared them by boiling for many hours, or even steaming in a pressure cooker. When they were thoroughly cooked, the "fingers" (the frond bases from previous years' growth) were broken off, peeled and eaten with grease [**t'aaw** (S)] or sugar. They are said to be very sweet-tasting, somewhat like yams or sweet potatoes (Newcombe 1897; Norton 1981; Solomon Wilson, Florence Davidson, George Young, Maude Moody). (This information may also pertain to larger rootstocks of sword fern; see following species.)

Swanton (1905b) recorded a story in which the hero painted his face with a design of this fern to make himself look beautiful.

## Sword Fern

*Polystichum munitum* (Kaulf.) K.B. Presl; Spleenwort Family (Aspleniaceae)

This dark green, coarse fern was generally called **ts'aagul** (S), **ts'aagwaal** (M), **ts'áagwaal** (A) (GY, WM, EW, MM; Newcombe 1897, 1901; Norton 1981), a term also sometimes applied to spiny wood fern (see previous species). Chief Willie Matthews was careful to distinguish them, noting that **saagwaal** (M) applied to wood fern and **ts'aagwaal** to sword fern, but others seemed to confuse these terms or use them interchangeably. Sword fern fronds were called **ts'aagwaal-xil** (M) by

**Left:** Sword fern.

**Right:** Deer fern.

Chief Matthews and Florence Davidson. The rootstocks of sword fern were generally called **snanjang**, at least in the Skidegate dialect, but some people called them **sk'yaaw** (S), a term used by others for wood fern rootstocks. George Young and Watson Pryce, however, were emphatic in stating that **sk'yaaw**, and not **snanjang** (S), pertained to sword fern rootstocks. The latter, they said, applied to wood fern rootstocks. They considered both types to be edible. George Young, Watson Pryce, Willie Matthews and the elders of the Xaad Kil (Haida language) curriculum group also used the term **ta.an sky'aaw** (S, M) for sword fern rootstocks (Marianne Ignace, personal communication 2003); this was also applied by some people to bracken fern rhizomes.

Florence Davidson said that **sk'yaaw** referred to the larger, edible rootstocks (apparently wood fern, but possibly also large-rooted specimens of sword fern), the tops of these being called **sk'yaaw xil** (M). The smaller rootstocks, too small to be eaten, were called **snaal jaad**, **sanaal jaad** (M) ('scabby-woman/girl'). This latter term was also reported by Keen (1898) and Newcombe (1897). This term apparently applied to small-rooted wood fern, sword fern and other ferns such as deer fern (*Blechnum spicant* [L.] Roth). This last, in its own family (Blechnaceae), was often associated with sword fern. It was called **ts'aagul** (variant: **ts'agwul**) by George Young and other Skidegate elders, and its small rootstock was called **snaal jaad**/ **sanaal jaad** by Florence Davidson.

***Kaagan jaad*** **[Mouse Woman] with sword fern; painting by Gitkinjuaas (also known as Giitsxaa).**

Sword fern is an important Haida medicine, and also plays a prominent role in Haida narratives. The word for shrew (sometimes called 'mouse'), **jigul 'awG̲a**, **jiigwal 'awG̲a** or **Kaagan jaad** ('Mouse Woman') (S), **jagul 'aww** (M) translates as 'fern-mother' (Swanton, 1911). In one story, the "hero" of the story helps a shrew to cross a log. The shrew [or mouse] disappears under a clump of ferns, and when the man draws the ferns aside, he finds the painted house front of the 'fern-mother,' with planks sewn together in the old style. The 'fern-mother' calls him "grandson" and gives him supernatural medicine (Swanton 1905b, 1908a). Similar episodes occur in other Haida stories (See also Williams-Davidson 2017).

## Bracken Fern

*Pteridium aquilinum* (L.) Kuhn; Hay-scented Fern Family (Dennstaedtiaceae)
**hlt'an'anda** (S) (Swanton, various notes and plant collection; Newcombe 1901—JE); **saagun** (S) (JE); **ts'aagwaal hlk̲'a.aay** (M) (JE)

The long, black rhizomes of bracken fern were eaten after cooking. Some people called them **taG̲ansk'yaaw** (S), **ta.ansk'yaaw** (M) (Curtis 1916; Willie Matthews). George Young and Watson Pryce called bracken (fronds and rhizomes) **snanjang xil** (S), whereas Becky Pearson used this term for sword fern leaves. Another name is **saagun** (S) (JE), and, in Massett, **ts'aagwaal hlk̲'a.aay** (M) (Florence Davidson—JE).

Bracken rhizomes were dug in the fall and steamed in underground pits or, in recent times, in large pots, and eaten with eulachon grease [**t'aaw** (S)] as a dressing, according to Amanda Edgars, Maude and Agnes Moody and Curtis (1916).

**LEFT: Bracken fern.**

**RIGHT: Bracken rhizomes.**

Licorice fern.

## Licorice Fern

*Polypodium glycyrrhiza* D.C. Eat.; Polypody Family (Polypodiaceae)
**glaayingwaal, glaay.yangwal** (S), **glaaying'waal,** or **dlaayéngwaal** (M), **gláamaal, dláamaal** (A) (Norton 1981; JE)

This name, applying to the whole plant or specifically the rhizomes ("roots"), was known to all of the elders consulted, and was also recorded by Newcombe (1901) and Curtis (1916). Newcombe (1897), however, gave this term only for Massett and recorded the term "**tsagwal**" for Skidegate. Florence Davidson noted that if one was referring specifically to the leaves, or fronds, she could say **dlaayéngwaal-xil**.

The long, greenish rhizomes are sweet-tasting, and were sometimes used by people out in the bush as a mouth sweetener. Several of the elders pointed out that if one drinks water after chewing the rhizomes, it will taste exceedingly sweet. Kaigani Haida often use them to flavour Labrador-tea (*Rhododendron groenlandicum*). Licorice fern is widely valued by Northwest Coast peoples, including Haida, as a medicine for colds and sore throats. Sometimes the fresh rhizomes are chewed and the juice swallowed, or they may be boiled and the solution drunk for coughs, including whooping cough. The Haida use licorice fern in a variety of other medicinal preparations as well.

## "Mossy Growth": Lichens, Liverworts and Mosses

### "Crow's Whiskers" Lichens or Old Man's Beard or "Beard Moss"

*Alectoria sarmentosa* (Ach.) Ach., *Usnea longissima* Ach., and *Usnea barbata* (L.) F.H. Wigg.

**k'aalts'idaa liisg̲a** (S, N), **k'aalts'adaa liijaa** (M) ('crow's mountain goat wool'; **liis** 'mountain goat wool' is now obsolete in S, M; originally borrowed from Tsimshian—JE) (GY; Newcombe 1897, 1901; EW, EM, FD); or **k'aalts'idaa gyaa'adg̲a** (S) ('crow's blanket'; see **giiya'ad** 'blanket') (EM—less commonly used); or "**k!al.jîda**" [**k'aalts'idaa**] (M) (Newcombe 1897)

Almost all the elders I talked with held an association between these light-green, hair-like lichens and crows. The metaphor of "mountain goat wool" apparently derives from the Tsimshian practice of collecting mountain goat wool from bushes (JE). "Crow's whiskers" lichens were used medicinally by the Haida in a variety of ways.

A dark-coloured relative, *Bryoria capillaris* (including related species), was called **hlk̲'am.aal k̲aj** (M) ('bough hair') by Willie Matthews, but this name was not used by Florence Davidson. Boas (1891) applied the name **k'aalts'idaa liisg̲a** to *Parmelia* sp. (now *Hypogymnia*).

### "Cloud" Lichens

*Platismatia glauca* (L.) Culb. & C. Culb. (syn. *Cetraria glauca* [L.] Ach.)

**ts'uu liisg̲a** (S) ('red-cedar goat wool') (GY; AY; not recognized by BP); or"**inku*nhu*tkwiawe**" ('light clouds') [**hlk'inx̲a k̲wii'awaay**; see (Newcombe 1897, 1901)]

*Lobaria pulmonaria* (L.) Hoffm., *Lobaria oregana* (Tuck.) Müll. Arg. (lung lichens)

**k̲ayd gyaa'ad** (S) ('tree blanket'); or **hlk'inx̲a k̲wiiawaay, hlk'inx̲a k̲wii'awaay** (S) ('forest cloud'); or **xil k̲wii.awaa** (M) ('cloud leaves/medicine'; identification uncertain) (FD); or "**kinhau**" (possible **hlk'inx̲a**—JE) ("*Sticta* spp.") (Newcombe 1901)

*Peltigera canina* (L.) Willd., *Peltigera polydactylon* (Necker) Hoffm., *Peltigera aphthosa* (L.) Willd. (dogtooth lichen and relatives: pelt lichens)

**xil k̲wiiawaa, xil k̲wii'awaa** (S), **xil k̲wii.awaa** (M) ('cloud leaves/medicine') (MM, GY, FD); or **hlk'inx̲a k̲wiiawaay, hlk'inx̲a k̲wii'awaay** (S) ('forest cloud') (EW); or **gihlgah**l (M) ('twist' as when making twine—JE) (WM, EM—for *Peltigera aphthosa* only; not known to FD); or **t'iis xil, t'iis xilee** (M) ('rock leaf') (WM—for *Peltigera canina*; not known to FD)

**Left: Old man's beard lichen (*Usnea longissima*).**

**Right: Lung lichen (*Lobaria pulmonaria*).**

George Young noted that there are several different leafy "cloud" lichens in the woods, including the first two, which grow on tree branches, and the last types (*Peltigera* spp.), which grow on the ground. He said that one kind had "little white things" on it, and was good to eat if these were removed.

Emma Wilson told me that her Haida name was "cloud" [**k̲wii'aawaa**; see **k̲wii'aaw** 'cumulus cloud,' related to the verb **k̲wiiG̲a** 'scud, blow along (of clouds)'—JE]. Cumulus clouds were frequently mentioned in Haida narratives. Cloud Woman was the name of a supernatural being whom **X̲uya** [Raven] married (John Sky, as told to Swanton 1905b:126). Cloud patterns were drawn on boxes and sides of canoes as crests. Mats were also edged in cloud patterns (Swanton 1905b). The "cloud" lichens are so named because of their resemblance to cumulus clouds.

The lung lichens (*Lobaria pulmonaria* and *L. oregana*) and the pelt lichens (*Peltigera* spp.) are ingredients in several different Haida medicine mixtures.

## Other Lichens

Newcombe (1897 1901) recorded the name **xil tl'a.aang** (M, A) (**tl'a** probably classifier; root word unidentified—JE) (Newcombe 1897) for British soldiers lichen (*Cladonia bellidiflora* [Ach.] Schaerer) in both Massett and Alaska Kaigani dialects, and noted that the "red ends [were] dipped into human milk and applied to sore eyes," information which he credited to Reverend J.H. Keen. He also gave the name "**kinhau**" to *Sticta* spp., a foliose lichen that is similar to lung lichen, but gave no further details. Another unidentified lichen mentioned by Newcombe is "**hluani**" (**hluuaanii**), which was boiled as a medicine. Both Swanton (1905b) and Newcombe (1901) refer to a plant called "**sk̲enáwasLia**" (**skiida wasliia**) and "**gutsginá wasLia**" (**gudgina wasliia**) ("a lichen") respectively. Swanton says that it was steamed with deer bones (apparently as a food). Possibly it is *Bryoria fremontii* (Tuck.) Brodo & D. Hawksw. (syn. "*Alectoria jubata*"), the edible black tree lichen eaten by the Tsimshian and many other groups, mostly interior (Boas 1916; Turner 1995). Emma Matthews recognized one of the reindeer lichens (*Cladina pacifica* [Ahti] Hale & W.L. Culb.) from her berry-picking trips, and called it **k̲'al.aa skusaang.u** (M) (literally 'muskeg [special]-roots'), but knew of no use for it.

## "Seal's-Tongue" Liverwort, or Cone-Head Liverwort

*Conocephalum conicum* (L.) Dumort

**x̲ud t'aang.alg̲a** (S), **x̲u t'aangal** (M) ('hair-seal's tongue'; borrowed from Tsimshian **x̲u** 'hair-seal,' according to Boas 1891; or see **x̲ud** 'harbour seal' S; and **t'aang.al** 'tongue' S)

Virtually all of the elders I talked with recognized this flat, branching, green liverwort. The Kwakwa̲ka̲'wakw (Southern Kwakiutl) name for this plant is similar, meaning "tongue on the ground" (Turner and Bell 1973). This plant, which gives off a distinctive odour, is used in a variety of medicinal preparations.

**"Seal's-tongue" liverwort.**

## Mosses (General)

Oregon feather moss.

**k'inxaan** (S), **k'in.aan** (M), **k'ín.aan** (A)
Poking moss between cracks [in a cabin]: **kiits'ixang** (S)

The general names for mosses and moss-like plants (gen. Bryophytes) were known to all of the elders. In addition, Chief Willie Matthews and other elders distinguished a number of different types by adding modifiers to the general name:

- **kiid k'in.anee** (M) [**kaayd k'inxaan** (S)] ('moss growing on trees') for *Kindbergia oregana* (Sull.) Ochyra (syn. *Eurhynchium oreganum* [Sull.] Jaeg.), Oregon feather moss, because it grows under trees;
- **hlii.ng k'in.anee** (M) [**hllng.aa k'inxaan** (S)] ('root moss') for *Hylocomium splendens* (Hedw.) Br. Evr.; grows long, like a root;
- **k'in.aan hlt'aamdalaa** (M) [**k'inxaan hlt'aamdalaa** (S)] ('tall moss') for *Rhytidiadelphus triquetrus* (Hedw.) Warnst.;
- **k'al.aa k'in.anee** (M) [**kal.aa k'inxaan** (S)] ('muskeg moss') for *Sphagnum* spp. and other muskeg mosses; and
- **k'in.aan gangaa** (M) [**k'inxaan gang.'ah** (S)] ('thick moss') for thick cushions of moss, such as *Sphagnum* growth out in the muskeg.

Sphagnum mosses.

Mosses were used for a variety of household purposes: for stuffing pillows and mattresses, for making sanitary napkins and baby diapers, and for chinking cabins and houseboards. They were also soaked in water, then placed in a fire to generate steam for softening and moulding wood, as in making bentwood cedar boxes (Newcombe 1902). Newcombe specified one particular type of moss, "branch moss," named "**wit**" (or possibly **wiid**), which was used in box-making. George Young recalled that on camping trips, mosses were gathered in large quantities to use as bedding.

---

## Seaweeds and Other Marine Plants

All kinds of seaweeds on the shore were called **gaay taay dang.Gwaal** (S) ('flotsam and jetsam along the high water line'—JE) (Newcombe 1901). Seaweeds from the deeper waters (e.g., *Constantinea subulifera* Setchell, and coralline algae, *Corallina* spp.) were called **chaaGan xilaay, tsaGan xilaay** ('deep-water leaves') by George Young, a term also known to Kathleen Hans. Chief Willie Matthews applied the terms "**chaanstul**" (**chaan** is possibly **tsa.àn**—JE) and **tsa.àn hlk'am.alee.uu 'iija**

Marine plants and algae important to the Haida: rockweed at the top, eel-grass in the middle, sac seaweed at the bottom, and giant kelp frond underneath.

(literally 'it's an underwater branch'—JE) to coralline algae. Coralline algae were recognized as originating from deeper water, and although they were familiar to most people, they were not known by the people I spoke with to have any use.

## Common Rockweed, or Sea Wrack

*Fucus distichus* L.
**t'al** (S, M), **t'ál** (A)

The name **t'al** was recorded by Newcombe (1898) and Boas (1891), and is still widely known. The swollen double receptacles are called **t'al k̲aw** (**k'aaw**) (S, M), **t'ál k̲áw** (A) (literally '**t'al** eggs'). Newcombe (1898) reported that fresh rockweed was eaten with herring spawn on it. This seaweed was widely used as a medicinal poultice. George Young said that this was originally a Tsimshian medicine and was learned from them by his people at Skedans, who had close contact with them.

## Sac Seaweed

*Halosaccion glandiforme* (Gmelin) Ruprecht
**t'a sk'at'uuga** (S) (literally 'popping by stepping on'—JE) (GY, KH), **stla skaajuu**, **stla tl'anii** (uncertain) (M) (literally 'nipple' or 'cow's teat') (WM; not used by FD); or **sk'aang k'iis** (M) (literally 'fish's air bladder') (FD)

This seaweed consists of a cluster of elongated, water-filled bladders or sacs attached to the rocks in the lower tidal zone. Emma Matthews recalled that when she was a child, they used to play with these, squirting water out of the ends and pretending to milk a cow [**muus muus**]. She commented, "When I was small we used to play around the beach, and we knew every name of things like that." George Young applied the same name to *Leathesia* (see next species).

**Deformed seaweed (t'a sk'at'uuga - S).**

## Deformed Seaweed

*Leathesia difformis* (L.) Areschoug

This was called **t'a sk'at'uuga** by George Young and Ernie Wilson (see previous species), who both remembered that as children they liked to step on the plants to make them pop. Willie and Emma Matthews gave it the name "sponge" [**sk̲waank'aa**, **sk̲unk'aa**] because of its resemblance to this marine organism; "when it gets dried it's like a sponge, same as white people's sponge" (Chief Willie Matthews).

## Giant Kelp

*Macrocystis pyrifera* (L.) C. Agardh

**ngaal**, **ng.aal** (S, M), **ngáal** (A) (refers to entire plant, and to fronds, with or without herring eggs)

Entire plant, or for some just small floats at the base of the fronds: **k'aay** (S, M), **k'áay** (A)

Herring roe deposited on kelp leaves: **k'aaw** (S)

Picking herring roe from kelp: **k'aawdang** (S)

Cake of dried kelp (possibly with herring eggs): "**x̲aaydaa gulG̲a**" ('Haida tobacco') (Boas 1891; GK)

**Above: Herring eggs on giant kelp.**

**Right: Herring eggs drying on giant kelp.**

The large, "bumpy" fronds of this seaweed are used as collectors of herring spawn, and the name **ngaal** is widely known in all three major dialects. The second, **k'aay**, was also generally known to the elders consulted. **Ngaal** applies to giant kelp fronds with or without herring spawn on them. The herring spawn on kelp is called **k'aaw** (S, M), **k'áaw** (A), the name used for herring roe in any form, fresh or dried. This is a favourite food, still gathered in quantity. George Young stated that sometimes people ate the kelp fronds without herring eggs, cutting them up in strips, but he noted that these were definitely inferior to those with herring eggs.

**Picking Herring Eggs on Kelp, and Edible Seaweed**
by Becky Pearson

Do you want to know how we pick fish eggs? We go out on boats and we get them by those islands. We pick the thick ones and then we salt some and we dry some and we also freeze some. They spawn on the kelp. When it gets thick on the kelp we pick it. It takes a couple of days to get thick on the kelp. When we take it off the boat we spread some of it out on the beach and we also put it in plastic bags and freeze it. When it gets dry we put them together and bundle them up. The bundles have to be of uniform size. We barter it for grease. The grease is expensive and so are the fish eggs. We harvest seaweed [see edible seaweed, *Pyropia abbottiae*] too. When we pick the seaweed it's five dollars for a five-pound [2.3 kilogram] pail. We even sell it to one another; we don't get the seaweed here in Skidegate. We get the seaweed from Massett and we also get some from the mainland. When we went to get seaweed [before] we had to go to Cumshewa Inlet—there's where we used to have to get it. They don't do that anymore. When we had small gasboats we used to go to Cumshewa and get it and dry it right there. When it's dry we bring it over here and we put some of it in the stove and we fix it differently. We used to sell that too. (from article by Levine 1973, which gives both original Haida text and Pearson's English translation)

The herring spawn on kelp is generally gathered in June and may be eaten fresh, but is more often preserved. K̲ii'iljuus (Barbara Wilson) explained that there are two kinds of **ngaal**: one kind, from the strong tidal areas offshore, is very tough, whereas the other, from the inner islands and rocky areas close to shore, is feather-light. When the thin type is dried, even with the herring eggs on it, you can almost see right through it. Niis Wes (Chief Skedans, Ernie Wilson) said that there is a place near Cumshewa where the thin type grows, and people like to harvest it from there. It is also found in some places near Alliford Bay and **sgaay yas**. The thin kind is preferred by the Haida for eating because it is more tender. For commercial harvest for export to Japan, however, the thicker fronds, from places where the tides and currents are strong, are preferred because they remain intact and do not easily rip.

For preserving, the kelp fronds with herring roe may be sun-dried, either whole or in thin strips. The whole roe-covered fronds may be packed in barrels or buckets with salt or, as is commonly done nowadays, frozen. One method of cooking them is to fry them in a little grease, turning them over, until both sides are slightly browned and the kelp turns from brown to green. Then they are served with bread or toast and eaten with a knife and fork or with the fingers. They are also served in small pieces as hors d'oeuvres. They have a rich, salty taste and a texture like that of other types of fish roe, such as caviar, with the added flavour and texture of the kelp.

**Fresh herring eggs on kelp, edible as shown or ready for drying or freezing.**

The Massett people do not have ready access to herring spawn, and hence generally obtain theirs from the Skidegate people or from the west coast of Graham Island (Chief Willie Matthews).

The commercial market for **k'aaw** has expanded tremendously in recent years, because North American herring roe is now widely sought by the Japanese. The prices they are willing to pay raise serious concerns about the overexploitation of this traditional aboriginal resource. In the spring of 1991, for example, a 180-gram (6-ounce) box of dried "Herring Roe on Kelp" (Watashi brand; packaged in USA) was selling at the duty-free shop at the Sea-Tac Airport, Seattle, for US $24. In February 2001, this product was no longer being sold at the shop. Control of the lucrative roe-on-kelp market is a matter of concern, and there are ongoing struggles between Indigenous Peoples, who have always used this resource, and industry and government, which seek to impose their jurisdiction over it (continuing to this day: 2021).

Newcombe (1901) notes that some of the short kelps, such as *Alaria marginata* Postels & Ruprecht, were also used on occasion to collect herring spawn, and were eaten together with the spawn, but not alone. Newcombe (1901) recorded the term **ng.aal Ga'aan, ng.aal Ga'aanda** (S) for "brown kelp—*Alaria*" said by JE's consultants to consist of a single thick, brown, wide frond per stipe and to dry up at low tide. It was said to be found at the mouth of the Watan River (JE). Swanton (1905b) recorded a similar term for "seaweeds." Swanton (1908a, 1911) also recorded the related term **ngaalaagaas** (M) for "broad seaweeds" (**ngaalaa** 'have giant kelp on'—JE). These terms may therefore be applicable generally to kelp-like seaweeds or to all seaweeds, or may simply have not been fully identified by Newcombe and Swanton. Some were called by the same name as giant kelp, but George Young referred to a species of *Laminaria* as **hlkyaama** (S), a name generally applied to bull kelp (*Nereocystis*); see next species. Skidegate elders also provided the terms **kaajaanda** ('hairy kelp with **k'aaw**/herring roe'); this is apparently feather boa kelp (*Egregia menziesii* [Turner] Areschoug). Another kind of kelp, also apparently used to collect herring roe, is called **taayjanda** ('flat hairy kelp with **k'aaw**) (S).

In Haida stories, there are many references to seaweeds, some apparently specifically to giant kelp. For example, Swanton (1905b) records several stories alluding to "**ngálagas**" ("broad seaweeds"; **ngaalaagaas**—JE; see previous paragraph for analysis) growing on canoes or supernatural ocean beings. In one story, piles of elk skins obtained by a chief's son from undersea shamans turned into piles of seaweed, apparently giant kelp fronds, when taken onto dry land. In the same story, boxes of grease were transformed into ordinary bull kelp heads filled with water, and the canoe carrying these articles turned into a rotten log.

**Bull kelp.**

## Bull Kelp, Bullwhip Kelp or Common Kelp

*Nereocystis luetkeana* (Mertens) Postels & Ruprecht
Whole plant: **hlk̲yaama** (S), **hlk̲aa.m** (M), **hlk̲áam** (A)
Fishing line of kelp: **tl'agaay** (S), **tl'agayee**, **tl'age.ee**, **tl'agee** (M), **tl'agiyáay** (A)
[from **tl'aga** 'soak' (verb)—JE]
Kelp stipe: **hlk̲aa.m sdlaa.n** (M) (JE)

These terms were recorded by Newcombe (1901), Swanton (1905b, 1908a) and John Enrico, and were known to and used by George Young, Kathleen Hans, Florence Davidson and the other elders consulted. The names for the kelp plant apparently also pertain to "a tall, rough seaside grass" (see American dune grass, *Leymus mollis*), according to Swanton (1905b:148) in a story told by John Sky.

The hollow bulbs and upper stipes of bull kelp, dried and cured, were used as

*Two-Headed Kelp and the Undersea World*; painting by Gitkinjuaas (also known as Giitsxaa).

storage vessels for grease [**t'aaw** (S)] and dogfish oil (Dawson 1880; Swanton 1905b). On fishing and sea mammal hunting expeditions, canoes were anchored to kelp plants offshore. The long, thin, solid sections of kelp stipes were washed in fresh water, dried and cured and used as fishing line and rope. Adam Bell (personal communication to Marianne Boelscher 1980) noted that kelp from Lepas Bay is very strong and good for fishing lines. The stipes were soaked in fresh water, then boiled, then soaked again, then pulled hard and left, and pulled hard again and left again. The day before it was to be used for fishing, it was soaked to make it flexible. Newcombe (1897) noted that formerly a Haida fisherman owned a number of kelp lines of various lengths, for example, one of 200 fathoms (365 m), two of 50 fathoms (90 m) and one of 10 fathoms (18 m). These could be spliced together in the combination required for particular circumstances. To catch deep-water fish, such as black cod, about 10 people would tie their longest kelp lines together, and all their hooks (up to 100 or so) were fastened at the end. The lines always had to be soaked for a while before use to make them flexible.

### Haida Kelp Game

There are four players, divided into two teams of two people each. A number of bull kelp stalks are cut into foot-long (30 cm) pieces. These are placed upright in the ground at either end of a clear space 20 feet (~6 m) long. The teams are positioned at opposite ends of the field. Sharpened salmonberry sticks are thrown from a crouching position at the opponent's kelp stalks in an effort to hit them and split them open. The teams take turns at throwing. One kelp stalk of each team is very small. If an opponent strikes this one, he wins all the other kelp stalks, and therefore wins the game immediately. (Described by Newcombe 1902)

In Haida narratives, a two-headed kelp floating on the surface of the ocean often marked the entrance to the home of a powerful supernatural ocean being. For example, in the story "Sounding-Gambling-Sticks" (Swanton 1905b:52), the following episode occurs, where the hero of the story, who lost all his family possessions from gambling, was drifting about on the ocean on a cedar beam.

### Sounding-Gambling-Sticks and the Two-headed Kelp

Now he floated about. Many nights passed over him ... By and by something said to him: "Your powerful grandfather asks you to come in." He looked in the direction of the sound ... He saw only the ripples where it had gone down. He was floating against a two-headed kelp. Then he again covered his face, and something spoke to him as before. Now he looked through the eyeholes in his marten-skin blanket. After he had looked for a while ... a grebe's beak came out and [the bird said] at the same time: "Your powerful grandfather asks you to come in." Then he took his gambling-stick bag, grasped the kelp head, and went down on it. It was a two-headed house pole on which he started down ... When he stood in front of the house his grandfather invited him inside: "Come in, grandchild. I have news, grandson, that you came floating about in search of me as soon as you lost your father's town." Then he entered, and he gave him food. He had fasted ever since he lost his father's town in gambling ... The supernatural grandfather then helped the young man, giving him the power to regain all he had lost. (Swanton 1905b:52)

### Edible Seaweed, or Red Laver

*Pyropia abbottiae* (V. Krishnamurthy) S.C. Lindstrom and related spp.
**sG̲yuu** (S), **sG̲iw** (M), **sG̲íw** (A)
Picking seaweed: **sG̲yuudang** (S)

**Red laver seaweed.**

This is apparently the most common and widely used species of the *Pyropia* (formerly *Porphyra*) group of edible seaweeds, which are related to the Japanese **nori**, a prized delicacy whose cultivation in Japan is a multi-billion-dollar industry (see Turner 2003). The Haida gather this seaweed from the rocks at low tide in May. It can be eaten fresh, but is usually sun-dried. Purplish green when fresh, it turns black when it dries. Seaweed from inner island areas, which is ready to pick early in the season and is considered the best quality, being sweet-tasting, is called **didxwa sG̲yuu** (S) by the Skidegate elders, whereas the outer island seaweed, ready to pick later and of inferior taste and quality, is called **k'aat'xwa sG̲yuu** (S). When seaweed is about to go "bad," it turns from a purply green colour to reddish brown and becomes tougher. It is called **gup** (S). According to the Skidegate elders, you can pick it from the same places where the good seaweed is growing, but you have to know the colours and avoid picking the older, browner seaweed.

Formerly, for winter use, the seaweed was partially dried in the sun in large sheets, then folded up and pressed into cedar boxes in layers interspersed with red-cedar boughs. It was then weighted with rocks and allowed to form a dense cake called **sG̲iw tl'ang.andaa** ('flat seaweed'—JE) in the Massett and Alaska Kaigani dialects, according to Florence Davidson and Newcombe (1897). Newcombe noted that this was the only seaweed made into cakes by the Haida:

> Taken from a quantity freshly gathered at Skincuttle, but transported to Skidegate, where it is not found of such tender quality. It is dried in the sun, pressed into square cakes and preserved for winter use, being much relished in soups and stews.

The prepared seaweed cakes were then chopped into small pieces on a special block, using a sharp adze. For serving, the pieces were boiled in a box using red-hot rocks, and a few spoonfuls of eulachon grease were mixed in. The resulting mixture was described by Dawson (1880) as having the consistency of tea or soup. Maude Moody recalled that boiled seaweed was often served with halibut heads. It was believed that a young girl at puberty should never eat seaweed, or she would get diarrhea when she grew older (Swanton 1905a).

Edible seaweed is commonly gathered in the vicinity of Massett, although Dawson (1880) reported that it is frequent on the southern islands, and Becky Pearson said that people used to get it from Cumshewa (Levine 1973). The Skidegate people often obtain it from friends and relatives in Massett (Maude Moody, Becky Pearson). It is still sold and traded within the community (see under giant kelp,

**Above: Red laver, an edible seaweed.**

**Right: Seaweed with salmon eggs, and herring roe on kelp: nutritious Haida foods.**

*Macrocystis pyrifera*). The Haida traded their seaweed cakes, along with canoes and dried halibut, to the Tsimshian in exchange for dried berries, eulachon grease and dried eulachon from the Skeena River (Curtis 1916).

Norton (1981:438) noted that among the Kaigani Haida, many families formerly kept five-gallon (20 litre) tins of dried seaweed for using as snacks, or for cooking with vegetables or in soups. "Today [early 1980s] this is an expensive and prestigious food and friends or relatives in the "lower 48" states feel quite fortunate if someone sends them a gift of dried seaweed."

The name **sG̲yuu "gyuanda"** (uncertain—JE) ("Eating-Seaweed-Puts-Grease-Vessel-Down-When-Half-Empty," or simply "Seaweed-Eater") belonged to the wife of a house owner at Cumshewa (Newcombe 1902).

Another type of edible *Pyropia*, **sing.G̲a** (S), **sangga**, **sanga** (M), **sángg** (A) (literally 'winter'), or **sing.G̲a sG̲iiwaay** (S), **sangg sxiiwee** (M), **sángg sG̲íiwaay** (A) (literally 'winter seaweed'), is known in English as "winter seaweed," as contrasted with *Pyropia abbottiae*, which is called "summer seaweed." Specimens of "winter seaweed" have been identified (Dr. Sandra Lindstrom, personal communication 1991) as other species of *Pyropia*, a mixture of *Pyropia lanceolata* (Setchell & Hus) S.C. Lindstrom and *Pyropia torta* (V. Krishnamurthy) S.C. Lindstrom. The former is smaller and somewhat greenish, and is gathered in March, "when the sun shines." It is black when dry and is said to taste very good and sweet (Florence Davidson). Newcombe (1898) also referred to **sangg sxiiwee**, a dark brown shiny seaweed collected at half-tide in March. The young plants, about 2 in (5 cm) high, were rolled up and eaten fresh, but not dried in cakes, according to his sources.

## Sea Lettuce and Other Green Seaweeds and Freshwater Algae

*Ulva lactuca* Postels et Ruprecht and other related species

**sg̲inaaw**, **sg̲iinaaw** (S, M), **sg̲ináaw** (A) (GY; FD); or **g̲andll sg̲inawaay** (S only) for *Ulva intestinalis*, 'growing in a river' (GY); or **k̲'aats'** (M), **k̲'áats'** (A) (Boas 1890; J. Williams, 1962) ("*Porphyra* [*Pyropia*] *lanciniata*," from Tlingit; not on Haida Gwaii—JE); or **gup** (S) (also apparently applied to brownish *Pyropia* seaweed that is too old to eat)

These names are general for green water weeds, including *Ulva lactuca*, *Monostroma* spp., *Ulva intestinalis* L. and freshwater filamentous green algae such as *Spirogyra*. Sea lettuce is said to be similar to the edible seaweed, only a different colour (Williams 1962). These green water plants apparently had no use for the Haida.

## Eelgrass and Seagrasses

*Zostera marina* L. and *Phyllospadix* spp.; Pondweed Family (Naiadaceae)

**t'aanuu**, **t'anuu** (S, M), **t'anúu** (A)

A bunch of eelgrass drifted ashore: **gaytaysgid** (S)

Cutting with a knife through eelgrass or sand: **k̲'iijuu** (S)

Eelgrass is a marine plant with long, ribbon-like, emerald green leaves and fleshy, whitish to orange "roots" (rhizomes) that anchor it in sand and mud below tide level in shallow bays and inlets. Its relatives, the seagrasses, are similar, but have tougher, narrower leaves and generally grow in less sheltered areas of the coast.

T'anu is the site of a Haida village named after eelgrass (or seagrass). Also known as Old Kloo, it is situated on the east coast of Moresby Island. The people who lived there, the "**t'anuu x̲àaydag̲aay**" ("seagrass [eelgrass] people"—JE), were said to be fond of swimming in the sea (Harrison 1925). All of the elders I talked with recognized eelgrass, and knew of its association with the village of T'anu.

Eelgrass, and undoubtedly seagrass as well, was harvested with herring eggs on it, then the eggs were eaten with or without the leaves (Newcombe 1897; Willie and Emma Matthews, Florence Davidson). These plants were used all along the coast as collectors for herring eggs, and the leaf bases and rhizomes of eelgrass were also eaten (Turner 1995). Newcombe (1897) noted that the "roots" were formerly eaten raw or cooked by the Haida. Eelgrass rhizomes were also used medicinally by Haida, according to George Young and a man named Richard interviewed by Swanton (1905a:44).

## Unidentified Seaweeds

There are various other types of seaweeds having Haida names, including a fine brown algae called **tsa.àn k'in.anee** (M) ('underwater moss') (FD, but later rejected by her—JE), and a dark brown seaweed occasionally used to collect herring eggs, but not preferred for this purpose, called **x̲uya sk'yuug̲a, x̲uya sk'yuug̲aay** (S) ('Raven's mustache' seaweed) (Becky Pearson), which John Enrico notes may be *Desmarestia intermedia* Postels & Rupr. Another is called **k̲ajaanda, k̲aajanda** (S), **k̲as janda, k̲a jand, k̲aj janda** (M), **k̲as jánd** (A) (see **k̲aj** 'hair'; **jinda** (S), **janda** (M) 'be long'—JE) (Watson Pryce, Florence Davidson), evidently *Egregia menziesii*, according to Skidegate elders (see entry for giant kelp). Swanton (1905b) recorded a story by Walter McGregor relating to the origin of gathering herring eggs, which alludes to 'Raven's mustache' (see under western hemlock, *Tsuga heterophylla*).

Another unidentified seaweed is one recalled by Ed Calder, which he described as yellowish brown and "hanging in bunches like bananas." When he was fishing at Kiusta Village, off Langara Island, he collected this plant, which is only obtainable at zero tide, to treat muscular pains. He said it does not grow around Skidegate. Florence Davidson also knew of this seaweed, and called it **sdlagu tliidaang.wee** (M) (**sdlagu** 'land otter'). She said it was "like kelp" and that it was placed on hot rocks to make a steam bath. This plant was identified by Florence Davidson, working with John Enrico, as sea staghorn (*Codium fragile* [Suringar] Hariot).

---

# Freshwater Aquatic Plants

Pondweed (*Potamogeton epihydrus* Raf. and related species), a freshwater relative of eelgrass, was called **g̲andll xilg̲a** (S) ('water-leaves/medicine') by George Young, who said that any water plants could be called by this name. He knew of no particular use for them. Another aquatic plant, called **t'aanuu sguunx̲uulaa** (S) ('fragrant eelgrass'—JE), or "**agun'x̲ila**" (M) [probably **g̲agan xilee** (M)—JE; identified by FD as "something growing on the beach"] was recorded by Keen (1898), Newcombe (1897, 1901) and Curtis (1916), and identified by Newcombe as wild cress (*Cardamine angulata*) in the mustard family (see under "Leafy Herb" Plants). Florence Davidson did not recall what this plant looked like. Elizabeth Collinson described a plant growing in wet places having three leaves and a long root (a description possibly fitting marsh buckbean—*Menyanthes trifoliata* L. in the buckbean family, Menyanthaceae); it was used medicinally.

## Yellow Pond-Lily, or "Water-Lily"

*Nuphar polysepala* Engelm. (Engelm.) O.E Beal; Water-lily Family (Nymphaeaceae)

**xil gaaydllgins** (S), **xil giidlagang** (M), **xil gíidlagáng** (A) (all literally 'floating-leaves/medicine'); or **x̲iila gaaydlging, k̲'aayda xil gaaydllgins, xiila gaydllgyang** (S) ('water-lily root')

Yellow pond lilies at Mayer Lake.

"Water-lily" was known by its Haida name to all of the present-day elders, and the name was also recorded by Newcombe (1897). Boas (1891) applied this name to marsh-marigold, *Caltha biflora*, but this was apparently a case of mistaken identification (see also under buttercups). The name for yellow pond-lily pertains to its habit (floating leaves), habitat (water) and medicinal importance. The "roots" (rhizomes), which are long and thick and grow in the mud at the bottom of ponds and lake edges, were, as of the early 1970s, and still are, a widely used herbal medicine. They are collected from shallow pools in the muskeg, or from the edges of lakes such as Skidegate and Mayer lakes. Each "root" is as thick as a person's arm. Many Haida elders consulted, including Elizabeth Collinson, George Young, Emma Wilson, Ed Calder and Maude and Agnes Moody, were aware of the various medicinal uses of this plant, and medicinal uses were also recorded by Newcombe (1897, 1901). Around 1900, "Water-lily" was the crest of the Kaigani Kasaowak family (Newcombe 1902).

The name of another freshwater aquatic plant, marsh cinquefoil (*Potentilla palustris* [L.] Scop.), was recorded by Newcombe (1897) as "**sanix̲ila**" (probably **saanii xilaay**—JE), a term similar to that given by Chief Willie Matthews and Keen (1898) for branchless horsetail (*Equisetum hiemale*): "**saanxila**" (M). Newcombe noted that the stem of marsh cinquefoil was used as a medicine for consumption.

Marten's fire.

## A Terrestrial Alga

Newcombe (1897, 1901) referred to a certain "red fungus," **k'ùu ts'aanaawaa** (M) ("Marten's fire") [marten: **k'uuxuu** (S)], which he collected on the northwest side of a rock fort near Nang Sdins (Ninstints). His notation (1897), as follows, was for a specimen seen at "Nagas" on June 7, 1901: "encrusting the vertical wall of the natural rock fort in large brilliant red patches. Changes colour in drying." Some people have speculated that it is a lichen, such as *Caloplaca* or *Xanthoria*. However, in June 1995, a specimen obtained from this same area near **Nans Dins** (Ninstints) was sent to mycologist Dr. Brenda Callan. She and botanist Dr. Adolf Ceska confirmed its identification: it is neither a fungus nor a lichen, but a terrestrial alga, *Trentepohlia aurea* (L.) Martius (Chlorophyta).

---

## "Tree Biscuits" and Other Fungi

### Bracket Fungi, Shelf Fungi or Tree Fungi

including many members of the polypore group: *Ganoderma applanatum* (Pers. ex Wallr.) Pat., *Fomitopsis pinicola* (Sw. ex Fr.) Karst. and related species of tree fungi

**gyallgas naan<u>g</u>a**, **gyaalagas naan<u>g</u>a** (S) ('pilot-biscuit's grandmother'); or **kug gilgee** (M) or **kug <u>g</u>alaanggaa** (M) ('wood pilot-biscuit'; see **kug** 'firewood,' mostly Alaskan; resembles Tlingit 'rotten wood'—JE) (FD; Newcombe 1901, 1906); or **<u>k</u>iid gilgee** (M) ('tree pilot-biscuit') (FD; EM applied this name to lung lichen, Lobaria pulmonaria)

The names "pilot-biscuit's grandmother" and "wood pilot-biscuit" for tree fungi were known generally to the Haida elders I consulted. Since "pilot biscuits" are a product introduced to the Haida during the trade era, either the name is recent in origin or, more likely, the pilot biscuit was originally named from its resemblance to tree fungus, and not the other way around. Then, as pilot biscuits gained salience in

**Bracket fungus (*Ganoderma applanatum*).**

*Tree Fungus Man and Xuya* [Raven]; painting by Gitkinjuaas (also known as Giitsxaa).

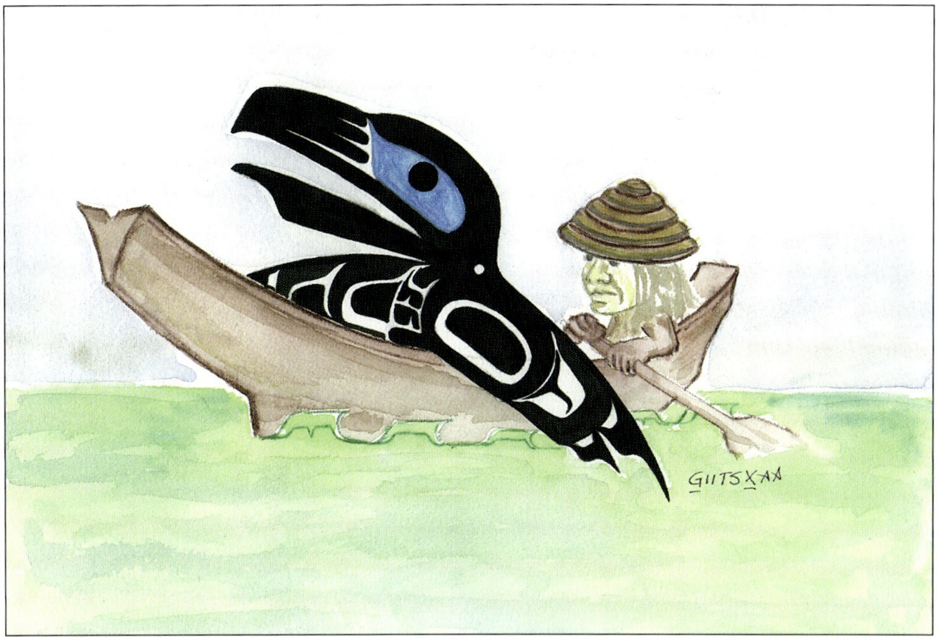


Haida life, there was a semantic shift from the original meaning to the more modern meaning. Newcombe (1901) translated the name as "grandmother's pilot-biscuit." It is interesting that the Tlingit word for bracket fungus, **aas daa gáadli** (Alaska Native Language Dictionaries 2003), also means "tree biscuit" (Boas 1891). Another name, heard recently, for tree fungus is "bear's beard."

Chief Willie Matthews was the only one who gave a name to turkey tails (*Trametes versicolor* [L.: Fr.] Pilat). He used a descriptive phrase, **kiid gaabee.uu 'iijaa** ('it's tree scallops'—JE), but knew of no particular use for it. The other elders simply considered it to be a small, or young, type of "pilot-biscuit's grandmother."

In September 1990, I asked Florence Davidson about the chicken-of-the-woods fungus (*Laetiporus sulfureus* [Fr.] Murr.) I found. She called it by the same name as the other tree fungi and was surprised to hear it was edible.

Tree fungus, presumably *Ganoderma applanatum*, whose undersurface can be used to draw on when fresh, played an important role in a Haida narrative about the origin of women. This story is pictorially represented in an argillite plate carving (slate dish No. 17952, Field Museum of Natural History, Chicago) designed and made by Charlie Edenshaw (Florence Davidson's father and famous Haida artist) in 1894. (In 1973, a replica of this plate was carved for me by Edenshaw's grandson, Claude Davidson, who also drew a graphic of the design—see page 73.) C.F. Newcombe purchased the original carving from Edenshaw and described it as showing "**nang kilsdlaas** [Raven] in the act of collecting women's genitalia on the first rock which appeared in the Haida country (called **xaagi**). This was in the far south. Up to that time the only people were men. Raven speared the parts and threw them at the men so they landed on their parts, making them so ashamed that they ran away and hid, because they grew up so quickly. Raven as seen with his cloak of feathers is steered by a man made of the fungus called 'wood biscuit' ... " In a later version (1906), Newcombe refers to the female genitalia as "women of the rock chitons."

One version of the story, originally told to Swanton by John Sky (American Philosophical Society Library Manuscript; Swanton 1905b:126), then retranslated by John Enrico, is given below.

### Tree Fungus, Xuya 's [Raven's] Steersman

**Xuya** [Raven] wanted to go on a journey to a certain reef to fetch "certain short objects," which were female genitalia: "Then they say he left there. While he was going along, they say he managed to pick up his sister. He let her off at his wife's place. Then they say he left. He asked Junco to be crew for him and took him with him. He also took a spear. The female genitalia were climbing on each other on the reef there [like chitons].* When the canoe got near it, Junco became deranged. Then Raven went back with him, they say. He asked Steller's Jay [**kl'aay kl'aay**] to be crew for him and set out with him, too. When they got near it, Steller's Jay too just flapped his wings around. Raven failed with everything [that he asked to go with him] and he drew a design on a bracket fungus and sat it in the stern. Then, 'Keep your eyes open and backpaddle every once in a while,' he said to him. Then he left with him. When the canoe got near the roof, the fungus just shook its head.

He [**Xuya**] speared a big and a little one [female genitalia] and put them aboard and went back with them. He landed and summoned his wife and stuck one on her. Then he put one on his sister too. **Siwaas** [his sister] cried. Then he said to her, 'But your little one will be safe [from me]!'"** (translation of Swanton's Haida, from Enrico 1995:63)

* This reef is said to be **kaw gwaayaay** (Pudendum Island), a bare rock just south of Newberry Point (JE).

** Note from JE: Raven here refers to lineage exogamy. Nevertheless, he soon tricks his sister into having sex. Swanton noted here that women of the Raven moiety, to which Raven and his sister belonged, were said to behave less promiscuously than Eagle women, hence the description of **Siwaas**'s genitals as "little."

## Indian Paint Fungus

*Echinodontium tinctorium* Ell. & Everh.

Indian paint fungus, showing the bright-red inside, powdered to produce a pigment.

Newcombe (1903) recorded the name "**tsigwán**" (perhaps **tsigwáan**—JE) (A) [**chiigwan** (S)] for Indian paint fungus, as well as the face paint made from it. The fungus, which grows on tree bark, especially hemlock, was used as a cosmetic paint and sunburn preventative by the Haida and other First Peoples (Turner 1998). Newcombe (1897) originally identified the paint fungus as a species of *Polyporus*. Haida use of the powdered paint fungus was also mentioned by Dawson (1880) and Chittenden (1884). The Haida were said to have imported it from the Tsimshian. As a cosmetic, it was dried, powdered and mixed with pitch. It was said to "enrich and preserve the complexion" (Newcombe 1897). To prevent sunburn, it was roasted, ground between stones into a dark brownish powder and rubbed on the face over grease or fat. The powder soon turned black and resembled dried blood, according to Dawson (1880:107B). This powdered fungus was also used medicinally, according to Newcombe (1897).

Fly agaric, a poisonous mushroom, which grows on Haida Gwaii.

## Mushrooms

Mushrooms, or "toadstools," are called **st'aw daajing.<u>G</u>a**, **st'aaw daajing** (S); **st'all naay** (S); **st'aw dajaangaa**, **st'aaw daajing** ('owl hat'), **k'ak'u dajaangaa** ('owl hat') or **kaagan daajing** (S), **kagann dajaangaa** (M) ('mouse hat') (JE; Skidegate elders). Mushrooms were apparently not eaten traditionally by the Haida, although many species grow in Haida Gwaii, including spectacular specimens of the poisonous and hallucinogenic fly agaric (*Amanita muscaria* [L.: Fr. ] Pers.). Newcombe (1901) translated "**gyallgas naan<u>G</u>a**" as "toadstool," a name commonly applied to tree fungi by the Haida elders, but not to mushrooms in general.

## Puffballs

*Lycoperdon perlatum* Pers. and related species

Puffballs are called **<u>k</u>aw tsik'uus** [some say **k'aaw ts'iik'uus**] (S), **<u>k</u>aw tsagwiid** (M)—for puffballs (from **tsigud**, **tsagud** 'sacklike object burst'; **<u>k</u>aw** 'egg'). This term was also recorded by Newcombe (1897) for the Alaskan Haida. When Florence Davidson was small, she was warned not to touch puffballs because they might hurt her eyes (from the spores getting into her eyes and causing irritation). Nevertheless, the Kaigani Haida, like other First Peoples across North America, used the spore powder externally as a medicine for sores and other skin ailments.

# Reflections and Conclusions

**RIGHT:** Poles at Kay Llnagaay, June 2001.

**OPPOSITE PAGE:** Pole raising at Kay Llnagaay ("Sea-Lion Town"). In June 2001, six poles were raised in succession, representing each of the six major villages of the southern Haida: Nansdins (Ninstints), Hlgaagilda (Skidegate), T'aanuu, Skedans, Cumshewa and Ts'aahl. The figures represent each village's crests, its lineage and its history. The poles were each carved by different artists and their assistants. Here, the Hlgaagilda pole, carved by Norman Price, is being raised. The Ts'aahl pole, by Garner Moody, stands in the foreground. This is the site of the Kay Llnagaay Heritage Centre, which showcases Haida culture and botanical knowledge in perpetuity.

Plants are meaningful and relevant to practically everyone in all human cultures. Because they are essential for life and are found virtually everywhere in diverse forms and types, they present a universal focus that is of mutual interest to people. With plants as a topic, people can readily find a shared reality and a common subject for communication. Because of this, to be both a botanist and an ethnobotanist is exciting and rewarding; few things are more gratifying than to learn about and share ideas and information with others on a subject of common relevance and interest.

The Haida with whom I have had the privilege of working and learning from have all, both consciously and unconsciously, shared with me a deep knowledge, understanding and appreciation of the plants around them. Collectively, they and their predecessors—those working with John Swanton, Charles Newcombe and other earlier researchers—have contributed specific information and names for over 150 different kinds of wild plants of Haida Gwaii and neighbouring areas.

In many cases, their knowledge is not necessarily unique, but rather, it is representative of that of the Indigenous Peoples of their generations. In other instances, the information they have given is unique to themselves and their own particular backgrounds and experiences. Both types of knowledge, knowledge that is widely known to several or many, as well as that restricted to only a few or to a single individual, are critically important. As integral components of the culture, language and worldview of Haida past and present, this knowledge is essential to sustaining and nurturing Haida into the future.

However, this knowledge is inextricably bonded to the plants themselves, and to the lands and waters in which they grow. They cannot be separated, one from the other. Knowledge of a medicine or a material, away from the context of the plant from which it derives and the place where it is found, is only a fragment of the whole. The people, the culture, the language, the plants, the animals, the land, the marshes and lakes, the ocean, the past and the future are all pieces, strands in a great and multi-dimensional fabric, a wonderful system. Take away any parts of the whole, and the whole fabric becomes distorted.

This is the most compelling reason that the Haida are so determined to remain the watchers, the Guardians of Haida Gwaii, and to retain their rights to these lands.

The Haida are clear in their assertions that they have never relinquished control of their land to anyone through treaty negotiation, or through war. Therefore, they still have an inherent right to these lands, to the places they occupy and all the resources therein. In general, the Haida do not feel that the government, company officials, researchers or environmentalists are adequately voicing their concerns or considering their needs and desires in trying to make decisions relating to the land. It is clear that comprehensive jurisdictional disputes must be settled in the near future. I hope that by providing details of knowledge about the plant world, some of the original and continuing relationships between the Haida and the land will become clear.

Reinstatement of some of the traditional Haida ways, with their underlying philosophies of connectedness among the people, the trees and all other living things of the land and the sea, will undoubtedly help all people—Haida and others alike—to live with less impact on the land (Turner and Wilson 2008).

Gwaa<u>G</u>anad, in an eloquent statement called "Speaking in the Haida Way," expressed her views as a Haida that serve as the essence of these basic concepts:

> So I want to stress that it's the land that helps us maintain our culture. It is an important, important part of our culture. Without that land, I fear very much for the future of the Haida nation. Like I said before, I don't want my children to inherit stumps. I want my children and my grandchildren to grow up with pride and dignity as a member of the Haida nation. I fear that if we take that land, we may lose the dignity and the pride of being a Haida ... (Gwaa<u>G</u>anad 1985)

Certainly, the rich traditions surrounding plants in all their forms, in both natural and spiritual realms, are part of the Haida Way, and always will be. From the life-sustaining nutrients in the greens, berries and roots to the sacred powers vested in the trees, the plants nourish the Haida and strengthen and validate their lifeways. May **<u>X</u>uya** (S), **Yaahl** (M) always protect Haida Gwaii, its plants, its animals and its people. *NJT, January 2021.*

# Epilogue

## Conservation of Culturally Important Plants of Haida Gwaii

By Kii'iljuus (Barbara Wilson)[1]

**Kii'iljuus han uu dii kiigahgaa.** (My name is Kii'iljuus.) I am of the Xaaydaa nation on **Xaaydaa Gwaay**/Haida Gwaii (formerly the Queen Charlotte Islands, British Columbia). During part of the past ten years [as of 1999] the Haida Gwaii Watchmen Program was a part of my responsibilities within the Gwaii Haanas National Park Reserve/Haida Heritage Site on the southern part of Haida Gwaii. One of my duties was to ensure that the Parks Canada staff and visitors to the Reserve/Heritage Site were knowledgeable about as many aspects of our culture, as well as of the protection of the land and water and creatures within these places. Destructive forces such as smallpox, TB, influenza, venereal diseases, residential schools, the Indian Act and other laws have had a profound impact on our nation and our knowledge base. We hope that this book will help to restore some of the knowledge of our ancestors from the past.

Here, I focus on Indigenous approaches to conservation of important plants of Haida Gwaii. Part of heritage conservation is the process of evaluation, protection and promotion of objects that are of significance to the people of a region or country, or the world. Plants are being evaluated, promoted and hopefully protected through the interpretation of issues and values. Today, as in the past, we use and pay respect to the plants large or small, as we do for other things used in our daily living. As with the people, plants have a life cycle of use and needs.

What are the uses of our plants and what are their needs? The uses are many. Examples of some uses are foods such as berries for vitamins, fern roots for starches, medicines in the form of soothers for throats, flowers as poultices or bush stalks as decongestants, and fibres for built portions of our lives.

What are the needs of all these plants? This is a critical question for us. Rest,

[1] Originally presented at the XVI International Botanical Congress, 1–7 August 1999, St. Louis, Missouri, symposium organized by Nan Vance and Nancy J. Turner: *Economically Important Plants: Use and Conservation Issues,* Aug. 5.

protection, appreciation and respect are a few of the values we need to give these generous fellow passengers through time. Here on Xaaydaa Gwaay (Haida Gwaii), protection from the impact of introduced species—whether marine or terrestrial, plants or animals—is desperately needed. Sitka black-tailed deer were introduced in the 1920s. Only 20-plus deer were introduced at the time. By 2000 their numbers were estimated to be well over 30,000.

Prior to the introduction of the deer, indigenous plants were part of the daily food and medicines of our Nation. With no indigenous predators of deer on the islands, humans and weather remain as the only deterrents to their multiplication. Indigenous plants are heavily browsed and opportunities for new growth are very scarce. Without a plan to protect these plants through a carefully planned and managed elimination or control through culling of deer, the traditional modes of conservation and production enhancement through burning, rotation or selective harvesting are just a dream.

Historically, hereditary leaders controlled the use of the various resources within their acknowledged territories. Areas were used on a rotational basis, as was the practice of burning or cutting to ensure abundance of berries and other plant resources. The leaders decided when people could or could not gather resources within their territories, as well as quantities to be taken. Now, with the impact of deer, as well as other exotics—beaver, rats, raccoons, Scotch broom—the indigenous plants, birds and mammals are in danger of disappearing. In some cases, this has already occurred.

Beavers threaten the mature **k'aay** trees (crab apple trees). The few species of endemic deciduous trees are indiscriminately eliminated as the introduced beaver attempt to use these trees in the building of their dams. Bogs and swamps are flooded and plants are drowned. Again, humans are the only predators available on these islands. The wild crab apple, bog cranberries and Labrador-tea, to name a few plants, are being lost. These fruits are traditionally used for showing respect and acknowledging the hereditary leaders within the nations of the Pacific Northwest. How was this done? They are delicacies served to those of high standing, especially at the potlatches. How do we manage the beaver? The dressing and curing of pelts is time-consuming and the economic benefits are no longer there, if they ever were.

Sea grasses from Europe are invading the inlets and bays. What will the impact of these plants be? Will the herring be able to adjust and use this grass to lay their spawn on? What about the introduced green crab? Will our Dungeness crab be able to withstand the impact of their inevitable encroachment? The Japanese oyster has already eliminated our original native oyster and taken over its niche. Furthermore, in the inlets close to the settlements, sewage is daily pumped into the sea with minimal processing. The tender seaweeds are no longer harvested from the traditional spots, as people are unsure of their safety or effects on their health.

Elders teach that respect and thanks for all things are a must. If we do not respect, give thanks to and protect these plants—the life-giving travellers that share

**Cedar-bark hat, expertly woven by Jiixaa (Gladys Vandal) of Skidegate.**

our journey—they will not be there for us. These marine and terrestrial gems provide and share their gifts of medicines, foods, fibres and wood.

As the introduced plants and animals impact the endemic plants, uses are minimized, since people are discouraged by lack of their availability and worry about their survival. As the use diminishes, the associated knowledge stands to be forgotten. If the plants are gone, what is the need of recipes, stories and endemic gardens? As with our language, stories, songs, names and lifestyle, the plants and their uses are very much a part of what makes us who we are.

**Aa haayad di kil dalang gudangs sGawdaagii dalang 'uu waddluuxaan gawíhl kil laa howa.** (I thank you all for listening to me speak.) **Dii hltíaaxwii kooyah isis,** Nancy, **howa.** To my precious friend, Nancy, thank you.

**Note:** In 2019 Kii'iljuus completed her master's degree at Simon Fraser University, having undertaken a community-led project on responses and adaptations to climate change (Wilson 2019). She continues to contribute in important ways to her community and to society in her ongoing work.

# References

Akrigg, G.P.V. and H.B. Akrigg. 1969. *1001 British Columbia Place Names*. Discovery Press, Vancouver, BC.

Alaska Native Language Dictionaries. (cited) 2003. Online at <http://www.alaskool.org/language/dictionaries/akn/dictionary.asp>. Based on *English-Tlingit Dictionary of Nouns,* originally published 1963, 1976 by C. Naish and G. Story; second edition reprinted 1996, copyright Sheldon Jackson College.

Bannerman, R.H., J. Burton and C. Wen-Chieh. 1983. *Traditional Medicine and Health Care Coverage*. World Health Organization, Geneva.

Berlin, B. 1971. Speculations on the growth of ethnobotanical nomenclature. Working Paper No. 29, Language-Behavior Research Laboratory, University of California, Berkeley.

Berlin, B. 1992. *Ethnobiological Classification: Principles of Categorization of Plants and Animals in Traditional Societies.* Princeton University Press, Princeton, NJ.

Berlin, B., D.E. Breedlove and P.H. Raven. 1968. Covert categories and folk taxonomies. *American Anthropologist* 70:290–99.

Berlin, B., D.E. Breedlove and P.H. Raven. 1973. General principles of classification and nomenclature in folk biology. *American Anthropologist* 75(1):214–42.

Berlin, B.P. Raven and D. Breedlove. 1974. *Principles of Tzeltal Plant Classification*. Academic Press, New York.

Blackman, M.B. 1982. *During My Time: Florence Edenshaw Davidson, a Haida Woman*. University of Washington Press, Seattle.

Blackman, M.B. 1990. Languages. Pages 240–60 in *Northwest Coast*, edited by W. Suttles. *Handbook of North American Indians,* Vol. 7. W.C. Sturtevant, ed. Smithsonian Institution, Washington, DC.

Boas, F. 1889. Fifth report on the Indians of British Columbia. Pages 5–97 in *Tenth Report on the Northwestern Tribes of Canada,* British Association for the Advancement of Science, Newcastle-upon-Tyne Meeting.

Boas, F. 1891. Vocabularies of the Tlingit, Haida, and Tsimshian languages. *Proceedings of the American Philosophical Society* 29:183–93.

Boas, F. 1916. Tsimshian mythology, based on texts recorded by Henry Tate. *Bureau of American Ethnology* 31*st Annual Report (*1909–1910*)*. Smithsonian Institution, Washington, DC.

Boyd, R.T. 1990. Demographic history, 1774–1874. Pages 135–48 in *Northwest Coast,* edited by W. Suttles. *Handbook of North American Indians,* Volume 7. W.C. Sturtevant, general editor. Smithsonian Institution, Washington, DC.

Brown, A.S. 1960. Physiography of the Queen Charlotte Islands. *Canadian Geographical Journal* 61:30–37.

Brown, D. *See* GwaaGanad.

Bursill-Hall, G.L. 1962. Unpublished field work in Haida linguistics. Personal communication. Department of Modern Languages, Simon Fraser University, Burnaby, BC.

Calder, J.A. and R.L. Taylor. 1968. *Flora of the Queen Charlotte Islands,* Part I. Monograph No. 4, Canada Department of Agriculture, Research Branch, Ottawa.

Chittenden, N.H. 1884. *Official Report of the Exploration of the Queen Charlotte Islands for the Government of British Columbia*. Victoria, BC.

Cole, D. and B. Lockner, editors. 1989. *The Journals of George M. Dawson: British Columbia,* 1875–1878, Volumes I and II. University of British Columbia Press, Vancouver.

Compton, B. 1993. The North Wakashan "wild carrots": clarification of some ethnobotanical ambiguity in Pacific Northwest Apiaceae. *Economic Botany* 47(3):297–303.

Curtis, E.S. 1916. *The North American Indian*, Volume II. *Nootka; Haida*. The Plimpton Press, Norwood, NJ.

Dawson, G.M. 1880. *Report on the Queen Charlotte Islands,* 1878. Geological Survey of Canada, Montreal, QC.

Deagle, G. 1988. Traditional west coast native medicine. *Canadian Family Physician* 34(July):1577–1580.

Deur, D. and N.J. Turner, editors. (2005). *"Keeping it Living": Traditions of Plant Use and Cultivation on the Northwest Coast of North America*. University of Washington Press, Seattle and UBC Press, Vancouver.

Duff, W. 1954. Preserving the talking sticks. *Digester* 30(6):10–12.

Duff, W. 1964. *The Indian History of British Columbia*, Volume I. *The Impact of the White Man*. Anthropology in British Columbia Memoir 5, Provincial Museum, Victoria, BC.

Duff, W. 1970. Unpublished research in Haida art. Personal communication. Department of Anthropology, University of British Columbia, Vancouver.
Duff, W. and M. Kew. 1958. Anthony Island: A home of the Haidas. In *Report for the Year* 1957. British Columbia Provincial Museum of Natural History and Anthropology, Victoria, BC.
Engelstoft, C. and L. Bland. 2002. Introduced species and restoration on Haida Gwaii. *Local Perspectives,* Part 1 (draft report). Alula Biological Consulting. For Council of Haida Nation Forest Guardians, funded by Terrestrial Ecosystems Restoration Program. Prepared for January 2002 workshop on introduced species of Haida Gwaii.
Enrico, J. 1980. Masset Haida phonology. Unpublished Ph.D. dissertation, University of California, Berkeley.
Enrico, J. 1992. *The Lexical Phonology of Masset Haida*. Research Paper No. 8, Alaska Native Language Center, Fairbanks.
Enrico, J., translator and editor. 1995. *Skidegate Haida Myths and Histories*. Haida Gwaii Museum Press, Skidegate, B.C. (Original versions published by Swanton 1905b)
Enrico, J. and W.B. Stuart. 1996. *Northern Haida Songs*. Studies in the Anthropology of North American Indians Series. University of Nebraska Press, Lincoln.
Fedje, D.W. and R.W. Mathewes (editors). 2005. *Haida Gwaii Human History and Environment from the time of the Loon to the Time of the Iron People*. UBC Press, Vancouver.
Gunther, E. 1945. *Ethnobotany of Western Washington*. University of Washington Press, Seattle. (Reprinted 1973).
GwaaG̱anad (Diane Brown). 1985. Speaking in the Haida way. Statement made before Honourable Mr. Justice Harry McKay in British Columbia's Supreme Court, November 6, 1985, on the application by Frank Beban Logging and Western Forest Products for an injunction to prohibit Haida picketing of logging. Later published in Andrus, V., C. Plant, J. Plant and E. Wright, editors. 1990. Pages 49–52 in *Home! A Bioregional Reader*. New Society Publishers, Gabriola Island, BC.
Harrison, C. 1895. Haida grammar. *Proceedings and Transactions of the Royal Society of Canada* i(2), Series 2:123–226.
Harrison, C. 1925. *Ancient Warriors of the North Pacific*. H.F. and G. Witherby, London, UK.
Heller, C.A. 1976. *Wild Edible and Poisonous Plants of Alaska*. Publication No. 28, Cooperative Extension Service, University of Alaska, College.
Hunn, E.S. 1982. The utilitarian factor in folk biological classification. *American Anthropologist* 84(4):830–47.
Jenness, D. 1934. Indian vikings of the North West Coast. *Canadian Geographical Journal* 8:235–46.
Kari, P.R. 1987. *Tanaina Plantlore, Dena'ina K'et'una: An Ethnobotany of the Dena'ina Indians of Southcentral Alaska*. National Park Service, Alaska Region, Anchorage.
Kavanagh, B. 1992. *Spirits Not Broken: The Haida People and the Fisheries Resource*. Centre for Sustainable Regional Development, University of Victoria, Victoria, BC.
Keely, P.B. 1980. Nutrient composition of selected important plant foods of the pre-contact diet of the Northwest Coast Native Peoples. Unpublished M.Sc. thesis, University of Washington, Seattle.
Keen, Reverend J.H. 1898. Plant specimens and their Haida names, sent to C.F. Newcombe. Unpublished notes, Newcombe Collection, Provincial Archives of BC, Victoria, BC.
Keen, Reverend J.H. ca. 1900. *Medicinal Plants of Q.C.I.* Unpublished manuscript, cited with permission of the American Museum of Natural History, New York.
Kess, J.F. 1968. A bibliography of the Haida language. *Canadian Journal of Linguistics* 14:63–65.
Krause, A. (E. Gunther, translator). 1956. *The Tlingit Indians.*. University of Washington Press, Seattle. (Originally published in German in 1885)
Kroeger, P., B. Kendrick, O. Ceska and C. Roberts. 2012. *The Outer Spores—Mushrooms of Haida Gwaii*. Mycologue Publications, Sidney, BC.
'Ksan, People of. 1980. *Gathering What the Great Nature Provided: Food Traditions of the Gitksan*. Douglas and McIntyre, Vancouver, and University of Washington Press, Seattle.
Kuhnlein, H.V. and N.J. Turner. 1987. Cow-parsnip (*Heracleum lanatum*): An indigenous vegetable of native people of northwestern North America. *Journal of Ethnobiology* 6(2):309–24.
Kuhnlein, H.V. and N.J. Turner. 1991. *Traditional Plant Foods of Canadian Indigenous Peoples: Nutrition, Botany and Use.* Food and Nutrition in History and Anthropology, Volume 8. S. Katz, series editor. Gordon and Breach Science Publishers, Philadelphia, PA.
Levine, R. 1973. Notes on a Haida text: 1. *The Charlottes: A Journal of the Queen Charlotte Islands* 2:28–32.

Levine, R.D. 1977. The Skidegate dialect of Haida. Unpublished Ph.D. dissertation, Columbia University, New York.
Marchant, C. 1981. The genus *Fritillaria* in British Columbia. *Davidsonia* 12(1):18–25.
Marles, R. 1984. The ethnobotany of the Chipewyan of northern Saskatchewan. Unpublished M.Sc. thesis, University of Saskatchewan, Saskatoon.
McCutcheon, A.R., S.M. Ellis, R.E.W. Hancock and G.N. Towers. 1992. Antibiotic screening of medicinal plants of the British Columbian native peoples. *Journal of Ethnopharmacology* 37:213–23.
McGregor, M. 1981. Native medicine in Southeast Alaska: Tsimshian, Tlingit, Haida. *Alaska Medicine* November/December:65–69.
Medical Services Branch. 1985. *Native Foods and Nutrition: An Illustrated Reference Resource.* Health and Welfare Canada, Ottawa, ON.
Meilleur, B.A. 1979. Speculations on the diffusion of *Nicotiana quadrivalvis* Pursh to the Queen Charlotte Islands and adjacent Alaskan Mainland. *Syesis* 12:101–4.
Newcombe, C.F. 1897. Unpublished notes on Haida plants. C.F. Newcombe Accession 1897–47, Department of Anthropology (Belinda Kaye, Registrar for Loans and Archives), American Museum of Natural History, New York.
Newcombe, C.F. 1898–1913. Unpublished papers. Provincial Archives of British Columbia, Victoria, BC.
Niblack, A.P. 1890. The Coast Indians of southern Alaska and northern British Columbia. Pages 225–386, Report of the U.S. National Museum for 1888. Smithsonian Institution, Washington, DC.
Norton, H.H. 1981. Plant use in Kaigani Haida culture: Correction of an ethnohistorical oversight. *Economic Botany* 35(4):434–49.
Sapir, E. 1923. The phonetics of Haida. *International Journal of American Linguistics* 2:143–58.
Scagel, R.F. 1967. *Guide to Common Seaweeds of British Columbia.* Handbook No. 27, British Columbia Provincial Museum, Victoria, BC.
Schofield, W.B. 1993. *Some Common Mosses of British Columbia.* Royal BC Museum, Victoria, BC.
Scudder, G.G.E. and N. Gessler, editors. 1989. *The Outer Shores.* Queen Charlotte Islands Museum Press, Second Beach, Skidegate, BC.
Skidegate Elders and Skidegate Haida Immersion Program (SHIP). 2016. *HlG̲aagilda X̲aayda Kil K̲'aalang. SHIP X̲aayda Kil Glossary.* Published, translated and recorded by the Elders of HlG̲aagilda X̲aayda Kil Naay: Skidegate Immersion Program.
Steedman, Scott and Jisgang, Nika Collison, editors. 2011. *That which makes us Haida – the Haida Language.* Haida Gwaii Museum Press, Skidegate, Haida Gwaii.
Stewart, H. 1977. *Indian Fishing: Early Methods on the Northwest Coast.* University of Washington Press, Seattle.
Stewart, H. 1984. *Cedar: Tree of Life to the Northwest Coast Indians.* Douglas and McIntyre, Vancouver, BC.
Stockton, S., A.J. Gaston and J.L. Martin. 2001. Where have all the flowers gone? The impact of introduced black-tailed deer on the shoreline vegetation of Haida Gwaii, British Columbia. Pages 31–42 in *Laskeek Bay Research* 10. A.J. Gaston, editor. Laskeek Bay Conservation Society, Queen Charlotte City, BC.
Suttles, W., editor. 1990. *Northwest Coast. Handbook of North American Indians,* Volume 7. W.C. Sturtevant, general editor. Smithsonian Institution, Washington, DC.
Swan, J. 1885. Report on the explorations and collections in the Queen Charlotte Islands, British Columbia. Pages 137–46 in *Annual Report of the Smithsonian Institution.*
Swanton, J.R. 1903. The Haida calendar. *American Anthropologist* 5:331–35.
Swanton, J.R. 1905a. Contributions to the ethnology of the Haida. *Memoirs of the American Museum of Natural History* 8(1).
Swanton, J.R. 1905b. *Haida Texts and Myths, Skidegate Dialect.* Bureau of American Ethnology Bulletin No. 29. Smithsonian Institution, Washington, DC.
Swanton, J.R. 1908a. Haida texts: Masset dialect. *Memoirs of the American Museum of Natural History* 14(2).
Swanton, J.R. 1908b. Social condition, beliefs, and linguistic relationship of the Tlingit Indians. *Bureau of American Ethnology 26th Annual Report.* Smithsonian Inst., Washington, DC.
Swanton, J.R. 1911. Haida. In *Handbook of American Indian Languages.* F. Boas, editor. Bureau of American Ethnology Bulletin No. 40. Smithsonian Institution, Washington, DC.
Swanton, J.R. 1912. Haida songs. *Publication of the American Ethnological Society* 3:1–63.
Swanton, J.R. 1913. A Haida food plant [*Lupinus littoralis*]. *American Anthropologist* 15:543–44.
Taylor, R.L. and B. MacBryde. 1977. *Vascular Plants of British Columbia.* University of British Columbia Press, Vancouver.

Thompson, L.C. and M.D. Kinkade. 1990. Languages. Pages 30–51 in *Northwest Coast*, edited by W. Suttles. *Handbook of North American Indians,* Volume 7. W.C. Sturtevant, general editor. Smithsonian Institution, Washington, DC.

Turner, N.J. 1973. The ethnobotany of the Bella Coola Indians of British Columbia. *Syesis* 6:193–220.

Turner, N.J. 1974. Plant taxonomic systems and ethnobotany of three contemporary Indian groups of the Pacific Northwest (Haida, Bella Coola and Lillooet). *Syesis*, Supplement 7.

Turner, N.J. 1982. Traditional use of devil's-club (*Oplopanax horridum*; Araliaceae) by Native Peoples in western North America. *Journal of Ethnobiology* 2(1):17–38.

Turner, N.J. 1984. Counter-irritant and other medicinal uses of plants in Ranunculaceae by native peoples in British Columbia and neighbouring areas. *J. Ethnopharmacology* 11:181–201.

Turner, N.J. 1987. General plant categories in Thompson and Lillooet, two Interior Salish languages of British Columbia. *Journal of Ethnobiology* 7(1):55–82.

Turner, N.J. 1989. "All berries have relations": Midlevel folk plant categories in Thompson and Lillooet Interior Salish. *Journal of Ethnobiology* 9(1):69–110.

Turner, N.J. 1995. *Food Plants of Coastal First Peoples*. Royal British Columbia Museum Handbook. University of British Columbia Press, Vancouver.

Turner, N.J. 1998. *Plant Technology of First Peoples in British Columbia*. Royal British Columbia Museum Handbook. University of British Columbia Press, Vancouver.

Turner, N.J. 1999. "Time to burn": Traditional use of fire to enhance resource production by Aboriginal Peoples in British Columbia. Pages 185–218 in *Indians, Fire and the Land in the Pacific Northwest.* R. Boyd, editor. Oregon State University Press, Corvallis.

Turner, N.J. 2003. The ethnobotany of "edible seaweed" (*Porphyra abbottiae* Krishnamurthy and related species; Rhodophyta: Bangiales) and its use by First Nations on the Pacific Coast of Canada. *Canadian Journal of Botany* 81(2):283–93.

Turner, N.J. 2014. *Ancient Pathways, Ancestral Knowledge: Ethnobotany and Ecological Wisdom of Indigenous Peoples of Northwestern North America*. (2 vols.). McGill-Queen's, Montreal, QC.

Turner, N.J. and M.A.M. Bell. 1973. The ethnobotany of the southern Kwakiutl Indians of British Columbia. *Economic Botany* 27(3):257–310.

Turner, N.J. and A. Davis. 1993. "When everything was scarce": The role of plants as famine foods in northwestern North America. *Journal of Ethnobiology* 13(2):171–201.

Turner, N.J. and B.S. Efrat. 1982. *Ethnobotany of the Hesquiat Indians of Vancouver Island*. Cultural Recovery Paper No. 2, British Columbia Provincial Museum, Victoria, BC.

Turner, N.J., L.M. Johnson Gottesfeld, H.V. Kuhnlein and A. Ceska. 1992. Edible wood fern rootstocks of western North America: solving an ethnobotanical puzzle. *J. Ethnobiology* 12(1):1–34.

Turner, N.J. and R. Hebda. 2012. *Saanich Ethnobotany: Culturally Important Plants of the W̱SÁNEĆ' People.* Royal BC Museum, Victoria.

Turner, N.J. and H.V. Kuhnlein. 1983. Camas (*Camassia* spp.) and riceroot (*Fritillaria* spp.): Two liliaceous "root" foods of the Northwest Coast Indians. *Ecol. Food & Nutrition* 13:199–219.

Turner, N.J. and S. Peacock. 2005. Solving The Perennial Paradox: Ethnobotanical Evidence for Plant Resource Management on the Northwest Coast. Chapter 4, pp. 101–50, In. *"Keeping it Living"*..., D. Deur and N.J. Turner, eds. University of Washington Press, Seattle, WA.

Turner, N.J., R.Y. Smith and J.T. Jones. (2005). "A fine line between two nations": Ownership Patterns for Plant Resources among Northwest Coast Indigenous Peoples—Implications for Plant Conservation and Management. Chapter 5, pp. 151–80, In: *"Keeping it Living"*..., edited by D. Deur and N.J. Turner, U Washington Press, Seattle and UBC Press, Vancouver.

Turner, N.J. and R.L. Taylor. 1972. A review of the Northwest Coast tobacco mystery. *Syesis* 5:249–57.

Turner, N.J., J. Thomas, B.F. Carlson and R.T. Ogilvie. 1983. *Ethnobotany of the Nitinaht Indians of Vancouver Island*. Occas. Paper No. 23, British Columbia Provincial Museum, Victoria, BC.

Turner, N.J., L.C. Thompson, M.T. Thompson and A.Z. York. 1990. *Thompson Ethnobotany: Knowledge and Usage of Plants by the Thompson Indians of British Columbia*. Memoir No. 3, Royal British Columbia Museum, Victoria, BC.

Turner, N.J. and P. von Aderkas. 2009. *The North American Guide to Common Poisonous Plants and Mushrooms*. Timber Press, Portland, OR.

Turner, N.J. and B. Wilson (K̲ii'iljuus). 2008. The culture of forests: Haida Traditional Knowledge and Forestry in the 21st Century. In: *Wild Foresting: Practicing Nature's Wisdom* (pp. 130–37), edited by A. Drengson and D.M. Taylor. Island Press, Washington, DC.

Vila, B., F. Guibal and J.L. Martin. 2001. Impact of browsing on forest understory in Haida Gwaii: A dendro-ecological approach. Pages 62–73 in *Laskeek Bay Research* 10. A.J. Gaston, editor. Laskeek Bay Conservation Society. Queen Charlotte City, BC.

Vitt, D.H., J.E. Marsh and R.B. Bovey. 1988. *Mosses, Lichens and Ferns of Northwest North America*. Lone Pine Publishing, Edmonton, AB.

Williams, J. 1962. Haida. Skidegate Mission, BC. From tapes recorded by G. Bursill-Hall, Simon Fraser University, Burnaby, BC.

Williams-Davidson, T.-L. 2017. *Out of Concealment. Female Supernatural Beings of Haida Gwaii*. Heritage House, Victoria, BC.

Wilson, K̲ii'iljuus B. 2019. *Daman gud.ad t'alang hllG̲ang.gulX̲ads Gina Tllgaay* (Working together to make it a better world). MA thesis, Simon Fraser University, Burnaby, BC.

# Appendices

## Appendix 1. Haida Language Symbols

The symbols in this book that represent sounds in **X̲aaydaa Kil/X̲aad Kil** (Haida language) are based on those developed by the Elders of the Skidegate Haida Immersion Program (SHIP) and the Massett language program, and are used with respect and appreciation.

Haida and English share a number of sounds, but others are distinctive for Haida, and must be represented by special symbols or combinations of English alphabet characters. The following orthography and linguistic description is similar to that used by John Enrico, with the following exceptions: Enrico's **r** is replaced by an underlined **G̲**; Enrico's **c** is replaced by **x**, and his **x** is replaced by underlined **x̲**. His **q** is replaced by underlined **k̲**, since one standard convention is to underline the sounds made with the root of the tongue as opposed to similar sounds made with the back of the tongue.

### X̲aaydaa Kil/X̲aad Kil Sounds

**Sounds made with the lips:**

**p** **gup**—an inedible seaweed
**m** **mahlG̲aa**—seed

**Sounds made with the front of the tongue:**

**d** **daga**—sea lice
**t** **taawla**—rainbow
**t'** **t'a**—chiton
**n** **naa**—building
**'n** **s'nall**—scab

**The J class:**

**j** **jiit'la**—elderberries
**ts** **tsiina**—fish
**ts'** **ts'i-ts'i**—carrot
**s** **suu**—lake

**The DL class:**

**dl** **dlaada**—halibut eggs
**tl** **tluu**—canoe, boat
**t'l** **t'luu**—wedge
**hl** **hlaayii**—highbush cranberries
**l** **laguus**—mat
**'l** **'laanaa**—town, village

**Sounds made with the back of the tongue:**

**g** **gul**—tobacco
**k** **kwaay**—hips
**ng** **ngaa**—look here
**x** **xaal**—copper

**Sounds made with the root of the tongue:**

**G̱** **G̱aan**—berry, fruit
**ḵ** **ḵaal**, **ḵal**—alder
**ḵ'** **ḵ'aax̱ada**—dogfish
**x̱** **x̱angajii**—shadow

**Sounds made with the vocal cords:**

**'** **'aal**—paddle
**h** **hilG̱udaG̱aang**—strawberries

## Haida Vowels and Pitch

**Short vowels:**

**i** **gidG̱a**—child
**x̱idiid**—bird
**u** **kun**—whale, nose
**G̱uda**—box
**a** **mad**—mountain sheep
**k'uda**—lips

**Long vowels:**

**ii** **giidG̱ii**—your child
**x̱iidG̱ii**—down
**uu** **suu**—lake
**aa** **k'aad**—deer

**Low pitch:**

**x̱ax̱a**, **x̱aax̱aa**—mallard duck

**High pitch:**

**jii'daal**—roots on uprooted tree

## L Sound

**Low-pitch L sound:**

**tladaG̱aaw**—mountain
**sdlagu**—land otter

**High-pitch L sound:**

**tliix̱an**—later
**tlii**—sew
**dliina**—devilfish arm
**hll.nga**—spruce roots

## Consonants

**b** voiced syllable initially, voiceless syllable finally
**p** aspirated (borrowed)
**m**
**'m** glottalized **m** (rare; exclamations only)
**d** voiced syllable initially, voiceless syllable finally
**t** aspirated
**t'** glottalized **t**
**n**
**'n** glottalized **n**
**j** as in English **judge**, voiced syllable initially, voiceless as in English **wits**
**ch** aspirated; as in English **chew** [sometimes **ts**]
**ts'** glottalized **ts**
**s**
**dl** roughly as in English **waddle**, voiced initially, voiceless finally
**tl** aspirated; roughly as in English **bottle**
**tl'** glottalized **tl**
**hl** voiceless **l**, similar to Welsh **ll**, Icelandic **hl**
**l**
**'l** glottalized
**l**
**g** voiced initially, voiceless finally
**k** aspirated
**k'** glottalized **k**
**ng**

- **x** palatal-velar fricative, like in German **Ich** [Enrico: **c**]
- **G̲** (different values in Massett, Skidegate; voiced uvular stop in S, pharyngealized glottal stop in M; Massett has borrowed back the Skidegate value as a rare distinct sound, also represented as **G̲** [Enrico: **r**]
- **k̲** voiceless aspirated uvular stop [Enrico **q**]
- **k̲'** glottalized uvular stop [Enrico **q'**]
- **x̲** (different values in Massett, Skidegate; uvular fricative in S, pharyngeal fricative in M; Massett has borrowed back the Skidegate sound in a few words) [Enrico **x**]
- **'** glottal stop, as in "**Hawai'i**" (in Hawaiian); all English (and Haida words beginning with a vowel actually begin with a glottal stop.
- **h**
- **y**
- **w**
- (**.**) Period stands for an unlinked C slot (one can look at this as an abstract syllable boundary).

**Massett (and Alaskan) vowels:**

**a, aa**
**i, ii**
**u, uu**
**e, ee**
very rare **oo**
Syllabic resonants are very common in M, occasional in A. Even in M, they do not occur as such in underlying structure.

**Skidegate vowels:**

- **i, ii** **i** includes the surface value of morphophonemic schwa after the non-lateral affricate series **j**, **ch/ts**, **ts'**, **s**
- **u, uu**
- **l, a** representing schwa: **l** occurs only after a lateral segment, **a** elsewhere
- **a, aa** representing **a**, **aa**: **a** (in contrast with schwa) is found only after the two affricate series and the glides **y**, **w**
- very rare **ee**
- very rare **oo**
- long syllabic **ll**
- Except for syllabic **l**, syllabic resonants do not occur.

**Initial syllable lengthening:**
Skidegate has a simple phonological rule of **initial syllable lengthening** which automatically lengthens a short vowel in any work-initial open syllable. This is most dramatic when an open syllable is created by suffixation, so that one has pairs like **k̲'an** 'grass,' **k̲'anaay** 'the grass' (or, for that matter, **k̲'anaa** 'grassy'); the last two words have phonetically long vowels [**a:**] in their initial open syllables while the base noun has schwa. Once one recognizes this rule, words in the northern and southern dialects are found to be more similar than previously available transcriptions would suggest.

**Pitch:**
For the most part (except for some exceptional long low-tone vowels and very few exceptional short high-tone vowels), tone in the Canadian dialects doesn't need to be explicitly marked—it automatically follows from syllable structure (it is the few unpredictable cases that give rise to a tone system). Alaskan has a pitch accent system, not a tone system (in such a system, every high pitch—or accent—needs to be marked).

# Appendix 2. Haida Food Plants

Listed Alphabetically by scientific name; parentheses (X) for use imply restricted or inferred use only. (See also Turner 1995 for descriptions of these species.)

## A) Root vegetables

| HAIDA NAME(S) | SCIENTIFIC NAME/ COMMON NAME | Raw | Cooked | Stored |
|---|---|---|---|---|
| **sk̲il tawaatl'lx̲aay** (S), **sk̲il taw**, **sk̲il tuu** (M), **sk̲íidaw** (A) | *Calypso bulbosa* (calypso, or false ladyslipper) [RARE; NOT RECOMMENDED] | X | X | - |
| **hlk'uux̲aay** (S), **hlk'ung.iid**, **hlk'ungiid** (M) | *Claytonia sibirica* ssp. *bulbifera* (syn. *Montia sibirica* ssp. *bulbifera*) (Siberian miner's-lettuce) (?) | X | X | - |
| **gyaagyaa k̲'al sguna** (S) and other terms | *Conioselinum gmelini* ("wild carrot") | X | X | X |
| **sk'yaaw** (S,M), **sk'yáaw** (A) | *Dryopteris expansa* (spiny wood fern) - rootstocks | (X) | X | (X) |
| **tl'laal** (S), **tl'ii'aal** (M), **tl'íi.aal** (A) | *Epilobium angustifolium* (fireweed) | (X) | (X) | - |
| **'inhling** (S) ; **stla k̲'iist'aa** (M, A) | *Fritillaria camschatcensis* (northern rice-root) | X | X | X |
| **taG̲ansk'ya** (S), **ta.ansk'yaaw**, **ta.ansk'yaa** (M) | *Lupinus littoralis* (beach lupine) | (X) | X | X |
| **ganduu** (S), **gúnduu** (A) | *Lupinus nootkatensis* (Nootka lupine) | (X) | X | X |
| **hlgun, hlguun** (S,M), **hlgún** (A) | *Lysichiton americanus* (skunk-cabbage) (starvation food; generally TOXIC) | (X) | (X) | - |
| **ts'aagul** (S), **ts'aagwaal** (M), **ts'áagwaal** (A) | *Polystichum munitum* (sword fern) | - | X | (X) |
| **ts'i'aal, ts'iiaal** (S), **ts'a.al**, **ts'a'al** (M), **k̲'wíi ts'a.aláay** (A) | *Potentilla egedii* (Pacific silverweed) | (X) | X | X |
| **saagun** (S); **ts'aagwaal hlk̲'a.aay** (M) | *Pteridium aquilinum* (bracken fern) | - | X | X |
| **naa'a** (S) | *Trifolium wormskioldii* (springbank clover) | (X) | X | X |
| **G̲udangxaal** (S), **G̲udang.aal, G̲udang'al** (M), **G̲udáng.aal** (A) | *Urtica dioica* (stinging nettle) – rhizomes | - | (X)? | - |
| **t'anuu, t'aanuu** (S,M), **t'anúu** (A) | *Zostera marina* (eelgrass) | X | X | (X) |

## B) "Green vegetables"

| HAIDA NAME(S) | SCIENTIFIC NAME/ COMMON NAME | Raw | Cooked | Stored |
|---|---|---|---|---|
| **ngaal Ga'aan, ngaal Ga'aanda** (S) | *Alaria marginata* and other species (short kelp) – eaten with herring spawn | X | X | X |
| **hlk'uuxaay** (S), **hlk'ung.iid, hlk'ungiid** (M) | *Claytonia sibirica* (Siberian miner's lettuce) – leaves | X? | - | - |
| **kaajaanda, kajaanda** ('hairy kelp with **k'aaw**/herring roe') (S) | *Egregia menziesii* (feather boa kelp) | (X) | (X) | (X) |
| **tl'laal** (S), **tl'ii'aal** (M), **tl'íi.aal** (A) | *Epilobium angustifolium* (fireweed) | X | (X) | - |
| **k'ada sGawGa** (S), **dal xaww** (M) and other terms | *Equisetum telmateia* (giant horsetail) | X | - | - |
| **hlk'iid** (S, M,), **hlk'íid** (A) | *Heracleum maximum* (cow-parsnip) | X | (X) | (X) |
| **hlgun, hlguun** (S,M), **hlgún** (A) | *Lysichiton americanus* (skunk-cabbage) (special rare stalks; generally TOXIC) | (X) | (X) | = |
| **ngaal** (S,M), **ngáal** (A) | *Macrocystis pyrifera* (giant kelp) (eaten with or without herring eggs) | X | X | X |
| **sk'aaxaay** (S), **sk'aang.iid** (M), **sk'aang. iid** (A) | *Maianthemum dilatatum* (wild lily-of-the-valley) – shoots | (X)A | (X)A | - |
| "goose-tongue" - see also *Triglochin* | *Plantago maritima* (seaside plantain) | X? | - | - |
| **sGyuu** (S), **sGiw** (M); **sGíw** (A) | *Pyropia abbottiae* (red laver, summer seaweed) | (X) | X | X |
| **singga sGiiwaay** (S), **sangg sxiiwee** (M), **sángg sGíiwaay** (A) | *Pyropia lanceolata* (winter seaweed) | (X) | X | X |
| **singga sGiiwaay** (S), **sangg sxiiwee** (M), **sángg sGíiwaay** (A) | *Pyropia torta* (winter seaweed) | (X) | X | X |
| **k'úng hlk'a'ii** (S), **k'unhla hlk'a.aay** (M) | *Rosa nutkana* (Nootka wild rose) – shoots | (X)? | - | - |
| sprouts: **kaysgwaan** (S), **dangaldagaa, dangaldgaa** (M), **"stl'agudiisalay"** (A) | *Rubus parviflorus* (thimbleberry) – shoots | X | (X) | - |
| sprouts: **ts'ixaal, ts'iixaal** (S); **ts'asaal** (M); **ts'a.áal, tsa'**áal (A) | *Rubus spectabilis* (salmonberry) – shoots | X | (X) | - |
| **tl'aangk'uus** (S), **tl'aak'uus, tl'aak'uuj** (M), **tláak'uj, tl'áak'us** (A) | *Rumex aquaticus* var. *fenestratus* (western dock) – leaves, stalks | (X) | X | (X) |
| Haida name unknown | *Sarcocornia pacifica* (sea asparagus) (recent) | (X) | X | X |
| **saad GaanGa, shaad GanGa** (S), **saad Gaanaa** (M), **"sa'ián"** (A) | *Sedum divergens* (stonecrop) | X | (X) | - |

Continued ...

CONTINUED ...

| | | | | |
|---|---|---|---|---|
| **hlgid.un t'aangal** (M) | *Triglochin maritima* (arrowgrass) (can be TOXIC when mature) | X | X | - |
| **Gudangxaal** (S), **Gudang.aal, Gudang'al** (M), **Gudáng.aal** (A) | *Urtica dioica* (stinging nettle) – greens (recent) | - | X | X |

## C) Fruits

| HAIDA NAME(S) | SCIENTIFIC NAME/ COMMON NAME | Raw | Cooked | Stored |
|---|---|---|---|---|
| **Gaan xaw'laa** (S), **Gaan xaw'laa, Gaan xawulaa** (M), **Gáan xáw'laa** (A) | *Amelanchier alnifolia* (saskatoon berry) | X | (X) | (X) |
| **tllGaanGa** (S), **dinax** (M) | *Arctostaphylos uva-ursi* (kinnikinnick) | X | X | (X) |
| **ts'ik'ab, ts'ik'ap** (S), **ts'iik'ab** or **ts'iik'abaa, ts'iik'ab xil** (M), **ts'íik'ab** (A) | *Cornus canadensis, C. unalaschkensis* (bunchberry) | X | X | X |
| **"kanhla," "wakla,"** or **"wahla"** ? | *Crataegus douglasii* (black hawthorn) | X | - | - |
| **xa skaa.awaa** (M) and other terms | *Empetrum nigrum* (crowberry) | (X) | (X) | - |
| **hilGudaGaang, hil GudaGang** (S), **hillda. aang** (M), **hildaGáang** (A) | *Fragaria chiloensis* (seaside strawberry) | X | X | (X) |
| **sk'idGaan** (S), **sk'idaan, sk'id'aan** (M), **sk'itáan** (A) | *Gaultheria shallon* (salal) | X | X | X |
| **siGan** (S), **sa.an** or **sa'an** (M); **sa'áan** (A) | *Maianthemum dilatatum* (wild lily-of-the-valley) | (X) | X | X |
| **k'ay** (S, M), **k'áy** (A) | *Malus fusca* (Pacific crab apple) | X | X | X |
| **GalGun, GalGwan** (S), **Gal.un** (M), **Gál. un** (A) | *Ribes bracteosum* (grayberry, stink currant) | X | X | X |
| **GudGa gi Gayd (-hlk'a'ii)** (S), **xaayuwaa** (M), **xáayuwaa** (A) and other terms | *Ribes lacustre* (swamp gooseberry) | (X) | (X) | (X) |
| **k'iit'agwaand** (S), **k'iit'agwaand** (M), **k'íit'gwaang** (A) and other terms | *Ribes laxiflorum* (trailing currant) | X | X | X |
| **k'ung** (S), **k'unhla, k'unhl** (M), **k'únhl** (A) | *Rosa nutkana* (Nootka wild rose) | (X) | (X) | - |
| **k'aaxu ts'alaangGa** (S), **k'a.àw ts'alaangaa** (M); **k'aawts'aláangaa** (A) | *Rubus chamaemorus* (cloudberry) | X | X | X |
| **gugadiis** (S), **stl'a gudiis** (M), **"stl'a gudíis"** (A) | *Rubus parviflorus* (thimbleberry) | X | X | X |

CONTINUED ...

| | | | | |
|---|---|---|---|---|
| **tllgaa GaanGa** (S), **tl'aaytl'aay GaanGa** (S), **tl'ants'uud Gaanaa** (M), **tl'ants'uud Gaanaa** (A) | *Rubus pedatus* (trailing raspberry) | (X) | (X) | (X) |
| **sk'awGaan, sk'aawGan** (S), **sk'aw.aan** (M), **sk'aw.áan** (A) | *Rubus spectabilis* (salmonberry) | X | X | X |
| **jitl'l, jiitl'** (S), **jatl'a, jatl'** (M), **jatl'** (A) | *Sambucus racemosa* (red elderberry) | (X) | X | X |
| **'as** (S), **xagutl'iid** (M), **xagutl'íid** (A) | *Shepherdia canadensis* (soapberry) (not growing on Haida Gwaii) | (X) | X | X |
| "**hukia**," **xa k'ayaa** (M), **xa k'ayaa** (A) | *Sorbus sitchensis* (mountain-ash) | (X) | (X) | (X) |
| **st'aw GaanGa** (S), **st'aw Gaanaa** (M), **st'áw Gáanaa** (A) | *Streptopus amplexifolius* (twistedstalk) | (X)A | - | - |
| **hlGiid** (S,M), **hlGíid** (A) | *Taxus brevifolia* (Pacific yew) (caution; see under Poisonous Plants | (X) | - | - |
| **hldaan** (S, M), **hldáan** (A) | *Vaccinium alaskaense* (Alaska blueberry) | X | X | X |
| **hldaan** (S, M), **hldáan** (A) | *Vaccinium ovalifolium* (oval-leaved blueberry) | X | X | X |
| **dah** (S,M,A) | *Vaccinium oxycoccos* (bog cranberry) | (X) | X | X |
| **sGidllGuu, sGiidllguu** (S), **sGidlùu** (M), **sGidluu** (A) | *Vaccinium parvifolium* (red huckleberry) | X | X | X |
| **Gaan xaw'laa, Gaan xaw.ulaa** (M) – also saskatoon berry | *Vaccinium uliginosum* (bog blueberry) | X | X | X |
| **sk'agi tsaay** (S), **skaga tsaay, sk'ag tsaay** (M), **sk'ag tsáay** (A) | *Vaccinium vitis-idaea* (lingonberry) | X | X | X |
| **hlaayi** (S), **hlaa.i, hlaayaa** (M), **hláay** (A) | *Viburnum edule* (highbush cranberry) | (X) | X | X |
| **xuyaa tluuGa** (S), **yaahl tluwaa** (M), **yáahl tluwáay** (A) | *Vicia nigricans* ssp. *gigantea* (giant vetch) | (X) | (X) | - |

## D) Tree inner bark

| HAIDA NAME(S) | SCIENTIFIC NAME/ COMMON NAME | Raw | Cooked | Stored |
|---|---|---|---|---|
| **kayd** (S), **kiid** (M), **kíid** (A); edible inner bark: **sGaalaak'uu ts'ii** (S) | *Picea sitchensis* (Sitka spruce) | X | X | X |
| **k'aang** (S, M); **k'aáng** (A); edible inner bark: **xi** (S), **xiga**, **xig**, **xi** (M), **xi** (A) | *Tsuga heterophylla* (western hemlock) | X | X | X |

## E) Casual or emergency foods

**k'anhl'l, k'anhll** (S), "**wakla**" or "**wahla**" ? (*Crataegus douglasii;* black hawthorn)—fruits eaten casually
**t'al** (S, M), **t'ál** (A) (*Fucus distichus*; rockweed, or sea wrack)—sometimes eaten with herring eggs
**hlgun, hlguun** (S, M), **hlgún** (A) (*Lysichiton americanus;* skunk-cabbage)—roots and young shoots eaten in emergencies (potentially TOXIC)
**x̲udaan** (S, M) (*Stachys chamissonis* var. *cooleyae;* hedge nettle) (?)—stems apparently chewed as nibble
Unidentified ground lichen—eaten
**x̲uya tluuG̲a** (S), **yaahl tluwaa** (M), **yáahl tluwáay** (A) (*Vicia nigricans* ssp. *gigantea;* giant vetch)—young peas eaten in small amounts by some

## F) Beverage plants

*Matricaria matricarioides* (pineappleweed)—plants (recent—A)
**x̲àayda tiiG̲a, k̲'using.a xilG̲a** (S), **xil k̲agann** (M), **xíl k̲agan** (A) (*Rhododendron groenlandicum;* Labrador-tea)—leaves
**k̲'ung** (S), **k̲'unhla, k̲'unhl** (M), **k̲'únhl** (A) (*Rosa nutkana;* wild rose)—hips

## G) Flavourings and/or sweetenings and/or confections

"**kaigigunlkai**" (S), **k̲'iit'agwaandaa hlk̲'a.aay** (M)—and other terms (*Ribes laxiflorum;* trailing currant)—leaves used to flavour seaweed
**dlaaying'waal** (S), **dlaaying'waal** (M), **dláamaal** (A) (*Polypodium glycyrrhiza*; licorice fern)—rhizomes used as mouth sweetener; used to flavour Labrador-tea
**saad G̲aanG̲a, shaad G̲anG̲a** (S), **saad G̲aanaa** (M), "**sa'ián**" (A) (*Sedum divergens;* stonecrop)—fleshy leaves chewed as mouth freshener
**st'aw G̲aanG̲a** (S), **st'aw G̲aanaa** (M), **st'áw G̲áanaa** (A) (*Streptopus amplexifolius;* twisted-stalk)—roots used as flavouring in salads (Alaska, or Kaigani only)

## H) Plants for smoking or chewing

"**sk̲'utsgai**" (S), **tllG̲aanG̲a hlk̲'a'ii** (S), **dinax̲ hlk̲'a.aay** (M) (*Arctostaphylos uva-ursi;* kinnikinnick)—toasted leaves smoked
**x̲àaydaa gulG̲a** (S), **x̲àadas gulaa** (M), **x̲aadas guláa** (A) (*Nicotiana quadrivalvis* variety; Haida tobacco)—plants formerly cultivated by Haida, Tlingit and Tsimshian and chewed with lime

**k̲ayd, k̲aayd** (S), **k̲iid** (M), **k̲íid** (A) (*Picea sitchensis*; Sitka spruce)—**k̲'aas, k̲'aaji** (S), **k̲'aas, k̲'aaj** (M), **k̲'áas** (A) (pitch) chewed

**chaanaang, tsaanaang** (S), **sgiisga, sgiisg** (M) (*Salix* spp.; willow)—leaves possibly used as tobacco

## I) Plants used in food gathering or preparation

**xil sgunx̲ulaa** (S), or **ts'ats'a k̲'ukamm** (M) and other terms (*Achillea millefolium;* yarrow)—stems used as roasting skewers for smoke-drying clams

**t'al** (S, M), **t'ál** (A) (*Fucus distichus*; rockweed or sea wrack)—sometimes used to gather herring eggs

**sk'iid, sk'iidg̲aan xil** (S), **sk'iihla, sk'iihl, sk'iihla hlk̲'a.aay** (M) (*Gaultheria shallon*; salal)—leaves and branches used in cooking pits, and in storage of dried salmon

**hlgun, hlguun** (S, M), **hlgún** (A) (*Lysichiton americanus*; skunk-cabbage)—large leaves used for wrapping food in cooking pits, drying berries on and other food-related uses (not edible)

**ngaal** (S, M), **ngáal** (A) (*Macrocystis pyrifera;* giant kelp)—fronds used to gather herring eggs

**t'aanuu, t'anuu** (S, M), **t'anúu** (A) (*Phyllospadix* spp.; seagrasses—also eelgrass)—fronds used to gather herring eggs

**gugadiis xil** (S), **stl'a gudiis xil, stl'a gudiis hlk̲'a.aay** (M), **stl'a gudíis hlk̲'a.íi, stl'a gudíis xil** (A) (*Rubus parviflorus*; thimbleberry)—leaves used in cooking and storage pits

**sk̲'aw** (S), **sk̲'aw hlk̲'a.aay, sk̲'aw.aan hlk̲'a.aay** (M), **sk̲'áw, sk̲'áw hlk̲'a.íi, sk̲'áw.aan hlk̲'a.íi** (A) (*Rubus spectabilis;* salmonberry)—leaves used for wiping fish, and in storage

**k'u'iid** (S) (*Symphoricarpos albus*; waxberry, or snowberry)—branches used as roasting skewers, fish spreaders

**ts'uu** (S, M), **ts'úu** (A) (*Thuja plicata*; western red-cedar)—branches used as roasting skewers, fish spreaders

**k̲'aang** (S, M), **k̲'aáng** (A) (*Tsuga heterophylla;* western hemlock)—boughs used to collect herring eggs

**t'aanuu, t'anuu** (S, M), **t'an˙u** (A) (*Zostera marina;* eelgrass)—fronds sometimes gathered with herring eggs

**Right:** Spruce pitch (*Picea sitchensis*; **k̲'aas - S, M**), chewed as gum.

**Below left:** Herring eggs on rockweed (*Fucus distichus*; **t'al - S, M**), approximately life-sized. See also pages 196–97.

**Below right:** **Giant kelp (ngaal - S, M; ngáal - A)**; fronds are used for gathering herring eggs.

# Appendix 3. Plants Considered Poisonous or Irritating

*Empetrum nigrum* (crowberry) [**x̲a skaa.awaa** (M) and other terms]—berries edible, but said to cause ruptures if too many eaten

*Heracleum maximum* (cow-parsnip) [**hlk'iid** (S, M), **hlk'íid** (A)]—stems and leaves contain phototoxic skin irritant; young shoots must be peeled before eating

*Kalmia microphylla* (bog laurel) [**g̲agan xil** (M)]—known to be poisonous, and potentially confused with Labrador-tea (*Rhododendron groenlandicum* ) [**x̲àayda tiig̲a, k̲'usinga xilg̲a** (S), **xil k̲agann** (M), **xíl k̲agan** (A)], which was used as beverage

*Lonicera involucrata* (black twinberry) [**x̲uya g̲aang̲a** (S), **yaahl g̲aanaa** (M), **yáahl g̲áanaay** (A), **k'aalts'idaa g̲aang̲a** (S)]—berries considered inedible for people

*Lupinus littoralis, Lupinus nootkatensis* (lupines) [**tag̲ansk'ya** (S), **ta.ansk'yaaw, ta.ansk'yaa** (M); **ganduu** (S), **gúnduu** (A)]—roots not specifically known to be poisonous for Haida, but contain toxic alkaloids, and should not be used in quantity (Turner and von Aderkas 2009)

*Lycoperdon perlatum* (puffball) [**k̲aw tsik'uus** (S), **k̲aw tsagwiid** (M)]—spores said to be harmful to eyes

*Lysichiton americanus* (skunk-cabbage) [**hlgun, hlguun** (S, M), **hlgún** (A)]—leaves poisonous to eat

*Oplopanax horridus* (devil's-club) [**ts'iihlinjaaw** (S), **ts'iihlanjaaw** (M) **ts'íihlanjaaw** (A)]—spines highly irritating

*Ribes lacustre* (swamp gooseberry) [**g̲udg̲a gi g̲ayd (-hlk̲'a'ii)** (S), **x̲aayuwaa** (M), **x̲áayuwaa** (A) and other terms]—spines highly irritating

*Sambucus racemosa* (red elderberry) [**jitl'l, jiitl'** (S), **jatl'a, jatl'** (M), **jatl'** (A)]—raw fruits may cause nausea if eaten; other parts of plant poisonous; used as purgative

*Streptopus amplexifolius* (twisted-stalk) [**st'aw g̲aang̲a** (S), **st'aw g̲aanaa** (M), **st'áw g̲áanaa** (A)]—most people consider berries inedible

*Symphoricarpos albus* (waxberry) [**k'u'iid g̲aang̲a** (S)]—berries considered poisonous

*Taxus brevifolia* (western yew) [**hlg̲iid** (S, M), **hlg̲íid** (A)]—seeds, leaves poisonous; fleshy part surrounding seed can be eaten, but may cause sterility in women

*Veratrum viride* (false hellebore) [**gwaayk'yaa, gwaayk'ya** (S), **gwaayk'aa** (M), **gwáayk'aa** (A)]—highly toxic

# Appendix 4. Haida Plant Materials

(See also Turner 1998 for descriptions of these species.)

## A) Woods for implements, containers and construction

*Acer glabrum* (Rocky Mountain maple) [**sin** (S), **san** (M)] (traded)—gambling sticks
*Alnus crispa* (Sitka alder) [**k̲'aahl'a** (S), **ka'as, ka.as, ka'aj** (M), **kaas** (A)]—some small items
*Alnus rubra* (red alder) [**k̲aal, k̲al** (S, M), **k̲ál** (A)]—wood widely used for carving
*Betula papyrifera* (paper birch) [**adtagii** (A)] (traded)—some items
*Cornus stolonifera* (red-osier dogwood) [**sgiisgi** (S), **sg̲id x̲aadaal** (M)]—branches for frames and racks
*Lonicera involucrata* (black twinberry) [**xuya g̲aang̲a hlk̲'a'ii** (S)]—gambling sticks
*Malus fusca* (Pacific crab apple) [**k'anhl'l, k'aanhll, k'anhll** (S), **k'ayanhla, k'a'inhla** (M), **k'ayánhl** (A)]—strong, tough wood
*Picea sitchensis* (Sitka spruce) [**k̲aayd, k̲ayd** (S), **k̲iid** (M), **k̲íid** (A)]—wood for general construction, fish hooks
*Pseudotsuga menziesii* (Douglas-fir) [**vu'aga** (S)] (driftwood)—occasional use when available
*Rubus spectabilis* (salmonberry) [**sk̲'aw** (S), **sk̲'aw hlk̲'a.aay, sk̲'aw.aan hlk̲'a.aay** (M), **sk̲'áw, sk̲'áw hlk̲'a.íi, sk̲'áw.aan hlk̲'a.íi** (A)]—sticks to flatten cedar-bark sheets for roofing
*Salix* spp. (willows) [**tsaanaang** (S), **sgiisga, sgiisg** (M)]—small items
*Symphoricarpos albus* (waxberry) [**k'u'iid** (S)]—sticks for skewers, etc.
*Thuja plicata* (western red-cedar) [**ts'uu** (S, M), **ts'úu** (A)]—very important; wide variety of uses
*Tsuga heterophylla* (western hemlock) [**k̲'aang** (S, M), **k̲'aáng** (A)]—wood for general construction
*Vaccinium* spp. (blueberries and huckleberries) [**hldaan** (S, M), **hldáan** (A); **sg̲iidllg̲uu hlk̲'aay.yii** (S), **sg̲idlúu hlk̲'a.aay** (M)]—wood for pegs, nails
*Xanthocyparis nootkatensis* (yellow-cedar) [**sg̲aahlaan** (S), **sg̲ahlaan** (M), **sg̲ahláan** (A)]—wood widely used for carving; also for shipbuilding

## B) Woods for specialized fuels

*Alnus rubra* (red alder) [k̲aal, k̲al (S, M), k̲ál (A)]—fuel for smoking fish
*Malus fusca* (Pacific crab apple) [k'anhl'l, k'aanhll, k'anhll (S), k'ayanhla, k'a'inhla (M), k'ayánhl (A)]—fuel for smoking fish
*Picea sitchensis* (Sitka spruce) [kayd, kaayd (S), kiid (M), kíid (A)]—general fuel
*Thuja plicata* (western red-cedar) [ts'uu (S, M), ts'úu (A)]—very important kindling

## C) Fibres and fibrous materials

*Carex obnupta* (tall basket sedge) [k̲'an (S, M), k̲'án (A)—general for grasses]—leaves possibly used in basketry
*Epilobium angustifolium* (fireweed) [tl'laal (S), tl'ii'aal (M), tl'íi.aal (A)]—stem fibre for cordage, netting
*Juncus effusus* (common rush) [k̲'an (S, M), k̲'án (A)—general for grasses]—stems possibly used in basketry
*Leymus mollis* (American dune grass) [k̲'an (S, M), k̲'án (A)—general for grasses]—stems for basket imbrication
*Nereocystis luetkeana* (bull kelp) [hlk̲yaama (S), hlk̲aa.m (M), hlk̲áam (A)]—stipes for fishing line
*Picea sitchensis* (Sitka spruce) [kayd, kaayd (S), kiid (M), kíid (A)]—roots for baskets, hats, lashing
*Thuja plicata* (western red-cedar) [ts'uu (S, M), ts'úu (A)]—inner bark, withes; sheets of bark for roofing and walls of temporary structures
*Tsuga heterophylla* (western hemlock) [k̲'aang (S, M), k̲'aáng (A)]—roots for lines
*Urtica dioica* (stinging nettle) [g̲udangxaal (S), g̲udang.aal, g̲udang'al (M), g̲udáng.aal (A)]—stem fibre for cordage, netting
*Xanthocyparis nootkatensis* (yellow-cedar) [sg̲aahlaan (S), sg̲ahlaan (M), sg̲ahláan (A)]—inner bark for hats, baskets, clothing, blankets

## D) Dyes, stains, paints, preservatives

*Alnus rubra* (red alder) [k̲aal, k̲al (S, M), k̲ál (A)]—bark for red, orange, brown dyes and stains
*Echinodontium tinctorium* (Indian paint fungus) ["tsigwán" (? tsigwáan—JE) (A)]—dried, powdered, and mixed with pitch as face paint
*Picea sitchensis* (Sitka spruce) [kayd, kaayd (S), kiid (M), kíid (A)]—pitch [k̲'aas, k̲'aaji (S), k̲'aas, k̲'aaj (M), k̲'áas (A)] for protective coating, caulking

## E) Miscellaneous useful materials

(See also Appendix 2-I, Plants used in food gathering or preparation.)

*Alnus rubra* (red alder) [**ḵaal, ḵal** (S, M), **ḵál** (A)]—charcoal for tattooing

*Equisetum* spp. (horsetails) [**ḵ'ada sg̱awg̱a** (S), **dal x̱aw** (M) and other terms]—stems used as abrasive for polishing wooden items

*Gaultheria shallon* (salal) [**sk'iid, sk'iidg̱aanxil** (S), **sk'iihla, sk'iihl, sk'iihla hlḵ'a.aay** (M)]—leafy stems for soapberry whippers; also floral decorations (recent)

*Halosaccion glandiforme* (sac seaweed) [**t'a sk'at'uuga** (S), **sk'aangk'iis** (M)]—played with by children

*Leathesia difformis* (deformed seaweed) [**t'a sk'at'uuga** (S)]—played with by children

*Lysichiton americanus* (skunk-cabbage) [**hlgun, hlguun** (S, M), **hlgún** (A)]—roots as bait for halibut hooks; leaves as surface for drying berries, etc.

*Menziesia ferruginea* (false azalea) [**ḵ'as, ḵ'aas** (S, M, A)]—charcoal for tattooing

Mosses, especially *Sphagnum* spp. [**k'inx̱aan, k'iinx̱aan** (S), **k'in.aan** (M), **k'ín.aan** (A)]—used for their absorbent qualities and for bedding

*Nereocystis luetkeana* (bull kelp) [**hlḵyaama** (S), **hlḵaa.m** (M), **hlḵáam** (A)]—hollow, cured bulbs used to stored grease and dogfish oil; plants used to anchor canoes and as ropes; stipe sections used in throwing game

*Picea sitchensis* (Sitka spruce) [**ḵayd, ḵaayd** (S), **ḵiid** (M), **ḵíid** (A)]—used in test of strength

*Polystichum munitum* (sword fern) [**ts'aagul** (S), **ts'aagwaal** (M), **ts'áagwaal** (A)]—dried fronds used for bedding and food storage; fronds formed basis of basketry pattern

*Pteridium aquilinum* (bracken fern) [**saagun** (S); **ts'aagwaal hlḵ'a.aay** (M)]—dried fronds used for bedding and food storage

*Rubus spectabilis* (salmonberry) [**sḵ'aw** (S), **sḵ'aw hlḵ'a.aay, sḵ'aw.aan hlḵ'a.aay** (M), **sḵ'áw, sḵ'áw hlḵ'a.íi, sḵ'áw.aan hlḵ'a.íi** (A)]—sticks used for throwing spears in a game

*Salix* spp. ("pussy willows") [**chaanaang, tsaanaang** (S), **sgiisga, sgiisg** (M)]—household decoration

*Sambucus racemosa* (red elderberry) [**jitl'l/jiitl' hlḵ'a'ii, staay** (S), **stiid, stiid-xil, stiid-hlḵ'a.aay** (M), **stiid** (A) and other terms]—stem pith attached to arrows to stun birds

*Tsuga heterophylla* (western hemlock) [**ḵ'aang** (S, M), **ḵ'aáng** (A)]—boughs for temporary shelters, and for fish weirs

## Appendix 5. Haida Medicinal Plants

These plants are listed in alphabetical order of their scientific names, as a means of demonstrating the diversity of plant medicines and the depth of Haida knowledge about and use of the plants of Haida Gwaii. One or more—often many—medicinal applications have been documented for each of the species listed here. Many of these plants are from the forest and some are threatened by poor forestry practices, introduced species and other encroachments. They need to be protected for future generations of Haida and others who might need them.

*Achillea millefolium* (yarrow) [**xil sgunx̲ulaa** (S), or **ts'ats'a k̲'u kamm** (M)]
*Alectoria sarmentosa* (old man's beard lichen) [**k'aalts'idaa liisG̲a** (S, N), **k'aalts'adaa liijaa** (M)]
*Alnus rubra* (red alder) [**k̲aal, k̲al** (S, M), **k̲ál** (A)]
*Ambrosia chamissonis* (beach wormwood) [**sk̲'iina xil** (S), **xil sk'yaawaa** (M) and other terms]
*Arctostaphylos uva-ursi* (kinnikinnick) ["**sk̲'utsgai**" (S), **tllG̲aanG̲a hlk̲'a'ii** (S), **dinax̲ hlk̲'a.aay** (M)]
*Cardamine angulata* (wild cress) [**G̲aaG̲an xil, "tanuskunlwa"** (S), **G̲agan xilee** (M)]
*Cardamine oligosperma* (western bitter cress) [**danhlaa xilee** (M)]?
*Cladonia bellidiflora* (British soldiers lichen) [**xiltl'a.aang** (M, A)]
*Codium fragile* (sea staghorn) [**sdlagu tlíidaang.wee** (M)]
*Conocephalum conicum* ("seal's-tongue" liverwort) [**x̲ud t'aang.alG̲a** (S), **x̲u t'aangal** (M)]
*Echinodontium tinctorium* (Indian paint fungus) ["**tsigwán**" (? **tsigwáan**—JE) (A)]
*Empetrum nigrum* (crowberry) [**x̲a skaa.awaa hlk̲'a.aay** (M) and other terms]
*Epilobium angustifolium* (fireweed) [**tl'laal** (S), **tl'ii'aal** (M), **tl'íi.aal** (A)]
*Epilobium glandulosum* (willowherb) [no Haida name given]
*Equisetum hiemale* (branchless horsetail) [**dal x̲aww, saan xila** (M)]
*Fauria crista-galli* (deer cabbage) [**G̲asaa** (M,A)]
*Fragaria chiloensis* (seaside strawberry) [**hillda.aang xil**, or **hillda.aang hlk̲'a.aay** (M)]
*Fritillaria camschatcensis* (northern riceroot) [**'inhling** (S); **stla k̲'iist'aa** (M, A)]
*Fucus distichus* (rockweed, or sea wrack) [**t'al** (S, M), **t'ál** (A)]
*Gaultheria shallon* (salal) [**sk'iid, sk'iidgaanxil** (S); **sk'iihla, sk'iihl, sk'iihla hlk̲'a.aay** (M)]
*Geum macrophyllum* (large-leaved avens) [**gaalu(u)ga(a)k'u(u)** (S)]
*Heracleum maximum* (cow-parsnip) [**hlk'iid** (S, M), **hlk'íid** (A)]
*Heuchera chlorantha* (alumroot) [**xu'aji xilG̲a** (S), **xuu.uj xilee** (M)]
*Juniperus communis* (common juniper) [**k̲ayda kax̲awaay** (S), **hlk̲'am.aal** (M) and other terms]
*Kalmia microphylla* (swamp laurel) [**G̲agan xil** (M)] (TOXIC)

*Leymus mollis* (dune grass) [k̲'an (S, M), k̲'án (A)—general for grasses]

*Lobaria oregana* (Oregon lung lichen) [k̲ayd gyaa'ad or hlk̲'inx̲a k̲wii'awaay (S), xil k̲wii.awaa (M)]

*Lobaria* spp. ("cloud" lichen) [k̲ayd gyaa'ad, hlk̲'inx̲a k̲wii'awaay (S), xil k̲wii.awaa (M)]

*Lonicera involucrata* (black twinberry) [x̲uya gaannga hlk̲'a'ii (S)]

*Lycoperdon perlatum* (puffball) [k̲aw tsik'uus (S), k̲aw tsagwiid (M)]

*Lycopodium clavatum* (running club-moss) [k'aad dlljigawaay (S), k'aad dlajgaa.wee (M), k'áad dlajgáa.waay (A)]

*Lysichiton americanus* (skunk-cabbage) [hlgun, hlguun (S, M), hlgún (A)]

*Maianthemum dilatatum* (wild lily-of-the-valley) [sk'aax̲aay (S), siig̲an hlk̲'a'ii (S), sa.an xil, sa.an hlk̲'a.aay, sk'aang.iid (M), sk'aang.iid (A)]

*Malus fusca* (Pacific crab apple) [k'anhl'l, k'aanhll, k'anhll (S), k'ayanhla, k'a'inhla (M), k'ayánhl (A)] (bark, leaves POTENTIALLY TOXIC)

*Moneses uniflora* (single delight) [xilg̲uga (S), xilaawg (M)]

*Nereocystis luetkeana* (bull kelp) [hlk̲yaama (S), hlk̲aa.m (M), hlk̲áam (A)]

*Nuphar polysepala* (yellow pond-lily) [xil gaaydllgins (S), xil gii dlagang (M), xíl gíi dlagáng (A)]

*Oplopanax horridus* (devil's-club) [ts'iihllnjaaw, ts'iihlinjaaw (S), ts'iihlanjaaw (M), ts'íihlanjaaw (A)]

*Peltigera* spp. (dogtooth lichens) [xil k̲wiiawaa (S), xil k̲wii.awaa (M) and other terms]

*Picea sitchensis* (Sitka spruce) [k̲ayd, k̲aayd (S), k̲iid (M), k̲íid (A)]—pitch [k̲'aas, k̲'aaji (S), k̲'aas, k̲'aaj (M), k̲'áas (A)]

*Pinus contorta* (lodgepole pine) [ts'ahl (S), ts'ahla, ts'ahl (M), ts'ahl (A)]

*Plantago major* (broad-leaved plantain) ['laanaa hlguna (S), 'laanaa hlgun (M)]

*Polypodium glycyrrhiza* (licorice fern) [dlaaying'waal (S), dlaaying'waal (M), dláamaal (A)]

*Polystichum munitum* (sword fern) (?) [ts'aagul (S), ts'aagwaal (M), ts'áagwaal (A)]

*Populus balsamifera* ssp. *trichocarpa* (cottonwood) [tsaanaang (S, M), tsáanaang (A)] (Alaska)

*Potentilla palustris* (marsh cinquefoil) ["sanix̲ila," (?saanii xilaay—JE]

*Ranunculus occidentalis* and other spp. (buttercups) [doctor xilg̲a, daktaa xilg̲a (S), "doctor xilee" (M)]

*Rhododendron groenlandicum* (Labrador-tea) [x̲àayda tiig̲a, k'usinga xilg̲a (S), xil k̲agann (M), xíl k̲agan (A)]

*Ribes bracteosum* (stink currant) [g̲alg̲un xil, g̲alg̲wan xil (S), g̲ál.un hlk̲'a.aay (M)]

*Ribes laxiflorum* (trailing currant) ["kaigigunlkai" (S), k'iit'agwaandaa hlk̲'a.aay (M) and other terms]

*Rubus spectabilis* (salmonberry) [sk̲'aw (S), sk̲'aw hlk̲'a.aay, sk̲'aw.aan hlk̲'a.aay (M), sk̲'áw, sk̲'áw hlk̲'a.íi, sk̲'áw.aan hlk̲'a.íi (A)]

*Rumex aquaticus* var. *fenestratus* (western dock) [**tl'aangk'uus** (S), **tl'aak'uus, tl'aak'uuj** (M), **t'láak'uj, tl'áak'us** (A)]
*Sambucus racemosa* (red elderberry) [**jitl'l/jiitl' hlk'a'ii, stay** (S), **stiid, stiid-xil, stiid-hlk'a.aay** (M), **stiid** (A) and other terms]
*Sedum divergens* (stonecrop) [**saad GaanGa, shaad GanGa** (S), **saad Gaanaa** (M), "sa'ián" (A)]
*Streptopus amplexifolius* (twisted-stalk) [**st'aw GaanGa** (S), **st'aw Gaanaa** (M), **st'áw Gáanaa** (A)]
*Taraxacum officinale* (common dandelion)
*Taxus brevifolia* (western yew) [**hlGiid** (S, M), **hlGíid** (A)]
*Tsuga heterophylla* (western hemlock) [**k'aang** (S, M), **k'áang** (A)]
*Urtica dioica* (stinging nettle) [**Gudangxaal** (S), **Gudang.aal, Gudang'al** (M), **Gudáng.aal** (A)]
*Usnea* spp. (old man's beard lichen) [**k'aalts'idaa liisGa** (S, N), **k'aalts'adaa liijaa** (M)]
*Vaccinium parvifolium* (red elderberry) [**sGidllGu/sGiidlgu hlk'a'ii** (S), **sGidlúu hlk'a.aay** (M)]
*Veratrum viride* (false hellebore) [**gwaayk'yaa, gwaayk'ya** (S), **gwaayk'aa** (M), **gwáayk'aa** (A)] (HIGHLY TOXIC)
*Viburnum edule* (highbush cranberry) [**hlaayaa hlk'a'ii** (S), **hlaayaa hlk'a.aay** (M)]
*Zostera marina* (eelgrass) [**t'aanuu, t'anuu** (S, M), **t'anúu** (A)]

---

## Appendix 6. Plants Having a Role in Traditional Beliefs and/or Stories of the Haida

NOTE: The reader can find detailed information about these roles under the specific writeups on these plants.

*Acer glabrum* (Rocky Mountain maple) [**sin** (S), **san** (M)]—canoe material in story
*Alnus rubra* (red alder) [**kaal, kal** (S, M), **kál** (A)]—supernatural woman
*Aquilegia formosa* (red columbine) [**dall(-xil)-sGid** (M)]—believed to cause rain if picked
*Campanula rotundifolia* (blue harebell) [**dall(-xíl)-Guhlahl** (M)]—believed to cause rain if picked
*Dodecatheon jeffreyi* (shooting star) [**dall(-xil)** (M)]—believed to cause rain if picked
*Dryopteris expansa* (spiny wood fern) [**sk'yaaw** (S, M), **sk'yáaw** (A)]—mentioned in story as a face-paint design
*Fritillaria camschatcensis* (northern riceroot) [**'inhling** (S); **stla k'iist'aa** (M, A)]—used in story to "vanquish" salmon people

*Ganoderma applanatum* (tree fungus), or other similar species [**gyallgas naanGa** (S), **kug gilgee, kug Galaanggaa, kiid gilgee** (M)]—role as steersman for **Yaahl** (M) [Raven] in Haida "Origin of Women" story

"Grass" [**k'an** (S, M), **k'án** (A)]—frequently mentioned in stories

*Juniperus communis* (common juniper) [**kayda kaxawaay** (S), **hlk'am.aal** (M) and other terms]—used as medicine; all had to be drunk, or it would not work

*Lathyrus japonicus* (beach pea) [**xuya tluuGa** (S), **yaahl tluwaa** (M), **yáahl tluwáay** (A)]—"**Xuya**'s (S) [Raven's] canoe" in story of **Xuya**/Raven Travelling (see also *Vicia gigantea*)

*Leymus mollis* (American dune grass) [**hlkyaama** (S)]—featured in several stories, including "Master of Stories" narrative

*Lonicera involucrata* (black twinberry) [**xuya GaanGa hlk'a'ii** (S)]—gambling-stick material in story

*Lupinus littoralis* (beach lupine) [**taGansk'ya** (S), **ta.ansk'yaaw, ta.ansk'yaa** (M)]—food of ancient supernatural beings

*Lysichiton americanus* (skunk-cabbage) [**hlgun, hlguun** (S, M), **hlgún** (A)]—supernatural plant; gave gift of salmon to hero in Haida story

*Maianthemum dilatatum* (wild lily-of-the-valley) [**siGan** (S), **sa.an** or **sa'an** (M), **sa'áan** (A)]—food of supernatural beings in story

*Malus fusca* (Pacific crab apple) [**k'ay** (S, M), **k'áy** (A)]—food of supernatural beings; ceremonial use for women at puberty and in mourning

*Moneses uniflora* (single delight) [**xilGuGa** (S), **xilaawg** (M)]—plant eaten for luck by supernatural characters in stories

*Nereocystis luetkeana* (bull kelp) [**hlkyaama** (S), **hlkaa.m** (M), **hlkáam** (A)]—double-headed kelp known as marker of entrance to undersea home of a supernatural being in stories

*Nicotiana quadrivalvis* var. *multivalvis* (Haida tobacco) [**xàaydaa gulGa** (S), **xàadas gulaa** (M), **xaadas guláa** (A)]—mentioned many times in narratives; said to be first planted by **Xuya**'s [Raven's] sister

*Nuphar polysepala* (yellow pond-lily) [**xil gaay dllgins** (S) , **xil gii dlagang** (M), **xíl gíi dlagáng** (A)]—family crest (Kaigani)

*Oplopanax horridus* (devil's-club) [**ts'iihllnjaaw, ts'iihlinjaaw** (S), **ts'iihlanjaaw** (M) **ts'íihlanjaaw** (A)]—often mentioned in stories as used by shamans for protection against evil and to gain supernatural help; features in origin of Chief Weah's family name

*Picea sitchensis* (Sitka spruce) [**kayd, kaayd** (S), **kiid** (M), **kíid** (A)]—cones, needles feature in **xuya** (S), **yaahl** (M), **yáahl** (A) [Raven] story; used by dancers

*Polystichum munitum* (sword fern) [**ts'aagul** (S), **ts'aagwaal** (M), **ts'áagwaal** (A)]—associated with shrews and mice, which are in several stories; Fern Woman is a prominent supernatural being

*Potentilla egedii* (silverweed) [**ts'i'aal, ts'iiaal** (S), **ts'a.al, ts'a'al** (M), **k̲'wíi ts'a.aláay** (A)]—food of Goose Woman in story

"Raven's mustache" (unidentified seaweed) [**x̲uya sG̲yuuG̲a** (S)]—poor material for harvesting herring eggs in one story

*Rubus spectabilis* (salmonberry) [**sk̲'aw** (S), **sk̲'aw hlk̲'a.aay, sk̲'aw.aan hlk̲'a.aay** (M), **sk̲'áw, sk̲'áw hlk̲'a.íi, sk̲'áw.aan hlk̲'a.íi** (A)]—frequently mentioned in stories, in a variety of roles

*Sambucus racemosa* (red elderberry) [**jitl'l/jiitl' hlk̲'a'ii, staay** (S), **stiid, stiid-xil, stiid-hlk̲'a.aay** (M), **stiid** (A) and other terms]—"roots" name of a gambling stick in one story

Seaweeds—various kinds mentioned in stories

*Scirpus microcarpus* ("cut-grass") [**x̲uya sG̲awG̲a** (S)]—apparently "Raven's knife" in a Haida story

*Shepherdia canadensis* (soapberry) [**'as** (S), **x̲agutl'iid** (M), **x̲agutl'íid** (A)]—common food of supernatural beings

*Streptopus amplexifolius* (twisted-stalk) [**st'aw g̲aanG̲a** (S), **st'aw g̲aanaa** (M), **st'áw G̲áanaa** (A)]—called "witch/screech owl berries"

*Trifolium wormskioldii* (wild clover) [**naa'a** (S)]—rhizomes eaten by Goose Woman in story

*Tsuga heterophylla* (western hemlock) [**k̲'aang** (S, M), **k̲'aáng** (A); edible inner bark: **xi** (S) **xiga, xig, xi** (M), **xi** (A)]—inner bark highly important food of supernatural beings; needles feature in some stories

*Urtica dioica* (stinging nettle) [**G̲udangxaal** (S), **G̲udang.aal, G̲udang'al** (M), **G̲udáng.aal** (A)]—mentioned in some stories

*Veratrum viride* (false hellebore) [**gwaayk'yaa, gwaayk'ya** (S), **gwaayk'aa** (M), **gwáayk'aa** (A)]—often mentioned in Haida stories, as used by shamans for protection against evil and to gain supernatural help

*Viburnum edule* (highbush cranberry) [**hlaayi** (S), **hlaa.i, hlaayaa** (M), **hláay** (A)]—berries highly important food of supernatural beings; most frequently mentioned plant food in Haida stories

*Vicia nigricans* ssp. *gigantea* (giant vetch) [**x̲uya tluuG̲a** (S), **yaahl tluwaa** (M), **yáahl tluwáay** (A)]—"Raven's canoe" in Haida story (see *Lathyrus*)

*Viola* spp. (wild violets) [**daal sgii** (S)]—believed to cause rain if picked

*Xanthocyparis nootkatensis* (yellow-cedar) [**sG̲aahlaan** (S), **sG̲ahlaan** (M), **sG̲ahláan** (A)]—family crest; featured in stories

*Zostera marina* (eelgrass) [**t'anuu, t'aanuu** (S, M), **t'anúu** (A)]—name of village of T'aanuu on Moresby Island; food of Goose Woman in story

# Appendix 7. Examples of Plants Associated with Animals

*Alectoria sarmentosa* (old man's beard lichen) [**k'aalts'idaa liisG̲a** (S, N), **k'aalts'adaa liijaa** (M)]—associated with crows

*Calypso bulbosa* (calypso) [**sk̲il tawaatl'lx̲aay** (S), **sk̲il taw**, **sk̲il tuu** (M), **sk̲íidaw** (A)]—named "black cod grease"

*Carex macrocephala* (dune sedge) [**x̲ahlk'ats'a hlk̲'a.aay**]—called "porcupine plant" by one woman (because of its prickliness)

*Conocephalum conicum* (liverwort) [**x̲ud t'aangalG̲a** (S), **x̲u t'aangal** (M)]—called "seal's tongue"

*Crataegus douglasii* (black hawthorn) [**k'anhl'l, k'anhll** (S), "**wakla**," or "**wahla**" ?]—berries food of crows

*Eriophorum* spp. (cotton-grasses) [**hltanG̲waay** (S), **hlk'yaanàa t'amdalaa (M)**]—known as deer's food

*Fauria crista-galli* (deer cabbage) [**G̲asaa** (M, A)]—known as deer's food

*Fragaria chiloensis* (seaside strawberry) [**hillda.aang xil**, or **hillda.aang hlk̲'a.aay** (M)]—known as favourite food of deer and cattle, which have eliminated much of it since their introduction

*Heuchera chlorantha* (alumroot) [**xu'aji xilG̲a** (S), **xuu.uj xilee** (M)]—named 'grizzly-bear leaves/medicine'

*Lathyrus japonicus* (beach pea) [**x̲uya tluuG̲a** (S), **yaahl tluwaa** (M), **yáahl tluwáay** (A)]—"**x̲uya**'s (S) [Raven's] canoe" in story of **X̲uya**/Raven Travelling (see also *Vicia gigantea*)

*Lonicera involucrata* (black twinberry) [**x̲uya G̲aanG̲a** (S), **yaahl G̲aanaa** (M), **yáahl G̲áanaay** (A) ('raven's-berry'); or **k'aalts'idaa'G̲aanG̲a** (S)]—berries food of ravens and crows

*Lycopodium clavatum* (running club-moss) [**k'aad dlajgaa.wee** (S), **k'aad dlajgaa.wee** (M), **k'áad dlajgáa.waay** (A)]—called "deer's belt"

*Lysichiton americanus* (skunk-cabbage) [**hlgun, hlguun** (S, M), **hlgún** (A)]—known as food for deer and bear

"Mushrooms, general" [**st'aw dajingG̲a** (S); **st'aw dajaangaa** ('owl hat'), **k'ak'u dajaangaa** ('owl hat'), **kagann dajaangaa** ('mouse hat') (M)]—apparently associated with owl and mouse

*Plantago maritima* (seaside plantain)—called "goose tongue" by some

*Potentilla egedii* (silverweed) [**ts'i'aal, ts'iiaal** (S), **ts'a.al, ts'a'al** (M), **k̲'wíi ts'a.aláay** (A)]—known as food for geese

*Rubus pedatus* (trailing raspberry) [**tl'ants'uud aanaa** (M)]—called "Steller's jay berries"

*Rubus spectabilis* (salmonberry) [**sk̲'awG̲aan, sk̲'aawG̲an** (S), **sk̲'aw.aan** (M), **sk̲'aw.áan** (A)]—berries ripened by singing of Swainson's thrush

*Streptopus amplexifolius* (twisted-stalk) [**st'aw g̱aang̱a** (S), **st'aw g̱aanaa, taan xaanaa** (M), **st'áw g̱áanaa** (A)]—called "witch/saw-whet owl berries" in Skidegate, and sometimes "black bear berries" in Massett

*Triglochin maritima* (salt-grass) [**hlgid.un t'aangal** (M)]—called "goose tongue"

*Usnea* spp. (old man's beard lichen) [**k'aalts'idaa liisg̱a** (S, N), **k'aalts'adaa liijaa** (M)]—associated with crows

*Vaccinium vitis-idaea* (lingonberry) [**sk'agi tsaay** (S), **skaga tsaay, sk'ag tsaay** (M), **sk'ag tsáay** (A)]—called "dog-salmon eggs"

*Veratrum viride* (false hellebore) [**gwaayk'yaa, gwaayk'ya** (S), **gwaayk'aa** (M), **gwáayk'aa** (A)]—said to be bear's food right after its winter sleep (TOXIC)

*Viburnum edule* (highbush cranberry) [**hlaayaa hlk'a'ii** (S), **hlaayaa hlk'a.aay** (M)]—known as deer's food; deer have reduced its abundance since they were introduced

*Vicia nigricans* ssp. *gigantea* (giant vetch) [**x̱uya tluug̱a** (S), **yaahl tluwaa** (M), **yáahl tluwáay** (A)]—"Raven's canoe" in Haida story (see *Lathyrus*)

*Viola adunca* (blue violet)—called "seagull's flowers" [**sk'in hlaawersgaay** (M)] by one woman

---

## Appendix 8. Unidentified Haida Plants

Listed in alphabetical order of their Haida names.

**x̱aad** (S)—a plant whose name was recorded by Swanton (1905a—"x̱at") and was taken [as a charm or medicine] to bring one property and luck. When a man ate this medicine, he sometimes saw Property-Woman and then became wealthy. Florence Davidson had not heard of a plant by this name.

**x̱aad gina, x̱aadgiina** (S) (Swanton 1905a)—this is another medicine, not the same as the previous one, but similar. Swanton (1905a) recorded a story in which a man mistook this plant for "x̱at" and ate it. He became wealthy anyway and assumed the name "He-Who-Obtained-Property-by-Eating-x̱aad gina."

**hlk'ung.iid** (M)—Swan (1885) described this as a small, succulent plant "looking like a small cactus," which was served to him by Mrs. Edenshaw at Kiusta, opposite Langara Island. It was gathered "in the swamp," and was slightly astringent. From the description—except the habitat—and from a rough sketch he included, the plant could be stonecrop (*Sedum divergens*), which was eaten by various peoples along the coast (Turner 1995). However, stonecrop was called by other Haida names (see entry for that plant). Another possibility is pearlwort (*Sagina maxima* A. Gray), a coastal species that occurs in "wet openings in alder thickets" and "sedge meadows below spring tide levels." On Langara Island it grows as "well-developed succulent plants" or as "large clumps of many upright plants" (Calder and Taylor 1968). Yet another edible succulent plant, which grows in salt marshes, is glasswort (*Sarcocornia pacifica*), which was eaten by the Alaskan Haida, after first being soaked in fresh water to remove some of the salt. It was also jarred for winter use (Margaret Blackman, personal communication 1971). The name **hlk'ung.iid** is cognate, at least in part, with the name **hlk'uuxaay** (S) (see Siberian miner's lettuce (*Claytonia sibirica*), but it apparently refers to a different plant.

**sG̲aa.n xilaa** (M) ('killer-whale leaves/medicine')—Florence Davidson recalled this plant as we were talking about wild lily-of-the-valley (*Maianthemum dilatatum*), and said, like that plant, it grows under salmonberry bushes, although she did not remember what it looked like. It was used for some kind of medicine.

**sdllgu xilG̲a** (S), **sdlagu xilee** (M) ('land-otter's medicine')—several of the elders I talked with recognized these names, but the identity of the plant itself is uncertain. Most simply called it some kind of "weed" or "flower." Emma Matthews, however, used it to refer to a small bog plant in the aster family, *Microseris borealis* (Bong.) Sch. Bip; she recalled seeing it when she went cranberry picking in the muskeg. She knew of no particular use for it.

"**yatlguutla**" (M) (?'raven woman' or 'raven daughter,' cf. **yaahl** 'raven' )—this name was recorded by Newcombe (1897), apparently referring to seabeach sandwort [*Honckenya peploides* (L.) Ehrh.]. No use was given for it.

---

## Appendix 9. General Botanical Terms in Haida

From John Enrico, Barbara Wilson, Dr. Diane Brown and Skidegate Haida elders.

Ashes: **hldalx̲id** (S)
Bark, outer: **k̲'uujii** (S)
Bark, thin (of bushes, herbaceous plants): **k̲'al, k̲'aal** (S, M), **k̲'al** (A) (also 'skin of fish, birds, mammals'—JE); not usually applied to tree bark, but was used on occasion for lodgepole pine bark
Basket: **skaayx̲an** (S)

Basket weaving: **kiiguu xaay** (S)
Berry, Fruit: **ḡaan, ḡaanaa** (S, M), **Ḡáanaay** (A)
Berries, mixed with sugar and grease: **ḵaayuuda** (S)
Berries, eating from the bush: **xiihl.hladang** (S)
Berries, eating unripe ones: **k'aanda gwang** (S)
Berries, to pick: **skaadang** (S)
Berries, picking with the stem: **hlḡwa k'uusda** (S); **hlkyan ḵ'aayxaa** (S) (large branches)
Blossom (see Flower)
Bough (butting into limb; 'needle-bearing branch of evergreen tree'): **hlḵ'ang'waal** (S), **hlḵ'am.aal** (M), **hlḵ'ám.aal** (A)
Branch, leaf bearing; Bush: **hlḵ'a'ii** (S), **hlḵ'a.aay** (M), **hlḵ'a.íi** (A)
Branch, of a tree: **ḵyaad klaajii** (S); **hlkyan ḵ'aayxaa** (S) (large branches)
Bushes (see Forest, Bushes)
Bushy: **hlk'wahljuu** (S)
Cones, evergreen and alder: **sk'aḡanda, sk'yuu'ul, sk'aḡanjuu, sk'yuu'u** (S), **stl'aas k'am.aal** (M), **stl'áas k'ám.aal** (A)
Digging stick for roots: **dllḡu** (S)
Flower: **xilaahgaay** (S), **xillee, xilayee** (M), **xiláay** (A) (nominalization of verb **xilaah**, **xila** 'bloom'—JE)
Forest, Bushes: **hlk'inxa, hlk'iinxaa, hlk'inxaayd** (S), **hlk'yaan** (sometimes translated by Newcombe as "stick"); or **ḵaayd ḵ'aaws** (S)
Fruit (see Berry)
Garden: **taawkiihl, taawkiihldan** (S)
Gardening: **taawk'ii** (S)
Grass, hay: **k'aan, ḵ'aan** (S)
Knot (of a tree): **klaajii** (S) ('root of a branch')
Leaf: **xil, xiil** (also 'medicine') (S, M)
Limb (branching, butting into trunk): **tlaas, tlaaji** (S), **tlaas, tlaaj** (M), **tláas** (A) (see also Branch, Bough)
Log, decayed: **k'aaxuu, ḵ'aaxuu** (S)
Medicine: **xil, xiil** (also 'leaf') (S, M)
Medicine man: **sḡaaga** (S)
Needles (of a coniferous tree): **t'aaw** (= hemlock needle) (S)
Pitch: **ḵ'aas, ḵ'aaji** (S), **ḵ'aas, ḵ'aaj** (M), **ḵ'áas** (A) ('gum, pitch, tar, wax, pitchwood')
Pitch, red: **ḵ'aas sluuts'a gid** (S)
Planting: **taaw k'iidaan, taawk'ii** (S) (see also Garden, Gardening)
Red tide: **chiitaawgaygiidas** (S)
Roots, general: **hllng.aa** (S) (but see more specific meaning for M, A cognates below); **skusaang.u** (M) ('any roots other than **hlii.ng**'), **skusáangwa** (A)
Roots, long, narrow, of evergreen tree (spruce in particular, but also hemlock, cedar): **hllng.aa** (S), **hlii.ng** (M), **hlíing** (A)
Roots, large, thick: **skusḡaanda, skusxaanda** (S) (see M, A terms for Roots, general)

Roots, picking: **giyaadii k̲aa** (S)
Seeds: **k'angii** (S) (stone of a fruit); or **mahlG̲aa, maahlga** (S)
Sliver, needle: **stlin** (S)
Tree: **k̲aayd** (= Sitka spruce) (S); trees: **hlk'iiyan k'aaws, k̲aayd k'aaws** (S)
Wood: **hlk'yaana, ts'aanu, ts'aanuud** (S)
Wood, rotten: **staanii** (S)

---

## Appendix 10. Introduced Vegetables and Fruits and Other Plant Products Having Haida Names

Listed alphabetically by English common name.

Apples (*Malus sylvestris* Mill.; syn. *Pyrus malus* L.): rose family (Rosaceae)—called "apples," **k'aay x̲aawla** 'sweet apple' (S), or **k'ay, k'aay** (S, M) after the native Pacific crab apple, *Malus fusca*, which is called **x̲àadas k'ayaa** (M) ('Haida apples') when necessary to distinguish them from the domesticated ones (EM, FD).

Bananas (*Musa* sp.); banana family (Musaceae)—**gina skaapdala** (S).

Beans (*Phaseolus vulgaris* L.); bean, or legume family (Fabaceae)—like peas, green beans are sometimes called **x̲uya tluuG̲a** or **k'uu sid xil** (S), **yaahl tluwaa** (M), **yáahl tluwáay** (A), after wild beach pea (*Lathyrus japonicus*) and giant vetch (*Vicia nigricans* ssp. *gigantea*), which were originally called by this name.

Blackberries (*Rubus* spp.); rose family (Rosaceae)—**tllgaa sk̲'aawG̲aanG̲a** (S). Himalayan blackberries (*Rubus armeniacus* Focke) are now common in and around Queen Charlotte City (JE) (see also salmonberry, *R. spectabilis*).

Carrot (*Daucus carota* L.); celery, or umbel family (Apiaceae)—**ts'its'i** (S), **ts'ats'a** (M), **ts'ats'** (A); see discussion under hemlock-parsley ("wild carrot"), *Conioselinum gmelini*.

Currants (*Ribes* spp.); gooseberry family (Grossulariaceae)—called **G̲al.un hlq'a.aay**) (M), the same as stink currant (*Ribes bracteosum*) (FD).

Gooseberries (*Ribes* spp.); gooseberry family (Grossulariaceae)—called **ginn x̲ayaa hlgamdalaa** (M) (literally 'round hard things with ligaments, or internal segments'—JE) (FD; JE).

Oats, rolled (*Avena sativa* L.); grass family (Poaceae)—**hlk'iid kaatsaa** (S) ('cow-parsnip seeds') (GY).

Onions (*Allium cepa* L.); lily family (Liliaceae)—**'aaniyaas** (M) (borrowed from English "onions") (FD).

Oranges (*Citrus sinensis* [L.] Osb.); citrus family (Rutaceae)—called **ginn q'al sgunaas** (M) ('thing with smelly skin'—JE).

Peas (*Pisum sativum* L.); bean, or legume family (Fabaceae)—like beans, are sometimes called **x̱uya tluuga, x̱uya kluuga** (S), **yaahl tluwáay** (M) ('raven's-canoe'), after wild beach pea (*Lathyrus japonicus*) and giant vetch (*Vicia nigricans* ssp. *gigantea*), which were originally called by this name.

Peppermint (*Mentha piperita* L.); mint family (Lamiaceae)—**xil sguunx̱uula** (S) ('leaves smell good')

Potatoes (*Solanum tuberosum* L.); nightshade family (Solanaceae)—called **sgawsiid, sgaawsid** (S), or **sguusiid** (M), **sgúusiid** (A). These names were said to have originated from the English words "good seed," learned at the time potatoes were first introduced to Haida Gwaii. An American seaman was said to have brought the first potatoes sometime between 1800 and 1820. By 1830, the Haida were already growing potatoes in large quantities for their own use and for trade to the Nass and Skeena people of the mainland. They also sold them to the Hudson's Bay Company and to passing fur-trading ships, and this allowed some Haida people to become very wealthy. For example, Newcombe (1902) referred to a mortuary pole for a man at Cumshewa, put up by his wife, "who ... was very rich, having much money in raising and selling potatoes to the villages in the neighbourhood." Dawson (1878, in Cole and Lockner 1989:472) noted, "*July* 18. Besieged by Indians with various things to sell this morning, curiosities, new potatoes about the size of wallnuts [sic] ..."

In January 2002, Primrose Adams gave me some Haida potatoes that her late husband, Victor Adams, had brought back with him from Alaska. He had been told by his Alaskan relatives that these potatoes originally came from Hawaii. They are elongated, with a light yellowish skin and white flesh. Some have small knobs, but most are regularly formed. Primrose said that a number of people, including those in her family, still grow these potatoes; they are delicious. A green potato that has been exposed to the light and is not good to eat is called **k'aa'anjuuwa** (S). They are said to be very similar to the Makah Ozette potatoes of Neah Bay.

Radish (*Rhaphanus sativus* L.), mustard family (Brassicaceae)—**ḵaadauu ḵ'uuhlii** (S).

Raspberry (*Rubus idaeus* L.), rose family (Rosaceae)—called **sḵ'awG̱aan, sḵ'aawG̱an, sk'awG̱an** (S); **sq'aw.aan giid'ii (hlq'a.aay), sq'aw.aan giidii** (M) ['salmonberry-baby(-bush)'], after salmonberry (*Rubus spectabilis*).

Rhubarb (*Rheum rhabarbarum* L.); knotweed family (Polygonaceae)—called **tl'aangq'uus** (S), **tl'aaq'uus, tl'aaq'uuj** (M), after "wild rhubarb" or western dock (*Rumex aquaticus* var. *fenestratus*). Rhubarb has been a common garden plant for many years and today is often used to make jam, sometimes mixed with strawberries, called "**tl'aaq'uus jáamgaa**" (M) (cf. English "jam"). Unlike "wild rhubarb," one should never eat the leaves of garden rhubarb because they are poisonous (Turner and von Aderkas 2009).

Rice (*Oryza sativa* L.); grass family (Poaceae)—called **'inhling ts'ing** (S) ('-teeth') after the rice-like bulblets of northern riceroot (*Fritillaria camschatcensis*) (not known to JE).

**Haida potatoes grown by Primrose Adams and family, 2002.**

Strawberry (*Fragaria* x *ananassa* Duch.); rose family (Rosaceae)—the berries are named **hilGudaGaang, hilGudaGang** (S), or **hillda.aang** (M), **hildaGáang** (A) and the plants **hillda.aang xil** (M) (FD), or **hillda.aang hlq'a.aay** (M) (WM, EM), after their wild counterpart (*Fragaria chiloensis*).

Tobacco (*Nicotiana tabacum* L.); nightshade family (Solanaceae)—called **gul, guul** (S, M), **gúl** (A) after the original Haida tobacco that was cultivated on Haida Gwaii in pre-contact times. Chewing tobacco is called **gul xaw'laa**, or **gul xaw.ulaa** (M only) ('sweet-tobacco'). The whole leaves of the native Haida tobacco were called **gul hlq'a.ang**, or **gul hlq'a'ang** (M) (JE). The first commercial tobacco was brought in as whole leaves and cigars by the Hudson's Bay Company. It was used for both chewing and smoking, and eventually replaced totally the indigenous tobacco (Solomon Wilson, George Young; Turner and Taylor 1972). Dawson (1880) noted that tobacco smoke, presumably of the commercial tobacco, was used to cleanse a house of sickness.

Turnip (*Brassica oleracea* L.); mustard, or crucifer family (Brassicaceae)—**yanahaw, yanaahuu** (S) (possibly from Chinook Jargon); or **'inuu** (M), **'inúu** (A) (swede turnip, rutabaga—JE) ('half'; cf. **inneweey q'al hlq'edaang** 'cut the turnip'). Turnips were introduced to the Haida early in the trading era. There are examples of Haida argillite pipes with carvings resembling half-turnips (emerging from the ground) with their leaves (Wilson Duff, personal communication 1971). Florence Davidson (cited in Blackman 1982:84) recalled, "My mother grew turnips in Masset, nothing but turnips, and she used to sell her turnip seeds."

**Northern riceroot (*Fritillaria camschatcensis*; inhling - S; stl'a k'iist'aa - M, A), flowers and bulbs.**

# Index

## English and Scientific Plant Names

(**Note:** Common names are generally listed under their primary term: e.g., Blueberry, Alaska, or Spruce, Sitka; in cases of ambiguity, names are cross-referenced. Appendices 1–7 are not indexed, because they represent summaries of information from the text.)

Figures in **bold face** indicate illustrations.


*Abies amabilis* 29
*Abies grandis* 29
*Abies lasiocarpa* 29
*Abies mertensiana* 94
*Acer glabrum* 29, 100, 107
*Achillea millefolium* 127, **159**, 160–61, 169
*Aconitum delphinifolium* 175
*Adiantum aleuticum* 186
*Agrostis aequivalvis* 177
*Agrostis palustris* 177
*Alaria marginata* 199
Alder 65
Alder, red 34, 57, 58, 60, 66, 69, 86, 87, 88, 102, **103**, 178
Alder, green (see Alder, Sitka)
Alder, Sitka 33, 34, 104
"*Alectoria jubata*" 194
*Alectoria sarmentosa* 192
Alga, terrestrial 207
Algae 61, 70, 79, 195–208
Algae, coralline 195
Algae, freshwater 205
Algae, green 205
*Allium cepa* 248
*Alnus rubra* 102, **103**, 178
*Alnus sitchensis* 104
*Alopecurus geniculatus* 177
Alumroot 70, 161
*Amanita muscaria* 211
*Ambrosia chamissonis* 159, **161**, 169
*Amelanchier alnifolia* **121**, 122
*Ammophila arenaria* 178
Apiaceae 136–37, 142–43, 248
Apple 46, 69, 248
Apple, crab (see Crab apple)
*Aquilegia formosa* 26, **31**, 171–72
Araceae 145–48
Araliaceae 153–55
*Arctostaphylos uva-ursi* **126**, 169
Arnica, heart-leaved 175
*Arnica cordifolia* 175
Arrow-grass 177, **180**
Arrow-grass Family 177, 180
Arum Family 145–48
*Aruncus dioicus* **107**, 108, 169
*Aruncus sylvester* 108
Ash, mountain (see Mountain-ash)
*Aspidium spinulosum* var. *dilatatum* (see *Dryopteris expansa*)
Aspleniaceae 185–90
*Asplenium trichomanes* 185
Aster Family 159–61, 175, 177
Asteraceae 159–61, 175, 177
*Athyrium filix-femina* 186
*Avena sativa* 248
Avens, large-leaved 169, **170**, 175
Azalea, false (see False azalea)

Balm of Gilead (see Cottonwood)
Bananas 248
Banana Family 248
"Beach carrot" 31
Beach pea (see Pea , beach)
Beach tansy (see Tansy, beach)
Beach wormwood (see Wormwood, beach)
Bean(s), domesticated 69, 149, 248
Bean Family 137–40, 149–50, 248
Bearberry (see Kinnikinnick; see also Twisted-stalk)
Bedstraw 33, 70, **164**, 169
Beets 43, 44
*Betula* sp. 100
*Betula papyrifera* 29
Betulaceae 102–4
Birch, paper 29, 100
Birch Family 101–4
Bitter cress, western (see Cress, western bitter)
Blackberries 248
Blackberry, Himalayan 248
Blackberry, trailing wild 116
Blackcap 45
Blechnaceae 189
*Blechnum spicant* **188,** 189
Blue-eyed grass 170
Blueberry, Alaska 34, 68, 121–22
Blueberry, bog 33, 121, 122
Blueberry, mountain 33
Blueberry, oval-leaved 34, 69, 121, 122
Blueberry, wild **43,** 44, 45, 48, 55, 67, 70
Boa, kelp (see Kelp, feather boa)
Bracken (see Fern, bracken)
*Brassica oleracea* 250

Brassicaceae 162, 250
Broom, Scotch 216
Bryophytes 79
*Bryoria capillaris* 192
*Bryoria fremontii* 194
Buckbrush 157
Bull kelp (see Kelp, bull)
Bulrush, small-flowered 178
Bunchberry 33, 34, 44, **130**, 131
Burnett, Canada 171
Buttercup 67, 170, 173, **174**, 175, 177
Buttercup, small-flowered 175
Buttercup, western 33, 173, **174**, 175
Buttercup Family 171–72, 173–75
Butterwort 171

Cabbage 44
*Cakile edentula* 169
*Caloplaca* 208
*Caltha biflora* 176, 207
Calypso 34, 42, 71, 170, **171**
*Calypso bulbosa* **170**, 171
*Campanula rotundifolia* 26, 169, 171, 172
Campanula Family 171–72
Campanulaceae 171–72
Caprifoliaceae 106–8, 109–11, 119, 127
*Cardamine* 151
*Cardamine angulata* 151, 162, 206
*Cardamine oligosperma* 151, **162**
*Carex canescens* 177
*Carex laeviculmis* 177
*Carex lenticularis* 177
*Carex macrocephala* 178
*Carex mertensii* 177, 178
*Carex obnupta* 177, 178
*Carex pauciflora* 177
Carrot(s) 43, 146, 248
"Carrot, wild" (see Hemlock-parsley)
Cascara 29
Cauliflower 135
Chard 44
Cedar, red- (see Cedar, western red-)
Cedar, western red- **10**, **23**, 29, **31**, 33, 34, 44, 49, 57, **58**, 60, 61, 68, 69, 71, 72, 73, 81-88, **83**, 85, 86, 118, 140, 217
Cedar, yellow- 33, 58, **59**, 68, 73, 80–81, **82**, 88
Celery Family 31, 136–37, 142–43, 248
*Cetraria glauca* (see *Platismatia glauca*)
*Chamaecyparis nootkatensis* (see *Xanthocyparis nootkatensis*)
*Chenopodium album* 169
Chenopodiaceae 144
Cherry 46, 105
Cherry, bitter 21
Chicken-of-the-woods fungus 209
Chocolate lily (see Riceroot, northern)
*Cicuta* spp. 137
Cinquefoil (see Silverweed, Pacific)
Cinquefoil, hairy 175
Cinquefoil, marsh 184, 207
*Cirsium brevistylum* **177**
*Cirsium* spp. 177
*Citrus sinensis* 248
Citrus Family 248
*Cladina pacifica* 194
*Cladonia bellidiflora* 193
*Claytonia sibirica* 171, **172**, 173, 245
*Claytonia sibirica* ssp. *bulbifera* 173
Cleavers (see Bedstraw)
Cloudberry 33, 44, 45, 56, 68, **79**, **128**, 129
Clover, springbank 33, 34, 42, 48, 51, 56, 67, **76**, **139**, 140, 141
Clover, white 170
Clover, wild (see Clover, springbank)
Club-moss 160, **184**, 185
Club-moss, fir 184
Club-moss, running **184**, 185
Club-moss Family 184–85
*Codium fragile* 206
Columbine, red 26, **31**, 33, 34, 171–72
*Conioselinum gmelini* **136**, 137, 248
*Conocephalum conicum* **194**
*Constantinea subulifera* 195
Coptis 175
*Coptis asplenifolia* 175
*Corallina* spp. 195
Coralroot 169
*Corallorhiza maculata* 169
Cornaceae 109, 130–31
*Cornus canadensis* **130**, 131
*Cornus sericea* 108, 109
*Cornus stolonifera* (see *Cornus sericea*)
*Cornus unalaschkensis* **130**, 131
Cotton-grass **33**, 70, 177, 179
Cottonwood, black 29, 101, 102, 119
Cow-parsnip 34, 43, 53, 69, 137, 142, **143**, 181
Crab apple, Pacific 33, 34, **44**, 45, 46, 48, 49, 51, 52, **56**, 57, 66, 69, 70, 72, 74, 88, 100, 101, 104, **105**, 106, 131, 132, 216
Crab apple, wild (see Crab apple, Pacific)
Cranberry 30, 44, 49, 74
Cranberry, bog 32, 33, 44, 48, 52, 69, **124**, 130, 216
Cranberry, lowbush (see Lingonberry)
Cranberry, highbush 34, **43**, 44, 45, 46, 48, 51, 52, 56, 66, 68, 69, 94, 105, **110**, 111, 119, 132
Cranberry, moss (see Lingonberry)
Cranberry, rock (see Lingonberry)
Crassulaceae 133
*Crataegus douglasii* 106, **108**
Cress, western bitter **162**
Cress, wild 162, 206
"Crow's whiskers" lichens 192, **193**
Crowberry 33, 69, **127**, 169
Crowberry Family 127

Cupressaceae 80–88, 106
Currant(s) 46, 55, 248
Currant, stink 34, 44, 48, 66, 111, **112**, 248
Currant, swamp (see Gooseberry, swamp)
Currant, trailing **112**, 113
"Cut-grass" 178
Cyperaceae 177–79
Cypress, yellow (see Cedar, yellow-)
Cypress Family 80–88, 106

*Dactylis glomerata* 178
Dandelion 175, 177
Deer cabbage 171
Deer fern (see Fern, deer)
Dennstaedtiaceae 190
*Deschampsia caespitosa* 178
*Desmarestia intermedia* 206
Devil's club **17**, **31**, 34, 53, 62, 63, 72, 74, **153**, **154**, 155
Dock, curly 143
Dock, western 43, 44, 69, 135, 143, **144**, 173, 250
*Dodecatheon jeffreyi* 172
Dogtooth lichen (see Lichen, dogtooth)
Dogwood, dwarf (see Bunchberry)
Dogwood, red-osier 34, 57, **108**, 109
Dogwood Family 109, 130, 131
Douglas-fir 29, 97
*Drosera rotundifolia* 151, **152**, 169
*Dryopteris austriaca* 187
*Dryopteris assimilis* 187
*Dryopteris dilatata* 187
*Dryopteris expansa* **187**, 188
Droseraceae 151–52
Dune grass, American (see Grass, American dune)
Dune sedge (see Sedge, dune)

*Echinodontium tinctorium* **211**
Eelgrass 33, 47, **196**, 205
*Egregia menziesii* 199, 206
Elderberry, red 34, 48, 100, **109**, 110
Elaeagnaceae 118–19
*Eleocharis macrostachya* 177, 178
*Elymus hirsutus* 178
*Empetrum nigrum* **127**, 169
*Epilobium angustifolium* 117, **162**, 163
*Epilobium glandulosum* 163
*Epilobium watsonii* 163
Equisetaceae 183–84
*Equisetum* 127, 160, 183–84
*Equisetum arvense* 183–84
*Equisetum hiemale* 184, 207
*Equisetum telmateia* **183**, 184
*Equisetum* spp. 183–84
Ericaceae 120, 121–27, 151, 155–57
*Eriophorum angustifolium* 177, **179**
*Eriophorum chamissonis* 177, 179
*Eurhynchium oreganum* (see *Kindbergia oregana*)
Evening-primrose Family 162–63
*Exobasidium vaccinii* **157**

Fabaceae 137–40, 149–50, 248
Fairy lamp-posts 175
False asphodel 170, 177, 178
False azalea 34, 156, **157**
False hellebore 34, **53**, 69, 77, 152, **153**, 155
False ladyslipper (see Calypso)
*Fauria crista-galli* 171
Fern(s) 74, 182, 183, 185–91
Fern, bracken 42, 46, 67, 69, 185, **190**
Fern, deer **188**, 189
Fern, lady 186
Fern, licorice 34, 46–47, 69, 70, **191**
Fern, maidenhair 186
Fern, oak 185
Fern, spiny wood 34, 42, 46, 67, **187**
Fern, sword 34, 42, 46, 69, **188**, **189**, 190
Figwort Family 176
Fir 29, 65, 127
Fir, Douglas- (see Douglas-fir)
Fir, true 29
Fireweed **15**, 34, 41, **42**, 43, 51, 60, 117, **162**, 163
Flowers (see "Haida Flowers")
Foamflower 170
*Fomes* spp. 68
*Fomitopsis pinicola* 208, 209, 210
Forget-me-not, water 171
"Fox berry" (see Cloudberry)
*Fragaria X ananassa* 250
*Fragaria chiloensis* **128**, 250
*Frangula purshiana* 29
*Fritillaria camschatcensis* **134**, 135, 143, 170, **250**
"Frog berry" (see Bunchberry)
*Fucus distichus* **196**
Fungi (fungus) 61, **208**, **209**, 211
Fungus, bracket **208**, **209**, 210
Fungus, shelf (see Fungus, bracket)
Fungus, Indian paint 60,
Fungus, red 207
Fungus, tree 68, **73**, 74, **208**, **209**, 210
Fungus, "wood biscuit" 210

*Galium aparine* **164**, 169
*Ganoderma applanatum* **208**, **209**, 210
*Ganoderma* spp. 68
*Gaultheria shallon* **120**
Geranium, wild 171, 173
*Geranium richardsonii* 171, 173
*Geum macrophyllum* 169, **170**, 175
Ginseng Family 153–55
Glasswort (sea asparagus) 33, **144**
*Glehnia littoralis* **31**, 137
*Glyceria occidentalis* 178
Goatsbeard **107**, 108, 169
Gooseberry 46, 69, 248
Gooseberry, swamp 53, 69, 108, 112, **113**

Gooseberry Family 111–14, 248
Goosefoot Family 144
"Goosetongue" 180
Grass(es) and Grass-like Plants 67, 76, 91, 173, 177–82
Grass, American dune 33, 69, 76, 180, **181**, 182, 185, 200
Grass Family 177, 178, 181–82, 250
Greyberry (see Currant, stink)
Grossulariaceae 111–14, 248
*Gymnocarpium dryopteris* 185

"Haida Flowers" 168–77
Haida tea (see also Labrador-tea) 30, **32**
*Halosaccion glandiforme* **31**, **196**
Harebell, blue 26, 31, 33, 169, 171–172
Hawthorn, black 34, 106, 108
Hay (see Grass)
Hay-scented Fern Family 190
Heather Family 120, 121–27, 151, 155–57
Hedge nettle 163, **164**, 170
Hellebore, false (see False hellebore)
Hellebore, green (see False hellebore)
Hemlock 68, 88
Hemlock, mountain 34, 97
Hemlock, western **29**, **33**, 34, 46, 47, 48, 51, 60, 71, 72, 76, 84, 89, 90, 93-97, **93**, **94**, **97**, 206
Hemlock-parsley 33, 42, 136, 137, 248
*Heracleum maximum* 137, 142, **143**, 181
*Heuchera chlorantha* 161
Highbush cranberry (see Cranberry, highbush)
*Holcus lanatus* 178
Honeysuckle Family 106–8, 109-111, 119, 127
*Honckenya peploides* 246
*Hordeum brachyantherum* 178
Horsetail(s) 60, 127, 160, 183–84
Horsetail, branchless 184, 207
Horsetail, common 69, 183–84
Horsetail, giant 43, 60, **183**, 184
Horsetail Family 183–84
Huckleberry 51, 157
Huckleberry, red **3**, 34, **43**, 44, 45, 48, 49, 51, 54, **55**, 118
Hudson's Bay tea (see Labrador-tea)
Hudson's Bay tea, Poisonous (see Swamp Laurel)
*Huperzia selago* 184
*Hylocomium splendens* 195
*Hypogymnia* sp. 192

"Indian celery" (see Cow-parsnip)
Indian paint fungus (see Fungus, Indian paint)
"Indian rhubarb" (see Dock, western)
"Indian rice" (see riceroot, northern)

Juncaceae 177
Juncaginaceae 177, 180
*Juncus articulatus* 177
*Juncus bufonius* 177
*Juncus effusus* 177, 178
*Juncus ensifolius* 177
*Juncus falcatus* 177
*Juncus* spp. 177
Juniper, common **106**
*Juniperus communis* **106**

*Kalmia microphylla* **155**, 156, 169
Kelp 48, 68, 206
Kelp, brown 199
Kelp, bull **24**, 33, 60, 61, 69, 72, 74, 95, 107, 142, 181, 182, 199, **200**, **201**, 202
Kelp, bullwhip (see Kelp, bull)
Kelp, common (see Kelp, bull)
Kelp, feather boa 199
Kelp, giant 33, 43, 47, 48, 49, 50, 51, 52, 69, **196**, **197**, 198–200, 204
Kelp, short 199
*Kindbergia oregana* 195
Kinnikinnick 33, 69, **126**, 169
Knotweed Family 143–44, 250

Labrador-tea 33, 47, 69, 70, 155, **156**, 191, 216
*Laetiporus sulfureus* 209
Lady fern (see Fern, lady)
Ladyslipper, false (see Calypso)
Lambsquarters 169
Lamiaceae 163, 248
*Laminaria* 199
*Lathyrus japonicus* **149**–50, 248
Laurel, swamp (see Swamp laurel)
Laver, red (see Seaweed, edible)
*Leathesia difformis* **197**
*Ledum* (see *Rhododendron*)
Legume Family 137–40, 149–50, 248
Lemon 70
Lettuce 44
*Leymus mollis* 180, **181**, 182, 185, 200
Lichen(s) 61, 68, 70, 79, 192–95
Lichen(s), "cloud" 192, **193**
Lichen, black tree 194
Lichen, British soldiers 193
Lichen, "crow's whiskers" 192, **193**
Lichen, dogtooth 68, 70, 192, 193
Lichen, lung 68, **193**, 208
Lichen, old man's beard 192, **193**
Lichen, reindeer 194
Licorice fern (see Fern, licorice)
Liliaceae 131–35, 152, 177
*Lilium columbianum* 134
Lily Family 131–35, 152, 177
Lily-of-the-valley, wild (see Wild Lily-of-the-valley)
Lingonberry 33, 44, 48, 52, 66, 71, 124, **125**
*Linnaea borealis* 127, 130, 169
Liverwort(s) 192–95
Liverwort, cone-head **194**

Liverwort, "seal's-tongue" **194**
*Lobaria oregana* 192, 193
*Lobaria pulmonaria* 192, **193**, 208
Loganberry 46
*Lonicera involucrata* 106–8, **107**
Lopseed Family 176
Lung lichen (see Lichen, lung)
Lupine 67
Lupine, beach 33, 46, 69, 132, 137, **138**, 139, 169
Lupine, Nootka 33, **138**, 139, 149
*Lupinus littoralis* 137, **138**, 139, 169
*Lupinus nootkatensis* **138**, 139, 149
*Luzula multiflora* 177
*Luzula parviflora* 177
*Lycoperdon perlatum* 211
Lycopodiaceae 184–85
*Lycopodium* 160, 184–85
*Lycopodium clavatum* **184**–85
*Lycopodium selago* 184
*Lysichiton americanus* **144**, 145–46, **147**, 148

*Macrocystis pyrifera* **197**, 198–200, 204
Madder Family 164
*Maianthemum dilatatum* **131**, 132
*Maianthemum racemosum* 132, 133
*Maianthemum stellatum* 132, **133**
Maidenhair Fern (see Fern, maidenhair)
Maidenhair Fern Family 186
*Malaxis paludosa* 171
*Malus fusca* 104–6, **105**, 248
*Malus sylvestris* 248
Maltberry (see Cloudberry)
Maple, Douglas (see Maple, Rocky Mountain)
Maple, Rocky Mt. 29, 100, 106, 119
"Mars apple" (see Cloudberry)
Marsh-marigold 175, 207
Marten's fire **207**, 208
*Matricaria matricarioides* 161
Melanthiaceae 152
Melanthium Family 152
*Mentha piperita* 248
*Menyanthes trifoliata* 206
*Menziesia ferruginea* 156, **157**
*Microseris borealis* 70, 246
*Mimulus guttatus* **176**
Miner's lettuce, Siberian 171, **172**, 173, 245
Mint, field 33
Mint (peppermint) 248
Mint Family 163, 248
Mission bells (see Riceroot, northern)
*Moneses uniflora* **151**, 154
*Monostroma* spp. 205
Monkeyflower, yellow 33, **176**
Monkshood 175
*Montia sibirica* (see *Claytonia sibirica*)
Montiaceae 171–73
Moss, mosses (and moss-like plants) 68, 76, 159, 192–95
Moss, "beard" (see Lichens, "crow's whiskers")
Moss, Oregon feather **195**
Moss, sphagnum 32, 184, **195**
Mountain-ash 100
*Musa* sp. 248
Musaceae 248
Mushroom(s) 68, 211
Mushroom, fly agaric **211**
Mustard Family 151, 162, 206
*Myosotis laxa* 171

*Nereocystis luetkeana* 181, 199, **200**, **201**, 202
Naiadaceae 205
Nettle, hedge (see Hedge nettle)
Nettle, stinging 34, 42, 44, 53, **59**, **158**, 159
Nettle Family 158-159
*Nicotiana quadrivalvis* 167
*Nicotiana quadrivalvis* var. *multivalvis* 165, **166**, **167**, 168
*Nicotiana tabacum* 250
Nightshade Family 165–68, 249, 250
*Nuphar polysepala* 175, 206, **207**
Nymphaeaceae 206–7

Oak 65
Oak, garry 101
Oats 248
*Oenanthe sarmentosa* 137
Old man's beard lichens (see Lichen, old man's beard; also "crow's whiskers")
Oleaster Family 118–19
Onagraceae 162–63
Onion(s) 148, 248
*Oplopanax horridus* **153**, **154**, 155
Oranges 248
Orchid, bog 171
Orchid Family 170–71
Orchidaceae 170–71
Orpine Family 133
*Oryza sativa* 250
"Owl berries" (see Twisted-stalk, common)
*Oxycoccos* spp. 124

Pacific silverweed (see Silverweed, Pacific)
*Parmelia* sp. 192
Parsnips 137
Pea(s), domesticated 69, 149, 248
Pea, beach 33, 68–69, 139, **149**–50, 248
Peach 105
Pear 46
Pearlwort 245
*Peltigera aphthosa* 192, 193
*Peltigera canina* 192, 193
*Peltigera polydactylon* 192, 193
Peppermint 248
*Phaseolus vulgaris* 248

Phrymaceae 176
*Phyllospadix* spp. 205
*Picea sitchensis* **29**, 88–93, **90, 91**
Pinaceae 88–98
Pine 65
Pine, lodgepole 33, 34, **98**
Pine Family 88–98
Pineappleweed 161
*Pinguicula vulgaris* 171
*Pinus contorta* **98**
*Pisum sativum* 248
*Plantago maritima* **180**
*Plantago major* **148**, 149, 161
Plantain, broad-leaved 34, 71, **148**, 149, 161
Plantain, seaside 33, **180**
*Platismatia glauca* 192, 193
Plum 46, 105
*Poa douglasii* 178
Poaceae 177, 178, 181–82, 250
Polygonaceae 143–44, 250
Polypodiaceae 191
*Polypodium glycyrrhiza* **191**
Polypody Family 191
Polyporaceae 209–10
Polypore (fungus) **208**, **209**, 210
*Polyporus* spp. 68, 211
*Polystichum munitum* **188, 189**, 190
Pond-lily, yellow **32**, 33, 67, 70, 168, 175, 206, **207**
Pondweed 206
Pondweed Family 205
*Populus balsamifera* ssp. *trichocarpa* 29, 102
*Porphyra* (see *Pyropia*)
Portulacaceae (see Montiaceae)
*Potamogeton epihydrus* 206
Potato(es) 42, 48, 49, 52, 137, 148, 165, **249**
*Potentilla egedii* 115, 140, **141**, 169
*Potentilla palustris* 184, 206
*Potentilla villosa* **175**
*Prunella vulgaris* 163, 169
*Prunus emarginata* 29
*Pseudotsuga menziesii* 97
Pteridaceae 186
*Pteridium aquilinum* 185, **190**
*Puccinellia pauciflora* 178
Puffballs 211
Purslane Family 172–73
"Pussy willow" 102
Pyrola, single-flowered (see Single Delight)
*Pyropia abbottiae* 26, 31, 198, 202, **203**, 205
*Pyropia lanceolata* 204
*Pyropia torta* 204
*Pyropia* spp. 204, 205
*Pyrus fusca* (see *Malus fusca*)
*Pyrus malus* 248

*Quercus garryana* 101

Radish 250
"Rain flowers" 171–72
Ranunculaceae 171–72, 173–75
*Ranunculus acris* 169
*Ranunculus occidentalis* 173, **174**, 175
*Ranunculus tenellus* (see *Ranunculus uncinatus*)
*Ranunculus uncinatus* 175
*Ranunculus* spp. 173
Raspberry 46, 65, 116, 250
Raspberry, wild 45
Raspberry, trailing 67, 70, 122, 127, **129**, 130
"Raven's berry" (see Twinberry, black)
Red-cedar (see Cedar, western red-)
*Rhamnus purshiana* (see *Frangula purshiana*)
*Rheum rhabarbarum* 250
*Rhodiola rosea* 133
*Rhododendron groenlandicum* **156**, 191
Rhubarb 44, 69, 143, 250
Rhubarb, Haida (see Dock, western)
Rhubarb, wild (see Dock, western)
*Rhytidiadelphus triquetrus* 195
*Ribes bracteosum* **112**, 113, 248
*Ribes lacustre* 108, **113**
*Ribes laxiflorum* **112**, 113
*Ribes* spp. 248
Rice 68, 136, 250
Riceroot, northern 33, 42, 48, 55, 67, 68, 70, **134**, 135, 143, 170, **250**
Rockweed, common 33, **196**
*Rosa nutkana* **13**, **117**, 170
Rosaceae 104–6, 107, 108, 114–17, 121, 127, 128–30, 140–41, 175, 248, 250
Rose 65, 69
Rose, wild **13**, 33, 34, 66, 69, **117**, 128–30, 162, 170
Rose Family 104–6, 107, 108, 114–17, 121, 127, 128–30, 140–41, 175, 248, 250
Roseroot stonecrop 133
Rubiaceae 164
*Rubus armeniacus* 248
*Rubus chamaemorus* **128**, 129
*Rubus parviflorus* **114**
*Rubus pedatus* 122, 127, **129**, 130
*Rubus spectabilis* **115**, 248, 250
*Rubus ursinus* 116
*Rubus* spp. 248
*Rumex acetosella* 144
*Rumex crispus* 143
*Rumex aquaticus* var. *fenestratus* 135, 143, **144**, 173, 250
Rush, common 178
Rush Family 177
Rutabaga 250
Rutaceae 248

Sac seaweed (see Seaweed, sac)
*Sagina maxima* 245
Salal 33, 34, **43**, 44, 45, 48, 49, 50, 51,

52, 54, 55, 60, 66, 93, 105, 114, **120**, 132
Salicaceae 101–2
*Salix* spp. 101–2
*Salix alba* 29
*Salix scouleriana* 101–2, 101
Salmonberry **34**, 43, 44, 48, 51, 52, 59, 67, **78**, 114, **115**, 116, 117, 162, 245, 248, 250
Salt-grass (see Arrow-grass)
*Sambucus racemosa* **109**, 110
Sandbur ragweed (see Wormwood, beach)
*Sanguisorba canadensis* 171
*Sarcocornia pacifica* **144**, 245
Saskatoon berry 33, 67, **121**
Salt-grass 33
Saxifragaceae 161
Saxifrage Family 161
*Scirpus microcarpus* 178
Scouring rush (see Horsetail) 184
Scrophulariacae (see Phrymaceae) 176
Sea asparagus (glasswort) 33, **144**
Sea lettuce 70, 205
Sea rocket 169
Sea staghorn 206
Sea wrack (see Rockweed, common)
Seabeach sandwort 246
Seagrass(es) 33, 205
Seagull's flowers 171, 172
Seaweed(s) 50, 67, 95, 100, 113, 195–208
Seaweed, deformed **197**
Seaweed, edible (see also Laver, red) 26, 44, 48, 51, 52, 68, 172, 198, 202, **203**, 205
Seaweed, green 205
Seaweed, sac **31**, 71, **196**
Seaweed, "summer" (see Seaweed, edible)
Seaweed, unidentified 206
Seaweed, winter 47–48, 204
Sedge(s) 177, 178
Sedge, dune 33, 178
Sedge, large-headed (see Sedge, dune)
Sedge, Mertens' 178
Sedge, tall basket 178
Sedge Family 177–79
*Sedum divergens* **133**, 245
*Sedum rhodiola* (see *Rhodiola rosea*)
*Shepherdia canadensis* **118**, 119
Self-heal 163, 169
Shooting star 172
Siberian miner's lettuce (see Miner's lettuce, Siberian)
Silverweed, Pacific 33, **42**, 48, 51, 56, 67, 76, **140**, **141**, 169
Single delight 34, **151**, 154
Single-flowered pyrola (see Single delight)
*Sisrynchium littorale* 169
"Skookum-root" (see False Hellebore)
Skunk-cabbage 33, 34, 44, 45, 46, **47**, 50, 53, 60, 69, 71, 74, 77, 120, 138, **144**, 145–46, **147**, 148, 157
*Smilacina* (see *Maianthemum*)
Snowberry (see Waxberry)
"Snowflowers" (see Single delight)
Soapberry **44**, 45, 46, 52, 100, 105, **118**, 119
Solanaceae 165–68, 249, 250
*Solanum tuberosum* **249**
Solomon's seal, false 132, 133
Solomon's seal, star-flowered 132, 133
Solomon's seal, two-leaved (see Wild Lily-of-the-valley)
Soopolallie (see Soapberry)
*Sorbus sitchensis* 100–101
Sourgrass 34, 144
*Sphagnum* spp. **195**
Sphagnum moss (see Moss, sphagnum)
Spinach 44, 143
Spiraea 65
*Spirogyra* 205
Spleenwort, maidenhair 185
Spleenwort Family 185, 186–90
Spruce, Sitka **7**, **29**, **34**, **35**, 46, 48, 49, 51, **59**, 60, 61, **63**, 66, 71, 76, 84, 88–93, **90**, **91**, 167
Spuds (see Potatoes)
*Stachys chamissonis* var. *cooleyae* 163, **164**, 170
Starflower, Arctic **170**
"Stick-potatoes" 137
*Sticta* spp. 192
Stinging nettle (see Nettle, stinging)
Stonecrop 33, **133**, 245
Strawberry 46, 69, 128, 250
Strawberry, seaside 33, 44, 48, 56, 69, **128**, 250
Strawberry, wild (see Strawberry, seaside)
*Streptopus amplexifolius* 108, 132, **133**, 170
*Streptopus roseus* 132
Sundew, round-leaved 33, 71, 151, **152**, 169
Sundew Family 151–52
Swamp laurel 33, 69, **155**, 156, 169
Swede (see Turnip)
Sweet potato 140, 141
"Sweet potato, wild" (see Silverweed, Pacific)
Sword fern (see Fern, sword)
*Symphoricarpos albus* **119**

*Tanacetum huronense* 159, **160**, 161
Tansy, beach 33, 159, **160**
*Taraxacum officinale* 175, 177
Taxaceae 98–100
*Taxus brevifolia* 98–100, **99**, 107
Thimbleberry **15**, 34, 43, 44, 45, 47, 48, 52, **114**
Thistle 71, **177**
Thistle, bull **177**
*Thuja plicata* 81–88, **83**, **85**, **86**
*Thelypteris limbosperma* 187
*Tiarella trifoliata* 169

Tiger lily 134
Toadstool 67–68, 211
Tobacco 69, 71, 74, 102, 165–68, 250
Tobacco, Haida 47, 52, 69, 102, 132, 165, **166**, **167**, 168
*Tolmeia menziesii* 169
*Trametes versicolor* 209
"Tree biscuits" (see Fungus, tree)
Tree fungus (see Fungus, tree)
*Trentepohlia aurea* **207**, 208
*Triantha glutinosa* 170, 177, 178
*Trientalis arctica* **170**
*Trifolium repens* 169
*Trifolium wormskioldii* **76**, 139–40
*Triglochin maritima* 177, **180**
*Tsuga heterophylla* **29**, 90, **93–97**, 206
*Tsuga mertensiana* 97
Turkey tails (fungus) 209
Turnip(s) 43, 250
Twinberry, black 34, 53, 54, 106–8, **107**
Twinflower 67, 70, 127, 130, 169
Twisted-stalk, common 34, 53–54, 67, 70, 77, 108, 132, **133**, 170

*Ulva* 70
*Ulva intestinalis* 205
*Ulva lactuca* 70, 205
Umbel Family 136, 142–43, 248
*Urtica dioica* **158**, 159
Urticaceae 158, 159
*Usnea barbata* 192
*Usnea longissima* 192, **193**

*Vaccinium alaskaense* 121–22
*Vaccinium ovalifolium* 121, **122**
*Vaccinium oxycoccos* **124**
*Vaccinium parvifolium* **123**
*Vaccinium uliginosum* 121, 122
*Vaccinium vitis-idaea* **125**
*Vaccinium* spp. 44
*Veratrum viride* 152, **153**
Vetch, giant 33, 68, 70, 139, **149–50**, 248
*Viburnum edule* 94, 110, 111
*Vicia nigricans* ssp. *gigantea* **149–50**, 248
*Viola adunca* 171, 172
*Viola glabella* 172
Violet, blue 172
Violet, wild 171, 172
Violet, yellow 171

Water plants 195–208
Water-hemlock 137
Water-lily 175, 206
Water-lily, Yellow (see Pond-lily, yellow)
Water-lily Family 206–7
Water-parsley 137
Waxberry 47, 54, 65, **119**, 170
Western red-cedar (see Cedar, western red-)
"Wild carrot" (see Hemlock-parsley)
Wild Lily-of-the-valley 34, 46, **131**, 132, 133
Wild rose (see Rose, wild)
"Wild snowdrops" (see Single delight)
Wild violet (see Violet, wild)
Willow 66, 68, 119
Willow, Scouler's 33, 101–2, **101**
Willow, weeping 29
Willow Family 101–2
Willowherb 163
Wood fern, spiny (see Fern, spiny wood)
Wormwood, beach 33, **161**, 169

*Xanthocyparis nootkatensis* 80–81, **82**
*Xanthoria* 208

Yarrow 33, 34, 47, 67, 69, 127, **159**, 160–61, 169
Yellow flowers 173–77
Yellow-cedar (see Cedar, yellow-)
Yew, western 34, **42**, 53, 57, **58**, 70, 98–100, **99**, 107, 119, 140, 141
Yew Family 98–100
Youth-on-age 170

*Zostera marina* **196**, 205

**The beautiful Mount Moresby, perfectly reflected in the calm morning waters of Cumshewa Inlet on July 4, 2010.**

# Index

## Haida Plant Names

(**Note**: Not all variants of all plant names are included in this index. Plant names are arranged alphabetically by pronunciation rather than by spelling. Appendices 1–7 are not indexed.) Figures in **bold face** indicate illustrations.


**adtagii** (Birch) 100
**ahxada** (Nettle fibre) **158**
**'ankos** (S) (Miner's lettuce, Siberian ?) **172**, 173
**'as** (S) (Soapberry) 45, 52, **118**, 119

**chaaGan xiilaay** (S) (Seaweeds, deep-water) 195
**chaanaang** (S, M) (see also **tsaanaang**) (Cottonwood; Willow) **101**, 102
**chiigwan** (S) (Fungus, Indian Paint) **211**
**chiijii k'waaluu** (S) (Cow-parsnip stalks) 142, **143**

**daal sgii** (S) (Violets, wild) 172
**daal sgilGa** (S) Columbine, red) 172
**dah** (S, M, A) (Cranberry, bog) 44, 48, 52, 69, **124**
**daktaa xilGa** (S) (Buttercups) 174
**dal xaw** (M) (Horsetails) 43, 60, **183**, 184
**dall-xil, daal-xil** (M) ("rain flowers"; Harebell, blue; Columbine, red, and other flowers) 26, **171**–72
**dall(-xíl)-Guhlahl** (Harebell, blue) 26, **31**, **171**
**dall(-xil)-sGid** (M) (Columbine, red) 26, **31**, 171–72
**dangaldagaa, dangaldgaa** (M) (Thimbleberry sprouts) 43, **114**
**danhl xil** (S), **danhlaa xilee** (M) (Cress, western bitter) **162**
**dinax** (M) (Kinnikinnick) 69, **126**
**dlaaying'waal** (M), **dláamaal** (A) (Fern, licorice) 46, 69, **191** [see also **glaaying'waal** (M), **gláamaal** (A)]
**"doctor" xilGa** (S), **"doctor" xilee** (M) (Buttercups) **174**
**duus-xil** (M) ("Pussy willow") 102

**gaaluuga k'uu** (S) (Avens, large-leaved) 175
**ganduu** (S) (Lupine, Nootka) 139
**gihlgahl** (M) (Lichen, "cloud") 192, 193
**giixida** (S), **gi.id** (M), **giid** (A) (Cedar bark) 60, 81
**gina skaapdala** (S) (Banana) 248
**gin q'al sgunaas** (M) (Orange) 248
**ginn xayaa hlgamdalaa** (M) (Gooseberries) 248
**glaayingwal** (S), **glaaying'waal** (M), **gláamaal** (A) (Fern, licorice) 46, 69, **191** [see also **dlaaying'waal** (M), **dláamaal** (A)]
**gudgina wasliia** (S) (Lichen ?; unidentified) 194
**gul, guul** (S, M); **gúl** (A) (Tobacco, Haida; Tobacco, commerical) 165, **166**, **167**, 168, 250
**gul 'awGa** (S) (Thistle) **177**
**gul xaw'laa, gul xaw.ulaa** (M) (Tobacco, chewing) 250
**gup** (S) (Seaweed, inedible; Sea lettuce) 203, 205
**gumdi jiikiis gedans xilaiyu** (S, M) (Forget-me-not; Butterwort) 171
**gúnduu** (A) (Lupine, Nootka) **138**
**guugadiis, gugadiis** (S) (Thimbleberry) **15**, 44, 47, 48, 52, **114**
**gwaayk'yaa** (S), **gwaayk'aa** (M), **gwáayk'aa** (A) (False hellebore) **53**, 69, 152, **153**
**gyaagyaa k'al sguuna** (S) (Hemlock-parsley) **136**, 137
**gyallgas naanGa, gyaalagas naanGa** (S) **208**, **209**, 210, 211

**Gaan, Gan** (S, M, A) (Berry; Fruit) 67
**Gaan xaw'laa** or **Gaan xaw.ulaa** (M), **Gáan xáw'laa** (A) (Saskatoon berry) 67, **121**
**Gaayang'waal-hlk'a.aay** (Common juniper) **106**
**Gada kidxaaw** (S) 108
**Gagan xil, Gaagan xil** (M) (Cress, wild) **162**, 206
**Gagan xill** (M) (Swamp laurel) **155**
**GalGun, GalGwan** (S), **Gal.un** (M), **Gál.un** (A) (Currant, stink) 44, 48, 111, **112**, 248
**Gandll sGinawaay** (S) (Seaweeds, green; *Enteromorpha, Spirogyra*) 205
**Gandll xilGa** (S) (Pondweed) 206
**Gasaa** (M, A) (Orchid, bog ?; Deer cabbage) 171
**Gawaa sk'ajaaw** (M) (Labrador-tea) **156**
**Gudangxaal** (S), **Gudang.aal, Gudang'al** (M), **Gudáng.aal** (A) (Nettle, stinging) 42, 44, 53, **59**, 60, **158**, 159
**GudGa gi Gayd (-hlk'a'ii)** (S) (Gooseberry, swamp) 53, **113**

**ha skáawaa** (A) (Crowberry) **127**

**hilgudaGaang** (S), **hillda.aang** (M), **hildaGáang** (A) (Strawberry, seaside; Strawberry, domesticated) 44, 48, 56, **128**, 250
**hukia (see xa k'ayaa ...)**

**hlaayii, hlaayi** (S), **hlaa.i, hlaayaa** (M), **hláay** (A) (Cranberry, highbush) 44, 45, 46, 48, 51, 52, 56, 69, **110**, 111
**hldaan** (S, M), **hldáan** (A) (Blueberry) 44, 45, 48, 51, 67, 70, 121, **122**
**hldaan gidga** (M), **hldáan gidga** (A) (Blueberry, Alaska) 121–22
**hldaan Gadaga** (S), **hldaan Gadaga** (M), **hldaan Gadga** (A) (Blueberry, oval-leaved) 121, **122**
**hlgid.un t'aangal** (M) (Arrow-grass; Plantain, seaside) **180**
**hlgun, hlguun** (S,M), **hlgún** (A) (Skunk-cabbage) 44, 45, 46, **47**, 50, 53, 60, 69, **144**, 145–46, **147**, 148
**hlGaabaluu** (S) (Thimbleberry) 114
**hlGiid** (S,M), **hlGíid** (A) (Yew, western) 53, 57
**hlii.ng k'in.anee** (M) (*Hylocomium* moss) 195
**hlk'iid** (S, M,), **hlk'íid** (A) (Cow-parsnip) 43, 53, 69, 142, 143
**hlk'iid giidGii** (S) (Water-parsley) 137
**hlk'iid hlkaamee** (M), **hlk'íid hlkáamaay** (A) (Cow-parsnip stalks) 142, **143**
**hlk'iid sgaawsidaay** (S) (Hemlock-parsley) **136**, 137
**hlk'inxa kwii'awaay** (S) (Lichen, "cloud") 192, 193
**hlk'inxa sgaawsidaay** (S) (Water-parsley; Hemlock-parsley) **136**, 137
**hlk'ung.iid** (M) (Miner's lettuce, Siberian?; or unidentified edible plant) **172**, 173, 245
**hlk'uuxaay** (S) (Miner's lettuce, Siberian ?; or unidentified edible plant) **172**, 173, 245
**hlk'yaanàa t'amdalaa** (M) (Cotton-grass) **179**
**hlk'yaan hlk'am.alee** (M) (Crowberry) **127**
**hlk'yaan sguusadee** (M) (Hemlock-parsley) **136**, 137
**hlkyaama** (S), **hlkaa.m** (M), **hlkáam** (A) (Grass, American Dune, Kelp, bull) 24, 60, 61, 69, **181**, 182, 199, **200**, **201**, 202
**hlk'am.aal, hlk'am.aal gin gyaa.alaas** (M) (Juniper, common) **106**
**hlk'am.aal kaj** (M) (Lichen) 192, 193
**hlinga, hlling.a** (S), **hlii.ng** (M); **hlíing** (A) (Spruce roots) **59**, 60, 61, 88–93, **90, 91**
**hlllng.a k'inxaan** (S) (*Hylocomium* moss) 195
**hltanGwaay** (S) (Cotton-grass) **179**
**hltanhlk'yaa** (S), **hltanhlk'a** (M), **hltánhlk'a** (A) (shredded cedar bark) 87
**hlt'amjaaw** (S) (Cotton-grass) **179**
**hlt'an'anda** (S) (Bracken fern, and other ferns) **185**
**hluuaanii** (S) (Lichen) 194

**'inhling** (S) (Riceroot, northern) 42, 48, 55, **134**, 135, 143, **150, 248**
**'inhling ts'ing** (S) (Rice) 250
**'inuu** (M), **'inúu** (A) (Turnip, Swede turnip, Rutabaga) 250

**jatl'a, jatl'** (M), **jatl'** (A) (Elderberry, red) 48, **109**, 110
**jitl'l, jiitl'** (S) (Elderberry, red) 48, **109**, 110

**kaadauu k'uuhlii** (S) (Radish) 250
**kaagan daajing** (S), **kagann dajaangaa** (M) (Mushroom) 68, **211**
**kagan lhk'a'ii** (S) ("Pussy willow") 102
**kamkamm** (M) (Yarrow) **159**, 160–61
**ka'as, ka.as, ka'aj** (M), **kaas** (A) (Alder, Sitka) 104
**kémdelaa** (M, A) (Yarrow) **159**, 160–61
**"kinhau"** (M) (Lichen) 193
**kl'aay kl'aay GaanGa** (S) (Raspberry, trailing) **129**, 130
**kug gilgee, kug Galaanggaa** (M) (Fungus, tree) **208**, **209**, 210
**kun'aan** (S), **kun.aan** (M) (Nettle roots) **158**, 159

**k'aad dlljigawaay** (S), **k'aad dlajgaa. wee** (M), **k'áad dlajgáawaay** (A) (Club moss, running) **184**, 185
**k'aalts'idaa GaanGa** (S) (Twinberry, black) 54, 106–8, **107**
**k'aalts'idaa gyaa'adGa** (S) (Lichen) 192, **193**
**k'aalts'idaa liisGa** (S, N), **k'aalts'adaa liijaa** (M) (Lichen) 192, **193**
**k'aaw** (S, M) (Herring eggs) 49, 50, 51, 52, **197**, 198–200, **231**
**k'aaw tsik'uus** (S) (Puffball) 211
**k'aay** (S, M) (Crab apple, Pacific) 70, 104–6, **105**, 216
**k'aay xaawla** (S) (apple) 248
**k'aayluus** (S) (Lemon, Sourgrass) 70
**k'ak'u dajaangaa** (S), (Mushroom) 68, 211
**k'anhl'l, k'anhll, k'anhla** (S) (Crab apple, Pacific; Hawthorn, black) 57, 100, 104–6, **105, 108**
**k'ay, k'aay** (S, M), **k'áy** (A) (Crab apple, Pacific; Apple, domesticated) **44**, 45, 46, 48, 51, 52, 69, 70, 104–6, **105**, 216, 248
**k'ayanhla, k'a'inhla** (M), **k'ayánhl** (A) (Crab apple, Pacific) 57, 104–6, **105**

**k'in.aan gangaa** (M) (*Sphagnum* moss) **195**

**k'in.aan hlt'aamdalaa** (M) (*Rhytideadelphus* moss) 195

**k'inx̲aan, k'iinx̲aan** (S), **k'in.aan** (M), **k'ín.aan** (A) (Mosses and moss-like plants) 68, **195**

**k'inx̲aan gang.'ah** (S) (*Sphagnum* moss) **195**

**k'inx̲aan hlt'aamdalaa** (S) (*Rhytideadelphus* moss) 195

**k'u'iid, k'u'iid G̲aanG̲a** (S) (Waxberry) 47, 54, **119**

**k'uu sid xil** (S) (Beans) 248

**k'ùu ts'aanaawaa** (M) ("Marten's fire"; *Trentepohlia*, an alga) **207**

**k̲ajaanda, k̲aajaanda** (S) (Seaweed; ?*Egregia*) 206

**k̲aajii hltanG̲waay** (S) (Cotton-grass) **179**

**k̲aayd, k̲ayd,** (S) (Spruce, Sitka; tree, general) 46, 48, **63**, 66, 88–93, **90, 91, 231**

**k̲aayd k'inx̲aan** (S) (*Kindbergia* moss) **195**

**k̲ayd gyaa'ad** (S) (Lichen, "cloud") 192

**k̲aayda kax̲awaay** (S) (Juniper, common) **106**

**k̲aal, k̲al** (S, M), **k̲ál** (A) (Alder, red) 57, 60, 69, 87, 102, **103**

**k̲al.aa k'inx̲aan** (S) (*Sphagnum* moss) **195**

**k̲as janda, k̲a jand, k̲aj janda** (M), **k̲as jánd** (A) (Seaweed; ?*Egregia*) 206

**k̲aw tsik'uus** (S), **k̲aw tsagwiid** (M) (Puffball) 211

**k̲aysgwaan** (S) (Thimbleberry sprouts) 43

**k̲ayluus** (S) (Sourgrass) 144

**k̲iid** (M), **k̲íid** (A) (Spruce, Sitka) 46, 48, 84, 88–93, **90, 91**

**k̲iid gaabee.uu 'iijaa** (M) (Turkey tails, fungus) 209

**k̲iid k'in.anee** (M) (*Kindbergia* moss) **195**

**k̲uuG̲a k'u'inda** (S) (Yarrow) **159**, 160–61

**k̲'aahl'a** (S) (Alder, Sitka)

**k̲'aajii, k̲'aaj** (S, M) (spruce pitch) 88, 89, **231**

**k̲'aang** (S, M); **k̲'aáng** (A) (Hemlock, western) 46, 47, 48, 60, 84, 93–97, **93, 94, 97**

**k̲'aas** (S, M) (spruce pitch) **63**, 88, 89, 92

**k̲'aats** (M), **k̲'áats'** (A) (Sea lettuce; Seaweeds) 205

**k̲'aax̲u ts'alaangG̲a, k̲'aax̲u ts'alaang. G̲a,** (S), **k̲'a.àw ts'alaangaa** (M); **k̲'aawts'aláangaa** (A) (Cloudberry) 44, 56, **128**, 129

**k̲'aayda xil gaay dllgins** (S) (Pond-lily, yellow) 175, 206, **207**

**k̲'aaydaG̲aangG̲a, k̲'aydaG̲aanG̲a** (S) (Currant, trailing) **112**, 113

**k̲'ada sG̲awG̲a** (S) (Horsetail, giant; Horsetail) 43, **183**, 184

**k̲'al.aa k̲'anee** (M) (Grass-like plants growing in muskeg) 178

**k̲'al.aa k'in.anee** (M) (*Sphagnum* moss; Club-moss, running) **184, 195**

**k̲'al.aa hlk̲'am.alee** (M) (Juniper, common) **106**

**k̲'al.aa skusaang.u** (M) (Lichen, reindeer) 194

**k̲'al.aa xilee** (M) (Harebell, blue) **171**, 172

**k̲'a'll hltanG̲waay** (S) (Cotton-grass) 71, **179**

**k̲'an** (S, M), **k̲'án** (A) (Grasses and grass-like plants) 67, 173, 177–82

**k̲'an hlgamG̲anda** (S) (Arrow-grass) **180**

**k̲'an sk'ang.andaa** (M) (Arrow-grass; Grass, American dune) **180, 181**, 182

**k̲'an tl'ang.andaa** (M) (Grass, American dune) **181**, 182

**k̲'as, k̲'aas** (S, M, A) (False azalea) 156, **157**

**k̲'iit'agwaand** (S), **k̲'iit'agwaand, k̲'iidgwaan, k̲'iit'agwaan** (M), **k̲'íitgwaang** (A) (Currant, trailing) **112**, 113

**k̲'u kamm** (M) (Yarrow) **159**, 160–61

**k̲'ung** (S), **k̲'unhla, k̲'unhl** (M), **k̲'únhl** (A) (Rose hips, buds) **13, 117**

**k̲'unhla xilaay** (M) (Rose flowers, wild) **13, 117**

**k̲'using.a xilG̲a** (S) (Labrador-tea) 47, **156**

**k̲'wíi ts'a.aláay** (A) (Silverweed, Pacific) 42, 56, 76, **140, 141**

**"lkanatxil," "lhkunetxil"** (S) (Miner's lettuce, Siberian ?) **172**, 173

**'laanaa hlgunG̲a** (S), **'laana hlgun** (M) (Plantain, broad-leaved) **148**

**'laanaa xilG̲a** (S) Plantain, broad-leaved) **148**

**madalaa.u, madlaaw (-xil/-hlk̲'a.aay)** (M) (Thimbleberry bush) **114**

**naa'a** (S) (Clover, springbank) 42, 48, 51, 56, **76, 139**, 140

**naw-sgaawsidaay xil ("na'uskausitaxil")** (S) (Hemlock-parsley) **136**, 137

**ngaal** (S, M), **ngáal** (A) (Kelp, giant) 43, 47, 49, 50, 52, 69, **197**, 198–200, **231**

**ngaal ga'aan, ngaal ga'aanda** (S) (Kelp, short; Kelp, brown) 199

**ngaalaagaas** (S) (Seaweed; Kelp, short) 200

**saad G̲aanG̲a, shaad G̲anG̲a** (S), **saad G̲aanaa** (M), **"sa'ián"** (A) (Stonecrop) **133**

**saagun** (S) (Fern, bracken) 42, 46, **190**

**saagwaal** (M) (Ferns, various; Fern, spiny wood) 185–91, **187**
**saahldajiigaay** (N), **"sahildjigai"** (M) (Buttercup, western) **174**
**saan xila** (M) (Horsetail, branchless) 184, 207
**saanii xilaay ?** (S) (Cinquefoil, marsh) 207
**sanaal jaad** (M) (Fern, sword; Fern, deer) 189
**sangg sxiiwee** (M), **sángg sGíiwaay** (A) (Seaweed, winter) 48
**sa.an, sa'an** (M), **sa'áan** (A) (Wild lily-of-the-valley) **131**, 132
**sdlagu tliidaang.wee** (M) (Seaweed, unidentified; sea staghorn?) 106
**sdllgu xilGa** (S), **sdlagu xill** (M) (unidentified medicinal plant) 245
**sgawsiid** (S), or **sguusiid** (M), **sgúusiid** (A) (Potatoes) 42, 52, **247**
**sgiisga, sgiisg** (M) (Willow) 101
**sgiisgii** (S) (Dogwood, red-osier; Willow) 57, **108**, 109
**sGaahlaan** (S); **sGahlaan** (M); **sGahláan** (A) (Cedar, yellow-) 58, 80-81, **82**
**sGaal ts'iit'ii sga, sGaal tsit'iisgu, sGaal hlaawersGa** (S) (Monkeyflower, yellow) **176**
**sGaalaak'uu ts'ii, skaalaak'uu ts'ii** (S) (edible inner bark of spruce) 46, 48, 88
**sGaana jaad xad.dalaa** (S) (Fern) 186
**sGaa.n xilaa** (M) (unidentified medicinal plant) 245
**sGid xaadaal** (M) (Dogwood, red-osier) 57, **108**, 109
**sGidGang.xal** (S) (Rose flowers, wild) **117**
**sGidllGuu, sGiidllguu** (S), **sGidlùu** (M), **sGidluu** (A) (Huckleberry, red) 44, 45, 48, 51, 54, **123**
**sGiid** (M) (Sedge, Mertens') 178
**sGiinaaw** (S, M), **sGináaw** (A) (Sea lettuce; Seaweeds, green) 205
**sGyuu** (S), **sGiw** (M); **sGíw** (A) (Seaweed, edible) 44, 48, 51, 52, 202, **203**, 205
**siGan, siiGan** (S) (Wild lily-of-the-valley) 46, **131**, 132
**sin** (S), **san** (M) (Maple, Rocky Mountain) 100, 107
**sing.Ga** (S), **sangga, sanga** (M), **sángg** (A), or **sing.Ga sGiiwaay** (S), **sangg sxiiwee** (M), **sángg sGíiwaay** (A) (Seaweed, winter) 47–48, 204
**skiida wasliia** (S) (Lichen?; unidentified) 194
**skil t'aaxul** (S) (Tobacco, Haida) 165, **166, 167**, 168
**sk'aang k'iis** (M) (Seaweed, sac) **196**
**sk'aang.iid** (M, A) (Wild lily-of-the-valley) **131**, 132
**sk'aaxaay** (S) (Wild lily-of-the-valley) **131**, 132
**sk'agi tsaay** (S), **skaga tsaay, sk'ag tsaay** (M), **sk'ag tsáay** (A) (Cranberry, lowbush) 44, 48, 52, **125**
**sk'idGaan** (S), **sk'idaan, sk'id'aan** (M), **sk'itáan** (A) (Salal) 44, 45, 48, 50, 51, 52, 54, 60, **120**
**sk'iid, sk'iidGaanxil** (S); **sk'iihla, sk'iihl, sk'iihla hlk'a.aay** (M) (Salal) 50, 60, **120**
**sk'in** (S, N) (Horsetail) 183, 184
**sk'yaw hlk'a.aay** (M) (Yarrow) **159**, 160–61
**sk'yaaw** (S, M), **sk'yáaw** (A) (Fern, spiny wood; Lupine, beach) 42, 46, 138, **187**, 188
**sk'yaaw k'ad.dalaa** (S) (Fern) 186
**skaalaak'uu ts'ii, sGaalaak'uu ts'ii** (S) (edible inner bark of spruce) 46, 48, 88
**skil tawaatl'lxaay, skil taawaatllxaay** (S), **skil taw, skil tuu** (M), **skíidaw** (A) (Calypso) 42, **170**, 171
**skwaank'aa, skunk'aa** (M) (Seaweed, deformed) **197**
**"sk'awGaan giidGii"** (Blueberry, bog: Boas' name) 122
**sk'aw.aan giid'ii (hlk'a.aay)** (M) (Raspberry, garden) 116, 250
**sk'awGaan** (S), **sk'aw.aan** (M), **sk'aw.áan** (A) (Salmonberry; Raspberry) **34**, 48, 51, 52, 67, **115**, 116, **117**, 248, 250
**sk'iina xil** (S) (Wormwood, beach) **161**
**sk'in hlaawersgaay** (M) (Violet, blue) 171
**snaal jad** (M) (Fern, sword; Fern, deer) 189–90
**snanjang, snanjaang, snanjang xil** (S) (Fern, sword, and other ferns) 185, 186, 190
**staay** (S) (Elderberry, red) 109
**stla skaajuu, stla tl'anii** (M) (Seaweed, sac) **196**
**stla k'iist'aa** (M, A) (Riceroot, northern) 42, 48, **55**, **134**, 135, 143, **150, 248**
**stladaal sgyann** (M) (Dock, western; Dock, curly) 143, **144**
**stl'agudiis** (M), **stl'agudíis** (A) (Thimbleberry) **114**
**styuu xihl kidxunang ?** (N) (Club-moss, running) 184
**st'all naay** (S) (Mushroom) **211**
**st'aw dajingGa, st'aaw daajing, st'all naay, st'aw dajaangaa** (S) (Mushroom) 68, **211**
**st'aw GaanGa** (S), **st'aw Gaanaa** (M), **st'áw Gáanaa** (A) (Twisted-stalk, common) 53–54, 67, 132, **133**
**st'uu GaanGa** (M) (Twisted-stalk, common) 132, **133**

**taan Gaanaa** (M) (Twisted-stalk, common; Goatsbeard) 108, 132, **133**
**taajaanda, taayjanda** (S) (Kelp, a kind of) 199
**ta.an sk'yaaw** (S, M) (Fern, sword) **188**, **189**, 190
**taGansk'yaa, taGansk'ya** (S), **ta.ansk'yaaw, ta.ansk'yaa** (M) (Fern, bracken; Lupine, beach) 46, 69, 137, **138**, 139, 189, **190**
**t'a sk'at'uuga** (S) (Seaweed, sac; Seaweed, deformed) **197**
**t'a'inaang k'uug** (M), **ta'ináang k'úug** (A) (Sundew, round-leaved) 151, **152**
**t'al** (S, M), **t'ál** (A) (Rockweed, common) **196**
**t'anuu** (S, M), **t'anúu** (A) (Eelgrass) **196**, 205
**t'anuu skuunxuula** ? (S) (unidentified aquatic plant; possibly Cress) 206
**t'aanuu, t'anuu** (S, M), **t'anúu** (A) (Eelgrass; Seagrasses) **196**, 205
**t'iis xil, t'iis xilee** (M) (Lichen, dogtooth) 192
**t'iisgu skaahlln** (S) (Cinquefoil, hairy) **175**
**t'iisgu skaahlln** (S) (Stonecrop) **133**
**tllgaa GaanGa** (S) (Blueberry, bog; Kinnikinnick; Lingonberry; Raspberry, trailing) 122, **126**, **129**, 130
**tllgaa sk'aawGaanGa** (S) (Blackberry, trailing wild) 116
**tllgaa xilGa** (S) (Twinflower) 127
**tlGaanGa** (S) (Kinnikinnick) **126**
**tl'aak'uus, tl'aak'uuj** (M), **t'láak'uj, tl'áak'us** (A) (Dock, western; Rhubarb) 43, 44, 143, **144**, 250
**tl'aangk'uus, tl'aang.k'uus** (S) (Dock, western; Rhubarb; see also Miner's lettuce, Siberian) 43, 44, 143, **144**, **172**, 173, 250
**tl'aay tl'aay GaanGa** (S) (Raspberry, trailing) **129**, 130
**tl'ants'uud Gaanaa (-xil)** (M,A) (Raspberry, trailing) 127, **129**, 130
**tl'laal(-xil)** (S), **tl'ii'aal** (M), **tl'íi.aal** (A) (Fireweed) **15**, 41, 43, 51, 60, **162**, 163
**tsaanaang** (S, M) (Willow, Cottonwood) (see **chaanaang**) 101–102
**"tsá-ahl"** ("small willow") 101
**tsàa.u salii xil k'anhlahl jahjuu** (M) (Tansy, beach) **160**, 161
**tsàa.u ts'áagwaal** (M) (Yarrow) **159**, 160–61
**tsàa.us k'un saagulee** (M) (Tansy, beach) **160**, 161
**tsa.àn hlk'am.alee.uu 'iija** (M) (Seaweeds, deep water) 195
**tsa.àn k'in.anee** (M) (unidentified seaweed, brown) 206
**tsaGan xilaay** (S) (Seaweeds, deep water) 195
**"tsigwán"** (Fungus, Indian paint) 60, **211**
**tsixu k'an** (S) (Grass, American dune) **181**
**ts'aagul** (S), **ts'aagwaal** (M), **ts'áagwaal** (A) (Fern, sword, Fern, spiny wood and other ferns) 42, 46, 185–91, **187**, **188**
**ts'aagwaal hlk'a.aay** (M) (Fern, bracken) 42, 46, **190**
**ts'ahl** (S); **ts'ahla, ts'ahl** (M) ('pine'); **ts'ahl** (A) (Pine, lodgepole) **98**
**ts'ahl tlaas** (M) (Crowberry) **127**
**ts'ahl t'awsgiid, ts'ahl t'awt'iis** (S); **ts'ahl t'awsgiid, ts'ahl t'uusgiid** (M); **ts'ahl t'áwsgad** (A) (Bedstraw) **164**
**ts a.al, ts'a'al** (M) (Silverweed, Pacific) **140**, **141**
**ts'asaal** (M); **ts'a.áal, tsa'áal** (A) (Salmonberry sprouts) 43, **115**
**ts'ats'a** (M), **ts'ats'** (A) (Carrot; Hemlock-parsley) **136**, 137, 248
**ts'ats'a k'u kamm** (M) (Yarrow) 47, **159**, 160–61
**ts'iihllnjaaw** (S), **ts'iihlanjaaw** (M) **ts'íihlanjaaw** (A) (Devil's-club) **17**, 53, 62, 72, **153**, **154**, 155
**ts'iik'ap, ts'ik'ab** (S), **ts'iik'ab** or **ts'iik'abaa, ts'iik'ab xil** (M), **ts'íik'ab** (A) (Bunchberry) 44, **130**, 131
**ts'its'i** (S) (Carrot) 248
**ts'ixaal, ts'iixal** (S) (Salmonberry sprouts) 43, **115**
**ts'i'aal, ts'iiaal** (S) (Silverweed, Pacific) 42, 48, 51, 56, 76, **140**, **141**
**ts'uu** (S, M), **ts'úu** (A) (Cedar, western red-) 57, **58**, 69, 81–88, **83**, **85**, 86
**ts'uu liisGa** (S) (Lichen, "cloud") 192

**wakla, wahla** (Hawthorn, black) **108**
**wiid ?** (S) (Moss, unidentified) 195

**xagutl'iid** (M), **xagutl'íid** (A) (Soapberry) 45, 52, **118**, 119
**xil** (S, M) **xìl** (A) (Leaf; Medicine) 66–67
**xil 'ang dan tiisdalls** (M) (Monkeyflower, yellow) **176**
**xil gaaydllgins** (S), **xil gii dlagang** (M), **xil gíi dlagáng** (A) (Pond-lily, yellow; Marsh-marigold ?) 175, 206, **207**
**xil k'anhlahl** (M) (Buttercups) 173, **174**, 175
**xil k'ud tl'an, "xilskutsklan"** (S) (Buttercup; Dandelion) 175, 177
**xil kagann** (M), **xíl kagan** (A) (Labrador-tea; sometimes Swamp laurel) 47, 155, **156**

xil kwiiawaa (S), xil kwii.awaa (M) (Lichen, "cloud") 192, 193
xil sgunxulaa, xil sguunxuula (S), xil sgun.ulaa (M) (Yarrow; Tansy, beach; Wormwood, beach; Mint, Peppermint) 47, **159**, 160–61, 248
xil sk'yaawaa (S, M) (Yarrow; Wormwood, beach) **159**, 160–61
xil tl'a.aang (M, A) (Lichen, British soldiers) 193
xil tl'xida (S) (Spleenwort, maidenhair) 185
xil ts'ahlsgidaa (S) (Bedstraw) **164**
xil xawaas ? (A) (Arnica, heart-leaved) 175
xudaan (S, M) (Hedge nettle), see also xudaan **163**
xu'aji xilGa, xuuaji xilGa (S), xuu.uj xilee (M) (Alumroot) 161

xa k'ayaa (M), xa k'ayaa (A) (Mountain-ash) 100–101
xa skaa.awaa (M) (Crowberry) **127**
xaad, "xat" (S) (unidentified medicine) 245
xaad gina, xaadgiina (S)) (unidentified medicine) 245
xaad(as) k'ayaa (M) (Crab apple, Pacific) 69, 104
xaadas tl'aak'ujaa (M) (Dock, western) 143, **144**
xaadas ts'ats'á (A) (Hemlock-parsley ?) **136**, 137
xaaydaa hlaawersGa, xaaydaa hlaawersGaay (S) (Haida flowers; Wildflowers, "Haida Flowers") 67, 169–77
xaayda gulGa (S), xaadas gulaa (M), xaadas guláa (A) (Tobacco, Haida) 47, 165, **166**, **167**, 168
xaayda tiiGa (S) (Labrador-tea) 47, **156**
xaayuwaa (M), xáayuwaa (A) (Gooseberry, swamp) 53, **113**
xahlk'ats'a hlk'a.aay (M) (Sedge, dune) 178
xang k'aadaawaa (M) (Salmonberry, red form) 115
xat (M) (unidentified medicine plant) 62
xi (S) xiga, xig, xi (M), xi (A) (edible inner bark of hemlock) 46, 48, 93
xil GuuGa (S), xilaawg (M) (Single delight, "snowflower") **151**
xud t'aang.alGa (S), xu t'aangal (M) (Liverwort, "seal's-tongue") **194**
xudaan (S, M) (Hedge nettle), see also xudaan 163, **164**
xuuguuga (Douglas-fir) 97
xuya GaanGa (S) (Twinberry, black; Crowberry) 53, 106, **107**, 108
xuya sGawGa (S) ("cut-grass") 178
xuya sGyuuGa (S) ("Raven's mustache" seaweed, unidentified) 206
xuya tluuGa, xuya kluuGa (S) (Pea, beach; Vetch, giant; Beans; Peas) **149–50**, 248

yaahl Gaanaa (M), yáahl Gáanaay (A) (Twinberry, black) 54, 106, **107**, 108
yaahl tluwaa (M), yáahl tluwáay (A) (Pea, beach; Vetch, giant; Beans; Peas) **149–50**, 248
yaanaang-xilgaa (S) (Yarrow; Horsetail, common; Crowberry; Currant, trailing) 69, 113, 159, 160–61, **183**, 184
yatlguutla (M) (probably Seabeach sandwort) 246
y'aanaang hlk'a'ii (S) (Club-moss, running) 184
yanahaw, yanaahuu (S) (Turnip, Swede turnip, Rutabaga) 250

**Cumshewa Inlet, on a quiet morning, looking eastward shortly after dawn on July 4, 2010.**